DISCOVERING
NEW TESTAMENT

DISCOVERING NEW TESTAMENT GREEK

Ian Macnair

Marshall Pickering

An Imprint of HarperCollins*Publishers*

Marshall Pickering is an Imprint of
HarperCollins *Religious*
Part of HarperCollins *Publishers*
77–85 Fulham Palace Road, London W6 8JB

First published in Great Britain
in 1993 by Marshall Pickering

1 3 5 7 9 10 8 6 4 2

Copyright © 1993 Ian Macnair

Ian Macnair asserts the moral right to be
identified as the author of this work

A catalogue record for this book is
available from the British Library

ISBN 0 551 02389-9

Photoset by
Rowland Phototypesetting Limited,
Bury St Edmunds, Suffolk
Printed and bound in Great Britain by
HarperCollins Manufacturing Glasgow

Contents

Preface

Because the New Testament was written in Greek the most important issues raised by the study of the New Testament can only be fully investigated in the original language. For example, we can discuss the way the Synoptic Gospels – Matthew, Mark and Luke – are related to each other, but that discussion will be superficial at best, or ill-informed at worst, unless we have direct access to the Gospels in Greek. Greek is essential for serious New Testament study.

The traditional approach to teaching New Testament Greek has been to cover the grammar as thoroughly as possible, using artificially constructed examples and exercises and a limited vocabulary. There are two problems associated with this approach.

Firstly, many students have little knowledge of English grammar and so they struggle with the grammatical concepts. The second problem is that, having fought valiantly to conquer the difficulties of the language, they then open the Greek New Testament, only to find that it is a strange new world in which the writers seem to pay little attention to the grammatical "rules" and either ignore the words in the vocabularies or alter them beyond all recognition.

In this book I have attempted to overcome these problems simply by concentrating on the target material. Explanations, examples and exercises are all based on the authentic Greek of the New Testament itself. Although the technical terms of Greek grammar have inevitably raised their ugly heads, I have tried to explain them in non-technical language, always using "real" Greek as a base.

I have included the word "discovering" in the title deliberately. Many of the exercises are of the "view and do" variety, based on observation and deduction, and answers are given to most of them so that you can monitor your own progress. I have included review exercises, for which answers are not provided, and these can be used by teachers to monitor the progress of their students. However, if you are working on your own most of them can be checked using a Greek New Testament.

When we learn our own language as infants we are exposed to quite complex structures and difficult words, many of which we cannot understand, but, as our knowledge develops, this exposure to "real" language prepares us to grasp it more quickly. Similarly, some things will not be explained in the earlier chapters of this book but later they will become clear. You should aim to go through it from start to finish at least twice, and you should not worry too much about what you don't understand the first time.

This book is not an end in itself but a means to understanding the Greek New Testament, and so it is never too early to start using your Greek Testament. You should also invest in a Greek-English dictionary and use it in conjunction with the course. I also recommend the use of a grammatical analysis.

I would like to acknowledge my debt to all those who have helped me to understand the Greek New Testament better. I owe much to my teachers, and probably even more to my students, in particular Janet Lucas, whose constructive criticism and advice first made me rethink my approach to the teaching of Greek. I am grateful to the publishers for their interest and to London Bible College for giving me a sabbatical in which to write, and for providing the resources to develop my teaching approach. Finally, thanks to my wife for her love and encouragement.

The New Testament is the word of God. May he be pleased to use this book to create a greater understanding of it, for the glory of his name.

IAN MACNAIR
6th December 1991

Face to face

1. προσωπον, ου n   face
2. θριξ, τριχος f   hair
3. μετωπον, ου n   forehead
4. οὐς, ὠτος n   ear
5. ὀφθαλμος, ου m   eye
6. ὀσφρησις, εως f   nose
7. σιαγων, ονος f   cheek
8. στομα, τος n   mouth
9. χειλος, ους n   lip
10. ὀδους, οντος m   tooth
11. γλωσσα, ης f   tongue

Body talk

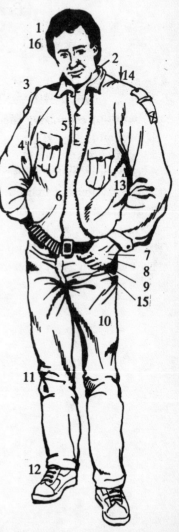

σωμα, τος n body

1. κεφαλη, ης f head
2. τραχηλος, ου m neck
3. ὠμος, ου m shoulder
4. ἀγκαλη, ης f arm
5. στηθος, ους n chest
6. ὀσφυς, υος f waist
7. πυγμη, ης f fist
8. χειρ, χειρος f hand
9. δακτυλος, ου m finger
10. σκελος, ους n leg
11. γονυ, γονατος n knee
12. πους, ποδος m foot
13. πλευρα, ας f side
14. νωτος, ου m back
15. ὀστεον, ου n bone
16. κρανιον, ου n skull

CHAPTER ONE

Preview

The letters of the Greek alphabet

Recognizing them

Writing them

Pronouncing them

Putting them in the correct order

CHAPTER ONE

Learning the ABG – the ABG?

As simple as

1.1 "It's as simple as ABC." Unfortunately learning the Greek alphabet is not quite as simple as that, but we could say it's "as simple as ABG". A, B and G are the first three letters of the Greek alphabet, written α, β, γ. This tells us two things about the alphabet straight away.

  1. Some letters are fairly easy to recognize (α = a, β = b).
  2. Some of the letters are quite different (γ = g). In fact a few, including γ, are downright misleading. βαγ is not "bay" but "bag".

The Vowels

1.2 Five of the Greek vowels are easily recognizable: α, ε, ι, ο, υ. Here are some English words which have been written using Greek letters. Write them out again in English. Do not go on to the material below the line until you have completed the exercise.

Exercise 1.2

βαγ βεγ βιγ βογ βυγ βιβ βοβ γαγ γιγ αγογ

1.3 The Greek language has two other vowels, η and ω. They are the long vowels, "e" and "o". It is unfortunate that they are so similar to the English letters "n" and "w". In English we do not distinguish between long and short vowels in writing, only in pronunciation. So we have the words "revere" and "hollow". If these words belonged to the Greek language their vowels would be ε/η and ο/ω.

Some more consonants

1.4   The consonants δ, κ and τ are fairly easy to recognize (δ = d, κ = k, τ = t). Not so obvious are μ, ν and ρ. μ is "m". If you ignore the "tail" it looks more like an "m". With ν and ρ you will need to give your brain some serious re-education. ν is "n" and ρ is "r". The following words are English words which have been written in Greek letters. Write them out again in English. (These "words" will help you to recognize Greek letters. They are not meant to be a guide to correct pronunciation.)

Exercise 1.4

γω γωατ βωατ βετ βηατ βεδ βηαδ βηακ βρηακ βανκ διγ μιτ μιντ μινκ μονκ κινκ δρινκ δρυνκ νοτ κνοτ μινδερ κινδερ μορταρ ρωαρ μαρκετ τανκαρδ νιβ κνοβ μιλκ ταλκερ

Alpha and omega

1.5   All the letters of the Greek alphabet have names, and although you need not try to learn them all at this stage, some of them are quite interesting in their own right. The first two letters of the alphabet are α (alpha) and β (beta). It's not hard to see which English word we get from them.

The first and last letters of the Greek alphabet are α (alpha) and ω (omega), hence the title "Alpha and Omega" – another way of saying "the First and the

Last" or "the Beginning and the End". See Revelation 1:8; 21:6; 22:13.

The names of the two vowels for "o" are "omicron" and "omega". The -μικρον part comes from a word meaning "small" and the -μεγα part comes from a word meaning "large". So the two letters are literally small "o" and large "o". Can you think of any other English words which have "micro" or "mega" in them?

P.S.

1.6 There are 24 letters in the Greek alphabet and we have now looked at 15 of them. The next three are π, σ and ψ. You may already be familiar with the mathematical symbol "pi", which is the name of the Greek letter "p", written π. It will probably take your brain some time to adjust to the idea that π and not ρ ("r") is the letter "p".

The Greek letter "s" is written σ, except at the end of a word when it is written ς. So "sister" in Greek letters would be σιστερ and "sisters" would be σιστερς.

When the sound "ps" occurs in Greek it is represented by a single consonant, written ψ. The word "saps" would be σαψ. The Greek word for a lie is ψευδος. That is why the English prefix "pseudo-" begins with a "p" and not an "s".

The last six

1.7 There are just six more letters to look at, and most of them are rather tricky. If you have studied mathematics you may have met some of them before. The letter "z" is ζ. With a bit of imagination you can see it as a "z" written in a shaky hand by someone with bad eyesight.

It is easy to confuse the letter ζ (z) with the letter ξ (x). If you examine them closely you will see that ξ (x) has an extra kink in it.

The letter "l" is written as λ in Greek. Before you tackle the last three consonants complete the next exercise, identifying the English words which have been written in Greek letters.

Exercise 1.7

ζοο ζεβρα ζωνε αξε αξλε οξ ψαλμ σαμε σομβρε σομβρερο σπαδε σπαδες σπαρε πρωβε βελλ βαλλ λαβελ σιξ μιξες ζιψ

1.8   The last three letters of the alphabet which we look at now all represent more than one letter in English.

The "ph" sound is written φ. "Ph" and "f" are not pronounced differently, but when English words have been derived from Greek words including the letter φ they contain the letters "ph" rather than "f". For example our word "philosophy" comes from φιλοσοφια.

You will need to be careful not to confuse φ (ph) and ψ (ps). The difference is that φ (ph) is a complete "o" with a line through it; ψ (ps) is like the letter υ, open at the top, with a line through it.

The "th" sound is written θ. The Greek word for God is θεος and from it we get "theology".

Greek has a "ch" sound, which is written χ. This is another annoying letter because it looks so much like our English "x". Our English word "character" comes from a Greek word χαρακτηρ, which means "exact representation", and occurs in Hebrews 1:3.

Writing the letters and putting them in the right order

1.9 The way to become fluent in reading Greek is to learn how to write it and speak it as well. It is also useful to know the correct alphabetical order of the letters since this will enable you to look up words in a dictionary more easily.

How do you speak a dead language?

1.10 The question of correct pronunciation is not very important for learning New Testament Greek. Some people argue that we should try to speak it in the same way as modern Greek, but the disadvantage of that is that many of the vowel sounds are similar and so the sounds themselves do not give us a clear idea of the way the words are written. Different writers offer slightly different pronunciations and there is no single "received pronunciation".

What is important is that you say the words as you learn them. How you say them is not so important. Saying the words out loud helps you to fix them in your memory. Repeat them over and over. I have found that students who become fascinated by the sound of words learn them much more quickly than students who are too scared to even try saying them out loud.

Mastering the alphabet

1.11   It is important to do the work in this chapter thoroughly because you are laying the foundations on which you will build all your future study. One of the most significant factors in learning is the part played by your subconscious mind. The process of learning begins to take place when you set aside time for reading and doing exercises, but when you go away and do something else that process does not stop. It goes on in your subconscious. So having breaks is just as important as having formal times of study. A good rule is "Little and Often". If you spend too much time in conscious learning your mind will grow tired and you will get things confused, but if you spend half an hour and then have a break your subconscious mind will sift and organize the material, and when you return to your formal study you will be ready to go on to the next stage. Remember

LITTLE AND OFTEN

A Strategy

1.12 So far we have looked at the letters in a fairly random order. It is time to work out a strategy for mastering the letters so that we can recognize words, write them and say them.

In section 1.13 you will find a chart with the following details.

Column 1 gives the names of the 24 letters.

Column 2 gives the small (lower case) letters.

Column 3 gives the pronunciation.

Column 4 gives the capital letters.

Column 5 gives the standard transliteration (the way in which a Greek letter is represented in English script).

Column 6 is a key to the notes in section 1.14.

Section 1.15 contains a guide to writing the letters. You will need a piece of paper with double lines for practising them yourself.

It is best to divide your work into about six stages. At each stage copy each of the lower case letters several times until you can write them out confidently, saying the name of the letter to yourself. Memorize the names of the letters as if they were a poem of about six lines:

1 Alpha beta gamma delta /
2 Epsilon zeta eta theta /
3 Iota kappa lambda /
4 Mu nu xi /
5 Omicron pi rho sigma tau /
6 Upsilon phi chi psi omega.

The alphabet in detail
1.13

1	2	3	4	5	6
Name of Letters	Small Letters	Pronunciation	Capital Letters	English	Notes
alpha	α	*a* as in part, past	A	a	
beta	β	*b*	B	b	
gamma	γ	*g* as in gold	Γ	g	1
delta	δ	*d*	Δ	d	
epsilon	ε	*e* as in let	E	e	2
zeta	ζ	*z* (*dz* in the middle of a word)	Z	z	
eta	η	*ay* as in pay	H	ē	2,6
theta	θ	*th* as in think	Θ	th	
iota	ι	*i* as in bit, or Ian	I	i	3
kappa	κ	*k*	K	k	
lambda	λ	*l*	Λ	l	
mu	μ	*m*	M	m	
nu	ν	*n*	N	n	
xi	ξ	*x*	Ξ	x	
omicron	o	*o* as in bottle	O	o	2
pi	π	*p*	Π	p	
rho	ρ	*r*	P	r	4,6
sigma	σ,ς	*s*	Σ	s	5
tau	τ	*t*	T	t	
upsilon	υ	*u* as in put	Y	u	6
phi	φ	*ph*	Φ	ph	
chi	χ	*ch* as in German *achtung*	X	ch	6
psi	ψ	*ps* as in tipsy	Ψ	ps	
omega	ω	*o* as in home	Ω	ō	2

Notes on the alphabet

1.14   (1) γ is equivalent to "g" and is pronounced hard, as in "gold", not soft as in "gentle". There is no letter "c" in Greek. A double γ (γγ) is pronounced "ng". Our word "angel" comes from the Greek ἀγγελος (pronounced "angelos", as if the first part were "angle" rather than "angel"). When combined with κ (k) or ξ (x) it sounds like an "n". So γκ is pronounced "nk" and γξ "nx".

  (2) The letters "e" and "o" have a short form and a long form. Be careful to distinguish them in pronunciation.

  (3) The letter iota does not have a dot above it.

  (4) ρ is not "p" but "r".

  (5) The letter "s" has two forms. σ is always used, except at the end of a word when ς is used. There is only one form for the capital letter.

  (6) Pay special attention to the capital letters H, P, Y, X. They are *not* equivalent to the English letters they resemble.

A guide to writing the letters

1.15   An arrow indicates the best place to begin the letter.

About capitals

1.16   It is not essential to learn Greek capital letters at this
point. Many of them are the same as their English
equivalents, although like the small letters, there are
some unfamiliar forms and some that are misleading.

In Greek capital letters are not used at the beginning
of every sentence. They are used as follows:

- at the beginning of a paragraph
- at the beginning of direct speech
- at the beginning of proper nouns (names, etc)

Some exercises on the alphabet

Exercise 1.17

1 The following strings of letters contain a deliberate
  mistake. See if you can spot the mistake in each.

EXAMPLE α β c δ ε

The cuckoo in the nest is "c". There is no letter
"c" in Greek.

Now try these:

    f ζ η θ ι
    ξ ο π q ρ
    υ φ χ ψ g
    j κ λ μ ν
    ζ η θ h ι

2 Put the above letters in order.
  The following strings of letters are in the wrong
  order. See if you can put them in the correct
  alphabetical order.

EXAMPLE ε α ο θ δ

The correct order is α δ ε θ ο

Now try these:

    υ ν ω ξ γ ζ
    η θ ε ψ λ π
    χ γ λ β τ μ
    ς δ ρ ο α φ
    ι γ ω κ ν σ

More about vowels

1.18   Normally each vowel is pronounced as a separate
sound. The word βιβλιον (biblion) means "book".
The three vowels are spoken as three separate
sounds, i.e. βίβ-λί-όν, pronounced "bib-lee-on".
However there are some combinations of vowels
which together form a single sound. The technical
term for these is diphthongs.

The word βουλομαι (boulomai) means "I wish". The
ου and the αι are spoken as single sounds, i.e. βού-λό
-μαί, pronounced "boo-law-my", *not* βό-ύ-λό-μά-í.
The ου and αι combinations are diphthongs.

Here is the complete list of vowel combinations
which are pronounced in this way. Some textbooks
describe the pronunciation of ει as "like **ei** in veil",
but it is helpful to distinguish between the sound of η
(ē) and ει. The difference is not crucial and you
should adopt the pronunciation you feel is most
natural for you.

1.19

αι	like **ai** in aisle	ηυ	like **eu** in feud
αυ	like **ow** in down	οι	like **oi** in oil
ει	like **ei** in Einstein	ου	like **ou** in through
ευ	like **eu** in feud	υι	like **we**

1.20   These combinations are only diphthongs in the order
given here; i.e. αι is one sound, but ια is two sounds.
The Greek word και has one syllable, pronounced
like **ky** in "sky", but δια has two, pronounced "dee-
ya".

Don't worry about recognizing which combinations
of vowels are diphthongs and which are not. You will
find that you recognize them intuitively.

Exercise 1.20

Rewrite these words in English letters and underline all the diphthongs. Use the charts in 1.13 and 1.19.

μαθηται διαβολος θαυμαζει κατευλογουμεν
κεραμιον κοινωνια λειτουργια λευκαινω
μετοικεσια τοιγαρουν

1.21 In a number of words you will find more than two vowels together and at this stage you may not be sure how to pronounce them. A helpful tip is that if the combination contains a diphthong it should be pronounced as a diphthong. For example the word πορνεια (porneia) has three syllables, πόρ-νεί-ά, *not* πορ-νέ-ί-ά. The word σκευους (skeuous) has two syllables, σκεύ-ούς, *not* σκέ-ύ-ό-ύς. The easier way of pronouncing a word is nearly always the correct way.

Vowels at the beginning of a word

1.22 If a word begins with a vowel it is written with a mark above the vowel called a "breathing", which may be a smooth breathing or a rough breathing.

The smooth breathing is like a small **c** written backwards above the vowel [']. It has no sound at all.
The rough breathing is written like a small **c** above the vowel ['] and gives a sound equivalent to the English letter "h".

Look carefully at these words with the equivalent English letters alongside:

● Words which begin with a smooth breathing.
ἀββα [abba]   ἐπιστολη [epistolē]   ἠλθον [ēlthon]
ἰχθυς [ichthus]   ὀφθαλμος [ophthalmos]
ὠτιον [ōtion]

- Words which begin with a rough breathing.

ἅγιος [hagios]   ἕτερος [heteros]   ἥλιος [hēlios]
ἱκανος [hikanos]   ὁδος [hodos]
ὑποκριτης [hupokritēs]   ὡσαννα [hōsanna]

- When a word begins with a vowel which is also a capital letter the breathing cannot go above it because of its size and so it is placed before the letter.

Ἀβρααμ [Abraam]   Ἑλλας [Hellas]   Ἠλιας [Ēlias]
Ἱεραπολις [Hierapolis]   Ὀνησιμος [Onēsimos]

- When a word begins with two vowels pronounced as one, a diphthong, the breathing goes over the second vowel. This rule applies even if the word begins with a capital letter.

αἰων [aiōn]   αἱμα [haima]   αὐτος [autos]
εἰρηνη [eirēnē]   εὐλογια [eulogia]
ηὑρισκεν [hēurisken]   οὑτος [houtos]
οἰκονομια [oikonomia]   Αἰγυπτος [Aiguptos]

1.23   Although the letter "r" is regarded as a consonant, in some languages it seems to take on some of the characteristics of a vowel. This is true of Greek, where the letter ρ (r) at the beginning of a word is written with a rough breathing. This is why the name of the letter is written with an "h", rho. This is also why some English words which have come into English from Greek begin with "rh" rather than "r", for example rhapsody, rhetoric and rheumatism.

ῥαββι [rabbi]   Ῥεβεκκα [Rebekka]

Some features of the letter iota

1.24   The vowel iota [ι] is sometimes written below another vowel. The technical name for this is "iota subscript". It is not pronounced, but it is part of the word and must be written. Here are a few examples.

ᾁδης [hạdēs] pronounced hah-days

σωζω [sọzō] pronounced so-dzo

δοξη [doxẹ] pronounced dock-say

1.25 Occasionally at the beginning of a word the letter iota is pronounced "y" rather than "i". The rule is that iota with a smooth breathing at the beginning of a word, followed by a vowel, is pronounced "y".

$$\text{ἰ + vowel = y. . .}$$

EXAMPLES:

Ἰησους, pronounced Yay-soos, is the Greek for "Jesus".
Ἰακωβος, pronounced Yak-oh-boss, is the Greek for "James", which in turn represents the Hebrew "Yacob" or "Jacob".

A guide to pronunciation

1.26 The following sentences are not Greek but are a guide to help you to pronounce Greek words properly.

1. ἀν ὀψιμαθ ἰς α λητ λερνερ.
   An opsimath is a late learner.

2. Λοχ Λωμονδ ἰς ἰν Σκοτλανδ.
   Loch Lomond is in Scotland.

3. ζιψ ἀρ πυτ ὀν γαρμεντς.
   Zips are put on garments.

4. ἀθλετιξ ἀνδ φυτβολ ἀρ βωθ σπωρτς.
   Athletics and football are both sports.

5. ἀ σκουλβοι ἀζ του ἀνδ φωρ του μηκ σιξ.
   A schoolboy adds two and four to make six.

6. στυδι μαι ἐξαμπλς φορ εὐσιγγ διφθογγς.
   Study my examples for using diphthongs.

7. ἰφ υἰ ἀνδ εὐ ἀρ ἰν ηὐρ αὐς υἰ καν λυκ αὐτ ὀν θε ἰαρδ.
   If we and you are in your house we can look out on the yard.

8. ἀν εἰ φορ ἀν εἰ ἀνδ ἀ τυθ φορ ἀ τυθ.
An eye for an eye and a tooth for a tooth.

Answers to Exercises

Exercise 1.2

bag beg big bog bug bib bob gag gig agog

Exercise 1.4

go goat boat bet beat bed bead beak break bank dig mit mint mink monk kink drink drunk not knot minder kinder mortar roar market tankard nib knob milk talker

Exercise 1.7

zoo zebra zone axe axle ox psalm same sombre sombrero spade spades spare probe bell ball label six mixes zips

Exercise 1.17

1 f, q, g, j, h

2 γ ζ ν ξ υ ω
ε η θ λ π ψ
β γ λ μ τ χ
α δ ο ρ ς φ
γ ι κ ν σ ω

Exercise 1.20

mathētai diabolos thaumazei kateulogoumen keramion

koinōnia leitourgia leukainō metoikesia toigaroun

REVIEW QUESTIONS

1. How many vowels are there in the Greek alphabet and what are they?

2. In what way are the first and last letters of the alphabet used in the Book of Revelation?

3. How many letters are there in the Greek alphabet?

4. What are the English equivalents of these letters?

   γ, ζ, η, λ, ν, ξ, π, ρ, σ, φ, χ, ψ, ω

5. What does the Greek word χαρακτηρ mean?

6. Why is it useful to know the correct order of the Greek letters?

7. Why is "Little and Often" a good rule for learning?

8. What is the pronunciation of γγ, γκ, γξ?

9. When are capital letters used in Greek?

10. Which combinations of vowels are pronounced as a single sound, and what is the technical name for them?

11. How is the punctuation of a word affected if it begins with a vowel?

12. If a word begins with a diphthong how is the punctuation affected?

13. What is unusual about the consonant ρ (r)?

14. What does "iota subscript" mean?

15. When is the letter ι (i) pronounced "y"?

16. What is the Greek word for "Jesus"?

REVIEW EXERCISES

ALPHABET SORT

The following words are in their English alphabetical order with the Greek equivalents alongside. Put the words in their correct Greek alphabetical order with the English alongside.

book	βιβλιον	– – – – – – – –	_____
child	τεκνον	– – – – – – –	_____
darkness	σκοτος	– – – – – –	_____
day	ἡμερα	– – – – –	_____
egg	ᾠον	– – – – – – – – –	_____
father	πατηρ	– – – – – – –	_____
fruit	καρπος	– – – – –	_____
garment	ἱματιον	– – – – – –	_____
grass	χορτος	– – – – – –	_____
house	οἰκος	– – – – –	_____
light	φως	– – – –	_____
man	ἀνθρωπος	– – – –	_____
mother	μητηρ	– – –	_____
night	νυξ	– – – –	_____
overseer	ἐπισκοπος	– – – – –	_____
root	ῥιζα	– – – – –	_____
slave	δουλος	– – – –	_____
soul	ψυχη	– – – – – –	_____
stone	λιθος	– – – – – –	_____

throne	θρονος	_ _ _ _	_____
tongue	γλωσσα	_ _ _	_____
tree	ξυλον	_ _ _ _ _ _	_____
water	ὑδωρ	_ _ _ _	_____
weed	ζιζανιον	_ _ _	_____

PEOPLE AND PLACES

In the lists below you will find 30 names of people and places in the New Testament. For each English name there is a Greek equivalent, but they have been jumbled up. Match the correct Greek words to their English counterparts. Some will be easier than others but there should be enough information to enable you to complete the exercise.

Agrippa	Πετρος
Andrew	Γαλιλαια
Antioch	Ἰσραηλ
Babylon	Σιμων
Barnabas	Ἰερουσαλημ
David	Δαυιδ
Elisabeth	Πιλατος
Festus	Φιλιππος
Philip	Βαρναβας
Galilee	Ἰακωβ
Isaac	Μαρια
Israel	Τιμοθεος
Jacob	Ἰσαακ
Jerusalem	Ἀντιοχεια
Jordan	Στεφανος
Lazarus	Ἰορδανης

Magdalene	Λαζαρος
Martha	Ἀνδρεας
Mary	Μαρθα
Nazareth	Σιλας
Peter	Τιτος
Pilate	Φηστος
Sidon	Βαβυλων
Silas	Ζεβεδαιος
Simon	Μαγδαληνη
Solomon	Σολομων
Stephen	Ἀγριππας
Timothy	Σιδων
Titus	Ἐλισαβετ
Zebedee	Ναζαρετ

CHAPTER TWO

Preview

CHAPTER TWO

Greek you know – Greek you don't know

You know more than you think

2.1 The Greek New Testament uses a vocabulary of 5,432 words, but you will discover that, just like the individual letters of the alphabet, some of them are quite easy to recognize. Try this little exercise.

Exercise 2.1

Write these words out again in the equivalent English letters, using the chart in section 1.13 of Chapter 1. Do you recognize any words we have adopted into English?

ἀγωνια ἀναθεμα ἀπολογια ἀποστολος ἀρωμα βαπτισμα βλασφημια γενεαλογια διαδημα εὐλογια ζηλος θεατρον καμηλος λαρυγξ μανια ὀρφανος παραβολη ῥαββι στιγμα τραυμα ὑποκριτης φιλανθρωπια χασμα ψαλμος ὡσαννα

2.2 Sometimes small changes have been made as words have migrated from Greek to English. Parts of Greek words may be dropped, such as the ending -α from διαδημα to give us "diadem", and the ending -ος from ὀρφανος to give us "orphan".

2.3 Some letters tend to change. We have seen already that γγ (gg) becomes "ng". So ἀγγελος comes into our language as "angel". It can also be translated "messenger". Another common change is from υ (u)

to "y". The Greek word μαρτυς (martus) enters English as "martyr". Its Greek meaning is "a witness", which throws interesting light on what witnessing could lead to in the early days of church history. The word γυμνος (gumnos) meant "naked" and from it our word "gymnasium" is derived. In the Greek games athletes stripped off completely when competing. A common prefix is συν (sun), "together", which turns up in many words beginning with the letters "sy": syllable, sympathy, symphony, synonym, syntax, synthetic and system. Sometimes κ (k) turns into a "c". The Greek word for "I hear" is ἀκουω (akouō), from which we get "acoustics".

2.4   One of the Greek words which has proved most useful in developing English words is λογος (logos), which has a wide range of meanings, including "word", "reason", "account", "matter". All our words ending in -logy use it. So, from θεος (theos), "God", we get theology. From ἀνθρωπος (anthrōpos), "man", we get anthropology. From χρονος (chronos), "time", we get chronology.

Exercise 2.4

Can you identify any English words which come from these? αὐτος (he, himself), βιος (life), γραφη (writing), ἀριθμος (number)

2.5   The gap between the Greek you know and the Greek you don't know may not be as great as you think. It is always helpful to try to connect what you are learning to something you know already. For example, ἐπι means "upon" and ταφος means "a grave"; put the two together and you get something written on a grave, an epitaph. When you come across the word ταφος again you may have forgotten what it means,

but a little thought about "taph" and "epitaph"
should bring the meaning back quickly.

View and do

2.6 The following exercise is in three parts.
1. Work out how the Greek words should be pronounced [sections 1.13 and 1.19]. It will be useful
to write the words out again using the equivalent
English letters.

2. Compare the English translation with the literal
equivalents of the Greek words.

3. Go on to the section, "For further study".

Exercise 2.6

1. ἀνδρα   οὐ   γινωσκω.
a man   not   I know.
I do not know a man (Luke 1:34).

2. ποθεν   με   γινωσκεις ;
from where   me   you know ?
                    [where "you" refers to one
                    person]
How do you know me? (John 1:48).

3. γινωσκει   με   ὁ   πατηρ.
(he) knows   me   the Father.
The Father knows me (John 10:15).

4. γινωσκομεν   το   πνευμα   της   ἀληθειας.
we know   the   spirit   of (the) truth.
We know the Spirit of Truth (1 John 4:6).

5. ἀπ' ἀρτι   γινωσκετε   αὐτον.
from now you know   him.
                    [where "you" refers to
                    more than one]
From now you know him (John 14:7).

6. γινωσκουσι με τα   ἐμα.
(they) know me (the) my own.
My own know me (John 10:14).

For further study

2.7   If you analyze the Greek words which refer to
"knowing" something or someone you will see that
they contain a constant element (γινωσκ) and an
ending which changes (-ω, -εις, -ει, -ομεν, -ετε,
-ουσι). Greek does have words for "I", "you" etc.,
but it does not always use them because the personal
endings already convey that information.

Exercise 2.7

Complete this chart by filling in the personal endings.
Note that Greek has two endings which represent
"you". One is singular, the other is plural.

γινωσκ__	I know	γινωσκ__	we know
γινωσκ__	you (s) know	γινωσκ__	you (p) know
γινωσκ__	he/she knows	γινωσκ__	they know

2.8   The ending which indicates "they" is more often
written with the letter ν (n) at the end -ουσιν.

Exercise 2.8

● πιστευω (pisteu ō) means "I believe". Give the
meaning of πιστευετε, πιστευομεν, πιστευεις,
πιστευουσιν.

● μενει (men ei) means "he remains". Give the
meaning of μενετε, μενω, μενομεν, μενεις.

- ἀποστελλουσι (apostell ousi) means "they send". Give the meaning of ἀποστελλεις, ἀποστελλει, ἀποστελλετε, ἀποστελλω.

- ἀκουω (akou ō) means "I hear". Give the meaning of ἀκουουσιν, ἀκουετε, ἀκουεις, ἀκουομεν.

Making statements and asking questions

2.9 In English, if we want to ask a question, we change the order of the words, or introduce an extra verb (do), and use a question mark (?).

STATEMENT You know.   You are knowing.
QUESTION Do you know? Are you knowing?

In Greek the same form of words is used whether it is a statement or a question. The only difference is that a Greek question mark is used. Look again at number 2 in Exercise 2.6 (John 1:48).

STATEMENT γινωσκεις.   You know.
QUESTION γινωσκεις;   Do you know?

You will have to make a conscious effort to persuade your brain that ; is a question mark in Greek, not a semicolon.

More about punctuation

Greek uses full stops (.) and commas (,) to divide sentences up. A break that is greater than a comma but less than a full stop is marked by a dot written above the line (·).

It uses apostrophes (') to show that a letter has dropped out, e.g ἀλλ' for ἀλλα, but it does *not* use them to mark possession.

There are no inverted commas; the beginning of direct speech is marked by a capital letter and the end has to be inferred from the context.

The mark above a vowel (¨) means that the vowel has to be pronounced separately. It is not common and occurs mainly in names, such as Ἡσαΐας (Ē-sa-i-as, four syllables), the Greek for "Isaiah".

Turning positives into negatives

2.10 In number 1 in Exercise 2.6 you will see that the positive statement is made negative by putting οὐ *in front of* the verb.

γινωσκω   I know
οὐ γινωσκω   I do not know

If the verb which follows begins with a vowel the negative becomes οὐκ before a smooth breathing, and οὐχ before a rough breathing.

οὐκ ἀκουω   I do not hear
οὐχ εὑρισκω   I do not find

Stems and endings

2.11 When you look up a verb in a Greek dictionary you will find it in the form which means "I ***". Here is a chart containing some of the verbs you have already met and some new ones.

ἀκουω, hear	ἀποστελλω, send	βλεπω, see
γινωσκω, know	γραφω, write	ἐχω, have
λεγω, say	μενω, remain	πιστευω, believe

Remember that the stem, the part that remains constant, identifies the basic meaning, and the ending can change for "I", "you", etc. When you learn new verbs you will find it helpful to recite them aloud using the six endings. First identify the stem by removing -ω, and then add each of the endings. This will fix a useful pattern in your mind and give you more fluency in reading.

Exercise 2.11

Use these texts to practise fluency in reading and speaking Greek. Then use what you have learned about stems and endings to identify the correct English translations for each text. Some verbs have been underlined to help you. Just to make it a little more challenging there are more English translations than Greek texts.

1. Ἀγαπητοι, οὐκ ἐντολην καινην <u>γραφω</u> ὑμιν ἀλλ' ἐντολην παλαιαν ἡν εἰχετε ἀπ' ἀρχης.

2. ἀλλα ὑμεις οὐ <u>πιστευετε</u>, ὁτι οὐκ ἐστε ἐκ των προβατων των ἐμων.

3. <u>γινωσκουσι</u> με τα ἐμα, καθως <u>γινωσκει</u> με ὁ πατηρ κἀγω <u>γινωσκω</u> τον πατερα.

4. ἐγω <u>ἀποστελλω</u> τον ἀγγελον μου προ προσωπου σου, ὁς κατασκευασει την ὁδον σου.

5. εἰπαν αὐτῳ, Οὐ καλως <u>λεγομεν</u> ἡμεις ὁτι Σαμαριτης εἰ συ και δαιμονιον <u>ἐχεις</u>;

6. εὐθυς κραξας ὁ πατηρ του παιδιου ἐλεγεν, <u>Πιστευω</u>· βοηθει μου τῃ ἀπιστιᾳ.

7. ἠλθεν γαρ Ἰωαννης μητε ἐσθιων μητε πινων, και <u>λεγουσιν</u>, Δαιμονιον <u>ἐχει</u>.

8. οἱ δε <u>λεγουσιν</u> αὐτῳ, Οὐκ <u>ἐχομεν</u> ὡδε εἰ μη πεντε ἀρτους και δυο ἰχθυας.

9. οὐ <u>πιστευεις</u> ὁτι ἐγω ἐν τῳ πατρι και ὁ πατηρ ἐν ἐμοι ἐστιν;

10. ὑμων δε μακαριοι οἱ ὀφθαλμοι ὁτι <u>βλεπουσιν</u>, και τα ὠτα ὑμων ὁτι <u>ἀκουουσιν</u>.

TRANSLATIONS

A. But why do you see the speck which is in your brother's eye?

B. I am sending my messenger before your face, who will prepare your way.

C. For John came neither eating nor drinking, and they say, "He has a demon."

D. But blessed are your eyes because they see, and your ears because they hear.

E. And they say to him, "We do not have here [anything] except five loaves and two fishes."

F. Immediately the father of the child crying out said, "I believe; help my unbelief."

G. They said to him, "Do we not say rightly that you are a Samaritan and you have a demon?"

H. My own know me, just as the Father knows me and I know the Father.

I. But you do not believe because you are not of my sheep.

J My sheep hear my voice and I know them and they follow me.

K. Do you not believe that I [am] in the Father and the Father is in me?

L. Beloved, I do not write you a new command but an old command which you had from the beginning.

Greek you don't know – English you do

2.12 The way in which the Greek language organizes things is largely unfamiliar to you, but as you come to study the Greek New Testament you are at an advantage, as there are many good translations available and much of the text is familiar to you in English.

Here is a very well-known passage from 1 Corinthians 11:23–26 set out in parallel in both Greek and English. Try to deduce which elements of the Greek text correspond to the English translation. But be warned: some words will appear where you least expect them.

²³Ἐγω γαρ παρελαβον	For I received
ἀπο του κυριου,	from the Lord,
ὃ και παρεδωκα ὑμιν,	what also I delivered to you,
ὁτι ὁ κυριος Ἰησους	that the Lord Jesus
ἐν τῃ νυκτι ᾑ παρεδιδετο	on the night in which he was betrayed
ἐλαβεν ἀρτον	took bread
²⁴και εὐχαριστησας	and having given thanks
ἐκλασεν και εἰπεν,	he broke [it] and said,
Τουτο μου ἐστιν το σωμα	"This is my body [of-me the body]
το ὑπερ ὑμων·	which is [literally "the"] for you;
τουτο ποιειτε	this do
εἰς την ἐμην ἀναμνησιν.	for my remembrance."
²⁵ὡσαυτως και το ποτηριον	Similarly also the cup
μετα το δειπνησαι λεγων,	after having supped saying,
Τουτο το ποτηριον	"This cup
ἡ καινη διαθηκη ἐστιν	is the new covenant
ἐν τῳ ἐμῳ αἱματι·	in my blood;
τουτο ποιειτε,	this do,
ὁσακις ἐαν πινητε,	as often as you drink,
εἰς την ἐμην ἀναμνησιν.	for my remembrance.
²⁶ὁσακις γαρ ἐαν ἐσθιητε	For as often as you eat
τον ἀρτον τουτον	this bread
και το ποτηριον πινητε,	and drink the cup,
τον θανατον του κυριου	the death of the Lord
καταγγελλετε	you proclaim
ἀχρις οὑ ἐλθῃ.	until he comes."

Exercise 2.12

1. What does γαρ (gar) mean? [Compare verses 23 and 26.]

2. What is the difference in meaning between το ποτηριον and τουτο το ποτηριον?

3. What is the meaning of εὐχαριστησας, and what English word is derived from it?

4. What is the difference in meaning between ὁ κυριος and του κυριου?

5. What is the meaning of μου (verse 24) and in what way is it related to ἐγω (verse 23)?

Answers to exercises

Exercise 2.1
agōnia (agony), anathema, apologia (apology), apostolos (apostle), arōma, baptisma (baptism), blasphēmia (blasphemy), genealogia (genealogy), diadēma (diadem), eulogia (eulogy), zēlos (zeal), theatron (theatre), kamēlos (camel), larugx (larynx), mania, orphanos (orphan), parabolē (parable), rabbi, stigma, trauma, hupokritēs (hypocrite), philanthrōpia (philanthropy), chasma (chasm), psalmos (psalm), hōsanna

Exercise 2.4
Autobiography, biography, autograph, arithmetic, biology, graphics. There are many "-graph" words, like photograph, and "auto-" words, like "autocratic".

Exercise 2.6
1. andra ou ginōskō.
2. pothen me ginōskeis?
3. ginōskei me ho patēr.
4. ginōskomen to pneuma tēs alētheias.

5. ap' arti ginōskete auton.
6. ginōskousi me ta ema.

Exercise 2.7

γινωσκ ω I know	γινωσκ ομεν we know
γινωσκ εις you (s) know	γινωσκ ετε you (p) know
γινωσκ ει he/she knows	γινωσκ ουσι they know

Exercise 2.8
you (p) believe, we believe, you (s) believe, they believe
you (p) remain, I remain, we remain, you (s) remain
you (s) send, he/she sends, you (p) send, I send
they hear, you (p) hear, you (s) hear, we hear

Exercise 2.11
1:L (1 John 2:7) 2:I (John 10:26)
3:H (John 10:14-15) 4:B (Matthew 11:10)
5:G (John 8:48) 6:F (Mark 9:24)
7:C (Matthew 11:18) 8:E (Matthew 14:17)
9:K (John 14:10) 10:D (Matthew 13:16)

The English sentences which were not used were A and J.

Exercise 2.12
1. γαρ means "for". It never comes first in a sentence or clause.
2. το ποτηριον means "the cup" and τουτο το ποτηριον means "this cup".
3. ευχαριστησας means "having given thanks". Our English word "eucharist" is derived from it.
4. ὁ κυριος means "the Lord" and του κυριου means "of the Lord".
5. μου means "of me"; μου το σωμα (of me the body) means "my body". The word ἐγω is related to it because it means "I".

REVIEW QUESTIONS

1. What kinds of changes have occurred as words have migrated from Greek to English?

2. What is the connection between the meaning of γυμνος and the English word derived from it, "gymnasium"?

3. What is the meaning of the prefix συν-?

4. What are some of the meanings of the Greek word λογος?

5. Why does the Greek verb have different endings, and which English words do they represent?

6. Why are there two endings representing "you" as the subject?

7. How does a Greek sentence indicate that a question is being asked?

8. In what ways is Greek punctuation (a) similar to English and (b) different from English?

9. How is a statement made negative in Greek?

10. What is the difference between οὐ, οὐκ and οὐχ?

REVIEW EXERCISE

CHOICE WORDS

Choose the correct words to fill the gaps in these texts from
the alternatives given.

και _____ (1) αὐτοις ὁ ᾿Ιησους,
    [λεγει λεγομεν λεγετε]

Ποσους ἀρτους _____ (2) ;
    [ἐχει ἐχομεν ἐχετε]

And Jesus *says* to them, "How many loaves *do you have*?"
            (Matthew 15:34)

οὐδεις _____ (3) οἰνον νεον εἰς
    [βαλλομεν βαλλουσιν βαλλει]
ἀσκους παλαιους.

No one *puts* new wine into old wineskins.   (Mark 2:22)

και _____ (4) προς
    [ἀποστελλουσιν ἀποστελλει ἀποστελλεις]
αὐτον τινας των Φαρισαιων και των ῾Ηρῳδιανων.

And *they send* to him
some of the Pharisees and the Herodians.   (Mark 12:13)

τῳ Σιμωνι ἐφη, _____ (5) ταυτην την
    [Βλεπω Βλεπομεν Βλεπεις]
γυναικα;

He said to Simon, "*Do you see* this woman?" (Luke 7:44)

την μαρτυριαν ἡμων οὐ _____ (6) .
    [λαμβανετε λαμβανομεν λαμβανω]

Our testimony *you* do not *receive*.   (John 3:11)

Οὐκετι δια την σην λαλιαν _____ (7) .
                              [πιστευετε πιστευομεν πιστευω]
We no longer *believe* because of what you say. (John 4:42)

ὁ πατηρ _____ (8) τους νεκρους.
         [ἐγειρεις ἐγειρει ἐγειρετε]
The Father *raises* the dead.   (John 5:21)

ἑνα πατερα _____ (9) τον θεον.
          [ἐχομεν ἐχετε ἐχουσιν]
We have one father, God.   (John 8:41)

Τίνα κατηγοριαν _____ (10) κατα του
               [φερομεν φερετε φερουσιν]
ἀνθρωπου τουτου;
What accusation *do you bring* against this man? (John 18:29)

Και _____ (11) αὑτη ἐκεινοι,
    [λεγω λεγουσιν λεγεις]
Γυναι, Τί _____ (12) ;
         [κλαιω κλαιουσιν κλαιεις]
And *they say* to her, "Woman, why *are you weeping*?"
                                                (John 20:13)

Σαουλ, Σαουλ, τί με _____ (13) ;
                    [διωκω διωκουσιν διωκεις]
"Saul, Saul, why *do you persecute* me?"   (Acts 9:4)

ὁ δε ἐφη, Ἑλληνιστι _____ (14) ;
          [γινωσκομεν γινωσκεις γινωσκουσιν]
And he said, "*Do you know* Greek?"   (Acts 21:37)

Οὐδεν κακον _____ (15) ἐν τῳ
      [εὑρισκετε εὑρισκομεν εὑρισκω]
ἀνθρωπῳ τουτῳ.

"*We find* nothing wrong in this man." (Acts 23:9)

καθως πανταχου ἐν παση ἐκκλησιᾳ
_____ (16) .
[διδασκεις διδασκουσιν διδασκω]
As *I teach* everywhere in every church. (1 Corinthians 4:17)

εἰτε οὐν _____ (17)
      [ἐσθιετε ἐσθιομεν ἐσθιω]
εἰτε _____ (18)
     [πινετε πινομεν πινω]
So whether *you eat* or *you drink* . . . (1 Corinthians 10:31)

ἐκ μερους γαρ _____ (19) και ἐκ
      [γινωσκετε γινωσκομεν γινωσκω]
μερους _____ (20) .
  [προφητευετε προφητευομεν προφητευω]
For *we know* in part and *we prophesy* in part.

                              (1 Corinthians 13:9)

_____ (21) δε παντας ὑμας λαλειν γλωσσαις.
[θελει θελομεν θελω]
Now *I want* you all to speak in tongues. (1 Corinthians 14:5)

Χριστος καταγγελλεται, και ἐν τουτῳ _____ (22) .
          [χαιρουσιν χαιρω χαιρει]
Christ is proclaimed, and in this *I rejoice*. (Philippians 1:18)

το δε ρημα κυριου _____ (23) εἰς τον αἰωνα.
      [μενουσιν μενω μενει]
But the word of the Lord *remains* for ever. (1 Peter 1:25)

τεκνια μου, ταυτα _____ (24) ὑμιν ἱνα μη
           [γραφουσιν γραφω γραφει]
ἁμαρτητε.

My little children, *I write* these things to you that you may
not sin.   (1 John 2:1)

WORDS TO LEARN

ἀγγελος   angel, messenger
ἀκουω   hear
ἀλλα (ἀλλ')   but
ἀποστελλω   send
βλεπω   see
γινωσκω   know
γραφω   write
ἐστιν (he, she, it)   is
ἐχω   have
θεος (usually ὁ θεος)   God*
'Ιησους (often ὁ 'Ιησους)   Jesus
και   and
λεγω   say
μενω   remain
ὁ κοσμος   the world
ὁ πατηρ   the father*
ὁ υἱος   the son*
οὐ, οὐκ, οὐχ   not
πιστευω   believe
το πνευμα   the spirit*

* Greek does not use capitals with these words but English
  does: God, Father, Son and Spirit.

CHAPTER THREE

Preview

Nouns: stems and endings

ὁ θεος υἱος κοσμος πατηρ

The cases and how they are used

Word order and word endings

Prepositions and the cases

Personal pronouns

ἐγω ἡμεις συ ὑμεις αὐτος αὐτη αὐτοι

CHAPTER THREE

The case of the different endings

Some detective work

3.1   Look at these English texts and their equivalents in
      Greek and see if you can spot a basic difference
      between English nouns and Greek nouns.
      CLUE: the word to look out for is "God", θεος,
      which is usually written with the word for "the", i.e.
      ὁ θεος.

1. God is light (1 John 1:5).
   ὁ θεος φως ἐστιν.

2. "I love God" (1 John 4:20).
   Ἀγαπω τον θεον.

3. The love of God (1 John 2:5).
   ἡ ἀγαπη του θεου.

4. God remains in him and he in God (1 John 4:15).
   ὁ θεος ἐν αὐτῳ μενει και αὐτος ἐν τῳ θεῳ.

5. This is the true God and eternal life (1 John 5:20).
   οὑτος ἐστιν ὁ ἀληθινος θεος και ζωη αἰωνιος.

3.2   Elementary, isn't it? Greek nouns have different
      endings. In English the noun "God" does not change
      its appearance, but in Greek θεος does. It changes to
      θεον (the**on**) in number 2, θεου (the**ou**) in number 3,
      and θεῳ (the**ọ**) in number 4. It may be easier to see
      what is happening if we substitute an English word
      which does change in this way, the pronoun "he".

God (θεος) is light.	i.e. HE is light.
I love God (θεον).	i.e. I love HIM.
The love of God (θεου).	i.e. HIS love.

The four basic endings

3.3   Just like the verbs we looked at in Chapter 2, Greek
        nouns have a stem which identifies the basic meaning
        of the word and is constant, and a set of different
        endings. The part which the noun plays in the
        sentence determines which ending is used. Look at
        this chart which gives the endings of some very
        common words. To make things easier I have left a
        gap between the stem and its endings, but in an
        actual text they would be written as one word without
        the gap.

	the (m)	God	son	world	father
1	ὁ	θε ος	υἱ ος	κοσμ ος	πατηρ
2	τον	θε ον	υἱ ον	κοσμ ον	πατερ α
3	του	θε ου	υἱ ου	κοσμ ου	πατρ ος
4	τῳ	θε ῳ	υἱ ῳ	κοσμ ῳ	πατρ ι

3.4   You will see that πατηρ (father) behaves differently
        from the other nouns in the chart. πατρος looks as if
        it should be ending 1, not ending 3. πατηρ is not the
        only word to behave like this, but fortunately there is
        a reliable way of telling whether -ος indicates ending
        1 or ending 3. Usually the definite article (the word
        "the") will be present, and that is a strong clue. So
        we have ὁ υἱος but του πατρος.

3.5   Look at these examples to see how the four endings
        are used.

1. ὁ πατηρ γινωσκει τον υἱον.   The Father
                                  knows the
                                  Son.

2. ὁ υἱος γινωσκει τον πατερα.   The Son
                                  knows the
                                  Father.

3. ὁ υἱος του θεου φιλει τον κοσμον.

The Son of God loves the world.

4. ὁ θεος λεγει τῳ κοσμῳ, Οὑτος ἐστιν ὁ υἱος μου.

God says to the world, "This is my Son."

A pattern emerging

3.6   You should be able to see a pattern emerging.

• Where a word is **the subject** of a verb it adopts **ending 1**. The subject is the one who is doing the action of the verb.

In example 1 it is *the Father* who knows; in examples 2 and 3 it is *the Son* who knows and loves. In example 4 it is *God* who loves.

• Where a word is **the object** of a verb it adopts **ending 2**. The object is rather quaintly described in some grammar books as "the sufferer of an action". In one of my grammar books the example which is given is "George kicked the dog" (where the dog is the object). However, the object does not always "suffer" quite as vividly as that!

In example 1 *the Son* is the object; in example 2 it is *the Father*, and in example 3 it is *the world*.

• Where we would use **of** or **'s** in English, Greek uses **ending 3**.

In example 3 the Greek for *of God* has ending 3. Note that the English could also have been written "*God's* Son". In English it is much more usual to talk about "Peter's wife" than "the wife of Peter", but to analyze Greek sentences it is more helpful to use a construction with "of".

• When something is done **to** or **for** somebody we refer to that person as the **indirect object**.

In example 4 *the world* is the indirect object, and in Greek ending 4 is used.

● Where a word is the **complement** of a verb it adopts **ending 1**.

If you look at what God says in example 4 you may be surprised by the structure: *"This* [ending 1] is *the Son* [ending 1]."* You may have expected that *"the Son"* would be the object and would have ending 2. The verb "to be" (e.g. is, was, will be, etc) has what is called a **complement**, not an object. Another example may help to clarify the difference between an object and a complement. Look at these two statements and the way they are analyzed. Notice whether the subject and object/complement are the same person or thing.

George kicked the dog.　[**A** (subject)
　　　　　　　　　　　　kicked **B** (object).]
George is a dog.　　　　[**A** (subject)
　　　　　　　　　　　　is **A** (complement).]

Exercise 3.6

Translate these sentences into English. Note that if there is no word with ending 1 before the verb the subject will be included in the verb's endings, i.e. "I. . .", "you. . .", etc.

1. ὁ υἱος φιλει (loves) τον πατερα.
2. ὁ πατηρ φιλει τον υἱον.
3. ὁ πατηρ και (and) ὁ υἱος φιλουσιν τον κοσμον.
4. ὁ υἱος του πατρος σῳζει (saves) τον κοσμον.
5. λεγω τῳ πατρι, Φιλω τον υἱον σου (of you).
6. φιλουμεν (we love) τον πατερα και γινωσκομεν τον υἱον του θεου.

[Some verbs adopt the ending -ουμεν rather than -ομεν to denote that "we" do something. More about this in Chapter 6.]

Word order and word endings

3.7   In English the key to the meaning is in the order of
       the words. Look at these simple sentences.

● The Father loves the Son.
● The Son loves the Father.

By changing the order of the words we have changed
the meaning. Now look at the same sentences in
Greek. You will see that the word order is flexible.

● The Father loves the Son. ὁ πατηρ φιλει τον υἱον.
                          OR   τον υἱον φιλει ὁ πατηρ.

● The Son loves the Father. ὁ υἱος φιλει τον πατερα.
                          OR   τον πατερα φιλει ὁ υἱος.

Because the meaning is contained in the endings, the
order of the words is not so important. In the
following exercise you will see that it is possible to be
even more flexible in word order.

Exercise 3.7

Look carefully at these sentences and give the English meanings.

1. φιλει τον υἱον ὁ πατηρ.
2. ὁ πατηρ τον υἱον φιλει.
3. τον υἱον του θεου οὐ φιλει ὁ κοσμος.
4. τον κοσμον φιλουσιν ὁ υἱος και ὁ πατηρ.
5. ὁ υἱος ἐστιν ὁ θεος.
6. ὁ υἱος οὐκ ἐστιν ὁ πατηρ.
7. φιλει ὁ υἱος τον πατερα.
8. σῳζει ὁ υἱος του θεου τον κοσμον.
9. λεγει ὁ κοσμος τῳ πατρι, Οὐ γινωσκομεν τον
   υἱον.
10. λεγει τῳ κοσμῳ ὁ υἱος, Τον πατερα οὐ
    γινωσκετε;

Back on the case

3.8   A noun will adopt different endings depending on the part it is playing in a sentence. The correct way to describe these changes is to say that the word is in a certain "case". So the real solution to the case of the different endings is that

---

> ## THEY ARE THE ENDINGS OF
> ## THE DIFFERENT CASES

3.9   There are four cases, corresponding to the four endings we have considered. Their names, in order, are **Nominative, Accusative, Genitive** and **Dative**. It is worth knowing these technical terms as they are used in dictionaries, commentaries, etc. A little bit of "nonsense" may help to sort out their significance:

I **nominate** the **accused** of **Genoa** for a **date**.

There is a fifth case called the **Vocative**, which is used when you address somebody, but it is hardly worth learning separately as it often has the same ending as the Nominative case. The word κυριος is one that has a separate vocative, κυριε.

They say to him, "Yes, **Lord**" (Matthew 9:28).
λεγουσιν αὐτῳ, Ναι **κυριε**.

Another use for the cases

3.10   Nominative (ending 1) and Accusative (ending 2) are used for the subject and object of a verb. Genitive (ending 3) is used for possession. These uses are very common.

Cases are also used after words called prepositions, words which "put things in their place". Here are some examples of prepositions in English: **into, from** and **in**.

- **into** the world, **from** the world, **in** the world

See what happens to these in the Greek language:

- εἰς τον κοσμον, ἐκ του κοσμου, ἐν τῳ κοσμῳ

The prepositions εἰς, ἐκ and ἐν do not change, but they cause a change in the case of the following words which they are "putting in place". The nominative case is never used with prepositions but the accusative, genitive and dative cases often are.

Exercise 3.10

Fill in the gaps in this review paragraph.

The nominative case is used for the _____ of a verb but is never used after a _____. The _____ case is used for the object of a verb and is also used after some prepositions. One of these is εἰς, meaning _____. The _____ case is used to show possession and is used after some prepositions. One of these is _____, meaning "from". The dative case is used for the _____ object, but more frequently in association with _____. One of these is ἐν, meaning _____.

Personal pronouns

3.11 Greek has a full set of personal pronouns, each with
      four cases. Study these examples and see how the
      chart has been filled in.

      ἐγω και ὁ πατηρ ἑν ἐσμεν.   I and the Father
                  (one we-are)   are one
                                    (John 10:30).

      το ποτηριον ὃ δεδωκεν μοι   The cup which the
      ὁ πατηρ.   Father has given
                                    to me (John 18:11).

      Φιλεις με;   Do you love me?
                                    (John 21:17).

      Βοσκε τα προβατα μου.   Feed my sheep
                                    (the sheep of-me)
                                    (John 21:17).

	1 Nominative	ἐγω
I/me	2 Accusative	με
	3 Genitive	μου
	4 Dative	μοι

There are alternative endings for accusative, genitive
and dative: ἐμε, ἐμου and ἐμοι.

View and do

3.12 Look carefully at these Greek texts with their English
      translations and complete the charts which follow.

Exercise 3.12

ὁ πατηρ ἡμων Ἀβρααμ ἐστιν.	Abraham is our father (John 8:39).
ἡμεις δε κηρυσσομεν Χριστον ἐσταυρωμενον.	But we preach Christ crucified. (1 Corinthians 1:23).
ὁ κοσμος οὐ γινωσκει ἡμας.	The world does not know us (1 John 3:1).
γινωσκομεν ὁτι μενει ἐν ἡμιν.	We know that he remains in us (1 John 3:24).

we/us

1	Nominative	ἡμεις
2	Accusative	＿＿＿
3	Genitive	＿＿＿
4	Dative	＿＿＿

ὁ βασιλευς σου ἐρχεται σοι.	Your king is coming to you (Matthew 21:5).
συ γινωσκεις ὁτι φιλω σε.	You know that I love you (John 21:17).

you (singular)

1	Nominative	συ
2	Accusative	＿＿＿
3	Genitive	＿＿＿
4	Dative	＿＿＿

δια τουτο μισει ὑμας ὁ κοσμος.   Because of this the world hates you (John 15:19).

Ἰδε ὁ βασιλευς ὑμων.   Behold your king (John 19:14).

ὑμεις ἐχετε κυριον ἐν οὐρανῳ.   You have a master in heaven (Colossians 4:1).

Ταυτα γραφω ὑμιν.   I write these things to you (1 John 2:1).

you (plural)

1	Nominative	ὑμεις
2	Accusative	_____
3	Genitive	_____
4	Dative	_____

αὐτος γαρ σωσει τον λαον αὐτου.   For he will save his people (Matthew 1:21).

ἐγω οὐ κρινω αὐτον.   I do not judge him (John 12:47).

ὁ θεος ἐν αὐτῳ μενει.   God remains in him (1 John 4:15).

he

1	Nominative	αὐτος
2	Accusative	_____
3	Genitive	_____
4	Dative	_____

ὁ δε οὐκ ἀπεκριθη αὐτη λογον.   But he did not answer [to] her a word.

. . . οἱ μαθηται αὐτου ἠρωτουν αὐτον λεγοντες, Ἀπολυσον αὐτην.   . . .His disciples asked him saying, "Send her away" (Matthew 15:23).

και εαν αυτη απολυσασα	And if she having divorced
τον ανδρα αυτης	her husband
γαμηση αλλον	marries another
μοιχαται.	she commits adultery
	(Mark 10:12).

she

	1 Nominative	αυτη
	2 Accusative	_____
	3 Genitive	_____
	4 Dative	_____

και εθεραπευσεν αυτους.	And he healed them
	(Matthew 4:24).
και αυτοι εν τω κοσμω εισιν.	And they are in the world
	(John 17:11).
εγω δεδωκα αυτοις τον λογον σου.	I have given your word to them
	(John 17:14).
ταφος ανεωγμενος ο λαρυγξ αυτων.	Their throat [is] an open grave (Romans 3:13).
	(grave open the throat of them)

they

	1 Nominative	αυτοι
	2 Accusative	_____
	3 Genitive	_____
	4 Dative	_____

A final note on the genitive

3.13 In Greek "my son" is usually expressed as "the son of me". The "of me" part is in the genitive case, whatever the case of "the son". Note how μου (my) remains constant in the following examples.

My son knows him.	ὁ υἱος μου γινωσκει αὐτον.
He knows my son.	αὐτος γινωσκει τον υἱον μου.
He is a friend of my son.	αὐτος ἐστιν φιλος του υἱου μου.
He is speaking to my son.	αὐτος λαλει τῳ υἱῳ μου.

Answers to exercises

Exercise 3.6

1. The Son loves the Father.
2. The Father loves the Son.
3. The Father and the Son love the world.
4. The Son of the Father saves the world.
5. I say to the Father, "I love your Son."
6. We love the Father and we know the Son of God.

Exercise 3.7

1. The Father loves the Son.
2. The Father loves the Son
3. The world does not love the Son of God.
4. The Son and the Father love the world.
5. The Son is God.
6. The Son is not the Father.
7. The Son loves the Father.
8. The Son of God saves the world.
9. The world says to the Father, "We do not know the Son."
10. The Son says to the world, "Do you not know the Father?"

**Did you spot the question mark in number 10?

Exercise 3.10

The nominative case is used for the <u>subject</u> of a verb but is never used after a <u>preposition</u>. The <u>accusative</u> case is used for the object of a verb and is also used after some prepositions. One of these is εἰς, meaning "<u>into</u>". The <u>genitive</u> case is used to show possession and is used after some prepositions. One of these is ἐκ, meaning "from". The dative case is used for the <u>indirect</u> object, but more frequently in association with <u>prepositions</u>. One of these is ἐν, meaning "*in*".

Exercise 3.12

we/us	1 Nominative	ἡμεις
	2 Accusative	ἡμας
	3 Genitive	ἡμων
	4 Dative	ἡμιν

you (singular)	1 Nominative	συ
	2 Accusative	σε
	3 Genitive	σου
	4 Dative	σοι

you (plural)	1 Nominative	ὑμεις
	2 Accusative	ὑμας
	3 Genitive	ὑμων
	4 Dative	ὑμιν

he	1 Nominative	αὐτος
	2 Accusative	αὐτον
	3 Genitive	αὐτου
	4 Dative	αὐτῳ

she

1	Nominative	αὐτη
2	Accusative	αὐτην
3	Genitive	αὐτης
4	Dative	αὐτῃ

they

1	Nominative	αὐτοι
2	Accusative	αὐτους
3	Genitive	αὐτων
4	Dative	αὐτοις

REVIEW QUESTIONS

1. What is the most significant difference between Greek nouns and English nouns?

2. How many basic endings does a Greek noun have?

3. What do these words mean?

   ὁ θεος υἱος κοσμος πατηρ

4. How would you usually be able to distinguish between υἱος (ending 1) and πατρος (ending 3)?

5. What is meant by the subject of a verb and what ending is used in Greek?

6. What is meant by the object of a verb and how is it usually identified in Greek?

7. When is the third noun ending used?

8. What is an indirect object and which ending is used for it in Greek?

9. How does a complement differ from an object?

10. Why is word order more flexible in Greek than in English?

11. What are the four main cases?

12. Which case often has the same endings as the nominative and what is it used for?

13. What are prepositions and in what way are they related to the cases of nouns?

14. What are the Greek personal pronouns?

15. How do the personal pronouns change to indicate the different cases?

REVIEW EXERCISES

SELECT AND TRANSLATE

Select the correct alternative and then translate the phrase.

1. [εἰς ἐν] τον κοσμον
2. [εἰς ἐν] τῳ κοσμῳ
3. [εἰς ἐκ] του πατρος
4. [εἰς ἐκ] τον πατερα
5. [ἐκ ἐν] του οὐρανου
6. [ἐκ ἐν] τῳ οὐρανῳ
7. εἰς [αὐτον αὐτου]
8. ἐν [αὐτης αὐτη]
9. ἐξ [αὐτης αὐτη]   ἐκ is written ἐξ before a vowel.
10. ἐν [αὐτων αὐτοις]
11. [ἐγω συ αὐτος] γινωσκεις
12. [ἐγω συ αὐτος] ἀκουω
13. [ἡμεις ὑμεις αὐτη] λεγομεν
14. [ἡμεις ὑμεις αὐτη] γραφει
15. [αὐτοι ἡμεις συ] μενουσιν
16. [αὐτοι ἡμεις συ] πιστευομεν
17. [ὑμεις ἐγω ἡμεις] βλεπετε
18. [ὑμεις ἐγω ἡμεις] ἐχομεν
19. [συ αὐτος ὑμεις] λεγει
20. [συ αὐτος ὑμεις] ἀποστελλετε

FILL THE GAPS

Words have been removed from these texts and must be put back in the correct places.

ἀποκριθεις δε Σιμων Πετρος εἰπεν, *** εἰ ὁ Χριστος ὁ *** του *** του ζωντος.

Simon Peter said in answer, "*You* are the Christ the *Son* of the living *God*" (Matthew 16:16).

[θεου Συ υἱος]

σαρξ και αἱμα οὐκ ἀπεκαλυψεν *** ἀλλ' ὁ *** μου ὁ *** τοις οὐρανοις.

Flesh and blood has not revealed [it] *to you* but my *Father in* heaven (Matthew 16:17).

[ἐν πατηρ σοι]

ἰδου *** ἀποστελλω τον ἀγγελον *** προ προσωπου ***.

Behold *I* send *my* messenger before the face *of you (Mark 1:2).*

[μου σου ἐγω]

Και εἰπεν ***, Ἀναστας πορευου· ἡ πιστις *** σεσωκεν ***.

And he said *to him*, "Rise, go. *Your* faith has made *you* well" (Luke 17:19).

[σε σου αὐτῳ]

ἀπεκριθη Ἰησους και εἰπεν ***, Ὁτι εἰπον *** ὁτι εἰδον *** ὑποκατω της συκης πιστευεις;

Jesus answered and said *to him*, "Because I said *to you* that I saw *you* under the fig tree do you believe?" (John 1:50).

[σε σοι αὐτῳ]

μη *** μειζων εἰ του πατρος *** Ἰακωβ, ὃς ἐδωκεν *** το φρεαρ;

Are *you* greater than *our* father Jacob, who gave the well *to us*? (John 4:12).

[ἡμων συ ἡμιν]

*** προσκυνειτε ὃ *** οἴδατε· *** προσκυνουμεν ὃ οἴδαμεν.

You worship what you do *not* know; *we* worship what we know (John 4:22).

[οὐκ ἡμεις ὑμεις]

*** ἐληλυθα *** τῳ ὀνοματι του πατρος ***, και οὐ λαμβανετε ***.

"*I* have come *in my* Father's name, and you do not receive *me* (John 5:43).

[ἐν με μου ἐγω]

Εἶπεν οὖν παλιν ***, *** ὑπαγω και ζητησετε ***, και ἐν τῃ ἁμαρτιᾳ *** ἀποθανεισθε.

So he said again *to them*, "*I* am going and you will seek *me*, and you will die in *your* sin" (John 8:21).

[με ἐγω αὐτοις ὑμων]

ἐστιν ὁ πατηρ *** ὁ δοξαζων ***, ὃν *** λεγετε ὁτι Θεος *** ἐστιν.

It is *my* Father who glorifies *me*, whom *you* say that "He is *our* God" (John 8:54).

[ἡμων μου με ὑμεις]

WORDS TO LEARN

αὐτη   she
αὐτος   he
αὐτοι   they
ἐγω   I
εἰς + accusative   into
ἐκ, (ἐξ) + genitive   from, (out) of
ἐν + dative   in, by, among
ἡ ἀγαπη   (the) love
ἡ ζωη   (the) life

ζωη αἰωνιος   eternal life
ἡμεις   we
λογος   word
οὐρανος (often plural, οὐρανοι)   heaven
οὑτος   this
συ   you (singular)
το προσωπον   face
σωζω   save
το φως   (the) light
ὑμεις   you (plural)
φιλω   I love

CHAPTER FOUR

Preview

Gender: masculine feminine and neuter

ἡ οἰκια διαθηκη το εὐαγγελιον

John 1:1–13

CHAPTER FOUR

What gender is your house?

Masculine feminine or neuter?

4.1 In English we don't have to worry too much about gender. Nouns that refer specifically to males are masculine, and those that refer to females are feminine. So "lion", "father" and "boy" are masculine and "lioness", "mother", and "girl" are feminine. Some nouns can refer to either male or female and they are said to have a common gender, words like "animal", "parent" and "child". Anything outside these categories is simply neuter, for example "den", "house", "toy".

In Greek many words which we would think of as neuter are either masculine or feminine. There is no hidden significance in this; the gender is often quite arbitrary. The words listed in section 3.3 are all masculine. That is predictable with "God", "son", and "father" but "world" is also masculine, which you may find surprising.

4.2 When you look up a noun in a Greek dictionary (sometimes called a lexicon) you will find it in this format:

οἶκος, ου m *house, home, family, household.*

The first two pieces of information give you the basic nominative singular form of the noun (οἶκος) along with the ending for the genitive singular (-ου). The third piece of information is the gender, here "m" for masculine. Then various English meanings are listed.

4.3   Here are some texts from the New Testament with their English meanings. Use them to refresh your memory about the endings of the different cases.

1. **ὁ οἶκος** μου οἶκος προσευχης κληθησεται.
                        a house of prayer will be called
   My house will be called a house of prayer
   (Mark 11:17).

2. μη ποιειτε **τον οἶκον** του πατρος μου οἶκον ἐμποριου.
                    the house of-the father of-me
   Do not make my Father's house a house of trade
   (John 2:16).

3. κατεσκευασεν κιβωτον εἰς σωτηριαν **του οἶκου** αὐτου
   He prepared an ark for [the] salvation of his house
   (Hebrews 11:7).

4. Μαριαμ δε ἐν **τῳ οἶκῳ** ἐκαθεζετο.
   But Mary sat in the house (John 11:20).

4.4   Now look at this text from Luke 10:7 with its English translation and see if you notice anything unexpected.

ἐν αὐτῃ δε τῃ οἰκιᾳ μενετε
ἐσθιοντες και πινοντες τα παρ' αὐτων·
ἀξιος γαρ ὁ ἐργατης του μισθου αὐτου.
μη μεταβαινετε ἐξ οἰκιας εἰς οἰκιαν.

But remain in the same house
eating and drinking what they provide;
for worthy [is] the labourer of his pay.
Do not go from house to house.

A different word for "house" has been used, οἰκια. It has a different set of endings. Can you complete this chart? Note that ἐξ is the same word as ἐκ, but the vowel at the beginning of οἰκιας makes it change from κ (k) to ξ (x).

Exercise 4.4

	the (f)	house	
1	ἡ	οἰκι α	nom
2	την	οἰκι _____	acc
3	της	οἰκι _____	gen
4	τῃ	οἰκι _____	dat

4.5 The way in which this word would appear in a dictionary is **οἰκια, ας** f *house, home, family, household*.

You will notice that the definite article (the) has a separate set of forms for feminine words. For example

ἐν τῳ οἰκῳ

In the house

ἐν τῃ οἰκιᾳ

4.6 There are feminine nouns with endings that copy the definite article almost exactly, such as **διαθηκη, ης** f *covenant*. You can see the similarity in these examples.

1. τουτο το ποτηριον ἡ καινη **διαθηκη** ἐστιν.
   This cup is the new covenant (1 Corinthians 11:25).

2. συντελεσω διαθηκην καινην, οὐ κατα **την διαθηκην** ἡν ἐποιησα τοις πατρασιν αὐτων.
   I will make a new covenant, not like the covenant which I made with their fathers (Hebrews 8:8–9).

3. τουτο ἐστιν το αἱμα μου **της διαθηκης**.
   This is my blood of the covenant (Mark 14:24).

4. αὐτοι οὐκ ἐμειναν ἐν **τῃ διαθηκῃ** μου.
   They did not remain in my covenant (Hebrews 8:9).

And now the good news

4.7   As well as masculine and feminine nouns Greek also
has neuter nouns. One of these is the word which
means "gospel" or "good news". If you pronounce it
correctly it should remind you of some familiar
English words. Here it is in its dictionary form.

εὐαγγελιον, ου n *good news, gospel*

The stem is εὐαγγελι *and the nominative singular*
ending is ον. With a small change from Greek υ (u) to
English "v" we can see the derivation of words like
evangelist, evangelism, etc. It is related to the word
ἀγγελος, ου m angel, messenger.

We see the genitive clearly in the opening of Mark's
Gospel:

Ἀρχη του εὐαγγελιου Ἰησου Χριστου υἱου θεου.
Beginning of the gospel of Jesus Christ Son of God.

See if you can identify the endings of the accusative
and dative from Mark 1:14–15.

ἠλθεν ὁ Ἰησους εἰς την Γαλιλαιαν κηρυσσων το
εὐαγγελιον του θεου και λεγων ὁτι Πεπληρωται
ὁ καιρος και ἠγγικεν [ēngiken] ἡ βασιλεια του θεου·
μετανοειτε και πιστευετε ἐν τῳ εὐαγγελιῳ.

Jesus came into Galilee preaching the gospel of God
and saying, "The time is fulfilled and the kingdom of
God is at hand; repent and believe in the gospel."

The endings for nominative and accusative are in fact
the same, -ον. The genitive ending is -ου and the
dative is -ῳ. This gives us one or two helpful hints to
remember.

1. In neuter words the nominative and accusative are
   always identical.
2. Neuter words tend to be more like masculine than
   feminine words in the way they are formed.

Now complete this chart by filling in the endings of εὐαγγελιον. Note that the definite article has already been printed correctly. The nominative and accusative are το (not τον).

Exercise 4.7

	the (n)	gospel	
1	το	εὐαγγελι ον	nom
2	το	εὐαγγελι ____	acc
3	του	εὐαγγελι ____	gen
4	τῳ	εὐαγγελι ____	dat

In the beginning

4.8 The following set of exercises is based on John 1:1–13. First practise reading the Greek text to make sure you can identify the words properly, but don't expect to understand what it means yet. Then go on to the exercises.

¹ Ἐν ἀρχῃ ἠν ὁ λογος, και ὁ λογος ἠν προς τον θεον, και θεος ἠν ὁ λογος. ²οὑτος ἠν ἐν ἀρχῃ προς τον θεον. ³παντα δι' αὐτου ἐγενετο, και χωρις αὐτου ἐγενετο οὐδε ἑν. ὁ γεγονεν ⁴ἐν αὐτῳ ζωη ἠν, και ἡ ζωη ἠν το φως των ἀνθρωπων· ⁵και το φως ἐν τῃ σκοτιᾳ φαινει, και ἡ σκοτια αὐτο οὐ κατελαβεν. ⁶Ἐγενετο ἀνθρωπος ἀπεσταλμενος παρα θεου, ὀνομα αὐτῳ Ἰωαννης· ⁷οὑτος ἠλθεν εἰς μαρτυριαν, ἱνα μαρτυρηςῃ περι του φωτος, ἱνα παντες πιστευσωσιν δι' αὐτου. ⁸οὐκ ἠν ἐκεινος το φως, ἀλλ' ἱνα μαρτυρηςῃ περι του φωτος. ⁹Ἡν το φως το ἀληθινον, ὁ φωτιζει παντα ἀνθρωπον, ἐρχομενον

εἰς τον κοσμον. ¹⁰ἐν τῳ κοσμῳ ἦν, και ὁ κοσμος δι᾽ αὐτου ἐγενετο, και ὁ κοσμος αὐτον οὐκ ἐγνω. ¹¹εἰς τα ἰδια ἦλθεν, και οἱ ἰδιοι αὐτον οὐ παρελαβον. ¹²ὁσοι δε ἐλαβον αὐτον, ἐδωκεν αὐτοις ἐξουσιαν τεκνα θεου γενεσθαι, τοις πιστευουσιν εἰς το ὀνομα αὐτου, ¹³οἳ οὐκ ἐξ αἱματων οὐδε ἐκ θεληματος σαρκος οὐδε ἐκ θεληματος ἀνδρος ἀλλ᾽ ἐκ θεου ἐγεννηθησαν.

Exercise 4.8

1. Translate this piece of "Grenglish" into English, referring to the Greek text printed above which contains the clues you need.

¹In the beginning was the word, and ὁ λογος ἦν with God, και ὁ λογος was θεος. ²He was ἐν ἀρχῃ προς τον θεον. ³Everything through him was made, and without him nothing ἐγενετο. What was made ⁴in him ἦν life, και ἡ ζωη ἦν the light of human beings; ⁵and το φως shines in the darkness, και ἡ σκοτια has not put it out.
⁶There was a man sent from θεου, whose name was John; ⁷οὑτος came for witness, that he might witness about the light, that all people might believe δι᾽ αὐτου. ⁸He οὐκ ἦν το φως, but [he came] ἱνα μαρτυρηςῃ περι του φωτος. ⁹He was the true φως, which gives light to every ἀνθρωπον, coming εἰς τον κοσμον. ¹⁰ἐν τῳ κοσμῳ ἦν, και ὁ κοσμος ἐγενετο δι᾽ αὐτου, και ὁ κοσμος did not know αὐτον. ¹¹ἦλθεν to his own home, and his own people did not receive αὐτον. ¹²But as many as received αὐτον, he gave to them the right to become children θεου, to those who believe in το ὀνομα αὐτου, ¹³who were born οὐκ of blood, nor of the will of the flesh, οὐδε ἐκ θεληματος of a husband, but ἐκ θεου.

2. Answer the following questions (in English) to familiarize yourself with the passage, referring to

both the Greek and your translation from the "Grenglish".

a) When is it stated that ὁ λογος already existed (verse 1)?
b) Who was he with (verse 2)?
c) What was made without him (verse 3)?
d) What was ἡ ζωη (verse 4)?
e) What does το φως do, and where (verse 5)?
f) Who was ἀπεσταλμενος παρα θεου (verse 6)?
g) Why did he come (verse 7)?
h) What was he not (verse 8)?
i) How is το φως described (verse 9)?
j) What was made by ὁ λογος (verse 10)?
k) To whom did ὁ λογος come (verse 11)?
l) Who received the right to become τεκνα θεου (verse 12)?
m) In what way did their relationship with God change (verse 13)?

3. What do these words mean?

ἠν (verse 1), παντα (verse 3), ἀνθρωπων (verse 4), κατελαβεν (verse 5), ἀπεσταλμενος (verse 6), πιστευσωσιν (verse 7), ἀληθινον (verse 9) ἐγνω (verse 10), ἠλθεν (verse 11), ἐλαβον (verse 12), θεληματος (verse 13), ἐγεννηθησαν (verse 13)

4. Find a word or expression in the same verse which is roughly opposite to these.

οὐδε ἑν (verse 3), το φως (verse 5), ἐκ θεληματος ἀνδρος (verse 13)

5. Say whether these "Grenglish" statements are true to the meaning of the verses they refer to.

a) God became ὁ λογος (verse 1).
b) The word was in the beginning προς τον θεον (verse 2).

c) Everything was made χωρις αὐτου (verse 3).

d) In him was σκοτια (verse 4).

e) ἡ ζωη shines in the darkness (verse 5).

f) John was ἀπεσταλμενος παρα θεου (verse 6).

g) John came ἱνα παντες πιστευσωσιν εἰς αὐτον (verse 7).

h) John was το φως (verse 8).

i) The true light ἠν ἐρχομενον εἰς τον κοσμον (verse 9).

j) The world δι' αὐτου οὐκ ἐγενετο (verse 10).

k) His own παρελαβον αὐτον (verse 11).

l) He gave the right to become God's children τοις πιστευουσιν εἰς το ὀνομα αὐτου (verse 12).

m) God's children were born ἐκ θεληματος σαρκος (verse 13).

6. Supply what is missing in these dictionary entries.

ἀρχη, ης f _____   ἀνθρωπος, _____ m
                           man, human being

_____, ης f life   φως, φωτος n _____

φαινω _____   δια (or δι') + gen. _____

χωρις + _____ without   _____ + gen. about

Notes on John 1:1–13

4.9   θεος ἠν ὁ λογος, verse 1. This statement is sometimes misunderstood. It seems to be saying, "The word was a god," but that is not what it means. "God" is usually expressed as ὁ θεος, and "the word was God" could have been written

ὁ λογος ἠν ὁ θεος.

But because of the flexibility in Greek word order that could be translated "the word was God" or "God was the word". Sometimes Greek writers did not mind being ambiguous, but if they wanted to make the meaning unambiguous they removed the definite article from the complement (here θεος) and placed it immediately before the verb (ἠν), hence θεος ἠν ὁ λογος – "the word was God".

οὐδε ἑν (oude hen), verse 3, is literally "not-even one-thing".

ὁ γεγονεν, verse 3, may be linked with the earlier part of verse 3 or (as here) with verse 4. If the full stop is placed after γεγονεν at the end of verse 3 it means "nothing was made . . . that was made", and then verse 4 begins, "In him was life".

αὐτο οὐ κατελαβεν, verse 5, "has not put it out", understands the verb in the sense "overcome" but the verb can also mean "understand". This would give the different sense of "has not understood it". The New English Bible and the Revised English Bible have rather cleverly retained the two possibilities in their translation, "the darkness has never mastered it".

ὀνομα αὐτῳ Ἰωαννης, verse 6, is literally "name to him John".

ἀλλ' ἱνα, verse 8. We need to add something to make this verse read smoothly in English. The sense is ἀλλ' ἠλθεν ἱνα, i.e. "but **he came** that . . .".

Verse 9 can be understood in two ways. My "Grenglish" takes the subject as part of **ἠν**, "he was"; **ἐρχομενον**, "coming" then goes with **παντα ἀνθρωπον**, "every human being". This way of understanding the Greek lies behind the King James Version, *That was the true Light, which lighteth every man that cometh into the world.*

However most modern translators understand it differently. They take **το φως το ἀληθινον**, "the true light", as the subject and link **ἐρχομενον**, "coming" with **ἠν**, "was". The Revised Standard Version, for example, translates, *The true light that enlightens every man was coming into the world.*

Your knowledge of Greek should enable you to understand why these two interpretations are possible. Here is the text again, written in two ways, to highlight the difference.

1. ἦν το φως το ἀληθινον, ὃ φωτιζει παντα ἀνθρωπον (accusative masculine) ἐρχομενον (accusative masculine) εἰς τον κοσμον.

2. το φως το ἀληθινον (nominative neuter), ὃ φωτιζει παντα ἀνθρωπον, ἦν ἐρχομενον (nominative neuter) εἰς τον κοσμον.

Answers to exercises

Exercise 4.4

	the (f)	house	
1	ἡ	οἰκια	nom
2	την	οἰκιαν	acc
3	της	οἰκιας	gen
4	τῃ	οἰκιᾳ	dat

Exercise 4.7

	the (n)	gospel	
1	το	εὐαγγελιον	nom
2	το	εὐαγγελιον	acc
3	του	εὐαγγελιου	gen
4	τῳ	εὐαγγελιῳ	dat

Exercise 4.8

1. Check your translation with a modern English translation.

2. a) In the beginning. b) God. c) Nothing. d) ἡ ζωη (the life) was the light of human beings. e) το φως (the light) shines in the darkness. f) A man called John. g) To witness about the light. h) The light. i) The true light which gives light to every human being. j) The world. k) His own home and his own people l) All who received him and believed in his name. m) They were born of God, becoming his children.

3. ἠν was, παντα everything, ἀνθρωπων of human beings, κατελαβεν put out, ἀπεσταλμενος sent, πιστευσωσιν might believe, ἀληθινον true, ἐγνω knew (οὐκ ἐγνω did not know), ἠλθεν came, ἐλαβον received, θεληματος will, ἐγεννηθησαν were born.

4. Verse 3: οὐδε ἐν nothing – παντα everything
   Verse 5: το φως the light – ἡ σκοτια the darkness
   Verse 13: ἐκ θεληματος ἀνδρος of the will of a husband –
   ἐκ θεου of God.

5. a) No. b) Yes. c) No. d) No. e) No. The light, το φως, shines in the darkness. f) Yes. g) No. He came that all might believe δι' αὐτου, through him, not εἰς αὐτον, in him. h) No. i) Yes. j) No. k) No. l) Yes. m) No.

6. ἀρχη, ης f beginning ἀνθρωπος, ου m man, human being

   ζωη, ης f life φως, φωτος n light

   φαινω, shine δια (or δι') + gen. through

   χωρις + gen. without περι + gen. about

REVIEW QUESTIONS

1. How does Greek differ from English in the gender of nouns?

2. In what format do nouns appear in a Greek dictionary?

3. What is a lexicon?

4. Is there any difference in meaning between οἰκος and οἰκια?

5. What gender is διαθηκη and what does it mean?

6. What gender is εὐαγγελιον and what does it mean?

7. What are the distinguishing features of neuter nouns?

Questions on John 1:1–13

8. What do these nouns mean and what gender are they?
   λογος θεος ἀρχη σκοτια μαρτυρια φως κοσμος ὀνομα

9. What do these prepositions mean and what case follows them?
   ἐν προς δια (δι') χωρις παρα περι εἰς ἐκ (ἐξ)

10. What is the meaning of θεος ἠν ὁ λογος and is it ambiguous?

11. What is the meaning of αὐτο οὐ κατελαβεν and is it ambiguous?

12. In what ways can verse 9 be understood and how does the gender of the words affect the meaning?

REVIEW EXERCISES

THREE TOO MANY

One word is missing from each of the texts below and only one of the four words supplied is the right one.

1. και ἐλθοντες εἰς την *** εἰδον το παιδιον.

   And when they came into the house they saw the child (Matthew 2:11).

   [οἰκια οἰκιαν οἰκιας οἰκιᾳ]

2. και λαμπει πασιν τοις ἐν τῃ ***.

   And it gives light to all in the house (Matthew 5:15).

   [οἰκια οἰκιαν οἰκιας οἰκιᾳ]

3. ᾠκοδομησεν αὐτου την *** ἐπι την πετραν.

   He built his house on the rock (Matthew 7:24).

   [οἰκια οἰκιαν οἰκιας οἰκιᾳ]

4. ἀπηλθεν εἰς τον *** αὐτου.

   He went to his house (Matthew 9:7).

   [οἰκος οἰκον οἰκου οἰκῳ]

5. τα προβατα τα ἀπολωλοτα *** Ἰσραηλ.

   the lost sheep of (the) house of Israel (Matthew 10:6).

   [οἰκος οἰκον οἰκου οἰκῳ]

6. εἰσηλθεν εἰς τον *** του θεου.

   He went into the house of God (Matthew 12:4).

   [οἰκος οἰκον οἰκου οἰκῳ]

7. οὐκ οἰδατε γαρ ποτε ὁ κυριος της *** ἐρχεται.

   For you do not know when the master of the house is coming (Mark 13:35).

   [οἰκου οἰκιας οἰκῳ οἰκιᾳ]

8. ἐν Βηθανιᾳ ἐν τῃ *** Σιμωνος του λεπρου.
   In Bethany in the house of Simon the leper (Mark 14:3).
   [οἰκου οἰκιας οἰκῳ οἰκιᾳ]

9. σημερον γαρ ἐν τῳ *** σου δει με μειναι.
   For today I must stay in your house (Luke 19:5).
   [οἰκου οἰκιας οἰκῳ οἰκιᾳ]

10. ὁ ζηλος του *** σου καταφαγεται με.
    Zeal for your house will consume me (John 2:17).
    [οἰκου οἰκιας οἰκῳ οἰκιᾳ]

11. και ἐπιστευσεν αὐτος και ἡ *** αὐτου ὁλη.
    And he and all his house believed (John 4:53).
    [οἰκια οἰκιᾳ οἰκου οἰκῳ]

12. ὁ δε δουλος οὐ μενει ἐν τῃ *** εἰς τον αἰωνα.
    But the slave does not remain in the house for ever
    (John 8:35).
    [οἰκια οἰκιᾳ οἰκου οἰκῳ]

13. Μαριαμ δε ἐν τῳ *** ἐκαθεζετο.
    But Mary sat in the house (John 11:20).
    [οἰκια οἰκιᾳ οἰκου οἰκῳ]

14. ἐν τῃ *** του πατρος μου μοναι πολλαι εἰσιν.
    In my Father's house are many rooms (John 14:2).
    [οἰκια οἰκιᾳ οἰκου οἰκῳ]

15. Σολομων δε οἰκοδομησεν αὐτῳ *** .
    But Solomon built a house for him (Acts 7:47).
    [οἰκος οἰκον οἰκου οἰκῳ]

16. και εἰσηλθομεν εἰς τον *** του ἀνδρος.

   And we went into the man's house (Acts 11:12).

   [οἰκος οἰκον οἰκου οἰκῳ]

17. εἰδεν τον ἀγγελον ἐν τῳ *** αὐτου σταθεντα.

   He saw the angel standing in his house (Acts 11:13).

   [οἰκος οἰκον οἰκου οἰκῳ]

18. σωθησῃ συ και πας ὁ *** σου.

   You will be saved, and all your house (Acts 11:14).

   [οἰκου οἰκιας οἰκος οἰκιαν]

19. ἠλθεν ἐπι την *** της Μαριας της μητρος
   Ἰωαννου.

   He went to the house of Mary the mother of John
   (Acts 12:12).

   [οἰκου οἰκιας οἰκος οἰκιαν]

20. ἐβαπτισθη και ὁ *** αὐτης.

   She was baptized, and her house (Acts 16:15).

   [οἰκου οἰκιας οἰκος οἰκιαν]

AND NOW THE GOOD NEWS

Translate these phrases into English.

1. το εὐαγγελιον της βασιλειας   (Matthew 4:23).

2. ἐν τῳ εὐαγγελιῳ του υἱου αὐτου   (Romans 1:9).

3. το εὐαγγελιον μου δια Χριστου Ἰησου

                                       (Romans 2:16).

4. το εὐαγγελιον του θεου   (Romans 15:16).

5. το εὐαγγελιον του Χριστου   (Romans 15:19).

6. ἐν Χριστῷ Ἰησου δια του εὐαγγελιου

(1 Corinthians 4:15).

7. ἐν τῷ εὐαγγελιῳ του Χριστου (2 Corinthians 10:14).

8. ἐν ἀρχῃ του εὐαγγελιου   (Philippians 4:15).

9. το εὐαγγελιον ἡμων   (1 Thessalonians 1:5).

10. δια του εὐαγγελιου ἡμων   (2 Thessalonians 2:14).

WORDS TO LEARN

ἀνθρωπος, ου m   man, mankind, people
ἀρχη, ης f   beginning
βασιλεια, ας f   kingdom
Γαλιλαια, ας f   Galilee
δια + genitive   through
διαθηκη, ης f   covenant
ἐσθιω   eat
εὐαγγελιον, ου n   gospel, good news
ἠν   (he, she, it) was
Ἰωαννης, ου m   John
οἰκια, ας f   house, household
οἰκος, ου m   house, household
περι + genitive   about, concerning
πινω   drink
ποτηριον, ου n   cup
προς + accusative   with, to
προσευχη, ης f   prayer
σκοτια, ας f   darkness
σωτηρια, ας f   salvation
Χριστος, ου m   Christ, Messiah

CHAPTER FIVE

Preview

Forming plurals

οἱ πατερες υἱοι αἱ ἁμαρτιαι τα δαιμονια

Families of nouns

Family 1

Family 2

Family 3

The definite article

Luke 14:25–27

πιστις χαρις

CHAPTER FIVE

Family matters

One is not enough

5.1 So far we have looked at the singular forms of nouns like father, and son, but we need to know how to recognize the plural forms as well. In English the most common way of forming a plural is to add **s** to the singular: father → fathers, son → sons.

In Greek it is not so simple because each of the cases has a different ending for the plural.

Exercise 5.1

In this exercise you are going to discover the plural endings of the words for "father", "son", "sin" and "demon". Analyze the texts and complete the charts.

πατηρ, πατρος m *father*

οἱ πατερες ἡμων ἐν τῳ ὀρει τουτῳ προσεκυνησαν.	Our fathers worshipped on this mountain (John 4:20).
ὁ θεος των πατερων ἡμων ἐδοξασεν τον παιδα αὐτου Ἰησουν.	The God of our fathers glorified his servant Jesus (Acts 3:13).
Ἡ σκηνη του μαρτυριου ἠν τοις πατρασιν ἡμων ἐν τη ἐρημῳ.	The tent of witness was for our fathers in the desert (Acts 7:44).

ὁ θεος του λαου τουτου
Ἰσραηλ ἐξελεξατο τους
πατερας ἡμων.

The God of this people
Israel chose our fathers
(Acts 13:17).

οἱ	πατερες
___	_____
___	_____
___	_____

υἱος, ου m *son*

οὗτοι εἰσιν οἱ υἱοι
της βασιλειας.

These are the sons of the
kingdom (Matthew 13:38).

Τοτε προσηλθεν αὐτῳ ἡ μητηρ
των υἱων Ζεβεδαιου.

Then the mother of the
sons of Zebedee came to
him (Matthew 20:20).

και παραλαβων τον Πετρον και
τους δυο υἱους Ζεβεδαιου
ἠρξατο λυπεισθαι και
ἀδημονειν.

And taking Peter and
the two sons of Zebedee
he began to be sorrowful
and to be troubled
(Matthew 26:37).

τον λογον ὁν ἀπεστειλεν
τοις υἱοις Ἰσραηλ . . .
ὑμεις οἰδατε.

The word which he sent
to the sons of Israel . . .
you know (Acts 10:36,37).

οἱ	υἱοι
___	_____
___	_____
___	_____

ἁμαρτια, ας f *sin* [like οἰκια]

εἰ δε Χριστος οὐκ ἐγηγερται . . . But if Christ has not been
ἐτι ἐστε ἐν ταις ἁμαρτιαις raised . . . you are still
ὑμων. in your sins
(1 Corinthians 15:17).

ἐν ᾧ ἐχομεν την ἀπολυτρωσιν, In whom we have
την ἀφεσιν των ἁμαρτιων. redemption, the
forgiveness of sins
(Colossians 1:14).

Τινων ἀνθρωπων αἱ ἁμαρτιαι The sins of some people
προδηλοι εἰσιν. are obvious
(1 Timothy 5:24).

ἐξομολογεισθε οὐν ἀλληλοις Therefore confess to one
τας ἁμαρτιας. another the [i.e. your] sins
(James 5:16).

αἱ	ἁμαρτιαι
____	_____
____	_____
____	_____

δαιμονιον, ου n *demon* [like εὐαγγελιον]

οἱ δε Φαρισαιοι ἐλεγον, But the Pharisees were
'Εν τῳ ἀρχοντι των δαιμονιων saying, "By the prince of
ἐκβαλλει τα δαιμονια. demons he casts out
demons" (Matthew 9:34).

ἁ θυουσιν, δαιμονιοις και What they sacrifice they
οὐ θεῳ θυουσιν. sacrifice to demons and not to
God (1 Corinthians 10:20).

και τα δαιμονια πιστευουσιν
και φρισσουσιν [phrissousin].

Even the demons believe
and tremble (James 2:19).

τα	δαιμονια
____	_____
____	_____
____	_____

Nouns and their families

5.2   Greek nouns can be thought of as belonging to three different families, each of which has certain family characteristics – similarities which they share. There are also individual differences which persist in spite of the family likeness. Traditionally these families have been referred to as the "declensions", but I think that the idea of families is much more helpful.

In the charts below representatives of the families have been chosen to illustrate both the similarities and the differences within them.

Each column lists the four cases, singular first and then plural. In the plural the vocative is always the same as the nominative but in the singular it is sometimes different and the separate singular form is given where appropriate.

Family 1 [also known as the first declension]

		1.1	1.2	1.3	1.4	1.5	1.6
		fem.	fem.	fem.	masc.	masc.	masc.
		γραφη Scripture	καρδια heart	γλωσσα tongue	μαθητης disciple	νεανιας young man	Σατανας Satan
SING	N.	γραφη	καρδια	γλωσσα	μαθητης	νεανιας	Σατανας
	V.				μαθητα	νεανια	Σατανα
	A.	γραφην	καρδιαν	γλωσσαν	μαθητην	νεανιαν	Σαταναν
	G.	γραφης	καρδιας	γλωσσης	μαθητου	νεανιου	Σατανα
	D.	γραφη	καρδια	γλωσση	μαθητη	νεανια	Σατανα
PLUR	N.V.	γραφαι	καρδιαι	γλωσσαι	μαθηται	νεανιαι	
	A.	γραφας	καρδιας	γλωσσας	μαθητας	νεανιας	
	G.	γραφων	καρδιων	γλωσσων	μαθητων	νεανιων	
	D.	γραφαις	καρδιαις	γλωσσαις	μαθηταις	νεανιαις	

Family likeness

- In the plural the endings of the cases do not differ.
- In the singular forms γραφη and καρδια the only difference is the use of **η** or **α** in the endings.
- μαθητης and νεανιας also follow a similar pattern, deviating only in the genitive and vocative singular.
- Words like γραφη, καρδια and γλωσσα are always feminine; words like μαθητης, νεανιας and Σατανας are always masculine.

Individual differences

- καρδια and γλωσσα go their different ways in the genitive singular. The distinguishing factor is the last letter of the stem, **ι** in καρδι-α, and **σ** in γλωσσ-α. The rules are

▶ If the stem ends in a vowel (or **ρ**) it behaves like καρδια and retains the **α** throughout the singular.

▶ If the stem ends in a vowel (other than **ρ**) it behaves like γλωσσα, and switches to **η** in the genitive and dative singular.

Nouns like καρδια are much more common than nouns like γλωσσα.

- Nouns like Σατανας with the unusual **-α** ending in the genitive singular are rare. Like the νεανιας group most of them are people's names, e.g. Ἀνδρεας, ου m *Andrew,* Ἰουδας, α m *Judas.* Again, it is the last letter of the stem that signals the way they behave.

We have already met some words which belong to this family in previous chapters:
διαθηκη (section 4.6) behaves like γραφη; οἰκια (section 4.4) and ἁμαρτια (section 5.1) behave like καρδια.

Family 2 [also known as the second declension]

		2.1	2.2	2.3
		m/f	masc.	neut.
		λογος word	Ἰησους Jesus	ἐργον work
SING	N.	λογος	Ἰησους	ἐργον
	V.	λογε	Ἰησου	
	A.	λογον	Ἰησουν	ἐργον
	G.	λογου	Ἰησου	ἐργου
	D.	λογῳ	Ἰησου	ἐργῳ
PLUR	N.V.	λογοι		ἐργα
	A.	λογους		ἐργα
	G.	λογων		ἐργων
	D.	λογοις		ἐργοις

Family likeness

- The genitive and dative endings of λογος and ἐργον are identical in both singular and plural.
- The accusative singulars of λογος and ἐργον are the same.
- All nouns which follow the pattern of ἐργον are neuter.

Individual differences

- The nominative forms of λογος and ἐργον differ in both singular and plural.
- Although most of the nouns like λογος are masculine there are some which are feminine, e.g. ἐρημος, ου f *desert*. "In the desert" is ἐν τῃ ἐρημῳ.
- λογος and ἐργον represent a pattern which is followed by many nouns, but Ἰησους is a unique item. Note the dative singular Ἰησου very carefully. "In Jesus" is ἐν Ἰησου.

  Several of the nouns we have already met belong to this family: θεος, υἱος and κοσμος (section 3.3) and οἰκος (section 4.4) behave like λογος; εὐαγγελιον (section 4.7) and δαιμονιον (section 5.1) behave like ἐργον.

Family 3 [also known as the third declension]

		3.1	3.2	3.3	3.4	3.5	3.6	3.7
		m/f	m/f	m/f	fem.	masc.	neut.	neut.
		ἐλπις	πατηρ	ἰχθυς	πολις	βασιλευς	σωμα	ὀρος
		hope	father	fish	city	king	body	mountain
SING	N.	ἐλπις	πατηρ	ἰχθυς	πολις	βασιλευς	σωμα	ὀρος
	V.		πατερ	ἰχθυ	πολι	βασιλευ		
	A.	ἐλπιδα	πατερα	ἰχθυν	πολιν	βασιλεα	σωμα	ὀρος
	G.	ἐλπιδος	πατρος	ἰχθυος	πολεως	βασιλεως	σωματος	ὀρους
	D.	ἐλπιδι	πατρι	ἰχθυϊ	πολει	βασιλει	σωματι	ὀρει
PLUR	N.V.	ἐλπιδες	πατερες	ἰχθυες	πολεις	βασιλεις	σωματα	ὀρη
	A.	ἐλπιδας	πατερας	ἰχθυας	πολεις	βασιλεις	σωματα	ὀρη
	G.	ἐλπιδων	πατερων	ἰχθυων	πολεων	βασιλεων	σωματων	ὀρων
	D.	ἐλπισιν	πατρασιν	ἰχθυσιν	πολεσιν	βασιλευσιν	σωμασιν	ὀρεσιν

Notes on family 3

- Types 3.1, 3.2 and 3.3 contain both masculine and feminine nouns, and 3.1 is the pattern which has the biggest "following".

- The 3.6 pattern is equivalent to the 3.1 pattern for neuter nouns.

- Types 3.1 and 3.6 do not have a nominative singular ending. The stem only appears in the accusative singular in 3.1, and in the genitive singular in 3.6. This is why the dictionary form of nouns identifies the genitive as well as the nominative singular. Changes sometimes occur to the stem in the dative plural.

- Type 3.2 represents a small group containing only two other words, μητηρ, μητρος f *mother,* and θυγατηρ, θυγατρος f *daughter.* Notice that there are minor changes in the stem as well as the endings, which is unusual.

- Type 3.3 is not a large group and varies from 3.1 only in the accusative singular. The mark above the ι in ἰχθύϊ simply shows that it is pronounced ích-thú-í, not ích-thuí.

- Types 3.4 and 3.5 vary considerably from the 3.1 pattern, but they show marked similarities to each other. Nouns of the 3.4 pattern are nearly all feminine and the 3.5 group are all masculine.

- You have to look hard to see how type 3.7 got into this family. Nouns in this category are always neuter.

Never ending endings

5.3   It may seem that there is no end to the endings of these different nouns. To make things worse the families use the same endings in different ways.

A noun ending in -ος could be
- type 2.1 nominative singular
- type 3.1, 3.2, 3.3 or 3.6 genitive singular
- type 3.7 nominative or accusative singular

A noun ending in -ας could be
- type 1.2 genitive singular
- type 1.1, 1.2, 1.3, 1.4 or 1.5 accusative plural
- type 1.5 nominative singular
- type 3.1, 3.2 or 3.3 accusative plural

A noun ending in -η could be
- type 1.1 nominative singular
- type 3.7 nominative or accusative plural

A very useful little article

5.4   If all this seems hopelessly confusing don't despair. There is a reliable way of sorting out the different endings. The context of the passage will often give you a strong clue to the case of a noun, but an even better guide is the presence of the definite article (the word for "the").

The words λογος, πατρος and ἔθνος might look alike but with the definite article their different identities become clear: ὁ λογος (2.1), του πατρος (3.2) and το ὁρος (3.7).

The potential confusion of νεανιας and καρδιας is removed when the definite article appears: ὁ νεανιας (1.5), της καρδιας (1.2 genitive singular) and τας καρδιας (1.2 accusative plural).

It is worth learning the forms of the definite article thoroughly and looking out for them whenever you translate from the Greek New Testament.

The complete pattern of the definite article

	MASCULINE	FEMININE	NEUTER
	ὁ	ἡ	το
SINGULAR	τον	την	το
	του	της	του
	τῳ	τῃ	τῳ
	οἱ	αἱ	τα
PLURAL	τους	τας	τα
	των	των	των
	τοις	ταις	τοις

An extremely indefinite article

5.5   Greek does not have an indefinite article (the word "a" or "an" in English). The noun alone is used. So πατηρ can be translated "father" or "a father" according to the context.

Filling the gaps

Exercise 5.6

In this exercise you will need to refer to the charts in sections 5.2 and 5.4. You have also been given some nouns listed according to their family identity. Using this information work out the correct forms of the words that have been omitted from Luke 14:25–27 below.For example the first missing word is "father" (πατηρ) and the context tells you that it is the object of the verb "hate". The definite article (τον) confirms that you are looking for the accusative singular masculine form, which is πατερα.

1.1 ἀδελφη, ης f *sister*   ψυχη, ης f *life, soul*
1.4 μαθητης, ου m *disciple*
2.1 ἀδελφος, ου m *brother*   σταυρος, ου m *cross*
2.3 τεκνον, ου n *child*
3.1 γυνη, γυναικος f *wife, woman*
3.2 μητηρ, μητρος f *mother*   πατηρ, πατρος m *father*

Συνεπορευοντο δε αὐτῳ ὀχλοι πολλοι,	Now large crowds went with him
και στραφεις εἶπεν προς αὐτους·	and he turned and said to them,
Εἰ τις ἐρχεται προς με	"If anyone comes to me
και οὐ μισει τον __(1)__ ἑαυτου	and does not hate his father
και την __(2)__	and the (i.e. his) mother
και την __(3)__	and the wife
και τα __(4)__	and the children
και τους __(5)__	and the brothers
και τας __(6)__	and the sisters
ἐτι τε και την __(7)__ ἑαυτου,	and even his own life,
οὐ δυναται εἰναι μου __(8)__.	he cannot be my disciple.
ὁστις οὐ βασταζει τον __(9)__	Whoever does not carry the cross
ἑαυτου και ἐρχεται ὀπισω μου,	of himself and come after me,
οὐ δυναται εἰναι μου __(10)__.	cannot be my disciple."

Additional notes

- **προς**. In John 1:1–2 (Exercise 4.8) we saw that προς τον θεον meant "with God", but προς + acc. is used much more often to mean "to". It is an alternative way of expressing an indirect object. "He said to them" can be either εἰπεν αὐτοις or εἰπεν προς αὐτους.

- **ὀχλοι πολλοι**, "large crowds" is literally "crowds large". Greek again shows flexibility in the order of the words.

- **He [A] cannot be my disciple [A].** "Disciple" is a complement in this sentence not an object.

Grace and faith

5.7   The words "grace" (χαρις) and "faith" (πιστις) look as if they should behave in the same way. They are both from family 3 but their dictionary entry will show that they are from different parts of the family.

πιστις, εως f *faith*   χαρις, ιτος f *grace, favour*

πιστις is type 3.4 (like πολις) and χαρις is type 3.1 (like ἐλπις) but note that the genitive is χαριτος (not χαριδος).

Exercise 5.7

Write out the four forms of the singular of πιστις and χαρις.

For the accusative singular of χαρις you should have written χαριτα, and that is correct, but more often Greek writers used an alternative accusative singular, χαριν.

With abstract nouns like "grace" and "faith", things which you cannot see or touch physically, Greek tended to use the definite article. Hence ἡ χαρις is normally translated simply "grace" not "the grace".

Exercise 5.8

From the list of words supplied fill in the gaps in the texts below.

πιστει	πιστεως	πιστιν	πιστις	χαριν	χαρις
		χαριτι	χαριτος		

και ιδων ὁ Ἰησους την __(1)__ αὐτων εἰπεν τω παραλυτικω, Θαρσει, τεκνον, ἀφιενται σου αἱ ἁμαρτιαι.

And when Jesus saw their faith he said to the paralytic, "Take heart, child, your sins are forgiven" (Matthew 9:2).

ὁ δε Ἰησους στραφεις και ιδων αὐτην εἰπεν, Θαρσει, θυγατερ· ἡ __(2)__ σου σεσωκεν σε. και ἐσωθη ἡ γυνη ἀπο της ὡρας ἐκεινης.

But Jesus turning and seeing her said, "Take heart, daughter; your faith has made you well." And the woman was healed from that hour (Matthew 9:22).

Και Ἰησους προεκοπτεν ἐν τη σοφια και ἡλικια και __(3)__ παρα θεω και ἀνθρωποις.

And Jesus grew in wisdom and stature and favour with God and people (Luke 2:52).

Και παντες ἐμαρτυρουν αὐτω και ἐθαυμαζον ἐπι τοις λογοις της __(4)__ τοις ἐκπορευομενοις ἐκ του στοματος αὐτου και ἐλεγον, Οὐχι υἱος ἐστιν Ἰωσηφ οὑτος;

And they all testified to him and were amazed at the words of grace which came out from his mouth and they said, "Isn't this Joseph's son?" (Luke 4:22).

ὁτι ὁ νομος δια Μωϋσεως ἐδοθη, ἡ __(5)__ και ἡ ἀληθεια δια Ἰησου Χριστου ἐγενετο.

For the law was given through Moses, grace and truth came through Jesus Christ (John 1:17).

ἐχοντες δε το αὐτο πνευμα
της —(6)—
κατα το γεγραμμενον,
Ἐπιστευσα, διο ἐλαλησα,
και ἡμεις πιστευομεν,
διο και λαλουμεν.

Having the same spirit
of faith
according to what is written,
"I believed, therefore I spoke,"
we also believe,
and therefore we speak
(2 Corinthians 4:13).

Γνωριζομεν δε ὑμιν,
ἀδελφοι, την —(7)— του θεου
την δεδομενην ἐν ταις ἐκκλησιαις
της Μακεδονιας.

And we make known to you,
brothers, the grace of God
which was given in the churches
of Macedonia
(2 Corinthians 8:1).

Ἑαυτους πειραζετε εἰ
ἐστε ἐν τη —(8)—,
ἑαυτους δοκιμαζετε.

Examine yourselves [to see] if
you are in the faith,
test yourselves
(2 Corinthians 13:5).

Answers to exercises

Exercise 5.1

οἱ	πατερες
τους	πατερας
των	πατερων
τοις	πατρασιν

οἱ	υἱοι
τους	υἱους
των	υἱων
τοις	υἱοις

αἱ	ἁμαρτιαι
τας	ἁμαρτιας
των	ἁμαρτιων
ταις	ἁμαρτιαις

τα	δαιμονια
τα	δαιμονια
των	δαιμονιων
τοις	δαιμονιοις

Exercise 5.6
(1) πατερα (2) μητερα (3) γυναικα (4) τεκνα
(5) ἀδελφους (6) ἀδελφας (7) ψυχην
(8) μαθητης (9) σταυρον (10) μαθητης

Exercise 5.7

πιστις	χαρις
πιστιν	χαριτα (or χαριν)
πιστεως	χαριτος
πιστει	χαριτι

Exercise 5.8
(1) πιστιν   (2) πιστις   (3) χαριτι
(4) χαριτος   (5) χαρις   (6) πιστεως
(7) χαριν   (8) πιστει

REVIEW QUESTIONS

1. Why is forming plurals not so easy in Greek as in English?

2. What are the plural endings of ὁ πατηρ?

3. What are the plural endings of ὁ υἱός?

4. What are the plural endings of ἡ ἁμαρτια?

5. What are the plural endings of το δαιμονιον?

6. Why is it helpful to think of noun declensions as families, and how many families are there?

7. What do these words mean?

   γραφη καρδια γλωσσα μαθητης νεανιας Σατανας

8. How do γραφη and καρδια differ?

9. How do καρδια and γλωσσα differ? Which type is more common?

10. Are there many nouns like Σατανας?

11. Are nouns like λογος always masculine?

12. Are nouns like ἐργον always neuter?

13. How many other nouns follow the pattern of 'Ιησους?

14. Why do nouns of Family 3 have to be identified by the genitive singular as well as the nominative singular?

15. How many nouns behave like πατηρ?

16. Are nouns like πολις always feminine?

17. Are nouns like βασιλευς always masculine?

18. What factors help to establish the case, gender and family identity of words with ambiguous endings, such as λογος, πατρος and ἐθνος?

19. How is the indefinite article (a, an) expressed in Greek?

20. What two possible meanings can be represented by προς + accusative?

21. What are the two possible ways of expressing an indirect object in Greek?

22. In what way does Greek differ from English in the way abstract nouns appear?

REVIEW EXERCISES

ALL IN THE FAMILY

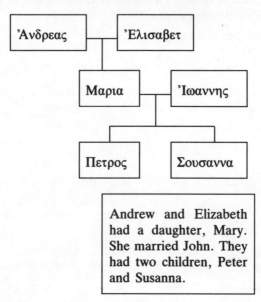

Andrew and Elizabeth had a daughter, Mary. She married John. They had two children, Peter and Susanna.

Read through this list of family facts and answer the following question.

ὁ Ἰωαννης ἐστιν ὁ ἀνηρ της Μαριας.

ἡ Μαρια ἐστιν ἡ γυνη του Ἰωαννου.

ὁ Ἰωαννης ἐστιν ὁ πατηρ του Πετρου και της Σουσαννης.

ἡ Μαρια ἐστιν ἡ μητηρ του Πετρου και της Σουσαννης.

ὁ Πετρος ἐστιν ὁ υἱος του Ἰωαννου και της Μαριας.

ἡ Σουσαννα ἐστιν ἡ θυγατηρ του Ἰωαννου και της Μαριας.

ὁ Πετρος και ἡ Σουσαννα εἰσιν τα τεκνα του Ἰωαννου.

ὁ Πετρος ἐστιν ὁ ἀδελφος της Σουσαννης.

ἡ Σουσαννα ἐστιν ἡ ἀδελφη του Πετρου.

ὁ Ἀνδρεας ἐστιν ὁ πενθερος του Ἰωαννου.

ἡ Ἐλισαβετ ἐστιν ἡ πενθερα του Ἰωαννου.

ἡ Ἐλισαβετ ἐστιν ἡ μαμμη του Πετρου.

What do these words mean?

ἀδελφη, ἀδελφος, ἀνηρ, γυνη, θυγατηρ, μαμμη, μητηρ, πατηρ, πενθερα, πενθερος, τεκνα, υἱος.

TRUE OR FALSE

Say whether each of these statements is true or false.

1. ἡ Μαρια ἐστιν ἡ θυγατηρ της Ἐλισαβετ.

2. ἡ Μαρια ἐστιν ἡ θυγατηρ του Ἀνδρεου.

3. ἡ Σουσαννα ἐστιν το τεκνον του Ἀνδρεου.

4. ἡ Ἐλισαβετ ἐστιν ἡ μητηρ του Πετρου.

5. ἡ Μαρια ἐστιν ἡ μαμμη της Σουσαννης.

6. ἡ Ἐλισαβετ ἐστιν ἡ μαμμη της Σουσαννης.

7. ὁ Ἀνδρεας ἐστιν ὁ ἀνηρ της Ἐλισαβετ.

8. ἡ Σουσαννα ἐστιν ἡ γυνη του Πετρου.

9. ὁ Πετρος οὐκ ἐστιν ὁ υἱος της Μαριας.

10. ὁ Ἀνδρεας ἐστιν ὁ πενθερος του Πετρου.

11. ὁ Πετρος και ἡ Σουσαννα εἰσιν τα τεκνα της Μαριας.

12. ἡ Μαρια οὐκ ἐστιν ἡ γυνη του Ἀνδρεου.

WORDS TO LEARN

ἀδελφη, ης f   sister
ἀδελφος, ου m   brother
ἁμαρτια, ας f   sin
βασιλευς, εως m   king
γλωσσα, ης f   tongue, language
γραφη, ης f   Scripture, writing (αἱ γραφαι, the Scriptures)
δαιμονιον ου n   demon
ἐλπις, ἐλπιδος f   hope
ἐργον, ου n   work, deed
ἰχθυς, ἰχθυος m   fish*
καρδια, ας f   heart
μαθητης, ου m   disciple
μητηρ, μητρος f   mother
νεανιας, ου m   young man
ὀρος, ους n   mountain
πιστις, εως f   faith
πολις, εως f   city, town
Σατανας, α m   Satan
σωμα, σωματος n   body
χαρις, χαριτος f   grace [acc. sing. often χαριν]

*[The sign of the fish derives from the days of the early church when the letters of the word were taken to stand for Ἰησους Χριστος Θεου Υἱος Σωτηρ, "Jesus Christ, Son of God, Saviour".]

CHAPTER SIX

Preview

CHAPTER SIX

Where the action is

Doing and being

6.1   Words which describe doing or being are called verbs and they are extremely powerful words. In Chapter 2 we learned that γινωσκω means "I know". It is made up of a stem, γινωσκ, which represents the basic meaning of the verb, and a set of changeable endings for "I", "you", etc.

Some words that went on a diet

6.2   There are some verbs that behave slightly differently from γινωσκω. Officially they are called "contracted" verbs because at some stage in their history they were longer words and their form was contracted, i.e. shortened. I prefer to think of them as words that went on a diet. Unfortunately the "diet" did not work out exactly and there are still one or two "bulges" visible.

The -εω *verbs*

6.3   The first group is represented by a verb which was once written φιλεω, meaning "I love". We can think of it as having three parts, φιλ-ε-ω, a regular stem, a regular set of endings and an extra ε. This extra ε disappeared, making the word shorter. In the process some of the endings were affected, but they are still fairly easy to identify.

Exercise 6.3

Put these jumbled forms into the correct order (I, you, etc). φιλειτε, φιλει, φιλουσιν, φιλω, φιλουμεν, φιλεις

Did you spot the different endings? They were **φιλουμεν** and **φιλειτε**. The old φιλεομεν dieted, and managed to get down to φιλουμεν, but never quite reached φιλομεν! φιλεετε got down to φιλειτε, but never reached φιλετε. The others were all more successful.

We can summarize the contractions by three simple "rules", which define what happened when the extra ε combined with the first letter of the endings.

ε + ε		→ ει
ε + ο		→ ου
ε + ω, η, ει or ου	→ the ε dropped out.

As a result o- at the beginning of an ending became ου- and ε- became ει-. So φιλεομεν became φιλουμεν and φιλεετε became φιλειτε. A long vowel (like ω) or a diphthong (like ει) "swallowed up" the extra ε so that it disappeared altogether.

In a dictionary verbs like this are listed in their "uncontracted" form, i.e. φιλεω, love.

The -αω and -οω verbs

6.4   Some verbs originally had an extra **α** or **o** in the middle, e.g. ἀγαπαω, (ἀγαπ-α-ω), meaning "I love", and πληροω (πληρ-ο-ω), meaning "I fill" or "I fulfil". They are not quite so easy to identify.

The rules of contraction for -αω verbs are:

α +	o, ω or ου (i.e. an "O" sound) →	ω
α +	ε, η (i.e. an "E" sound) →	α
α +	any combination with ι →	ᾳ
	(either on or below the line)	

The contraction of -οω verbs was made on a slightly different basis. the rules are:

o +	a long vowel →	ω
o +	a short vowel or ου →	ου
o +	any combination with ι →	οι
	(either on or below the line)	

It is much more important to practise recognizing the personal endings of these verbs than to try to learn the "rules of contraction". If you know the endings of γινωσκω thoroughly you should be able to recognize these "slimmed down" words as well.

Exercise 6.4

Try putting these jumbled forms into the correct order.

ἀγαπᾳ, ἀγαπωμεν, ἀγαπωσιν, ἀγαπω, ἀγαπας, ἀγαπατε

πληρουσιν, πληροι, πληρω, πληρουτε, πληροις, πληρουμεν

In a dictionary verbs like these are listed in their "uncontracted" form, i.e. ἀγαπαω, *love* and πληροω, *fill, fulfil*.

The verbs which are contracted from -ε- and -α- are much more frequent than those which are contracted from -o-, and so the various forms of φιλεω and ἀγαπαω are more important to learn.

Two words for loving

6.5   There are two words for "loving", φιλεω and ἀγαπαω. They both occur in John 21:15–17. See if you can translate this "Grenglish" text into English, using the information given in the Greek text as well.

Notes

(1) συ οἶδας (you know) is not an -αω verb, though you might think so. [Its ending does not have an iota subscript.]

(2) Although λεγει is present tense, "he says", it is often used in reporting past conversations and translated "he said".

Exercise 6.5

1   ¹⁵ Ὅτε οὖν ἠριστησαν

2   λεγει τῳ Σιμωνι Πετρῳ ὁ Ἰησους,

3   Σιμων Ἰωαννου, ἀγαπᾳς με πλεον τουτων;

4   λεγει αὐτῳ, Ναι κυριε,

5   συ οἶδας οτι φιλω σε.

6   λεγει αὐτῳ, Βοσκε τα ἀρνια μου.

7   ¹⁶ λεγει αὐτῳ παλιν δευτερον,

8   Σιμων Ἰωαννου, ἀγαπᾳς με;

9   λεγει αὐτῳ, Ναι κυριε,

10   συ οἶδας ὅτι φιλω σε.

11   λεγει αὐτῳ, Ποιμαινε τα προβατα μου.

12   ¹⁷λεγει αὐτῳ το τριτον,

13   Σιμων Ἰωαννου, φιλεις με;

14   ἐλυπηθη ὁ Πετρος ὅτι εἶπεν αὐτῳ το τριτον,

15   Φιλεις με;

16   και λεγει αὐτῳ, Κυριε, παντα συ οἶδας,

17   συ γινωσκεις ὅτι φιλω σε.

18   λεγει αὐτῳ ὁ Ἰησους, Βοσκε τα προβατα μου.

GRENGLISH TEXT

1 So when they had eaten breakfast

2 Jesus said to Simon Peter,

3 "Simon [son] of John, ἀγαπᾳς με more than these?"

4 He said to him, "Yes Lord,

5 you know that φιλω you."

6 λεγει αὐτῳ, "Feed my lambs."

7 λεγει αὐτῳ again the second time,

8 Σιμων Ἰωαννου, ἀγαπᾳς με;

9 λεγει αὐτῳ, Ναι κυριε,

10 συ οἰδας ὁτι φιλω σε.

11 λεγει αὐτῳ, "Tend my sheep."

12 λεγει αὐτῳ the third time,

13 Σιμων Ἰωαννου, φιλεις με;

14 ὁ Πετρος was grieved because he said to him το τριτον,

15 Φιλεις με;

16 και λεγει αὐτῳ, Κυριε, συ οἰδας everything,

17 συ γινωσκεις that φιλω σε.

18 λεγει αὐτῳ ὁ Ἰησους, "Feed τα προβατα μου."

Older commentaries often distinguish between the two verbs for "love" (and also the two verbs meaning "know"), but modern commentators tend to regard them as alternatives which are used for variation in style rather than for any subtle difference in meaning.

A very different set of endings

6.6 The endings of φιλεω, ἀγαπαω and πληρoω, though quite diverse, are based on the regular endings seen in γινωσκω, but some verbs use a different set of endings. An example of this type of verb is ἐρχομαι, "I come". The stem is ἐρχ- and -ομαι is the first of

the six endings. Here is the pattern with the endings
in bold type

ἐρχ **ομαι**	I come	ἐρχ **ομεθα**	we come
ἐρχ **η**	you (s) come	ἐρχ **εσθε**	you (p) come
ἐρχ **εται**	he/she/it comes	ἐρχ **ονται**	they come

Exercise 6.6

Using the information above match the following
Greek texts to the appropriate English translations.

1. ὑμεις δε ουκ οἰδατε ποθεν ἐρχομαι ἡ που
   ὑπαγω. ὑμεις κατα την σαρκα κρινετε.

2. ἐρχεται ὁ πονηρος και ἁρπαζει το ἐσπαρμενον
   ἐν τη καρδιᾳ αὐτου.

3. Ἐγω χρειαν ἐχω ὑπο σου βαπτισθηναι, και συ
   ἐρχη προς με;

4. λεγει αὐτοις Σιμων Πετρος, Ὑπαγω ἁλιευειν.
   λεγουσιν αὐτῳ, Ἐρχομεθα και ἡμεις συν σοι.

5. Προσεχετε ἀπο των ψευδοπροφητων, οἱτινες
   ἐρχονται προς ὑμας ἐν ἐνδυμασιν προβατων.

6. Εἰπατε τη θυγατρι Σιων, Ἰδου ὁ βασιλευς σου
   ἐρχεται σοι πραΰς και ἐπιβεβηκως ἐπι ὀνον.

7. Ἐτι αὐτου λαλουντος ἐρχονται ἀπο του
   ἀρχισυναγωγου λεγοντες ὁτι Ἡ θυγατηρ σου
   ἀπεθανεν.

A. "I have need to be baptized by you, and do
   you come to me?" (Matthew 3:14).

B. Beware of false prophets who come to you in
   sheep's clothing. (Matthew 7:15).

C. The evil one comes and snatches what was
   sown in his heart. (Matthew 13:19).

D. Say to the daughter of Zion, "Look, your king is coming, humble and riding on a donkey."
(Matthew 21:5).

E. While he was still speaking they came from the [home of the] ruler of the synagogue saying, "Your daughter has died." (Mark 5:35).

F. But you do not know where I come from or where I am going. You judge according to the flesh (i.e. by human standards) (John 8:14–15).

G. Simon Peter said to them, "I am going fishing." They said to him, "We are coming with you."
(John 21:3).

1	2	3	4	5	6	7

Our flexible friend

6.7   Verbs are very flexible parts of speech, which is why they are so powerful. They have a time element and are capable of describing events in the past, present or future. In English we use "auxiliary verbs" to alter the time reference, "helper" verbs which are added to the main verb.

e.g. They believe (present).
        They **will** believe (future).
        They believed or they **have** believed (past).

"Will" and "have" are auxiliary verbs.

Greek handles references to time in a different way, making changes to the main verb itself rather than introducing any "helpers".

Looking to the future

6.8   The basic way of turning a present into a future tense
in Greek is by inserting the letter **σ** between the stem
and the ending.

e.g. πιστευει.   He believes.
πιστευσει.   He will believe.

Here is an example from John 3:12.

εἰ τα ἐπιγεια εἰπον ὑμιν και οὐ **πιστευετε**,
πως ἐαν εἰπω ὑμιν τα ἐπουρανια **πιστευσετε**;

If I have told you earthly things and you do not
believe, how will you believe if I tell you heavenly
things?

6.9   With contracted verbs the extra letter again makes a
difference.

[φιλεω]   φιλει.   He loves.   φιλησει.   He will love.
[ἀγαπαω]   ἀγαπᾳ.   He loves.   ἀγαπησει.   He will love.
[πληροω]   πληροι.   He fulfils.   πληρωσει.   He will fulfil.

We now have three elements: a stem, a future
identifier, and an ending. Notice that with the future
tense of contracted verbs the extra letter has been
"swallowed up" in the middle rather than at the end,
and so the endings are not affected. They are simply
the regular endings we learned from γινωσκω: ω, εις,
ει, ομεν, ετε, ουσιν.

Here are some examples using these verbs:
μισεω, *hate*
ἀγαπαω, *love*
θανατοω, *put to death*.

Ἠκουσατε ὁτι ἐρρεθη, **Ἀγαπησεις** τον πλησιον σου
και **μισησεις** τον ἐχθρον σου.
You have heard that it was said, "*You shall love* your
neighbour and *you shall hate* your enemy."
(Matthew 5:43).

και επαναστησονται τεκνα επι γονεις και
θανατωσουσιν αυτους.
And children will rise up against parents and *will put*
them *to death*.
(Matthew 10:21).

6.10 Sometimes the end of the stem combines with the
future identifier. For example the verb βλεπω means
"I see". In theory the future should be βλεπσω, but
Greek already has a letter representing "ps" and so it
uses it. "I will see" is βλεψω. Similarly there is
already a letter which gives us a "ks" sound, ξ (x).
The verb ἡκω means "I come". Its future, "I will
come" is ἡξω (not ἡκσω). Look at these examples.
The basic form of the verb is given in brackets.

εαν δε πορευθω, πεμψω [πεμπω] αυτον προς υμας.
But if I go, I will *send* him to you (John 16:7).

ἡξει [ἡκω] ὁ κυριος του δουλου εκεινου εν ἡμερα
ἡ ου προσδοκα και εν ὡρα ἡ ου γινωσκει.
The master of that slave will *come* on a day when he
does not expect and at an hour which he does not
know (Matthew 24:50).

Exercise 6.10

Which of these would be the dictionary entry for
προσδοκα in Matthew 24:50, προσδοκεω, προσδοκαω, or προσδοκοω?

6.11 Sometimes the end of the stem "clashes" with the
identifier. The sound of the letters **β, γ, ζ, σ, τ, φ** and
χ combined with **σ** was not thought to be harmonious
and so the combination was not used. Look at these
examples to see what happened.

ὁ δε θεος της ειρηνης συντριψει [συντριβω] τον
Σαταναν ὑπο τους ποδας ὑμων εν ταχει.
And the God of peace will *crush* Satan under your
feet swiftly (Romans 16:20).

ἀνοιξω [ἀνοιγω] ἐν παραβολαις το στομα μου,
ἐρευξομαι [ἐρευγομαι] κεκρυμμενα ἀπο καταβολης
κοσμου.

I will *open* my mouth in parables, I will *declare* things
hidden from the foundation of the world
(Matthew 13:35).

Ἐγω βαπτιζω ἐν ὑδατι εἰς μετανοιαν, . . . αὐτος ὑμας
βαπτισει [βαπτιζω] ἐν πνευματι ἁγιῳ και πυρι.

I baptize with water leading to repentance, . . . he
will *baptize* you with the Holy Spirit and fire
(Matthew 3:11).

εὐ πραξετε [πρασσω].

You will *do* well (Acts 15:29).

και τουτο ὁ θεος ὑμιν ἀποκαλυψει [ἀποκαλυπτω].

This also God will *reveal* to you (Philippians 3:15).

Ὑποστρεψω [ὑποστρεφω] εἰς τον οἰκον μου ὁθεν
ἐξηλθον.

I will *return* to my house from which I went out
(Luke 11:24).

ἐκεινος ἐλεγξει [ἐλεγχω] τον κοσμον περι ἁμαρτιας
και περι δικαιοσυνης και περι κρισεως.

He will *convince* the world concerning sin and concerning righteousness and concerning judgement
(John 16:8).

The London Midland Northern Railway Verbs

6.12　Some verbs have a stem ending in the letters **λ, μ, ν** or
ρ (LMNR). Technically they are known as "liquid
verbs" but I think a mnemonic like "*L*ondon *M*id-
land *N*orthern *R*ailway" is more useful – the LMNR
verbs. They behave in a rather unexpected way in the
future tense. Note these two features.

● They do not use the identifier **σ** or any equivalent
of it.

- They adopt the endings used by contracted -εω verbs.

An example of this type of verb is ἀποστελλω, another word which means "I send". Compare the present and the future.

ἀποστελλω	I send	ἀποστελω	I will send
ἀποστελλεις	you send	ἀποστελεις	you will send
ἀποστελλει	he sends	ἀποστελει	he will send
ἀποστελλομεν	we send	ἀποστελουμεν	we will send
ἀποστελλετε	you send	ἀποστελειτε	you will send
ἀποστελλουσιν	they send	ἀποστελουσιν	they will send

Greek with an accent

6.13   In a printed text the Greek of the New Testament is written with accents. They are written above a vowel and there are three types, an acute [´], a grave [`] and a circumflex [ˆ]. The accents are not an essential part of the language and in general they can be ignored, but there are a few places where they are helpful. If you look closely at these accented texts which include the present and future of ἀποστελλω you will see that the -εω forms are always written with a circumflex accent over the ending.

Ἰδοὺ ἐγὼ ἀποστέλλω ὑμᾶς ὡς πρόβατα ἐν μέσῳ λύκων.

See, *I send* you as sheep in the midst of wolves (Matthew 10:16).

Ἀποστελῶ εἰς αὐτοὺς προφήτας καὶ ἀποστόλους.
I will send them prophets and apostles (Luke 11:49).

6.14   This distinction may not seem very important, but it becomes crucial in the case of a few verbs, such as μενω, "remain" and κρινω, "judge". The future of μενω is μενω, and the future of κρινω is κρινω. If you look closely at this chart you will see how useful the accents are in distinguishing between them. I have used μενω as a model.

μένω	I remain	μενῶ	I will remain
μένεις	you remain	μενεῖς	you will remain
μένει	he remains	μενεῖ	he will remain
μένομεν	we remain	μενοῦμεν	we will remain
μένετε	you remain	μενεῖτε	you will remain
μένουσιν	they remain	μενοῦσιν	they will remain

EXAMPLES

ἐὰν τὰς ἐντολάς μου τηρήσητε, **μενεῖτε** ἐν τῇ ἀγάπῃ μου, καθὼς ἐγὼ τὰς ἐντολὰς τοῦ πατρός μου τετήρηκα καὶ **μένω** αὐτοῦ ἐν τῇ ἀγάπῃ.

If you keep my commands, *you will remain* in my love,
just as I have kept my Father's commands
and *I remain* in his love (John 15:10).

οὐκ οἴδατε ὅτι οἱ ἅγιοι τὸν κόσμον **κρινοῦσιν;**
Do you not know that the saints *will judge* the world?
(1 Corinthians 6:2).

The rich young man

6.15   The story of Jesus' meeting with a rich young man is recorded in Matthew 19:16–22. Although it contains some unfamiliar features, you should know enough to be able to read the story with help.

Exercise 6.15

Read through the text, referring to the English translation alongside, and try to see how the structure of the Greek relates to the English. Complete the vocabulary items at the end by inserting the correct meanings.

¹⁶Καὶ ἰδοὺ εἷς προσελθὼν αὐτῷ
εἶπεν· Διδάσκαλε,
τί ἀγαθὸν ποιήσω
ἵνα σχῶ ζωὴν αἰώνιον;
¹⁷ὁ δὲ εἶπεν αὐτῷ·
Τί με ἐρωτᾷς περὶ τοῦ ἀγαθοῦ;

εἷς ἐστιν ὁ ἀγαθός·
εἰ δὲ θέλεις
εἰς τὴν ζωὴν εἰσελθεῖν,
τήρησον τὰς ἐντολάς.
¹⁸λέγει αὐτῷ· Ποίας;
ὁ δὲ Ἰησοῦς εἶπεν·
Τὸ Οὐ φονεύσεις,
Οὐ μοιχεύσεις,
Οὐ κλέψεις,
Οὐ ψευδομαρτυρήσεις,
¹⁹Τίμα τὸν πατέρα
καὶ τὴν μητέρα,
καί Ἀγαπήσεις τὸν πλησίον σου

ὡς σεαυτόν.
²⁰λέγει αὐτῷ ὁ νεανίσκος·
Πάντα ταῦτα ἐφύλαξα·
τί ἔτι ὑστερῶ;
²¹ἔφη αὐτῷ ὁ Ἰησοῦς·
Εἰ θέλεις τέλειος εἶναι,
ὕπαγε πώλησόν σου τὰ ὑπάρχοντα
καὶ δὸς τοῖς πτωχοῖς,
καὶ ἕξεις θησαυρὸν
ἐν οὐρανοῖς,
καὶ δεῦρο ἀκολούθει μοι.
²²ἀκούσας δὲ ὁ νεανίσκος
τὸν λόγον
ἀπῆλθεν λυπούμενος·
ἦν γὰρ ἔχων κτήματα πολλά.

And behold one approached him
and said, "Teacher,
what good thing shall I do
that I may have life eternal?"
And he said to him,
"Why do you ask me about the good?
There is one who is good.
And if you want
to enter into life
keep the commands."
He said to him, "Which?"
And Jesus said,
"[The] you shall not murder,
you shall not commit adultery,
you shall not steal
you shall not bear false witness,
honour your father
and your mother
and you shall love your neighbour
as yourself."
The young man said to him,
"All these I have kept;
what do I still lack?"
Jesus said to him,
"If you want to be perfect,
go, sell your possessions
and give to the poor,
and you will have treasure
in heaven,
and come, follow me."
And when the young man heard
the word
he went away grieving,
for he had many possessions.

Vocabulary

διδασκαλος, ου m _____ ποιεω, ___ ζωη, ης f _____,

ἐρωταω, ___ θελω, _____ ἐντολη, ης f _____

φονευω, _____ μοιχευω, _____ κλεπτω, _____

ψευδομαρτυρεω, _____ νεανισκος, ου m _____

ὑστερεω, _____ θησαυρος, ου m _____ λογος, ου m ____

κτημα, τος n _____

Answers to exercises

Exercise 6.3

φιλω φιλεις φιλει φιλουμεν φιλειτε φιλουσιν

Exercise 6.4

ἀγαπω ἀγαπας ἀγαπα ἀγαπωμεν ἀγαπατε ἀγαπωσιν

πληρω πληροις πληροι πληρουμεν πληρουτε
πληρουσιν

Exercise 6.5

1 So when they had eaten breakfast
2 Jesus said to Simon Peter
3 "Simon [son] of John, **do you love me** more than
these?"
4 He said to him, "Yes Lord,
5 you know that **I love you**."
6 **He said to him**, "Feed my lambs."
7 **He said to him** again the second time,
8 **"Simon son of John, do you love me?"**
9 **He said to him, "Yes, Lord,**

10 **you know that I love you."**
11 **He said to him,** "Tend my sheep."
12 **He said to him** the third time,
13 **"Simon son of John, do you love me?"**
14 **Peter** was grieved because he said to him **the third time,**
15 **"Do you love me?"**
16 **And he said to him, "Lord, you know** everything,
17 **you know** that **I love you."**
18 **Jesus said to him,** "Feed **my sheep."**

Exercise 6.6

1	2	3	4	5	6	7
F	C	A	G	B	D	E

Exercise 6:10

προσδοκαω

Exercise 6.15

διδασκαλος, ου m *teacher* ποιεω, *do* ζωη, ης f *life*
ἐρωταω, *ask* θελω, *want* ἐντολη, ης f *command*
φονευω, *murder* μοιχευω, *commit adultery*
κλεπτω, *steal* ψευδομαρτυρεω, *bear false witness*
νεανισκος, ου m *young man* ὑστερεω, *lack*
θησαυρος, ου m *treasure* λογος, ου m *word*
κτημα, τος n *possession*

REVIEW QUESTIONS

1. What are verbs?

2. Why are "contracted" verbs described in this way?

3. Are the endings of the contracted verbs slightly different or very different from regular endings?

4. What is the present tense of (a) φιλεω (b) ἀγαπαω (c) πληροω?

5. What are the two verbs meaning "love"? Is there any difference in meaning between them?

6. What are the alternative ways of translating λεγει? How would you know which is appropriate?

7. What does ἐρχομαι mean and what are the other parts of the present tense?

8. How do English and Greek differ in the way they form a future tense?

9. What is the future of these verbs?
   πιστευω φιλεω ἀγαπαω πληροω

10. What logical step is taken to form the future of verbs like βλεπω and ἡκω?

11. What changes occur in the future tense when a verb stem ends in these letters?

    β γ ζ σ τ φ χ

12. Why can "liquid" verbs be referred to as LMNR-verbs?

13. What features characterize the future tense of LMNR-verbs?

14. Is it safe to ignore accents and what value do they have?

15. In Matthew 19:18 is the future tense being used to make a statement or a command?

REVIEW EXERCISES

SINGULAR FOR PLURAL

The following verbs are all plural. Identify the meaning and give the corresponding singular form. For example, the first verb is πιστευομεν. It means "we believe" and the corresponding singular is πιστευω (I believe).

πιστευομεν, φιλειτε, πιστευετε, πληρουμεν, ἐρχονται, μισειτε, πεμπουσιν, ἀγαπωμεν, ἐρχομεθα, ἀγαπωσιν.

PLURAL FOR SINGULAR

These verbs are all singular. This time identify the meaning and give the corresponding plural form.

φιλω, ἀγαπᾳ, πληροις, ἐρχῃ, πεμπω, μισει, θανατω, ἀγαπᾳς, ἐρχεται.

PRESENT OR FUTURE

These verbs are all future. Identify the meaning and give the corresponding present form. For example, the first verb is πιστευσει. It means "he/she/it will believe" and the corresponding present tense is πιστευει (he/she/it believes).

ἀγαπησει, ἀνοιξομεν, ἀποκαλυψεις, ἀποστελειτε, βαπτισουσιν, ἐλεγξω, θανατωσετε, μισησομεν, πεμψει, πληρωσεις, πραξει, συντριψουσιν, ὑποστρεψει, φιλησομεν.

PICKING UP THE ACCENT

In this list of verbs you are given the basic meaning of the verb in brackets. Identify whether it is present or future by the accent, and translate accordingly.

[lift up] αἴρομεν
[kill] ἀποκτενοῦμεν
[throw] βαλεῖ
[raise] ἐγείρουσιν
[proclaim] καταγγέλλω
[judge] κρινῶ
[say] λέγεις
[remain] μένεις
[sow] σπερεῖς
[proclaim] καταγγελοῦμεν

[sow] σπείρουσιν
[lift up] ἀροῦσιν
[say] ἐρεῖτε
[sow] σπερῶ
[remain] μενοῦσιν
[throw] βάλλει
[lift up] αἴρουσιν
[raise] ἐγερεῖ
[judge] κρίνω
[kill] ἀποκτείνετε

PRESENT OR FUTURE

All the texts below are taken from the New Testament. The translation provided offers a choice of present or future tense. Pick the correct one for each text.

τον ἑνα μισησει και τον ἑτερον ἀγαπησει.

He [hates/will hate] the one and he [loves/will love] the other (Matthew 6:24).

ἀποστελει ὁ υἱος του ἀνθρωπου τους ἀγγελους αὐτου.

The Son of Man [sends/will send] his angels (Matthew 13:41).

φιλουσιν δε την πρωτοκλισιαν ἐν τοις δειπνοις.

They [love/will love] the place of honour at feasts (Matthew 23:6).

ἐγω ἀποστελλω προς ὑμας προφητας και σοφους και γραμματεις.

I [send/will send] you prophets and wise men and scribes (Matthew 23:34).

ἀγαπησεις τον πλησιον σου.

You [love/will love] your neighbour (Mark 12:31).

πεμψω τον υἱον μου τον ἀγαπητον.

I [send/will send] my beloved son (Luke 20:13).

πας γαρ ὁ φαυλα πρασσων μισει το φως.

For everyone who does what is evil [hates/will hate] the light (John 3:20).

ὁ γαρ πατηρ φιλει τον υἱον.

For the Father [loves/will love] the Son (John 5:20).

τίς ἐξ ὑμων ἐλεγχει με περι ἁμαρτιας;

Which of you [convicts/will convict] me of sin? (John 8:46).

τουτῳ ὁ θυρωρος ἀνοιγει και τα προβατα της φωνης αὐτου ἀκουει.

The gatekeeper [opens/will open] to him and the sheep hear his voice (John 10:3).

καθως ἀπεσταλκεν με ὁ πατηρ, κἀγω πεμπω ὑμας.

As the Father has sent me, I also [send/will send] you (John 20:21).

εἰ δε πνευματι τας πραξεις του σωματος θανατουτε, ζησεσθε.

But if by the Spirit you [put to death/will put to death] the deeds of the body, you will live (Romans 8:13).

εἰ γαρ ἑκων τουτο πρασσω, μισθον ἐχω.
For if I [do/will do] this willingly, I have a reward
(1 Corinthians 9:17).

ὁ ἀγαπων την ἑαυτου γυναικα ἑαυτον ἀγαπᾳ.
He who loves his own wife [loves/will love] himself
(Ephesians 5:28).

ὁ δε θεος μου πληρωσει πασαν χρειαν ὑμων.
And my God [fulfils/will fulfil] all your need (Philippians 4:19).

ἡμεις ἀγαπωμεν ὁτι αὐτος πρωτος ἠγαπησεν ἡμας.
We [love/will love] because he first loved us (1 John 4:19).

μισεις τα ἐργα των Νικολαϊτων.
You [hate/will hate] the deeds of the Nicolaitans
(Revelation 2:6).

ὁ ἀνοιγων και οὐδεις κλεισει, και κλειων και οὐδεις ἀνοιγει.
Who opens and no one will shut, and shuts and no one
[opens/will open] (Revelation 3:7).

και δωρα πεμψουσιν ἀλληλοις.
And they [send/will send] gifts to one another
(Revelation 11:10).

οὑτοι μισησουσιν την πορνην.
These [hate/will hate] the harlot (Revelation 17:16).

WORDS TO LEARN

ἀγαπαω love
ἀποκαλυπτω reveal
ἀποστολος, ου m apostle, messenger
βαπτιζω baptize
διδασκαλος, ου m teacher
δουλος, ου m slave, servant
ἐντολη, ης f command
ἐρχομαι come
θελω want, wish
θυγατηρ, θυγατρος f daughter
κρινω judge
μισεω hate
πεμπω send
Πετρος, ου m Peter
πληροω fill, fulfil
προβατον, ου n sheep
προφητης, ου m prophet
Σιμων, Σιμωνος m Simon
συν + dative with
φιλεω love

CHAPTER SEVEN

Preview

Adjectives

Case number and gender

ἀγαθος καλος

Word order

ἁγιος πονηρος

Adjective patterns 2–1–2, 3–1–3

πας

οὑτος ἐκεινος ὁλος

A translation exercise

CHAPTER SEVEN

Photofit words

Powers of description

7.1 One of the useful features of a language is its ability to describe people, objects or events. This can be done at great length, but there are single words which sum up particular characteristics and express them very succinctly – words like good, bad, impressive, unimpressive, noble, savage, kind, cruel, etc. They are called **adjectives**. Sometimes they stand next to the person or thing they are describing.

e.g. A **good** tree produces **good** fruit.

Sometimes they are further apart.

e.g. Look at that tree and its fruit. They are both **good**.

7.2 Adding adjectives to a sentence in English is fairly straightforward. Whether you are talking about a man or men, a woman or women, a tree or trees, they would all simply be described as "good". In Greek, however, the form of a noun depends on a number of factors. Which "family" does it belong to? Which "case" is it? Is it masculine, feminine or neuter? Are we talking about one or more than one? The answers to some of these questions affect not only the noun itself but also any adjectives that describe it. Greek adjectives are photofit words. They take on and reflect the main characteristics of the nouns they go with: their case, number and gender.

Adjectives and word order

7.3   Because the order of words is more flexible in Greek than in English an adjective can come before or after its noun.

"A **good** man" can be either ἀγαθος ἀνθρωπος or ἀνθρωπος ἀγαθος.

Remember that there is no word for "a" in Greek.

The same thing is true when we use the definite article.

"The **good** man" can be either ὁ ἀγαθος ἀνθρωπος
          or ὁ ἀνθρωπος ὁ ἀγαθος.

Notice how the definite article (ὁ) is repeated when the adjective comes after the noun (the man **the** good).

Some good examples

7.4   The adjectives ἀγαθος and καλος both mean "good". Look at these examples from the New Testament to see the way in which the characteristics of nouns are reflected in the adjectives which accompany them. Take time to sort out the order of the words, which is often different from English. Some vocabulary helps are included.

δενδρον, ου n tree   καρπος, ου m fruit

οὑτως παν δενδρον **ἀγαθον** καρπους **καλους** ποιει.
So, every **good** tree produces **good** fruits
(Matthew 7:17).

θησαυρος, ου m treasure ἐκβαλλω, bring out

ὁ **ἀγαθος** ἀνθρωπος ἐκ του **ἀγαθου** θησαυρου
ἐκβαλλει **ἀγαθα**.
The **good** man from the **good** treasure brings out **good**
[things] (Matthew 12:35).

ποιμην, ποιμενος m shepherd ψυχη, ης f life
τιθησιν "lays down" ὑπερ + gen. for
προβατον, ου n sheep

Ἐγω εἰμι ὁ ποιμην ὁ **καλος**. ὁ ποιμην ὁ **καλος** την
ψυχην αὐτου τιθησιν ὑπερ των προβατων.
I am the **good** shepherd. The **good** shepherd lays
down his life for the sheep (John 10:11).

καρποφορεω, bear fruit αὐξανομαι, increase
ἐπιγνωσις, εως f knowledge

ἐν παντι ἐργῳ **ἀγαθῳ** καρποφορουντες και
αὐξανομενοι τῃ ἐπιγνωσει του θεου.
Bearing fruit in every **good** work and increasing in the
knowledge of God (Colossians 1:10).

βλασφημεω, blaspheme ὀνομα, τος n name
το ἐπικληθεν ἐφ᾽ ὑμας = "which has been
given to you"

οὐκ αὐτοι βλασφημουσιν το **καλον** ὀνομα το
ἐπικληθεν ἐφ᾽ ὑμας;
Do they not blaspheme the **good** name which has
been given to you? (James 2:7).

Exercise 7.4

How is "the good man" expressed in Greek in Matthew 12:35? Write out the alternative way of expressing it.
How is "the good shepherd" expressed in Greek in John 10:11? Write out the alternative way of expressing it.

Not just copycat words

7.5   It would be convenient if adjectives were "copycat" words. At first it might look as if they are. "The good man" is ὁ ἀγαθος ἀνθρωπος. "The good men" would be οἱ ἀγαθοι ἀνθρωποι. However the adjective is not simply "copying" its noun but producing a "photofit" from the noun's data and using its own endings to make a match. Each adjective has a full set of its own endings, covering masculine, feminine and neuter, singular and plural and all the cases. Here is the pattern for ἀγαθος. The endings of καλος follow exactly the same pattern.

		Masculine	Feminine	Neuter
	nominative	ἀγαθ ος	ἀγαθ η	ἀγαθ ον
	accusative	ἀγαθ ον	ἀγαθ ην	ἀγαθ ον
SINGULAR	genitive	ἀγαθ ου	ἀγαθ ης	ἀγαθ ου
	dative	ἀγαθ ῳ	ἀγαθ η	ἀγαθ ῳ
	vocative*	ἀγαθ ε		
	nominative	ἀγαθ οι	ἀγαθ αι	ἀγαθ α
	accusative	ἀγαθ ους	ἀγαθ ας	ἀγαθ α
PLURAL	genitive	ἀγαθ ων	ἀγαθ ων	ἀγαθ ων
	dative	ἀγαθ οις	ἀγαθ αις	ἀγαθ οις

*ἀγαθε (masculine singular) is the only vocative with an ending which is different from the nominative.

7.6 In Colossians 1:10 when Paul writes ἐν παντι ἐργῳ ἀγαθῳ, the photofit works like this:

- What noun is ἀγαθος describing? ἐργῳ from ἐργον, ου n work
- What gender is needed? Neuter.
- Is it singular or plural? Singular.
- What case is it? Dative.
- What is the neuter singular dative of ἀγαθος? <u>ἀγαθῳ</u>.

In James 2:7 when he writes το καλον ὀνομα, the photofit works like this:

- What noun is καλος describing? ὀνομα from ὀνομα, τος n *name*.
- What gender is needed? Neuter.
- Is it singular or plural? Singular.
- What case is it? Accusative.
- What is the neuter singular accusative of καλος? <u>καλον</u>.

Adjectives in a dictionary

7.7 Adjectives like ἀγαθος and καλος appear in a dictionary with an indication of their feminine and neuter endings, i.e.

ἀγαθος, η, ον good
καλος, η, ον good

The masculine, feminine and neuter endings of these adjectives are the same as the endings of λογος, γραφη and ἐργον (section 5.2).

A slight variation

7.8 Before going on to this section review the notes on καρδια and γλωσσα in section 5.2, *Family 1*.

Many adjectives follow the pattern laid down by ἀγαθος, η, ον and many more follow a pattern that is different only in the feminine singular.Look at these two "dictionary entries" and the biblical examples which follow. Then go on to the exercise.

ἁγιος, α, ον holy
πονηρος, α, ον evil

μη not   ποιειν to do   θελημα, τος n will

μη ποιειν τα θεληματα σου ἐν τη ἡμερᾳ τη **ἁγιᾳ**
Not to do what you want on the holy day (Isaiah 58:13).

παραλαμβανω, take   διαβολος, ου m devil
πολις, εως f city

Τοτε παραλαμβανει αὐτον ὁ διαβολος εἰς την **ἁγιαν** πολιν.
Then the devil took him to the holy city (Matthew 4:5).

λυω, loose   ὑποδημα, τος n sandal
πους, ποδος m foot
τοπος, ου m place
ἐφ' ᾧ ἑστηκας "where you are standing"
γη, ης f ground, earth

Λυσον το ὑποδημα των ποδων σου, ὁ γαρ τοπος ἐφ᾽ ᾧ ἑστηκας γη **ἁγια** ἐστιν.
Loose the sandal from [literally, of] your feet, for the place where you are standing is holy ground (Acts 7:33).

δια τουτο therefore   ἀναλαβετε "take"
πανοπλια, ας f whole armour   ἱνα δυνηθητε "that you may be able"
ἀντιστηναι to stand   ἡμερα, ας f day

δια τουτο ἀναλαβετε την πανοπλιαν του θεου, ἱνα δυνηθητε ἀντιστηναι ἐν τη ἡμερᾳ τη **πονηρᾳ** (Ephesian 6:13).

ἀφελεῖ "will take away"   μερος, ους n share
ξυλον, ου n tree   ἀπο + gen. from
ζωη, ης f life   ἐκ + gen. from

ἀφελεῖ ὁ θεος το μερος αὐτου ἀπο του ξυλου της ζωης και ἐκ της πολεως της **ἁγιας**.
God will take away his share from the tree of life and from the holy city (Revelation 22:19).

Exercise 7.8

- Write out the four *feminine* singular forms of the adjective ἁγιος.
- Does the feminine singular of πονηρος have endings like καρδια or γλωσσα?

2–1–2 and 3–1–3 adjectives

7.9   A great many adjectives adopt the pattern of either ἀγαθος, η, ον or ἁγιος, α, ον. We may call this the 2–1–2 pattern because the masculine follows λογος from family 2, the feminine follows either γραφη or καρδια from family 1, and the neuter follows ἐργον from family 2.

7.10 There is another pattern, the 3–1–3 pattern, and we can illustrate it from the adjective which occurs most frequently in the New Testament (no less than 1244 times). Here is its dictionary entry and a chart showing all its forms.

πας, πασα, παν (genitive παντος, πασης, παντος) all, every

πας	πασα	παν
παντα	πασαν	παν
παντος	πασης	παντος
παντι	παση	παντι
παντες	πασαι	παντα
παντας	πασας	παντα
παντων	πασων	παντων
πασιν	πασαις	πασιν

The masculine and neuter forms belong to family 3 and behave like nouns of type 3.1 (masculine) and 3.6 (neuter).

The feminine forms behave like γλωσσα (1.3) in family 1; that is, they change from πασαν to πασης when they reach the genitive singular.

The prefix "pan", which is used in words like Pan-African and Pan-American, comes from this Greek word. Other English words which incorporate it include panorama, pantechnicon and pantomime.

Exercise 7.10

Each of the words in the box can be used once only to fill a gap in the Greek texts, all taken from Matthew's Gospel. Choose the correct "photofit", using the chart above. You will find that the definite article is a useful guide to identifying the correct form.

> πας παντι παντες παντας
> πασα πασαν παση πασαι πασας
> παν παντα πασιν

___(1)___ οὐν δενδρον μη ποιουν καρπον καλον ἐκκοπτεται και εἰς πυρ βαλλεται

Therefore *every* tree which does not produce good fruit will be cut down and thrown into the fire (3:10).

και δεικνυσιν αὐτῳ ___(2)___ τας βασιλειας του κοσμου και την δοξαν αὐτων.

And he showed him *all* the kingdoms of the world and the glory of them (4:8).

οὐδε Σολομων ἐν ___(3)___ τη δοξη αὐτου περιεβαλετο ὡς ἐν τουτων.

Not even Solomon in *all* his glory was dressed like one of these (6:29).

___(4)___ γαρ ταυτα τα ἐθνη ἐπιζητουσιν. οἰδεν γαρ ὁ πατηρ ὑμων ὁ οὐρανιος ὁτι χρῃζετε τουτων ἁπαντων.

For the Gentiles seek *all* these things. For your heavenly Father knows that you need all these things (6:32).

Οὐ ___(5)___ ὁ λεγων μοι· Κυριε, κυριε, εἰσελευσεται εἰς την βασιλειαν των οὐρανων, ἀλλ᾽ ὁ ποιων το θελημα του πατρος μου του ἐν τοις οὐρανοις.

Not *everyone* who says to me, "Lord, lord," will enter into the kingdom of heaven, but he who does the will of my father who is in heaven (7:21).

και ἰδου __(6)__ ἡ πολις ἐξηλθεν εἰς ὑπαντησιν τῳ Ἰησου.

And behold *all* the city came out to meet Jesus (8:34).

__(7)__ γαρ οἱ προφηται και ὁ νομος ἑως Ἰωαννου ἐπροφητευσαν.

For *all* the prophets and the law prophesied until John (11:13).

και αἱ ἀδελφαι αὐτου οὐχι __(8)__ προς ἡμας εἰσιν;

And his sisters, are they not *all* with us? (13:56).

και προσηνεγκαν αὐτῳ __(9)__ τους κακως ἐχοντας.

And they brought to him *all* who were unwell (14:35).

και κηρυχθησεται τουτο το εὐαγγελιον της βασιλειας ἐν ὀλη τη οἰκουμενη εἰς μαρτυριον __(10)__ τοις ἐθνεσιν, και τοτε ἡξει το τελος.

And this gospel of the kingdom will be preached in all the world as a testimony to *all* the nations, and then the end will come (24:14).

τῳ γαρ ἐχοντι __(11)__ δοθησεται και περισσευθησεται.

For to *everyone* who has it will be given and he will have more (25:29).

ἀπο δε ἑκτης ὡρας σκοτος ἐγενετο ἐπι __(12)__ την γην ἑως ὡρας ἐνατης.

From the sixth hour darkness came upon *all* the land until the ninth hour (27:45).

This and that

7.11   When "all" is used to describe something the order of words is slightly different from usual. We say "the good city" (not "good the city"), but we say "all the city"(not "the all city"). This difference is also seen in Greek.

the good city   ἡ ἀγαθη πολις
all the city   πασα ἡ πολις

7.12 Greek, however, uses the "all"-order with some other words. The words "this" and "that" can be used alone or with a noun.

ALONE: **This** is my house.

WITH A NOUN: **This** house belongs to me.

Here is how we would write these two sentences in Greek.

This is my house.   οὗτος ἐστιν ὁ οἰκος μου.

This house belongs to me.   οὗτος ὁ οἰκος ὑπαρχει μοι.

The first sentence is as we would expect, but something unexpected has happened in the second sentence. Instead of "this house" Greek has "this **the** house" (like "all the city"). In the same way we would refer to "that **the** house". There is one other word which behaves like this, usually translated "whole". Here are the "dictionary entries" for these four words with examples of the way they behave. Because of Greek's flexible word order there is again an alternative in which the adjective comes after the noun rather than before it.

πας, πασα, παν all, every
ὁλος, η, ον whole
ἐκεινος, η, ο that (plural those)
οὗτος, αὑτη, τουτο this (plural these)

παν το εὐαγγελιον   *or* το εὐαγγελιον παν
                      all the gospel

ὁλον το εὐαγγελιον   *or* το εὐαγγελιον ὁλον
                      the whole gospel

ἐκεινο το εὐαγγελιον   *or* το εὐαγγελιον ἐκεινο
                      that gospel

τουτο το εὐαγγελιον   *or* το εὐαγγελιον τουτο
                      this gospel

Here is an example from the New Testament itself, which illustrates three of these words in one sentence. I have included a very literal translation to illustrate the structure of the sentence.

ἐξηλθεν "went out"   φημη, ης f report
γη, ης f "district"

και ἐξηλθεν ἡ φημη αὑτη εἰς ὁλην την γην ἐκεινην.
And this report went out into the whole that district
(Matthew 9:26).

Another difference

7.13   The words "this" and "that" are different in another respect. The word "that" (ἐκεινος) is almost identical in its endings to ἀγαθος (section 7.5), but in the neuter singular the first two endings (nominative and accusative) are ἐκεινο. There is no ν (n) at the end.

ἐκεινος, η, o (that) is only slightly different, but οὑτος, αὑτη, τουτο (this) is very different. Fortunately when you read the New Testament you meet it so frequently you will soon become familiar with all its funny little ways.

Exercise 7.13

Here is a chart illustrating the pattern of οὑτος, αὑτη, τουτο, but it contains a few gaps. The "missing pieces" are all in the examples. See if you can complete the chart.

THIS			
	οὑτος	αὑτη	τουτο
	τουτον	———	τουτο
	———	ταυτης	τουτου
	τουτῳ	ταυτῃ	———

THESE			
	οὑτοι	αὑται	ταυτα
	τουτους	———	ταυτα
	———	τουτων	τουτων
	τουτοις	ταυταις	———

παχυνομαι grow dull   καρδια, ας f heart
λαος, ου m people

ἐπαχυνθη γαρ ἡ καρδια του λαου τουτου.

For this people's heart has grown dull (Matthew 13:15).

ἐγενετο it came to pass *(often not translated)*
ὁτε when   ἐτελεσεν "had finished"
παραβολη, ης f parable   μετηρεν he went
away   ἐκειθεν from there

Και ἐγενετο ὁτε ἐτελεσεν ὁ 'Ιησους τας παραβολας
ταυτας, μετηρεν ἐκειθεν.

And when Jesus had finished these parables, he went
away from there (Matthew 13:53).

εἶπαν they said   πρός + acc to
ὅτι (here introducing speech)   οὐδείς no one
ἐστιν there is   συγγενεια, ας f kindred
ὅς who   καλειται "is called"
ὀνομα, τος n name

καὶ εἶπαν πρὸς αὐτὴν ὅτι Οὐδεὶς ἐστιν ἐκ της
συγγενειας σου ὅς καλειται τῳ ὀνοματι τουτῳ.

And they said to her, "There is no one of your
relatives who is called by this name" (Luke 1:61).

λεγω say   ὅτι that   δυναται he is able
λιθος, ου m stone   ἐγειραι to raise
τεκνον, ου n child   Ἀβρααμ Abraham

λεγω γαρ ὑμιν ὅτι δυναται ὁ θεος ἐκ των λιθων
τουτων ἐγειραι τεκνα τῳ Ἀβρααμ.

For I tell you that God is able from these stones to
raise children to Abraham (Luke 3:8).

ἀναβαινω go up   ἑορτη, ης f festival
ἐμος, η, ον my   καιρος, ου m time
οὐπω not yet   πεπληρωται "is fulfilled"

ἐγω οὐκ ἀναβαινω εἰς την ἑορτην ταυτην, ὅτι ὁ ἐμος
καιρος οὐπω πεπληρωται.

I am not going up to this festival, because my time
has not yet fully come (John 7:8).

ἀλλ᾿ (= ἀλλα) but
ὑπερνικαω overcome completely
δια του ἀγαπησαντος ἡμας "through him
who loved us"

ἀλλ᾿ ἐν τουτοις πασιν ὑπερνικωμεν δια του
ἀγαπησαντος ἡμας.

But in all these things we are more than conquerors
through him who loved us (Romans 8:37).

This doesn't look right!

7.14   Even if you have filled in the chart correctly it will
probably still not look right. The genitive plural in
the feminine column is τουτων, which looks out of
place with all the ταυ- forms. Again, the nominative
and accusative plurals in the neuter column are
ταυτα, which looks out of place with all the του-
forms. Believe it or not there are some "rules" which
make sense of it all. It is not important to know them,
but it may satisfy your curiosity a little.

- The initial sounds are the same as those of ὁ, ἡ, το
(the).
- The endings are the same as the endings of
ἐκεινος, η, ο.
- If there is an "o" in the ending there is an "o" in
the stem. Hence τουτων but ταυτα.

Exercise 7.15

This is a translation exercise. The main vocabulary is provided and you should translate in two stages. First, identify the meanings of the words and make a fairly rough, literal translation. Then try to "polish up" what you have written, but without losing the meaning of the original Greek.

Vocabulary

Nouns

ἐντολη, ης f command
ἀρχη, ης f beginning
λογος, ου m word, message
σκοτια, ας f darkness

φως, φωτος n light

ἀδελφος, ου m brother
σκανδαλον, ου n stumbling-block, cause of sin
ὀφθαλμος, ου m eye

Adjectives

ἀγαπητος, η, ον beloved
καινος, η, ον new
παλαιος, α, ον old
ἀληθης (m/f) ἀληθες (n) true
(This adjective is similar to nouns of family 3, type 3.7.)
ἀληθινος, η, ον true

Verbs

γραφω write
ἐχω have (εἰχετε you had)
ἐστιν is (εἰναι to be)
ἀκουω hear (ἠκουσατε you heard)
παραγομαι disappear, pass away
  (Review section 6.6)
φαινω shine
ὁ λεγων εἰναι "he who claims to be"
μισεω hate (ὁ μισων he who hates)
ἀγαπαω love (ὁ ἀγαπων he who loves)
μενω remain
περιπατεω walk
οἰδα know (οἰδεν "he knows")
ὑπαγω go
τυφλοω blind
(ἐτυφλωσεν has blinded)

Other words

ἀλλ᾽ (= ἀλλα) but
ἀπ᾽ (= ἀπο) + gen. from
ὅν, ἥν, ὅ which (masc, fem, neut)
παλιν again
ἐν + dat. in

ὅτι because
ἤδη already
ἕως ἀρτι still (until now)
δε but, and (never comes first)
που where

⁷ Ἀγαπητοί, οὐκ ἐντολὴν καινὴν γράφω ὑμῖν
ἀλλ᾽ ἐντολὴν παλαιὰν ἣν εἴχετε ἀπ᾽ ἀρχῆς·
ἡ ἐντολὴ ἡ παλαιά ἐστιν ὁ λόγος ὃν ἠκούσατε.
⁸ πάλιν ἐντολὴν καινὴν γράφω ὑμῖν,
ὅ ἐστιν ἀληθὲς ἐν αὐτῷ καὶ ἐν ὑμῖν,
ὅτι ἡ σκοτία παράγεται καὶ τὸ φῶς τὸ ἀληθινὸν
ἤδη φαίνει.
⁹ Ὁ λέγων ἐν τῷ φωτὶ εἶναι
καὶ τὸν ἀδελφὸν αὐτοῦ μισῶν
ἐν τῇ σκοτίᾳ ἐστὶν ἕως ἄρτι.
¹⁰ ὁ ἀγαπῶν τὸν ἀδελφὸν αὐτοῦ ἐν τῷ φωτὶ μένει
καὶ σκάνδαλον ἐν αὐτῷ οὐκ ἔστιν·
¹¹ ὁ δὲ μισῶν τὸν ἀδελφὸν αὐτοῦ ἐν τῇ σκοτίᾳ
ἐστὶν
καὶ ἐν τῇ σκοτίᾳ περιπατεῖ
καὶ οὐκ οἶδεν ποῦ ὑπάγει,
ὅτι ἡ σκοτία ἐτύφλωσεν τοὺς ὀφθαλμοὺς αὐτοῦ.

Answers to exercises

Exercise 7.4

In Matthew 12:35 "the good man" is ὁ ἀγαθος ἀνθρωπος. The alternative would be ὁ ἀνθρωπος ὁ ἀγαθος.

In John 10:11 "the good shepherd" is ὁ ποιμην ὁ καλος. The alternative would be ὁ καλος ποιμην.

Exercise 7.8

- Nominative ἁγια
  Accusative ἁγιαν
  Genitive ἁγιας
  Dative ἁγιᾳ
- The feminine singular of πονηρος has endings like καρδια.

Exercise 7.13

THIS	οὑτος	αὑτη	τουτο
	τουτον	ταυτην	τουτο
	τουτου	ταυτης	τουτου
	τουτῳ	ταυτῃ	τουτῳ
THESE	οὑτοι	αὑται	ταυτα
	τουτους	ταυτας	ταυτα
	τουτων	τουτων	τουτων
	τουτοις	ταυταις	τουτοις

Exercise 7.15

The passage is 1 John 2:7–11. Look it up in the version of the Bible you are most familiar with. You will find it useful to compare different translations, such as the Revised Standard Version, which is fairly literal and the Good News Bible, which is more dynamic.

There are three ways of interpreting και σκανδαλον ἐν αὐτῳ οὐκ ἐστιν in verse 10. We can highlight the issues with a piece of "Grenglish".

And there is no **σκανδαλον** *in* **αὐτῳ**.

σκανδαλον is something which causes a person to stumble, that is, to sin. Here are the three possibilities.

(1) ἐν αὐτῷ means "in him". αὐτῷ is masculine. The reference is to the person who is walking in the light; he will not stumble.

(2) ἐν αὐτῷ means "in him" (masculine), but the person who is kept from stumbling is the brother. There is nothing in him that will cause his **brother** to stumble.

(3) ἐν αὐτῷ means "in it". αὐτῷ is neuter, and refers to the light, τῷ φωτι. There is nothing in **it** to cause anyone to stumble – the person or his brother.

REVIEW QUESTIONS

1. Why are adjectives less straightforward in Greek than in English?

2. In what way do adjectives illustrate the greater flexibility of word order in Greek?

3. What do ἀγαθος and καλος mean?

4. What are the two ways of expressing a phrase such as "the good man"?

5. Why is it more accurate to describe adjectives as "photo-fit" words rather than "copycat" words?

6. What is the full pattern of ἀγαθος, masculine, feminine and neuter, singular and plural, and all the cases?

7. How do adjectives appear in a dictionary entry?

8. What is the meaning of ἁγιος and in what way does its pattern differ from that of ἀγαθος?

9. Is there any difference between the endings of ἁγιος and πονηρος?

10. What is meant by the 2–1–2 pattern and the 3–1–3 pattern?

11. Why is πας such an important adjective to learn?

12. What is the full pattern of πας, masculine, feminine and neuter, singular and plural, and all the cases?

13. What are some of the ways in which πας can be translated into English?

14. In both Greek and English we say "all the city" not "the all city". Which other Greek adjectives adopt this word order, and what do they mean?

15. In what way do the neuter singulars of ἐκεινος and οὑτος differ from the neuter singular of ἀγαθος?

16. What are the "rules" which describe the behaviour of οὑτος?

REVIEW EXERCISES

DICTIONARY ENTRIES

Complete the dictionary entries for these adjectives with
-α,ον or -η,ον.

ἀγαπητος,_____ ,_____ beloved

ἀληθινος,_____ ,_____ true

ἀξιος,_____ ,_____ worthy

δεξιος,_____ ,_____ right

δευτερος,_____ ,_____ second

δικαιος,_____ ,_____ just, righteous

δυνατος,_____ ,_____ powerful, possible

ἐλευθερος,_____ ,_____ free

ἐσχατος,_____ ,_____ last

ἱκανος,_____ ,_____ sufficient

ἰσχυρος,_____ ,_____ strong

καθαρος,_____ ,_____ pure

καινος,_____ ,_____ new

κακος,_____ ,_____ bad

κυλλος,_____ ,_____ crippled

κωφος,_____ ,_____ dumb, deaf

μακαριος,_____ ,_____ happy, blessed

μικρος,_____ ,_____ small

μονος,_____ ,_____ only, alone

νεκρος,_____ ,_____ dead

νεος,_____ ,_____ new

παλαιος,_____ ,_____ old

παραλυτικος,_____ ,_____ paralyzed

πιστος,_____ ,_____ faithful, believing

πλουσιος,_____ ,_____ rich

πρωτος,_____ ,_____ first

πτωχος,_____ ,_____ poor

σοφος,_____ ,_____ wise

τριτος,_____ ,_____ third

τυφλος,_____ ,_____ blind

COMPLETING THE JIGSAW

The texts below with their English translations are like a jigsaw, with words as the pieces. You have been given the missing pieces and you have to put them in the correct places.

> ἀγαθα ἀγαθε ἀγαθη ἀγαθον ἀγαθος ἀγαθους
> ἁγια ἁγιον ἁγιος αὑτη ἐκεινας ἐκεινοι ὁλος
> παντας πονηρα πονηροι πονηρος πονηρου
> πονηρους ταυταις

Matthew 12:35

ὁ __(1)__ ἀνθρωπος ἐκ του __(2)__ θησαυρου ἐκβαλλει __(3)__ .

The *evil* man out of his *evil* treasure brings forth *evil* [things].

Matthew 22:10

και ἐξελθοντες οἱ δουλοι ___(4)___ εἰς τας ὁδους συνηγαγον ___(5)___ οὑς εὑρον, ___(6)___ τε και ___(7)___.

And *those* slaves went out into the streets and gathered *all* whom they found, both *evil* and *good*.

Matthew 22:40

ἐν ___(8)___ ταις δυσιν ἐντολαις ___(9)___ ὁ νομος κρεμαται και οἱ προφηται.

On *these* two commands the *whole* law hangs and the prophets.

Mark 10:17–18

ἐπηρωτα αὐτον, Διδασκαλε ___(10)___, τί ποιησω ἱνα ζωην αἰωνιον κληρονομησω; ὁ δε Ἰησους εἰπεν αὐτῳ, Τί με λεγεις ___(11)___; οὐδεις ___(12)___ εἰ μη εἰς ὁ θεος.

He asked him, "*Good* teacher, what shall I do that I may inherit eternal life?" Jesus said to him, "Why do you call me *good*? [There is] no one *good* except one, God."

Luke 11:13

εἰ οὐν ὑμεις ___(13)___ ὑπαρχοντες οἰδατε δοματα ___(14)___ διδοναι τοις τεκνοις ὑμων, ποσῳ μαλλον ὁ πατηρ ὁ ἐξ οὐρανου δωσει πνευμα ___(15)___ τοις αἰτουσιν αὐτον.

If you then being *evil* know to give *good* gifts to your children, how much more will the Father from heaven give [the] *Holy* Spirit to those who ask him.

Romans 7:12

ὥστε ὁ μεν νομος __(16)__ και ἡ ἐντολη __(17)__ και δικαια και __(18)__ .

So the law [is] *holy* and the commandment [is] *holy* and just and *good*.

Hebrews 10:16

__(19)__ ἡ διαθηκη ἥν διαθησομαι προς αὐτους μετα τας ἡμερας __(20)__ , λεγει κυριος.

This [is] the covenant which I will make with them after *those* days, says the Lord.

WORDS TO LEARN

ἀγαθος, η, ον   good

ἁγιος, α, ον   holy

[ὁ ἁγιος is often translated "the saint", οἱ ἁγιοι

"the saints".]

ἀπο (ἀπ', ἀφ') + genitive   from

δενδρον, ου n   tree

διαβολος, ου m   devil

ἐκεινος, η, ο   that (plural, those)

[ἐκεινος alone is often translated "he".]

ἡμερα, ας f   day

θελημα, θεληματος n   will, desire

καλος, η, ον   good

καρπος, ου m   fruit

κυριος, ου m   lord

νομος, ου m law

όλος, η, ον whole

όνομα, όνοματος n name

ότι that, because, (sometimes introducing direct speech)

ούτος, αύτη, τουτο this (plural, these)

[ούτος alone is also used with the meaning "he".]

πας, πασα, παν all, every

ποιεω do, make, produce

πονηρος, α, ον evil

[ό πονηρος often means "the evil one", i.e. the
devil.]

ψυχη, ης f soul, life

CHAPTER EIGHT

Preview

The verb: action in the past

The aorist tense: four elements

First aorist

ἐπιστευσα ἐδεξαμην

Second aorist

εἶπον ἐγενομην

Reference books

CHAPTER EIGHT

Reporting the action

Looking back in time

8.1   Much of the material in the New Testament is narrative, a report of events which took place in the past. So far we have concentrated on the way Greek verbs are used to describe the present and the future. It is time to investigate the way they handle events in the past.

8.2   Leaving aside all the exceptions, such as contracted verbs and LMNR verbs, we can express the tenses of the verb fairly simply.

PRESENT ACTION	Stem + endings	
e.g.	πιστευ|ω	I believe
	δεχ|ομαι	I receive
FUTURE ACTION	Stem + σ* + endings	
	(* or equivalent)	
e.g.	πιστευ|σ|ω	I will believe
	δεξ||ομαι	I will receive

To these we can now add the regular past tense, which for reasons we will come to later is called the AORIST tense.

PAST ACTION	ἐ* + stem + σ* + endings	
	(*or equivalent)	
e.g.	ἐ|πιστευ|σ|α	I believed
	ἐ|δεξ||αμην	I received

Four elements

8.3   The first element is the letter ἐ (with a smooth breathing because it stands at the beginning of the word). It is sometimes referred to as **the augment**. It is this, more than anything else, which identifies the verb as a past tense.

8.4   Verbs which already begin with a vowel do not use the extra ἐ but lengthen their own initial vowel if possible. Look at these examples.

ἀκουω	I hear	αἰτῶ (εω)	I ask
ἀκουσω	I will hear	αἰτησω	I will ask
ἤκουσα	I heard	ἤτησα	I asked
ἐγειρω	I raise		
ἐγερῶ (εω)	I will raise		
ἤγειρα	I raised		
ὁμολογῶ (εω)	I confess	οἰκοδομῶ (εω)	I build
ὁμολογησω	I will confess	οἰκοδομησω	I will build
ὡμολογησα	I confessed	ᾠκοδομησα	I built

- α → η   ε → η   ο → ω   αι → ῃ   οι → ῳ
- η, ι, υ, and ω do not change

8.5   The second element is the **stem**, which remains constant in all three tenses (except where the addition of σ forces an alteration).

The third element is the added σ or its equivalent. In sections 6.10 and 6.11 we noted the variations which occur in the future tense when the σ is combined with the letters π, κ, β, γ, ζ, σ, τ, φ and χ. The same changes take place in the aorist tense. e.g.

βλεπω I see   βλεψω I will see   ἐβλεψα I saw

8.6   The fourth element is an **ending** to indicate "I", "you", etc. The endings differ from ω, εις, ει, ομεν, ετε, ουσιν and ομαι, ῃ, εται, ομεθα, εσθε, ονται.

However if you have learned these endings which are used for present and future you will probably have developed an "instinct" for recognizing at least some of the new endings. Have a go at these multiple choice questions.

Exercise 8.6

- Does ἠκουσαμεν mean "he heard", "we heard" or "they heard"?
- Does ᾠκοδομησας mean "you (s) built", "we built" or "you (p) built"?
- Does ἐδεξασθε mean "I received", "he received" or "you (p) received"?

A Do It Yourself Chart

8.7 Analyze the texts and translations below and use the information to complete the chart of personal endings for the aorist tense.

- An unusual feature of πιστευω which you will see in these examples is that its object is not in the accusative case but the dative case. "I believe him" is πιστευω αὐτῳ (not αὐτον).

- In addition to δεχομαι I have used two other verbs:
  νιπτομαι I wash (aorist ἐνιψαμην)
  ψευδομαι I lie, tell lies (aorist ἐψευσαμην)

και εἰπεν ὁ ᾿Ιησους	And Jesus said
τῳ ἑκατονταρχῃ·	to the centurion:
῾Υπαγε, ὡς **ἐπιστευσας**	"Go. As **you have believed**
γενηθητω σοι.	let it be done for you"
	(Matthew 8:13).

ἦλθεν γαρ Ἰωαννης προς ὑμας
ἐν ὁδῳ δικαιοσυνης,
και οὐκ **ἐπιστευσατε** αὐτῳ.
οἱ δε τελωναι
και αἱ πορναι **ἐπιστευσαν**
αὐτῳ·

For John came to you
in [the] way of righteousness,
and **you did** not **believe** him.
But the tax-collectors
and the prostitutes **believed**
him (Matthew 21:32).

και **ἐπιστευσεν** αὐτος
και ἡ οἰκια αὐτου ὁλη.

And **he** himself **believed**
and his whole house
(John 4:53).

νυν γαρ ἐγγυτερον
ἡμων ἡ σωτηρια
ἠ ὁτε **ἐπιστευσαμεν**.

For now [is] nearer
our salvation
than when **we believed**
(Romans 13:11).

κατα το γεγραμμενον·
ἐπιστευσα, διο ἐλαλησα,
και ἡμεις πιστευομεν,
διο και λαλουμεν.

As it is written:
"**I believed** and so I spoke,"
we also believe,
and so we speak
(2 Corinthians 4:13).

ὁτε οὐν ἦλθεν εἰς την
Γαλιλαιαν,
ἐδεξαντο αὐτον οἱ Γαλιλαιοι.

So when he came into
Galilee,
the Galileans **received** him
(John 4:45).

ὁ δε εἰπεν αὐτοις·
Πηλον ἐπεθηκεν
μου ἐπι τους ὀφθαλμους
και **ἐνιψαμην** και βλεπω.

And he said to them,
"He put clay
on my eyes
and **I washed** and I can see"
(John 9:15).

οὐκ **ἐψευσω** ἀνθρωποις
ἀλλα τῳ θεῳ.

You have not **lied** to men
but to God (Acts 5:4).

οὑτος ἐστιν ὁ γενομενος
ἐν τῃ ἐκκλησιᾳ ἐν τῃ ἐρημῳ
. . .
ὁς **ἐδεξατο** λογια ζωντα
δουναι ἡμιν.

This is he who was
in the assembly in the desert
. . .
who **received** living oracles
to give to us (Acts 7:38).

οἱ δε προς αὐτον εἶπαν·
Ἡμεις οὐτε γραμματα περι
   σου **ἐδεξαμεθα**
ἀπο της Ἰουδαιας.

And they said to him,
"We have received no
   letters about you
from Judea" (Acts 28:21).

ἀλλα ὡς ἀγγελον θεου
ἐδεξασθε με,
ὡς Χριστον Ἰησουν.

But as an angel of God
you (p) **received** me,
as Christ Jesus
(Galatians 4:14).

Exercise 8.7

I believed	ἐπιστευσ_____
you (s) believed	ἐπιστευσ_____
he/she believed	ἐπιστευσ_____
we believed	ἐπιστευσ_____
you (p) believed	ἐπιστευσ_____
they believed	ἐπιστευσ_____

I received	ἐδεξ_____
you (s) received	ἐδεξ_____
he/she received	ἐδεξ_____
we received	ἐδεξ_____
you (p) received	ἐδεξ_____
they received	ἐδεξ_____

Exceptions are not the exception

8.8   One of the frustrating things about languages is the
       way they refuse to stick to the rules. Think of the
       simple past tense in English. You might formulate a
       rule that it usually adds **-ed** to the present.

       e.g. I pray   → I prayed
            I show   → I showed
            I delight → I delighted

       On the basis of this rule "I say" should become "I
       sayed", but it is "I said"; "I know" should become "I
       knowed", but it is "I knew"; "I fight" should become
       "I fighted", but it is "I fought". So what is the past
       tense of "I light"? "I lighted"? "I lought"? No, it is
       "I lit".

8.9   This variety of expression is also seen in the Greek
       language. Take the verb λεγω, *I say*. According to
       the rules its future and aorist ought to be λεξω,
       ἐλεξα, but they are not. Here is how it behaves.

       λεγω I say   ἐρῶ (εω) I will say   εἰπον I said

Exercise 8.9

Tick off the statements which are true of the tenses of
λεγω.
1. The present tense behaves like πιστευω.
2. The future has a different stem from the present.
3. The endings of the future follow LMNR verbs.
4. The aorist has a stem different from both present
   and future.
5. The aorist does not have the characteristic **σ**
   before the endings.
6. The aorist endings are different from the endings
   of ἐπιστευσα.

8.10 Yes, all those statements were true. Now look at these verbs.

βαλλω	I throw	βαλῶ (εω)	I will throw	ἐβαλον	I threw
ἐρχομαι	I come	ἐλευσομαι	I will come	ἦλθον	I came
λαμβανω	I accept	λημψομαι	I will accept	ἐλαβον	I accepted
ὁρῶ (αω)	I see	ὀψομαι	I will see	εἰδον	I saw
ἁμαρτανω	I sin	_____		ἡμαρτον	I sinned
μανθανω	I learn	_____		ἐμαθον	I learned

Exercise 8.10

- Which of the statements about λεγω in Exercise 8.9 are true of all these verbs as well? (Include statements about the future where applicable.)

- Formulate a new set of "rules" to cover the behaviour of these verbs.

Predictable endings

8.11 You can check your answers at the end of the chapter. What is clear is that when you try to formulate rules you end up with more exceptions than rules. Forms like ἐπιστευσα are called "first aorists" and forms like εἰπον are called "second aorists". We have not yet looked at the **endings** of these second aorists. The good news is that they are completely predictable. Once again they have a familiar ring and you may be able to put this jumbled list into the right order.

Exercise 8.11

εἰπεν εἰπετε εἰπον εἰπον εἰπομεν εἰπες

What is the correct order, "I said", "you (s) said", etc.?

8.12   You can confirm your answers by analyzing the second
        aorists in these texts.

και ἰδου ὁ ἀστηρ,
ὁν **εἰδον** ἐν τη ἀνατολη,
προηγεν αὐτους.

And behold the star,
which **they saw** in the east,
went ahead of them
(Matthew 2:9).

Κυριε, ποτε σε **εἰδομεν**
πεινωντα καὶ ἐθρεψαμεν,
ἠ διψωντα και ἐποτισαμεν;

Lord, when **did we see** you
hungry and feed [you],
or thirsty and give [you] drink?
(Matthew 25:37).

δια τουτο λεγω ὑμιν,
παντα ὁσα προσευχεσθε
και αἰτεισθε,
πιστευετε ὁτι **ἐλαβετε**
και ἐσται ὑμιν.

Therefore I say to you,
everything which you pray for
and ask,
believe that **you have received** [it].
and it will be yours.
(Mark 11:24).

και ἀποκριθεις **εἰπεν** αὐτοις·
Πορευθεντεςἀπαγγειλατε Ἰωαννη
ἁ **εἰδετε** και ἠκουσατε.

And in answer **he said** to them,
"Go and report to John
what **you saw** and heard."
(Luke 7:22).

και ἀναστας
ἠλθεν προς τον πατερα ἑαυτου.
Ἐτι δε αὐτου μακραν
ἀπεχοντος
εἰδεν αὐτον ὁ πατηρ αὐτου
και ἐσπλαγχνισθη
και δραμων
ἐπεπεσεν ἐπι τον τραχηλον αὐτου
και κατεφιλησεν αὐτον.

And having got up
he came to his father.
While he was still far away

his father **saw** him
and was filled with compassion
and running
he fell on his neck
and kissed him (Luke 15:20).

ὁσοι δε **ἐλαβον** αὐτον,
ἐδωκεν αὐτοις ἐξουσιαν
τεκνα θεου γενεσθαι.

But as many as **received** him,
he gave them power
to become children of God
(John 1:12).

ὁτι ἐκ του πληρωματος αὐτου
ἡμεις παντες **ἐλαβομεν**
και χαριν ἀντι χαριτος·

For from his fulness
we have all **received**
and grace upon grace
(John 1:16).

ἀπεκριθη Ἰησους
και **εἰπεν** αὐτῳ·
Ὁτι **εἰπον** σοι ὁτι **εἰδον** σε
ὑποκατω της συκης, πιστευεις;
μειζω τουτων ὀψῃ.

Jesus answered
and **said** to him,
"Because **I told** you that **I saw** you
under the fig tree, do you believe?
You will see greater things than
these" (John 1:50).

ταυτην την ἐντολην
ἐλαβον παρα του πατρος μου.

This command
I received from my father
(John 10:18).

εἰτα λεγει τῳ μαθητῃ·
Ἰδε ἡ μητηρ σου.
και ἀπ᾽ ἐκεινης της ὡρας
ἐλαβεν ὁ μαθητης αὐτην
εἰς τα ἰδια.

Then he said to the disciple,
"Behold your mother."
And from that hour
the disciple **took** her
into his own [home]
(John 19:27).

τίς γαρ σε διακρινει;
τί δε ἐχεις
ὁ οὐκ **ἐλαβες**;
εἰ δε και **ἐλαβες**,
τί καυχασαι
ὡς μη λαβων;

For who judges you superior?
What do you have
which **you did** not **receive**?
And so if **you received** [it],
why do you boast
as if you had not received [it]? (1
Corinthians 4:7).

γραψον οὐν ἁ **εἰδες**
και ἁ εἰσιν
και ἁ μελλει γενεσθαι
μετα ταυτα.

Write therefore what **you saw**
even the things which are
and the things which are to be
after these things
(Revelation 1:19).

Another Variety

8.13 Just as the *first aorist* comes in two varieties, ἐπιστευσα and ἐδεξαμην, so there is another variety of *second aorist* in addition to εἰπον. It can be illustrated in a very common and versatile verb, γινομαι, meaning *be, become, happen, come into being*, etc. Here are the present, future and aorist tenses.

γινομαι I become   γενησομαι I will become
ἐγενομην I became

In this chart you will see that the endings are not too different from the endings of ἐδεξαμην, but without the predominant **α-** in the endings and without the characteristic **-σ-** in front of them.

ἐγεν **ομην**	I became
ἐγεν **ου**	you (s) became
ἐγεν **ετο**	he/she became
ἐγεν **ομεθα**	we became
ἐγεν **εσθε**	you (p) became
ἐγεν **οντο**	they became

8.14 You will get some idea of the versatility of this verb from the English translations in these examples.

και ἰδου σεισμος μεγας **ἐγενετο** ἐν τη θαλασση, ὡστε το πλοιον καλυπτεσθαι ὑπο των κυματων, αὐτος δε ἐκαθευδεν.	And behold a great storm **arose** on the lake, so that the boat was swamped by the waves, but he was sleeping (Matthew 8:24).
Τοτε ἠρξατο ὀνειδιζειν τας πολεις ἐν αἱς **ἐγενοντο** αἱ πλεισται δυναμεις αὐτου, ὁτι οὐ μετενοησαν.	Then he began to denounce the cities in which **had been done** his greatest miracles, because they did not repent (Matthew 11:20).

παντα δι' αυτου ἐγενετο,	All things **were made** through him,
και χωρις αυτου ἐγενετο οὐδε ἑν.	and without him nothing **was made** (John 1:3).

Note παντα . . . ἐγενετο. Greek writers often used a *singular* verb after a *neuter plural* subject, literally "all things was made".

και ἐγενομην τοις Ἰουδαιοις ὡς Ἰουδαιος, ἵνα Ἰουδαιους κερδησω.	And to the Jews I **became** as a Jew, that I might win Jews (1 Corinthians 9:20).
οὐ διεκριθητε	Have you not made distinctions
ἐν ἑαυτοις και ἐγενεσθε κριται διαλογισμων πονηρων;	among yourselves and **become** judges with evil thoughts? (James 2:4).
ἐγενομην ἐν πνευματι ἐν τη κυριακη ἡμερᾳ και ἠκουσα ὀπισω μου φωνην μεγαλην ὡς σαλπιγγος.	I **was** in the Spirit on the Lord's day and I heard behind me a loud voice as of a trumpet (Revelation 1:10).
και ἐγενοντο ἀστραπαι	Then **there came** flashes of lightning
και φωναι και βρονται	and rumbling and peals of thunder
και σεισμος ἐγενετο μεγας,	and **there was** a great earthquake,
οἷος οὐκ ἐγενετο ἀφ' οὐ ἀνθρωπος ἐγενετο ἐπι της γης τηλικουτος σεισμος οὕτω μεγας.	such as has not **occurred** since man **existed** on the earth so terrible an earthquake so great (Revelation 16:18).

Memorization and Recognition

8.15   An important question is what you are going to do
with this rather bewildering collection of lists you are
accumulating. Should you learn them all so that you
can repeat them parrot-fashion? Not necessarily.
What is essential is that you should be able to
recognize and translate words as you come to them.
When you see the word πιστευομεν you probably
don't go through a list you've learned – πιστευω, I
believe; πιστευεις, you believe; πιστευει, he believes;
πιστευομεν – ah, that's it – we believe. With practice
you are able to recognize that a word ending in -ομεν
means "we" do something, and your knowledge of
the stem πιστευ- gives you the "believing" part. It
may be that in the early stages memorization is the
key to recognition, but in the long run it is far more
productive to read "real" texts, and pick up the clues
that give the meaning, than to recite endless, rather
boring, lists.

Exercise 8.15

In this exercise I want you to look carefully at the
verb forms that are given and try to use the "instinct"
which you are developing to recognize the meaning.
A basic meaning for each verb is supplied, and you
have to decide whether it is present, future, or past;
whether it is "I", "you", or whatever. Something
which makes this exercise harder is that you have
been given the words in isolation. In a real translation the context would also help you to identify the
meaning.

EXAMPLE: ἀκουσομεν, ἠκουσαμεν (hear) *We will
hear, we heard*

Now try these.

πιστευει, ἐπιστευσατε
(believe)
ἐδεξαμην, δεξεται (receive)
αἰτεῖτε, ἠτησα (ask)
ἐγεροῦμεν, ἐγειρουσιν (raise)
ὁμολογεῖς, ὡμολογησαν (confess)
οἰκοδομησετε, οἰκοδομει
(build)
νιπτονται, ἐνιψω (wash)
ψευδεσθε, ψευδονται (lie)

ἐρῶ, εἰπεν (say)
βαλλει, βαλεῖ (throw)
ἐρχομεθα, ἠλθετε (come)
λημψεται, ἐλαβον (take)
ὁρατε, εἰδετε (see)
ἁμαρτανουσιν, ἡμαρτες (sin)
ἐγενοντο, γινεσθε (become)

Naming of parts

8.16 A verb like πιστευω is very predictable and well-behaved; it follows the rules with its future, πιστευσω, and its aorist, ἐπιστευσα. A verb like λεγω is quite unpredictable. The basic stem λεγ- disappears after the present tense, followed first by ἐρῶ in the future and εἰπον in the aorist.

In a dictionary a regular verb like πιστευω would simply be listed under its present tense form, πιστευω. Where verbs are irregular, like λεγω, the different parts are listed for you.

A problem arises, of course, when you are translating from Greek to English. If you come across ἐπιστευσεν and you don't remember what verb it is from you can be looking up the dictionary forever under the E-section and you will never find it. It is under the Π-section.

There are several types of book which help students to deal with this problem.

- **An Analytical Lexicon**. This is a dictionary which lists not only the basic dictionary entry but also every form in which that word occurs in the New Testament in alphabetical order. So in this type of lexicon ἐπιστευσεν *would* appear under the E-section.

- **A Grammatical Analysis.** This is a type of commentary which gives information about the grammatical forms of the words in the New Testament specifically. Using a Grammatical Analysis is usually much quicker than looking up every word in a dictionary, even an analytical one.

- **A Commentary on the Greek Text.** Some New Testament Commentaries are based on the Greek text. The problem for the beginner is that they are usually very scholarly works and contain much more information than you can easily cope with. However, a knowledge of Greek will give you access to more advanced books and it is worth finding out what is available.

Answers to Exercises

Exercise 8.6

- ἠκουσαμεν means "we heard".
- ᾠκοδομησας means "you (s) built".
- ἐδεξασθε means "you (p) received".

Exercise 8.7

I believed	ἐπιστευσ **α**
you (s) believed	ἐπιστευσ **ας**
he/she believed	ἐπιστευσ **εν**
we believed	ἐπιστευσ **αμεν**
you (p) believed	ἐπιστευσ **ατε**
they believed	ἐπιστευσ **αν**

I received	ἐδεξ **αμην**
you (s) received	ἐδεξ **ω**
he/she received	ἐδεξ **ατο**
we received	ἐδεξ **αμεθα**
you (p) received	ἐδεξ **ασθε**
they received	ἐδεξ **αντο**

Exercise 8.9

All the statements are true of λεγω.

Exercise 8.10

- The statements which are true of all the verbs are:
2. The future has a different stem from the present.
5. The aorist does not have the characteristic σ before the endings.
6. The aorist endings are different from the endings of ἐπιστευσα.
- A possible set of rules is:
1. It is not possible to predict either the stem or the endings of the future and aorist from the present tense.
2. The aorist does not have an σ before the endings.
3. The aorist endings follow a regular pattern, which is different from the pattern of ἐπιστευσα.

Exercise 8.11

εἰπον	I said	εἰπομεν	we said
εἰπες	you (s) said	εἰπετε	you (p) said
εἰπεν	he/she said	εἰπον	they said

Note that εἰπον can mean either "I said" or "they said". Although this may look like a problem, in practice the context usually makes it clear which way it should be translated.

Occasionally Greek writers used 1st aorist endings with these verbs, e.g. εἶπαν, they said. It is just possible that they found it as confusing as we do!

Exercise 8.15

πιστευει, he/she believes

ἐδεξαμην, I received

αἰτεῖτε, you (p) ask

ἐγεροῦμεν, we shall raise

ὁμολογεις, you confess

οἰκοδομησετε, you (p) will build

νιπτονται, they wash

ψευδεσθε, you (p) lie

ἐρῶ, I will say

βαλλει, he/she throws

ἐρχομεθα, we come

λημψεται, he/she will take

ὁρατε, you (p) see

ἁμαρτανουσιν, they sin

ἐγενοντο, they became

ἐπιστευσατε you (p) believed

δεξεται he/she receives

ᾔτησα I asked

ἐγειρουσιν they raise

ὡμολογησαν they confessed

οἰκοδομει he builds

ἐνιψω you (s) washed

ψευδονται they lie

εἶπεν he/she said

βαλεῖ he/she will throw

ἤλθετε you (p) came

ἐλαβον I/they took

εἴδετε you (p) saw

ἥμαρτες you (s) sinned

γινεσθε you (p) become

REVIEW QUESTIONS

1. What are the component parts of a regular verb expressing action in the present?

2. What are the component parts of a regular verb expressing action in the future?

3. What are the component parts of a regular verb expressing action in the past (aorist tense)?

4. What is the augment and what does it identify?

5. What happens to the augment when a verb begins with a vowel?

6. What is the full pattern of endings for ἐπιστευσα and ἐδεξαμην?

7. What is the past tense (aorist) of λεγω?

8. What do these words mean, and which verbs (present tense) are they from?

   ἐβαλον, ἐμαθον, ὀψομαι, ἡμαρτον, ἠλθον, ἐλευσομαι, εἰδον, λημψομαι, ἐλαβον, βαλω.

9. What is the full pattern of endings for εἰπον and ἐγενομην?

10. Is ἐδεξαμην a first or a second aorist?

11. Is ἐγενομην a first or a second aorist?

12. What are some of the ways in which γινομαι can be translated into English?

13. Which is more important for language learning, memorization or recognition?

14. How does a dictionary help with irregular verbs?

15. What books are available to help with translation?

REVIEW EXERCISES

PRESENT FOR AORIST

What is the corresponding present of each of these? For example, the corresponding present of ἐπιστευσαμεν (we believed) is πιστευομεν (we believe).

ἐλαβον, εἶπες, εἶδεν, ἡμαρτομεν, ἐμαθετε, ἐβαλον.

AORIST FOR PRESENT

What is the corresponding aorist of each of these presents?

ποιουσιν, πιστευεις, φιλειτε, πεμπω, ἐρχεται, γινομεθα.

WHICH FITS?

Which of the words supplied fits correctly in the spaces in these texts? As a supplementary exercise you can identify the meaning of the words which have been rejected.

Luke 20:5

Ἐαν εἰπωμεν, Ἐξ οὐρανου, __(1)__ , Δια τί οὐκ __(2)__ αὐτῳ;

If we say, "From heaven," *he will say*, "Why *did you* not *believe* him?"

[ἐπιστευσας, ἐπιστευσατε, ἐρει, λεγει, λημψεται, πιστευσει]

John 14:26

ὁ δε παρακλητος, το πνευμα το ἁγιον, ὃ __(3)__ ὁ πατηρ ἐν τῳ ὀνοματι μου, ἐκεινος ὑμας διδαξει παντα.

But the Helper, the Holy Spirit, whom the Father *will send* in my name, he will teach you everything.

[ἐλευσεται, πεμψει, ὀψεται]

John 19:19

__(4)__ δε και τιτλον ὁ Πιλατος και ἐθηκεν ἐπι του σταυρου.

Pilate also *wrote* a title and put it on the cross.

[ἐγραψεν, ἐλαβεν, ἐσωσεν]

Acts 11:1

__(5)__ δε οἱ ἀποστολοι και οἱ ἀδελφοι οἱ ὀντες κατα την Ἰουδαιαν ὀτι και τα ἐθνη __(6)__ τον λογον του θεου.

Now the apostles and the brothers who were in Judea *heard* that the Gentiles also *had received* the word of God.

[δεξονται, ἐδεξαντο, ἐδεξασθε, ἐμαθον, ἠκουσαν, ἡμαρτον]

Acts 20:6

και __(7)__ προς αὐτους εἰς την Τρῳαδα ἀχρι ἡμερων πεντε.

And *we came* to them at Troas in five days.

[ἐβαλομεν, ἐλαβομεν, ἠλθομεν]

1 Corinthians 1:14

οὐδενα ὑμων __(8)__ εἰ μη Κρισπον και Γαϊον.

I baptized none of you except Crispus and Gaius.

[ἐβαπτισα, ἐβαπτισαν, ἐβαπτισεν]

Hebrews 1:9

__(9)__ δικαιοσυνην και __(10)__ ἀνομιαν.

You have loved righteousness and *you have hated* lawlessness.

[ἐγενου, ἐδεξω, εἰδες, ἐμισησας, ἐποιησας, ἠγαπησας]

STRAIGHT TRANSLATION

These verses contain some of the words you have learned. Some that you will not know are given with their meanings. You should first aim to understand the structure of the Greek. This will give you a rather "wooden" translation. The next stage is to find the best way of putting the verse into modern English, giving it vitality but without losing any accuracy. Finally, check your results with the work of "the professionals", i.e. a respected modern translation. It is always interesting to look at more than one and compare different approaches to the text.

John 4:46

ἦλθεν οὖν παλιν εἰς την Κανα της Γαλιλαιας ὁπου ἐποιησεν το ὑδωρ οἰνον.

παλιν again   ὁπου where   ὑδωρ, ὑδατος n water
οἰνος, ου m wine

John 12:34

Ἡμεις ἠκουσαμεν ἐκ του νομου ὁτι ὁ Χριστος μενει εἰς τον αἰωνα.
εἰς τον αἰωνα   for ever

John 14:28

ἠκουσατε ὁτι ἐγω εἰπον ὑμιν, Ὑπαγω και ἐρχομαι προς ὑμας.
ὑπαγω I go   ἐρχομαι is sometimes used with a future sense.

Acts 6:15

παντες οἱ καθεζομενοι ἐν τῳ συνεδριῳ εἰδον το προσωπον αὐτου ὡσει προσωπον ἀγγελου.

οἱ καθεζομενοι "who were sitting"   συνεδριον, ου n council   ὡσει like, as

1 Corinthians 2:12

ἡμεις δε οὐ το πνευμα του κοσμου ἐλαβομεν ἀλλα το
πνευμα το ἐκ του θεου.

δε and, but, sometimes not translated (never first in its
sentence)   λαμβανω accept, receive

1 Corinthians 4:17

δια τουτο ἐπεμψα ὑμιν Τιμοθεον, ὁς ἐστιν μου τεκνον
ἀγαπητον και πιστον ἐν κυριῳ.

δια τουτο for this reason   ὁς who

Ephesians 4:20

ὑμεις δε οὐχ οὑτως ἐμαθετε τον Χριστον.

οὑτως so, in this way

1 Thessalonians 3:2

και ἐπεμψαμεν Τιμοθεον τον ἀδελφον ἡμων και
συνεργον του θεου ἐν τῳ εὐαγγελιῳ του Χριστου.

συνεργος, ου m fellow-worker

Revelation 4:10

και βαλουσιν τους στεφανους αὐτων ἐνωπιον του θρονου
λεγοντες, Ἀξιος εἶ, ὁ κυριος και ὁ θεος ἡμων.

στεφανος, ου m crown   ἐνωπιον + gen. before
θρονος, ου m throne   λεγοντες saying   εἶ you are

Revelation 22:16

Ἐγω Ἰησους ἐπεμψα τον ἀγγελον μου μαρτυρησαι ὑμιν
ταυτα ἐπι ταις ἐκκλησιαις.

μαρτυρησαι to testify   ἐπι + dat. for (This preposition is
very versatile and it is safest to adjust the meaning to the
context.)

WORDS TO LEARN

ἀγαπητος, η, ον   beloved
ἁμαρτανω, aor. ἡμαρτον   sin
ἀξιος, α, ον   worthy
βαλλω, fut. βαλῶ (εω), aor. ἐβαλον   throw, cast
    (e.g. a net)
γη, ης f   earth, land, soil
γινομαι, fut. γενησομαι, aor. ἐγενομην   be, become
δεχομαι, fut. δεξομαι, aor. ἐδεξαμην   receive
δια + accusative   because of, on account of
    (cf. δια + gen., chapter 4)
δια τουτο   for this reason, therefore
διδασκω, fut. διδαξω, aor. ἐδιδαξα   teach
θρονος, ου m   throne
λαμβανω, fut. λημψομαι, aor. ἐλαβον   receive,
    accept, take
μανθανω, aor. ἐμαθον   learn
ὁραω, fut. ὀψομαι, aor. εἰδον   see
πιστος, η, ον   faithful, believing

SUPPLEMENT TO WORDS
ALREADY GIVEN
(chapter numbers in brackets)

Present	Future	Aorist	
ἀκουω (2)	ἀκουσω	ἠκουσα	[hear]
βαπτιζω (6)	βαπτισω	ἐβαπτισα	[baptize]
βλεπω (2)	βλεψω	ἐβλεψα	[see]
γραφω (2)	γραψω	ἐγραψα	[write]
πεμπω (6)	πεμψω	ἐπεμψα	[send]
πιστευω (2)	πιστευσω	ἐπιστευσα	[believe]
σῳζω (3)	σωσω	ἐσωσα	[save]
ἀγαπαω (6)	ἀγαπησω	ἠγαπησα	[love]
μισεω (6)	μισησω	ἐμισησα	[hate]
ποιεω (7)	ποιησω	ἐποιησα	[do, make]
φιλεω (6)	φιλησω	ἐφιλησα	[love]
πληροω (7)	πληρωσω	ἐπληρωσα	[fill, fulfil]
γινωσκω (2)	γνωσομαι	ἐγνων*	[know]

*The aorist of γινωσκω is *very* irregular. The pattern is ἐγνων ἐγνως ἐγνω ἐγνωμεν ἐγνωτε ἐγνωσαν.

ἐρχομαι (6)	ἐλευσομαι	ἠλθον	[come]
ἐσθιω (4)	φαγομαι	ἐφαγον	[eat]
ἐχω (2)	ἑξω (hexō)	ἐσχον	[have]
θελω (6)	θελησω	ἠθελησα	[want, wish]
κρίνω (6)	κρινῶ (εω)	ἐκρινα	[judge]
λεγω (2)	ἐρῶ (εω)	εἰπον	[say]
μένω (2)	μενῶ (εω)	ἐμεινα	[remain]
πινω (4)	πιομαι	ἐπιον	[drink]

CHAPTER NINE

Preview

Verbs: modes of action

Issuing commands: the imperative mood

Commands issued to the person or people you are talking to

Commands issued to someone else, or other people

Imperatives from πιστευω, φιλεω, ἀγαπαω, πληροω

Imperatives from ἐρχομαι, ἀρνεομαι, καυχαομαι, λυτροομαι

Neutral and continuous commands

Imperatives: present and aorist

CHAPTER NINE

Two ways of looking at it

A conversation

9.1 Read through this conversation. The numbers are there just to help you analyze it.

● Hello, where *do you live*[1]?

▶ *I live*[2] in Brighton.

● *Will you stay*[3] there?

▶ *I will stay*[4] there for a few years anyway.

● When *did you move*[5] there?

▶ *I moved*[6] in 1984.

● Why?

▶ *To be*[7] near the sea.

● If only *I lived*[8] at the seaside. Are you happy *living*[9] there?

▶ Oh yes. *Come*[10] and *see*[10] me sometime.

● *Don't be surprised*[10] if *I accept*[11] your offer.

9.2 Our old friend the verb is demonstrating its versatility again. In the examples numbered 1 to 6 the verbs are either making statements or asking questions. Past, present and future are all illustrated. This matches what we have discovered about the Greek verb so far: statements and questions; in the past (aorist), present or future tense.

But the repertoire of the verb is not exhausted by this. It can also be used to express a purpose (7), a wish (8), concurrent action (9), an invitation, command or prohibition (10), and something that *might* happen (11).

9.3   These different modes of the verb have technical
       terms: indicative (1 to 6), infinitive (7), optative (8),
       participle (9), imperative (10), and subjunctive (11).
       Collectively they are called the "modes" or more
       often the "moods" of the verb. It is not important to
       know all this technical jargon. What is important is to
       be able to recognize when a Greek verb is function-
       ing in one of these "modes" and to translate it
       accordingly.

Requests and commands

9.4   In the following examples you will discover how
       Greek handles commands.

       μετανοειτε και πιστευετε ἐν τῳ εὐαγγελιῳ.
       Repent and **believe** in the gospel (Mark 1:15).

       The verbs Mark is using are μετανοεω and πιστευω.
       In fact the commands are the same as the statements
       "you (p) repent" and "you (p) believe". Only the
       context indicates which they are.

       These commands are addressed to more than one
       person; they are **plural** commands. Greek can dif-
       ferentiate between a command to one person or
       more than one. Here is an example of the **singular**.

       λεγει αὐτῃ ὁ 'Ιησους· **Πιστευε** μοι, γυναι.
       Jesus said to her, "**Believe** me, woman" (John 4:21).

9.5   In addition to issuing commands to the person you
       are talking to, you can issue commands for someone
       else, or other people. Look at these examples, using
       the verbs ἀκουω and φευγω.

       ὁ ἐχων ὦτα **ἀκουετω**.
       He who has ears **let him hear** (Matthew 11:15).

       τοτε οἱ ἐν τῃ 'Ιουδαιᾳ **φευγετωσαν** εἰς τα ὀρη.
       Then **let** those in Judea **flee** to the mountains
       (Luke 21:21).

9.6   We can sum all this up in a chart.

πιστευ ε	believe (s)	πιστευ ετε	believe (p)
πιστευ ετω	let him believe	πιστευ ετωσαν	let them believe

9.7   The contracted verbs follow the same pattern with the usual adjustments. With commands the accents are not so helpful and I have left them out.
- From φιλεω (love)
φιλει, φιλειτω, φιλειτε, φιλειτωσαν
- From ἀγαπαω (love)
ἀγαπα, ἀγαπατω, ἀγαπατε, ἀγαπατωσαν
- From πληροω (fill, fulfil)
πληρου, πληρουτω, πληρουτε, πληρουτωσαν

9.8   Verbs which follow the pattern of ἐρχομαι (come) have their own distinctive endings when used for commands. Here is a chart.

ἐρχ ου	come (s)	ἐρχ εσθε	come (p)
ἐρχ εσθω	let him come	ἐρχ εσθωσαν	let them come

Exercise 9.8

In these examples the endings have been left off the commands. See if you can insert the correct endings. In the second text, Luke 21:21, a compound of ἐρχομαι is used – εἰσερχομαι, *enter*. This does not affect the endings.

1. καὶ ἀπεστειλεν τον δουλον αὐτου τῃ ὡρᾳ του δειπνου εἰπειν τοις κεκλημενοις,
   Ἐρχ――― ὅτι ἠδη ἑτοιμα ἐστιν.

   And he sent his servant at the hour of the feast to say to those who had been invited, **"Come** for it is now ready" (Luke 14:17).

2. τοτε οἱ ἐν τῃ Ἰουδαιᾳ φευγετωσαν εἰς τα ὀρη καὶ οἱ ἐν μεσῳ αὐτης ἐκχωρειτωσαν καὶ οἱ ἐν ταις χωραις μη **εἰσερχ**――― εἰς αὐτην.

   Then let those in Judea flee to the mountains and let those inside it depart and **let** those in the country not **enter** it (Luke 21:21).

3. καὶ εἰπεν αὐτῳ Ναθαναηλ·
   Ἐκ Ναζαρετ δυναται τι ἀγαθον εἰναι;
   λεγει αὐτῳ Φιλιππος, Ἐρχ――― καὶ ἰδε.

   And Nathanael said to him, "Can there be anything good from Nazareth?" Philip said to him, **"Come** and see" (John 1:46).

4. Ἐν δε τῃ ἐσχατῃ ἡμερᾳ τῃ μεγαλῃ της ἑορτης εἰστηκει ὁ Ἰησους καὶ ἐκραξεν λεγων·
   Ἐαν τις διψᾳ **ἐρχ**――― προς με καὶ πινετω.

   On the last great day of the feast Jesus stood and cried out saying, "If anyone is thirsty **let him come** to me and drink" (John 7:37).

9.9   There are some verbs in the "slimming club" that take endings like ἐρχομαι rather than like πιστευω. The rules of contraction outlined in chapter 6, sections 6.3 and 6.4, are applied to these verbs as well. Here are some samples.

● ἀρνεομαι *I deny*.
Statements: ἀρνουμαι, ἀρνῃ, ἀρνειται, ἀρνουμεθα, ἀρνεισθε, ἀρνουνται
Commands: ἀρνου, ἀρνεισθω, ἀρνεισθε, ἀρνεισθωσαν

● καυχαομαι *I boast*
Statements: καυχωμαι, καυχᾳ, καυχαται, καυχωμεθα, καυχασθε, καυχωνται
Commands: καυχω, καυχασθω, καυχασθε, καυχασθωσαν

● λυτροομαι *I redeem*
Statements: λυτρουμαι, λυτροι, λυτρουται, λυτρουμεθα, λυτρουσθε, λυτρουνται
Commands: λυτρου, λυτρουσθω, λυτρουσθε, λυτρουσθωσαν

Imperative knowledge

9.10   The technical term for the "command mode" is **the imperative**. It is not necessary to learn all the variations listed above. It will be enough to know thoroughly the imperative endings of πιστευω and ἐρχομαι. If you know them the others should be recognizable.

Make do

9.11 The verb ποιεω (which behaves like φιλεω, *love*) means "I make" or "I do". Look at these examples and, even with the limited knowledge you have of imperatives, you should be able to spot something unexpected.

1. εἰπεν δε αὐτῳ ὁ Ἰησους·
   Πορευου και συ **ποιει** ὁμοιως.

   And Jesus said to him,
   "Go and you **do** likewise" (Luke 10:37).

2. και μετα το ψωμιον τοτε εἰσηλθεν εἰς ἐκεινον ὁ Σατανας.
   λεγει οὐν αὐτῳ ὁ Ἰησους· Ὁ ποιεις **ποιησον** ταχιον.

   And after the dipped bread then Satan entered into him.
   So Jesus said to him, "What you are doing **do** quickly" (John 13:27).

3. Εἰτε οὐν ἐσθιετε εἰτε πινετε εἰτε τι ποιειτε, παντα εἰς δοξαν θεου **ποιειτε**.

   So whether you eat or drink or do anything, **do** everything for the glory of God
   (1 Corinthians 10:31).

4. Περι δε της λογειας της εἰς τους ἁγιους ὡσπερ διεταξα ταις ἐκκλησιαις της Γαλατιας, οὑτως και ὑμεις **ποιησατε**.

   Now concerning the contribution for the saints: as I gave instructions to the churches of Galatia, so you also **do** (1 Corinthians 16:1).

9.12 This is what the title of the chapter is about. When it comes to giving a command there are always two ways of doing it because there are two ways of looking at it. There is a form of the command which is "neutral" and there is a form which implies "go on doing this". If I were to say to someone, "Switch on the light please," that would be "neutral", a simple request. If I were to say to a child, "Be good," that would imply, "Be good – always."

Can you work out which is which in the examples in 9.11? Look at them again and look up the contexts in an English Bible.

9.13 John 13:27 and 1 Corinthians 16:1 contain "neutral" commands. Each time people were commanded to "do" something, but with no thought that they should go on doing it continually, Judas the betrayer and the Corinthian congregation taking a collection for a specific project.

In Luke 10:37 and 1 Corinthians 10:31 the idea is very much that the people should go on doing what they had been told. In the story of the good Samaritan the moral is "Go and do likewise," not just once but at every opportunity. The climax of 1 Corinthians 10 is a command expressed in the most general terms, "Do everything for the glory of God."

9.14   Here are charts with the second set of endings, using
       πιστευω and δεχομαι. [I have used δεχομαι because
       ἐρχομαι has a second aorist, ἠλθον, which behaves
       differently.]

πιστευσ ον	believe (s)	πιστευσ ατε	believe (p)
πιστευσ ατω	let him believe	πιστευσ ατωσαν	let them believe

δεξ ω	receive (s)	δεξ ασθε	receive (p)
δεξ ασθω	let him receive	δεξ ασθωσαν	let them receive

Aspect and context

9.15   If you remember the way statements are made in the
       present and aorist tenses you will not be surprised to
       find that the imperatives are also called **present**
       imperative and **aorist** imperative.

PRESENT IMPERATIVE	πιστευε, etc. (cf πιστευω	ἐρχου, etc. cf ἐρχομαι)
AORIST IMPERATIVE	πιστευσον, etc. (cf ἐπιστευσα	δεξω, etc. cf ἐδεξαμην)

The difference between the imperatives is not one of
time but of the **type** of action. The initial ἐ at the front
of ἐπιστευσα does denote the time of the action, "I
believed" – in the past. But you will see that in the
aorist imperative it has disappeared. The time factor
is no longer relevant; the difference is one of **aspect**.

9.16 It is quite hard to define "aspect". It has to do with the way an action is viewed. The aspect of the aorist tense has been described as "undefined", "completed", "instantaneous"; whereas the aspect of the present tense is said to be "durative", "continuous", "progressive".

The difficulty in reaching a satisfactory definition, which is also simple, is that many factors influence the meanings of words. Take a verb like "remain" for example. In what sense is it relevant to speak about different aspects? To remain is inevitably durative and continuous. Again, the context of a passage may make it clear that an action is continuous by including words like "always", "continually", etc. When that happens the aspect of the verb becomes less crucial.

However, with these cautions in mind, we can think of the aspect of the aorist as simple, neutral, undefined; and of the present as continuous, or progressive. Perhaps a visual symbol is more helpful than this wordy explanation.

AORIST   [●]

PRESENT [–––]

Exercise 9.16

Look carefully at these texts with their English translations. Fill in the appropriate symbol [●] or [–––] and think about why the writer used an aorist or a present imperative in each instance.

Παντα οὖν ὅσα ἐαν θελητε
ἱνα ποιωσιν ὑμιν οἱ
ἀνθρωποι,
οὑτως και ὑμεις **ποιειτε** [   ]
αὐτοις· οὑτος γαρ ἐστιν
ὁ νομος και οἱ προφηται.

So in everything whatever you want
that men should do to you,

you also should **do** likewise
to them. For this is
the law and the prophets
(Matthew 7:12).

και είπεν προς αυτους·
Παντως έρειτε μοι
την παραβολην ταυτην·
'Ιατρε, θεραπευσον σεαυτον·
όσα ηκουσαμεν γενομενα
εις την Καφαρναουμ
ποιησον [　　] και ώδε
εν τη πατριδι σου.

And he said to them,
"Doubtless you will tell me
this proverb:
Doctor, heal yourself;
what we have heard happened
in Capernaum
do here also
in your home town"
(Luke 4:23).

ουκετι ειμι άξιος
κληθηναι υίος σου·
ποιησον [　　] με
ώς ένα των μισθιων σου.

I am no longer worthy
to be called your son;
make me
like one of your hired servants (Luk
15:19).

και λαβων άρτον
ευχαριστησας έκλασεν
και εδωκεν αυτοις λεγων·
Τουτο εστιν το σωμα μου
το υπερ υμων διδομενον·
τουτο **ποιειτε** [　　]
εις την εμην αναμνησιν.

And having taken bread
having given thanks he broke [it]
and gave to them saying,
"This is my body
given for you;
do this
in remembrance of me"
(Luke 22:19).

λεγει ή μητηρ αυτου
τοις διακονοις·
῞Ο τι άν λεγη υμιν
ποιησατε [　　].

His mother said
to the servants,
"Whatever he says to you
do" (John 2:5).

ώς το φως έχετε,
πιστευετε [　　] εις το φως,
ίνα υίοι φωτος γενησθε.
ταυτα ελαλησεν 'Ιησους,
και απελθων εκρυβη απ'
αυτων.

"While you have the light,
believe in the light,
that you may become sons of light."
Jesus spoke these things,
and having departed hid from them
(John 12:36).

οί δε ειπαν·
Πιστευσον [　　] επι τον
κυριον

And they said,
"**Believe** on the Lord

'Ιησουν και σωθηση   Jesus and you will be saved,
συ και ὁ οἶκος σου.   you and your household"
                            (Acts 16:31).

Answers to exercises

Exercise 9.8
1. Ἔρχεσθε
2. εἰσερχεσθωσαν
3. Ἔρχου
4. ἐρχεσθω

Exercise 9.16
● ποιειτε [– – –] Matthew 7:12.
Jesus is giving a general guide to conduct, "the golden rule".

● ποιησον [●] Luke 4:23.
The people in the synagogue at Nazareth were asking Jesus to repeat what he had done in Capernaum.

● ποιησον [●] Luke 15:19.
The prodigal son's request was for a single action that would alter his status in the household.

● ποιειτε [– – –] Luke 22:19.
This command, given at the Last Supper, is to be obeyed as often as the Lord's Supper is observed.

● ποιησατε [●] John 2:5.
Mary's instructions to the servants were for the particular situation they faced at that time.

● πιστευετε [– – –] John 12:36.
Jesus' command to believe involved an ongoing commitment of faith, not just a moment of decision.

● Πιστευσον [●] Acts 16:31.
The drama of the scene in the Philippian jail is heightened by Paul's urgent command, "Believe" – right now.

REVIEW QUESTIONS

1. In what ways does the verb show its versatility?

2. Is it important to know the technical terms applied to the moods of the verb?

3. What is meant by "singular" and "plural" commands?

4. Why are there four forms of the command rather than just two?

5. What are the three other forms of command following (a) πιστευε (b) φιλει (c) ἀγαπα (d) πληρου?

6. What are the four forms of command derived from (a) ἐρχομαι (b) ἀρνεομαι (c) καυχαομαι (d) λυτροομαι?

7. Which imperative endings are most important to learn and why?

8. What are the two ways of looking at a command?

9. What are the other three forms of command following (a) πιστευσον (b) δεξω?

10. What is meant by "aspect"?

11. What other factors combine with aspect to determine the kind of action being described?

12. What aspects are conveyed by the present and aorist imperatives, and what visual symbols can be used to denote them?

REVIEW EXERCISES

DISPLACED VERBS

Some verbs have been removed from each of the following texts and you have to replace them correctly.

Matthew 13:17–18

ἀμην γαρ __(1)__ ὑμιν ὁτι πολλοι προφηται και δικαιοι ἐπεθυμησαν ἰδειν ἁ __(2)__ και οὐκ __(3)__ , και ἀκουσαι ἁ __(4)__ και οὐκ __(5)__ . ὑμεις οὐν __(6)__ την παραβολην του σπειραντος.

For truly I say to you that many prophets and just men desired to see what you see and they did not see [it], and to hear what you hear and they did not hear. Therefore hear the parable of the sower.

> ἀκουετε ἀκουσατε βλεπετε εἰδαν ἠκουσαν λεγω

Luke 7:8–9

και γαρ ἐγω ἀνθρωπος __(1)__ ὑπο ἐξουσιαν τασσομενος, ἐχων ὑπ᾽ ἐμαυτον στρατιωτας, και __(2)__ τουτω, Πορευθητι, και πορευεται, και ἀλλω, __(3)__ , και __(4)__ __, και τω δουλω μου, __(5)__ τουτο, και __(6)__ .

For I also am a man set under authority, having soldiers under me, and I say to this one, "Go," and he goes, and to another, "Come," and he comes, and to my slave, "Do this," and he does it.

> εἰμι ἐρχεται ᾽Ερχου λεγω ποιει Ποιησον

John 1:39

___(1)___ αὐτοις, ___(2)___ και ___(3)___ . ___(4)___ οὖν και
___(5)___ που ___(6)___ και παρ' αὐτῳ ___(7)___ την ἡμεραν
ἐκεινην.

He said to them, "Come and you will see." So they came and
saw where he was staying [literally, is staying] and they
remained with him that day.

εἶδαν ἐμειναν Ἐρχεσθε ἠλθαν λεγει μενει ὀψεσθε

Revelation 1:10–11

___(1)___ ἐν πνευματι ἐν τη κυριακη ἡμερᾳ και ___(2)___
ὀπισω μου φωνην μεγαλην ὡς σαλπιγγος λεγουσης, Ὀ
___(3)___ ___(4)___ εἰς βιβλιον και ___(5)___ ταις ἐπτα
ἐκκλησιαις, εἰς Ἐφεσον και εἰς Σμυρναν και εἰς Περγαμον
και εἰς Θυατειρα και εἰς Σαρδεις και εἰς Φιλαδελφιαν και εἰς
Λαοδικειαν.

I was in the Spirit on the Lord's day and I heard behind me a
great voice as of a trumpet saying, "What you see write in a
book and send to the seven churches, to Ephesus and to
Smyrna and to Pergamum and to Thyatira and to Sardis and
to Philadelphia and to Laodicea."

βλεπεις γραψον ἐγενομην ἠκουσα πεμψον

ONE TOO MANY

In these texts you have to select the correct verb from a
choice of two.

1. [ποιησατε/ποιησατω] οὖν καρπον ἀξιον της μετανοιας.
Therefore bear fruit worthy of repentance (Matthew 3:8).

2. και ὁ δικαιος δικαιοσυνην [ποιησατε/ποιησατω] ἐτι.
And let the righteous still do right (Revelation 22:11).

3. Ἀλλους ἐσωσεν, [σωσατω/σωσον] ἑαυτον.
He saved others, let him save himself (Luke 23:35).

4. Εἰ συ εἶ ὁ βασιλευς των Ἰουδαιων, [σωσατω/σωσον] σεαυτον.
If you are the king of the Jews, save yourself (Luke 23:37).

5. Οἱ ἀνδρες, [ἀγαπατε/ἀγαπατω] τας γυναικας ὑμων.
Husbands, love your wives (Ephesians 5:25).

6. ἑκαστος την ἑαυτου γυναικα οὑτως [ἀγαπατε/ἀγαπατω] ὡς ἑαυτον.
Let each love his own wife like this, as himself. (Ephesians 5:33).

7. τοτε λεγει αὐτοις, Περιλυπος ἐστιν ἡ ψυχη μου ἑως θανατου· [μεινον/μεινατε] ὡδε.
Then he said to them, "My soul is sorrowful unto death. Remain here" (Matthew 26:38).

8. [Μεινον/Μεινατε] μεθ᾽ ἡμων, ὁτι προς ἑσπεραν ἐστιν.
Stay with us, for it is towards evening. (Luke 24:29).

9. Γυνη ἐν ἡσυχιᾳ [μανθανετω/μανθανετωσαν] ἐν πασῃ ὑποταγῃ.
Let a woman learn in quietness in all submission
(1 Timothy 2:11).

10. [μανθανετω/μανθανετωσαν] δε και οἱ ἡμετεροι καλων ἐργων προϊστασθαι.
And let our people learn to apply themselves to good deeds
(Titus 3:14).

11. [μενε/μεινατε] ἐν ἐμοι, κἀγω ἐν ὑμιν.

Remain in me, and I in you (John 15:4).

12. συ δε [μενε/μεινατε] ἐν οἷς ἐμαθες.

But as for you, remain in the things you learned
(2 Timothy 3:14).

13. [πιστευε/πιστευετε] ὁτι ἐλαβετε, και ἐσται ὑμιν.

Believe that you have received [it] and it will be yours
(Mark 11:24).

14. πλην μη το θελημα μου ἀλλα το σον [γινεσθε/γινεσθω].

Nevertheless not my will but yours be done (Luke 22:42).

15. μιμηται μου [γινεσθε/γινεσθω] καθως κἀγω Χριστου.

Be imitators of me as I am of Christ (1 Corinthians 11:1).

A CHOICE OF ASPECT

The aim of this exercise is to investigate the aspect of some
New Testament imperatives. First identify whether the imperative is present or aorist tense. Then look up the context
in an English translation and try to analyze why that particular aspect was chosen. The examples come in pairs so that
you can compare them with each other.

1. ἀγαπαω

ἐγω δε λεγω ὑμιν, Ἀγαπατε τους ἐχθρους ὑμων.

But I say to you, "Love your enemies" (Matthew 5:44).

ἐκ καθαρας καρδιας ἀλληλους ἀγαπησατε ἐκτενως.

Love one another from a pure heart earnestly (1 Peter 1:22).

2. ἀκουω

Ἀκουε, Ἰσραηλ, κυριος ὁ θεος ἡμων κυριος εἰς ἐστιν.
Hear, Israel, the Lord our God, the Lord is one (Mark 12:29).

εἰπεν δε ὁ κυριος, Ἀκουσατε τί ὁ κριτης της ἀδικιας λεγει.
And the Lord said, "Hear what the unjust judge says"
(Luke 18:6).

3. βλεπω

ἀτενισας δε Πετρος εἰς αὐτον συν τῳ Ἰωαννῃ εἰπεν, Βλεψον
εἰς ἡμας.
Peter looking directly at him, with John, said, "Look at us"
(Acts 3:4).

ἑκαστος δε βλεπετω πως ἐποικοδομει.
Let each person take care how he builds on [it]
(1 Corinthians 3:10).

4. γινομαι

εἰ τις δοκει σοφος εἰναι ἐν ὑμιν ἐν τῳ αἰωνι τουτῳ, μωρος
γενεσθω.
If anyone among you thinks he is wise in this age, let him
become a fool (1 Corinthians 3:18).

παντα προς οἰκοδομην γινεσθω.
Let everything be done for building up (1 Corinthians 14:26).

5. διδασκω

Κυριε, διδαξον ἡμας προσευχεσθαι, καθως και Ἰωαννης
ἐδιδαξεν τους μαθητας αὐτου.
Lord, teach us to pray, as John also taught his disciples
(Luke 11:1).

Παραγγελλε ταυτα και διδασκε.
Command and teach these things (1 Timothy 4:11).

6. κρινω

μη κρινετε κατ' ὀψιν, ἀλλα την δικαιαν κρισιν κρινετε.

Do not judge by appearances, but judge with right judgement (John 7:24).

Λαβετε αὐτον ὑμεις και κατα τον νομον ὑμων κρινατε αὐτον.

You take him and judge him according to your law (John 18:31).

7. μενω

μεινατε ἐν τη ἀγαπη μου.

Remain in my love (John 15:9).

ἡ φιλαδελφια μενετω.

Let brotherly love continue (Hebrews 13:1).

8. πιστευω

λεγει τῳ ἀρχισυναγωγῳ, Μη φοβου, μονον πιστευε.

He said to the synagogue ruler, "Do not be afraid; only believe" (Mark 5:36).

ὁ δε 'Ιησους ἀκουσας ἀπεκριθη αὐτῳ, Μη φοβου, μονον πιστευσον.

When Jesus heard he answered him, "Do not be afraid; only believe" (Luke 8:50).

WORDS TO LEARN

ἀρτος, ου m bread, loaf
βιβλιον, ου n book
δικαιοσυνη, ης f righteousness
    ποιεω την δικαιοσυνην, do what is right
ἑαυτον,* gen. ἑαυτου, dat. ἑαυτῳ himself
    ἀρνησασθω ἑαυτον let him deny himself, (Luke 9:23).
    There is a feminine, ἑαυτην (ης, ῃ), and neuter, ἑαυτο
    (ου, ῳ) for "herself" and "itself".
    The plurals ἑαυτους (ων, οις), ἑαυτας (ων, αις), ἑαυτα
    (ων, οις) can mean "ourselves", "yourselves" or "them-
    selves" depending on the context. e.g.
    ἑαυτους ἐδωκαν πρωτον τῳ κυριῳ. They gave them-
    selves first to the Lord (2 Corinthians 8:5).
    παραστησατε ἑαυτους τῳ θεῳ. Present yourselves to
    God (Romans 6:13).
εἰσερχομαι come in, enter
ἐκκλησια, ας f church
ἐμαυτον* (ου, ῳ) myself
    ὑπερ αὐτων ἐγω ἁγιαζω ἐμαυτον. I sanctify myself for
    them (John 17:19).
ἐξουσια, ας f authority, power, right
ἐχθρος, ου m enemy
ἡμετερος, α, ον our
θεραπευω heal
μετα (μετ', μεθ') + genitive with
μετανοεω repent
μετανοια, ας f repentance
ὀπισω + genitive after (in time), behind (in place)
παραβολη, ης f parable, lesson
σεαυτον* (ου, ῳ) yourself
    φανερωσον σεαυτον τῳ κοσμῳ. Show yourself to the
    world (John 7:4).

σος, η, ον   your (singular)

ὑπερ + genitive   for, on behalf of

φωνη, ης f   voice, sound

*These words are accusative. They do not have a nominative.

SUPPLEMENT TO WORDS
ALREADY GIVEN
(chapter numbers in brackets)

Some verbs do not use the accusative case for their object.

ἀκουω (2), hear, is usually followed by the genitive case, especially if the object is a person.

> ἀκουει ἡμων. He hears us (1 John 5:14).

πιστευω (2), believe. When followed by the dative case it means to believe someone. When followed by εἰς + accusative it means to believe *in* someone.

> ἐπιστευσαν τη γραφη και τω λογω ὁν εἶπεν ὁ ᾿Ιησους.
> They believed the Scripture and the word which Jesus had said (John 2:22).

> Συ πιστευεις εἰς τον υἱον του ἀνθρωπου;
> Do you believe in the Son of Man? (John 9:35).

CHAPTER TEN

Preview

More about adjectives

πολυς μεγας

Using adjectives in comparisons

ἰσχυροτερος ἰσχυροτατος σοφωτερος σοφωτατος

πλειων πλειστος μειζων μεγιστος

Comparative and superlative

ἀληθης

Compound adjectives and αἰωνιος

Adverbs

Numbers

CHAPTER TEN

More powers of description

10.1 In chapter 7 we began to investigate the descriptive power of adjectives. It is worth reviewing it before going on with this chapter.

Words with an identity crisis

10.2 An adjective which appears frequently in the New Testament (over 400 times) is πολυς, πολλη, πολυ. It often occurs in the plural meaning *many*. In the singular it means *great*, in the sense of a large quantity. It will be obvious from this simple diction-ary entry that it does not follow the regular pattern of ἀγαθος, η, ον, though in fact it does not differ very much, as you will see from the chart.

πολυς	πολλη	**πολυ**
πολυν	πολλην	**πολυ**
πολλου	πολλης	πολλου
πολλῳ	πολλῃ	πολλῳ
πολλοι	πολλαι	πολλα
πολλους	πολλας	πολλα
πολλων	πολλων	πολλων
πολλοις	πολλαις	πολλοις

The only parts which vary from the regular 2–1–2 pattern are the first two cases, masculine and neuter. This word has invaded the English language in a big way. With a small change from "polu" to "poly" we get polyester, polystyrene, polytechnic, polythene, etc.

10.3   Study these New Testament examples carefully.

χαιρετε και ἀγαλλιασθε,
ὁτι ὁ μισθος ὑμων
πολυς ἐν τοις οὐρανοις·
οὑτως γαρ ἐδιωξαν τους
προφητας τους προ ὑμων.

Rejoice and be glad,
for your reward [is]
great in heaven;
for so they persecuted the
prophets who were before
you. (Matthew 5:12).

πολλοι ἐρουσιν μοι
ἐν ἐκεινη τη ἡμερᾳ·
Κυριε κυριε,
οὐ τῳ σῳ ὀνοματι
    ἐπροφητευσαμεν,
και τῳ σῳ ὀνοματι
δαιμονια ἐξεβαλομεν,
και τῳ σῳ ὀνοματι
δυναμεις **πολλας**
ἐποιησαμεν;

Many will say to me
on that day,
"Lord, lord,
in your name did we not
prophesy,
and in your name
cast out demons
and in your name
do **many** miracles?"
(Matthew 7:22).

και ἠκολουθησαν αὐτῳ
    ὀχλοι **πολλοι**, και
ἐθεραπευσεν αὐτους ἐκει.

And **large** crowds followed
him, and
he healed them there
(Matthew 19:2).

10.4 Another adjective which behaves very similarly to πολυς, πολλη, πολυ is μεγας, μεγαλη, μεγα. It also means *great*, but usually with the idea of importance not just size. It behaves like this.

μεγας	μεγαλη	**μεγα**
μεγαν	μεγαλην	**μεγα**
μεγαλου	μεγαλης	μεγαλου
μεγαλῳ	μεγαλῃ	μεγαλῳ
μεγαλοι	μεγαλαι	μεγαλα
μεγαλους	μεγαλας	μεγαλα
μεγαλων	μεγαλων	μεγαλων
μεγαλοις	μεγαλαις	μεγαλοις

Do you remember "small O" and "large O" from Chapter 1? They are the letters of the alphabet, ὀ-μικρον (μικρος, α, ον *small*), and ὠ-μεγα. You can also see the derivation of our English words megastar and megalomaniac.

10.5 Here are some more examples to study.

ὁ λαος ὁ καθημενος ἐν σκοτει	The people who sat in darkness
φως εἰδεν **μεγα**,	have seen a **great** light,
και τοις καθημενοις	and to those who sat
ἐν χωρᾳ και σκιᾳ θανατου	in the region and shadow of death
φως ἀνετειλεν αὐτοις.	light has dawned upon them (Matthew 4:16).

ἀκουων δε ὁ Ἀνανιας   And when Ananias heard
τους λογους τουτους   these words
πεσων ἐξεψυξεν,   he fell down and died,
και ἐγενετο φοβος **μεγας**   and a **great** fear fell
ἐπι παντας τους ἀκουοντας.   upon all who heard
    (Acts 5:5).

Στεφανος δε   But Stephen
πληρης χαριτος και δυναμεως   full of grace and power
ἐποιει τερατα και   did wonders and
σημεια **μεγαλα** ἐν τῳ λαῳ.   **great** signs among the
    people (Acts 6:8).

More and greater

10.6   In English if you want to compare two or more things you can do it by making adjustments to the adjective.

e.g. It is **small**. This is **smaller**. That is **smallest**.

The standard "rule" is to add **er** and **est** to the adjective, but we all know that the rule has many exceptions.

e.g. It is **bad**.   This is **worse**.   That is **worst**.
     It is **beautiful**.   This is **more beautiful**.   That is **most beautiful**.

10.7   In Greek there is a "standard" way of using adjectives in comparisons.

e.g. ἰσχυρος,   ἰσχυροτερος,   ἰσχυροτατος,
     α, ον   **α, ον**   **η, ον**
     strong   stronger   strongest

     σοφος,   σοφωτερος,   σοφωτατος,
     η, ον   **α, ον**   **η, ον**
     wise   wiser   wisest

[Where the first syllable before the ending is short, as in σο̱φος, there is a compensating **ω** in the comparative endings.]

10.8   It will come as no surprise to you to learn that this
        "rule" is not followed every time. The adjectives
        πολυς and μεγας do not follow this pattern in com-
        parisons. This is how they change.

πολυς, πολλη, πολυ   great, many
πλειων, ον   more
πλειστος, η, ον   most

μεγας, μεγαλη, μεγα   great
μειζων, ον   greater, greatest
μεγιστος, η, ον   greatest

10.9   The first thing to note is the second line of each set,
        πλειων and μειζων. They illustrate a pattern which
        we could call 3–3–3. All the forms are taken from
        Family 3. The masculine and feminine endings are
        identical and so **πλειων, ον** stands for πλειων (mas-
        culine and feminine) and πλειον (neuter). So it is
        more appropriate to express this pattern as 3–3.

MASCULINE & FEMININE	NEUTER
πλειων	πλειον
πλειονα	πλειον
πλειονος	πλειονος
πλειονι	πλειονι
πλειονες	πλειονα
πλειονας	πλειονα
πλειονων	πλειονων
πλειοσιν	πλειοσιν

Comparatively superlative

10.10   The technical name for forms like great, greater and greatest is **positive, comparative** and **superlative**. In English we have a preference for the superlative. We ought to say, "the greater of two" and "the greatest of more than two", but in practice we tend to say "the greatest", however many we are talking about.

In Greek the opposite happens. They had a preference for the comparative. So, for example, they tended to use the form μειζων, for both "greater" and "greatest". Look at these examples.

Ἀμην λεγω ὑμιν·	I tell you the truth
οὐκ ἐγηγερται	there has not arisen
ἐν γεννητοις γυναικων	among those born of women
μειζων Ἰωαννου του	a **greater** than John the
βαπτιστου·	Baptist;
ὁ δε μικροτερος	but the least
ἐν τη βασιλεια των οὐρανων	in the kingdom of heaven
μειζων αὐτου ἐστιν.	is **greater** than he
	(Matthew 11:11).

[There are two ways of saying "greater *than*" in Greek. You can say μειζων ἠ, or use the genitive, as here, "greater *of*".]

Ἐν ἐκεινη τη ὡρα	At that hour
προσηλθον οἱ μαθηται	the disciples came
τω Ἰησου λεγοντες·	to Jesus saying,
Τίς ἀρα **μειζων** ἐστιν	"Who then is **greatest**
ἐν τη βασιλεια των οὐρανων;	in the kingdom of heaven?"
	(Matthew 18:1).

10.11   The adjectives πολυς and μεγας do not represent a pattern which other verbs follow. Fortunately they keep their little "identity crisis" to themselves. The comparatives πλειων and μειζων, however, with their 3–3 pattern, are followed by a few others.

e.g. κρειττων, ον (sometimes written κρεισσων, ον) better   χειρων, ον worse

Another member of family 3

10.12 Near the end of chapter 7 you were introduced briefly to an adjective ἀληθης, ες *true*, which behaves similarly to nouns from family 3 (type 3.7). Here is its full pattern.

MASCULINE & FEMININE	NEUTER
ἀληθης	ἀληθες
ἀληθη	ἀληθες
ἀληθους	ἀληθους
ἀληθει	ἀληθει
ἀληθεις	ἀληθη
ἀληθεις	ἀληθη
ἀληθων	ἀληθων
ἀληθεσιν	ἀληθεσιν

There are several important adjectives which behave like ἀληθης.

e.g. ἀσθενης, ες weak, sick

μονογενης, ες only (in the sense of an only child)

πληρης, ες full

Here is a New Testament example using ἀσθενης.

ἐγενομην τοις **ἀσθενεσιν ἀσθενης**, ἱνα τους **ἀσθενεις** κερδησω· τοις πασιν γεγονα παντα, ἱνα παντως τινας σωσω.

To the **weak** I became **weak**, that I might win the **weak**;

I have become all things to all, that by all means I might win some (1 Corinthians 9:22).

Another variation

10.13   You will find one more variation, which can be illustrated by the adjective ἄπιστος. Its dictionary entry is:

ἄπιστος, ον unfaithful, unbelieving.

Its endings are just the same as ἀγαθος, η, ον except that the -ος endings are used for feminine as well as masculine. So the long way of writing it would be ἄπιστος, ἄπιστος, ἄπιστον. The adjectives which behave in this way are **compound adjectives**, that is, they combine different elements. The adjective πιστος, η, ον means "faithful" or "believing". So ἀ-πιστος, ον is a "compound" of the simple adjective preceded by a negative element.

Although it is not a compound, another adjective which also tends to behave in this way is αἰωνιος, ον eternal. Here are some examples. Help with vocabulary is provided.

οἰκοδομην ἐκ θεου ἐχομεν, οἰκιαν **ἀχειροποιητον αἰωνιον** ἐν τοις οὐρανοις.

We have a building from God, a house **not made with hands eternal** in the heavens (2 Corinthians 5:1).

οἰκοδομη, ης f building

ἀχειροποιητος, ον not made with hands

Ἐν ᾧ καὶ περιετμήθητε περιτομῇ **ἀχειροποιήτῳ**
ἐν τῇ ἀπεκδύσει τοῦ σώματος τῆς σαρκός,
ἐν τῇ περιτομῇ τοῦ Χριστοῦ.

In whom you were circumcised with a circumcision
made without hands in the putting off of the body of
flesh, in the circumcisión of Christ
(Colossians 2:11).

περιτεμνω circumcise
περιτομη, ης f circumcision
ἀπεκδυσις, εως f putting off
σαρξ, σαρκος f flesh

Exercise 10.13

A. Translate these Greek sentences into good English. Some help with vocabulary is provided.

1. εἶπον οὖν αὐτῷ οἱ Φαρισαιοι· Σὺ περι σεαυτου
   μαρτυρεις· ἡ μαρτυρια σου οὐκ ἐστιν ἀληθης.

οὖν so, therefore   Φαρισαιος, ου m Pharisee
μαρτυρεω witness, testify   περι + gen. about
σεαυτου (gen.) yourself
μαρτυρια, ας f witness, testimony

2. ὁ πιστευων εἰς τον υἱον ἐχει ζωην αἰωνιον·
    ὁ δε ἀπειθων τῳ υἱῳ οὐκ ὀψεται ζωην,
    ἀλλ᾽ ἡ ὀργη του θεου μενει ἐπ᾽ αὐτον.

> ὁ πιστευων he who believes   εἰς + acc. in
> ἐχω have   ζωη, ης f life
> ἀπειθεω disobey, not believe (+ dat.)
> ὀψομαι (future of ὁραω, see)
> ὀργη, ης f wrath   μενω remain
> ἐπι + acc. on

3. οὑτως γαρ ἠγαπησεν ὁ θεος τον κοσμον,
    ὡστε τον υἱον τον μονογενη ἐδωκεν,
    ἱνα πας ὁ πιστευων εἰς αὐτον
    μη ἀποληται ἀλλ᾽ ἐχῃ ζωην αἰωνιον.

> οὑτως . . . ὡστε so . . . that   ἀγαπαω love
> κοσμος, ου m world
> ἐδωκεν gave (from διδωμι)
> ἱνα so that
> πας ὁ πιστευων everyone who believes
> μη not   ἀποληται, from ἀπολλυμι perish
> ἐχῃ, from ἐχω have

B. Translate this "Grenglish" into English using both the Greek and the Grenglish texts.

Greek text

1   Τοις δε λοιποις λεγω ἐγω οὐχ ὁ κυριος·
2   εἰ τις ἀδελφος γυναικα ἐχει ἀπιστον
3   και αὐτη συνευδοκει οἰκειν μετ᾽ αὐτου,
4   μη ἀφιετω αὐτην·

5 και γυνη εἰ τις ἐχει ἀνδρα ἀπιστον
6 και οὗτος συνευδοκει οἰκειν μετ᾽ αὐτης,
7 μη ἀφιετω τον ἀνδρα.
8 ἡγιασται γαρ ὁ ἀνηρ ὁ ἀπιστος ἐν τῃ γυναικι
9 και ἡγιασται ἡ γυνη ἡ ἀπιστος ἐν τῳ ἀδελφῳ·
10 ἐπει ἀρα τα τεκνα ὑμων ἀκαθαρτα ἐστιν,
11 νυν δε ἁγια ἐστιν.
12 εἰ δε ὁ ἀπιστος χωριζεται, χωριζεσθω·
13 οὐ δεδουλωται ὁ ἀδελφος ἠ ἡ ἀδελφη ἐν τοις
   τοιουτοις·
14 ἐν δε εἰρηνῃ κεκληκεν ὑμας ὁ θεος.
15 τί γαρ οἰδας, γυναι, εἰ τον ἀνδρα σωσεις;
16 ἠ τί οἰδας, ἀνερ, εἰ την γυναικα σωσεις;

Grenglish text

1 But to the rest λεγω ἐγω οὐχ ὁ κυριος·
2 If a certain brother ἐχει an ἀπιστον wife
3 και she agrees to live with him,
4 let him not divorce αὐτην·
5 και if γυνη τις ἐχει an ἀπιστον husband
6 και οὗτος συνευδοκει οἰκειν μετ᾽ αὐτης,
7 μη ἀφιετω τον ἀνδρα.
8 For ὁ ἀνηρ ὁ ἀπιστος is sanctified ἐν τῃ γυναικι
9 και ἡγιασται ἡ γυνη ἡ ἀπιστος ἐν τῳ ἀδελφῳ·
10 otherwise your children would be unclean,
11 but now they are ἁγια.
12 But if ὁ ἀπιστος separates, χωριζεσθω·
13 ὁ ἀδελφος or the sister is not bound in such
   circumstances.
14 But ὁ θεος has called ὑμας to peace.
15 For how do you know, wife, if you will save τον
   ἀνδρα;
16 Or τί οἰδας, husband, εἰ την γυναικα σωσεις;

Adverbially speaking

10.14   In English if we want to form an adverb from an adjective the standard way of doing it is by adding **-ly** to the adjective.

e.g. true → truly, beautiful → beautifully, etc.

However there are exceptions. Sometimes a completely different word is used. The adverb from "good" is not "goodly" but "well".

i.e. It was a good job; he did it well.

Sometimes no change is made to the adjective at all, for example "little" and "late".

i.e. He came on the late train and so he arrived late.

10.15   Similarly in Greek there is a standard way of making adverbs out of adjectives. It is by replacing the ending with **-ως**.

e.g. καλος good   → καλως well
     ἀληθης true → ἀληθως truly

However it should come as no surprise to learn that Greek also has adverbs that are not constructed in this way.

e.g. ἀγαθος good → εὐ well

Some useful adverbs

10.16   These adverbs occur frequently in the New Testament.

here	ὡδε	there	ἐκει
then	τοτε	now	νυν or ἀρτι
never	οὐδεποτε	always	ἀει or παντοτε
today	σημερον	the next day	αὐριον
still	ἐτι	again	παλιν
in this way	οὑτως	immediately	εὐθυς or εὐθεως
first	πρωτον	also	και

Dealing with numbers

10.17 In a Greek text numbers are represented by words. Symbols (such as 1, 2, 3, etc) are not used. Even with books like 1, 2 and 3 John, Greek uses letters rather than numbers, e.g.

ΙΩΑΝΝΟΥ Α ('Ιωαννου Α – of John "A"), ΙΩΑΝΝΟΥ Β, ΙΩΑΝΝΟΥ Γ

It is useful to know some of the more common words representing numbers.

Number one

10.18 The word for "one" is a 3–1–3 adjective and agrees with the noun it is describing.

	Masculine	Feminine	Neuter
Nom	εἷς	μια	ἑν
Acc	ἑνα	μιαν	ἑν
Gen	ἑνος	μιας	ἑνος
Dat	ἑνι	μιᾳ	ἑνι

John 10:16

και γενησονται **μια** ποιμνη, **εἷς** ποιμην.
And there will be one flock, one shepherd.

ποιμνη, ης f flock.   ποιμην, ενος m shepherd.

John 10.30

ἑγω και ὁ πατηρ ἑν ἑσμεν.
I and the Father are one.

This is an interesting text. The word for "one" is not masculine, but neuter. As members of the Trinity Jesus and the Father are distinct persons, but one in essence.

Exercise 10.18

See if you can insert the correct form of εἰς μια ἐν in
these texts.

ἦν δε διδασκων ἐν ___(1)___ των συναγωγων ἐν τοις
σαββασιν.
Now he was teaching in *one* of the synagogues on the
sabbath (Luke 13:10).

ὅτι ___(2)___ ἀρτος, ___(3)___ σωμα οἱ πολλοι ἐσμεν,
οἱ γαρ παντες ἐκ του ___(4)___ ἀρτου μετεχομεν.
Because [there is] *one* bread, we [who are] many are
one body, for we all share in the *one* bread
(1 Corinthians 10:17).

Two three four

10.19 The word for "two" is δυο. The only time it changes
at all is when it is describing a noun in the dative
plural, when it becomes δυσι or δυσιν.

The word for "three" is τρεις, τρια. It is a 3–3
adjective.

	Masculine/Feminine	Neuter
Nom	τρεις	τρια
Acc	τρεις	τρια
Gen	τριων	τριων
Dat	τρισιν	τρισιν

The word for "four" is τεσσαρες, τεσσαρα. It is also
a 3–3 adjective.

	Masculine/Feminine	Neuter
Nom	τεσσαρες	τεσσαρα
Acc	τεσσαρας	τεσσαρα
Gen	τεσσαρων	τεσσαρων
Dat	τεσσαρσιν	τεσσαρσιν

Here are some examples of these numbers in the
New Testament.

Matthew 18:16

ἐαν δε μη ἀκουσῃ, παραλαβε μετα σου ἐτι **ἑνα** ἠ **δυο**, ἱνα ἐπι στοματος **δυο** μαρτυρων ἠ **τριων** σταθῃ παν ῥημα.

But if he does not listen, take with you one or two more, so that by the mouth of two witnesses or three every word may be established.

Revelation 7:1

Μετα τουτο εἰδον **τεσσαρας** ἀγγελους
ἑστωτας ἐπι τας **τεσσαρας** γωνιας της γης,
κρατουντας τους **τεσσαρας** ἀνεμους της γης.

After this I saw four angels
standing at the four corners of the earth,
holding back the four winds of the earth.

Five to twelve

10.20 The numerals 5 to 12 are constant and do not change.

five	πεντε
six	ἑξ
seven	ἑπτα
eight	ὀκτω
nine	ἐννεα
ten	δεκα
eleven	ἑνδεκα
twelve	δωδεκα

If you are familiar with geometrical terms there are plenty of hints for remembering these numbers – pentagons, hexagons, etc.

More useful numbers

10.21   Here are some other numbers. It is not an exhaustive
list because many numbers are not used in the New
Testament.

20	εἴκοσι
24	εἴκοσι τεσσαρες
30	τριακοντα
40	τεσσερακοντα (note the ε, τεσσ<u>ε</u>ρακοντα)
50	πεντηκοντα
60	ἑξηκοντα
70	ἑβδομηκοντα
72	ἑβδομηκοντα δυο
99	ἐνενηκοντα ἐννεα
100	ἑκατον
200	διακοσιοι, αι, α
300	τριακοσιοι, αι, α
400	τετρακοσιοι, αι, α
600	ἑξακοσιοι, αι, α
1,000	χιλιοι, αι, α
10,000	μυριοι, αι, α

Another way of expressing "thousands" is to use the
noun, χιλιας, αδος f thousand. e.g.

10,000	δεκα χιλιαδες
20,000	εἴκοσι χιλιαδες

Exercise 10.21

This is a little quiz to test both your general knowledge of the New Testament and your grasp of Greek
numbers. A word list is provided with all the answers
but not in the correct order.

δεκα δυο δυο δωδεκα εἱς ἑκατον ἑν ἑνδεκα
ἑξ ἑπτα μια ὀλιγοι πεντε τεσσαρα
τεσσερακοντα τρεις τρεις χιλια 100 1000

A. The number of disciples chosen by Jesus (Matthew 10:1)

B. The number of loaves used to feed the 5000 (Matthew 14:17)

C. The number of fish used to feed the 5000 (Matthew 14:17)

D. The number of men chosen for church administration (Acts 6:3)

E. The number of days (and nights) Jesus fasted in the desert (Matthew 4:2)

F. The number of witnesses cited in 1 John 5:7–8

G. The number of sheep owned by the man who went to seek the one that was lost (Matthew 18:12)

H. _____ κυριος, _____ πιστις, _____ βαπτισμα (Ephesians 4:5)

[κυριος, ου m lord πιστις, εως f faith βαπτισμα, τος n baptism]

I. The number of living creatures around the throne in heaven (Revelation 4:8)

J. The number of days allowed by the Jews for work (Luke 13:14)

K. The number of lepers who came to Jesus for cleansing (Luke 17:12)

L. The number of years which to the Lord are like a single day (2 Peter 3:8)

M. The number of disciples who stood up with Peter on the day of Pentecost (Acts 2:14)

N. The number of young men who appeared to the disciples after the ascension (Acts 1:10)

O. The number of days (and nights) Jonah was in the stomach of the great fish (Matthew 12:40)

P. The number of men commanded by a χιλιαρχος (commander)

Q. The number of men commanded by a ἑκατονταρχης (centurion)

R. The "number" who are chosen (Matthew 22:14)

Not even one

10.22   The New Testament does not contain the number
zero but there is a word for "none". It also means
"no one" and "nothing" depending on the context,
and it is composed of οὐδε (not even) + εἰς, μια ἐν
(one). The resulting word is οὐδεις, οὐδεμια, οὐδεν.
In contexts where the negative would be μη rather
than οὐ it takes the form μηδεις, μηδεμια, μηδεν.

Matthew 6:24

Οὐδεις δυναται δυσι κυριοις δουλευειν.
No one can serve two masters.

Answers to Exercises

Exercise 10.13

SECTION A

1. So the Pharisees said to him, "You are testifying
   about yourself; your testimony is not true"
   (John 8:13).

2. He who believes in the Son has eternal life;
   he who does not believe the Son will not see life,
   but the wrath of God remains on him (John 3:36).

3. For God so loved the world,
   that he gave his only Son,
   that everyone who believes in him
   should not perish but have eternal life (John 3:16).

SECTION B

1   But to the rest **I say, not the Lord,**
2   If a certain brother **has** an **unbelieving** wife
3   **and** she agrees to live with him,
4   let him not divorce **her;**

5 and if a certain woman has an unbelieving husband
6 and he agrees to live with her,
7 let her not divorce the husband.
8 For the unbelieving husband is sanctified in the
   wife
9 and the unbelieving wife is sanctified in the
   brother;
10 otherwise your children would be unclean,
11 but now they are holy.
12 But if the unbeliever separates, let him separate;
13 The brother or the sister is not bound in such
   circumstances.
14 But God has called you to peace.
15 For how do you know, wife, if you will save the
   husband?
16 Or how do you know, husband, if you will save
   the wife?

Exercise 10.18

(1) μια (2) εἱς (3) ἑν (4) ἑνος

ἠν δε διδασκων ἑν μια των συναγωγων ἑν τοις
σαββασιν.

Now he was teaching in *one* of the synagogues on the
sabbath (Luke 13:10).

ὁτι εἱς ἁρτος, ἑν σωμα οἱ πολλοι ἑσμεν, οἱ γαρ
παντες ἑκ του ἑνος ἁρτου μετεχομεν.

Because [there is] *one* bread, we [who are] many are
one body, for we all share in the *one* bread
(1 Corinthians 10:17).

Exercise 10.21

A. δωδεκα
B. πεντε
C. δυο
D. ἑπτα
E. τεσσερακοντα
F. τρεις
G. ἑκατον
H. εἱς κυριος, μια πιστις, ἑν βαπτισμα
I. τεσσαρα ζῳα
J. ἑξ
K. δεκα
L. χιλια
M. ἑνδεκα
N. δυο
O. τρεις
P. 1000
Q. 100
R. ὀλιγοι (few!)

REVIEW QUESTIONS

1. What does πολυς mean (a) in the singular (b) in the plural?

2. How does πολυς vary from the regular 2–1–2 pattern?

3. What does μεγας mean and how does it behave?

4. What is the standard way of modifying Greek adjectives when using them in comparisons?

5. How are comparisons made using πολυς and μεγας as the basic adjectives?

6. What are the technical terms for forms like great, greater, greatest?

7. In what way does Greek differ from English in expressing superlatives?

8. What does ἀληθης mean and what is the full pattern of its endings?

9. What is the dictionary entry for ἀπιστος and what is significant about it?

10. What is meant by compound adjectives and what characteristic do they share with αἰωνιος?

11. What is the standard way of forming an adverb in English?

12. What is the standard way of forming an adverb in Greek?

13. How does Greek represent numbers?

14. How does Greek represent the numbers 1 to 12?

15. What other numbers are found in the New Testament?

16. How does Greek represent nothing, none and no one?

REVIEW EXERCISES

IDENTIFICATION PARADE

In this line-up of missing adjectives you must find the words which fit the gaps in the following texts.

αἰωνιον δωδεκα ἑνος μεγα Μεγαλα μεγαλας μεγαλη
μεγας μειζων μονογενη μονογενης νεωτερας
νεωτερος νεωτερους ὁλην παντας παση πολλα
πολλοι πολλους

Matthew 8:26

ἐπετιμησεν τοις ἀνεμοις και τη θαλασση, και ἐγενετο
γαληνη ___(1)___.

He rebuked the winds and the sea, and there was a *great* calm.

Matthew 24:5

___(2)___ γαρ ἐλευσονται ἐπι τω ὀνοματι μου λεγοντες, Ἐγω
εἰμι ὁ Χριστος, και ___(3)___ πλανησουσιν.

For *many* will come in my name saying, "I am the Christ," and they will deceive *many*.

Mark 1:34

και δαιμονια ___(4)___ ἐξεβαλεν, και οὐκ ἠφιεν λαλειν τα
δαιμονια.

And he cast out *many* demons, and he did not allow the demons to speak.

Mark 13:2

και ὁ Ἰησους εἰπεν αὐτω, Βλεπεις ταυτας τας ___(5)___
οἰκοδομας;

And Jesus said to him, "Do you see these *great* buildings?"

Luke 8:42

θυγατηρ __(6)__ ἦν αὐτῷ ὡς ἐτων __(7)__ και αὐτη ἀπεθνησκεν.

He had an *only* daughter, about *twelve* years old, and she was dying.[An only daughter was to him]

Luke 14:16

ὁ δε εἶπεν αὐτῷ, Ἀνθρωπος τις ἐποιει δειπνον __(8)__ .

And he said to him, "A certain man made a *great* feast."

Luke 22:26

ὑμεις δε οὐχ οὑτως, ἀλλ' ὁ __(9)__ ἐν ὑμιν γινεσθω ὡς ὁ __(10)__ .

Not so for you, but let the *greatest* among you be like the *youngest*.

John 3:36

ὁ πιστευων εἰς τον υἱον ἐχει ζωην __(11)__ .

The one who believes in the Son has *eternal* life.

Acts 5:11

και ἐγενετο φοβος __(12)__ ἐφ' __(13)__ την ἐκκλησιαν και ἐπι __(14)__ τους ἀκουοντας ταυτα.

And *great* fear came upon the *whole* church and upon *all* those who heard these things.

Romans 5:12

δι' __(15)__ ἀνθρωπου ἡ ἁμαρτια εἰς τον κοσμον εἰσηλθεν και δια της ἁμαρτιας ὁ θανατος.

Through *one* man sin entered the world, and death through sin.

1 Timothy 5:1-2

πρεσβυτερῳ μη ἐπιπληξῃς, ἀλλα παρακαλει ὡς πατερα,
___(16)___ ὡς ἀδελφους, πρεσβυτερας ὡς μητερας, ___(17)___
ὡς ἀδελφας ἐν ___(18)___ ἁγνειᾳ.

Do not rebuke an older man, but exhort him as a father,
[treat] *younger* men as brothers, older women as mothers,
younger women as sisters, in *all* purity.

1 John 4:9

τον υἱον αὐτου τον ___(19)___ ἀπεσταλκεν ὁ θεος εἰς τον
κοσμον, ἱνα ζησωμεν δι' αὐτου.

God sent his *only* Son into the world, that we might live
through him.

Revelation 15:3

___(20)___ και θαυμαστα τα ἐργα σου, κυριε ὁ θεος ὁ
παντοκρατωρ· δικαιαι και ἀληθιναι αἱ ὁδοι σου, ὁ βασιλευς
των ἐθνων.

Great and wonderful [are] your works, Lord God the
Almighty;
Just and true [are] your ways, King of the Nations.

CLOZE ENCOUNTERS OF
THE GREEK KIND

One of the techniques used in learning modern languages is
the use of "cloze" exercises, where words are removed from
the text and the reader has to supply the missing words. This
is a difficult exercise but it helps you to get the "feel" of the
language you are learning. Below you will find the Greek
text of 1 Corinthians 1:18-25, in which Paul contrasts the
wisdom (σοφια) of the world with the folly (μωρια) of God,
seen in the preaching (κηρυγμα) of the cross (σταυρος).

The English translation has not been provided and the aim is
not to translate but to complete the Greek text using the list

of missing words and the clues contained in the structure of the text itself. If you find the exercise too difficult without the English translation then use one, but not before making an honest attempt without it.

άνθρωπων δυναμιν θεου Ἰουδαιοις κοσμου μεν μωρια μωριας σοφια σοφιαν σοφιας σοφος σοφωτερον σταυρου Χριστον

ὁ λογος γαρ ὁ του __(1)__
    τοις μεν ἀπολλυμενοις __(2)__ ἐστιν,
    τοις δε σῳζομενοις ἡμιν δυναμις __(3)__ ἐστιν.
γεγραπται γαρ,
    Ἀπολῶ την __(4)__ των σοφων
    και την συνεσιν των συνετων ἀθετησω.
που __(5)__ ;
που γραμματευς;
που συζητητης του αἰωνος τουτου;
οὐχι ἐμωρανεν ὁ θεος την σοφιαν του __(6)__ ;
ἐπειδη γαρ ἐν τη __(7)__ του θεου
οὐκ ἐγνω ὁ κοσμος δια της __(8)__ τον θεον,
εὐδοκησεν ὁ θεος δια της __(9)__ του κηρυγματος
    σωσαι τους πιστευοντας.
ἐπειδη και Ἰουδαιοι σημεια αἰτουσιν
και Ἑλληνες σοφιαν ζητουσιν,
ἡμεις δε κηρυσσομεν __(10)__ ἐσταυρωμενον,
    Ἰουδαιοις __(11)__ σκανδαλον,
    ἐθνεσιν δε μωριαν,
αὐτοις δε τοις κλητοις, __(12)__ τε και Ἑλλησιν
Χριστον, θεου __(13)__ και θεου σοφιαν,
ὁτι το μωρον του θεου __(14)__ των ἀνθρωπων ἐστιν,
και το ἀσθενες του θεου ἰσχυροτερον των __(15)__ .

WORDS TO LEARN

αἰωνιος, ον eternal
ἀληθης, ες true
ἀπιστος, ον unbelieving, unfaithful
δυναμις, εως f power, miracle
δυο, dat. δυσι(ν) two
δωδεκα twelve
εἱς, μια, ἑν one
θαλασσα, ης f sea, lake
θανατος, ου m death
ἰσχυρος, α, ον strong
λαλεω speak
μεγας, μεγαλη, μεγα great
μειζων, ον greater, greatest
μηδεις, μηδεμια, μηδεν no one, nothing, none
μικρος, α, ον small
οὐδεις, οὐδεμια, οὐδεν no one, nothing, none
πολυς, πολλη, πολυ large, many (pl.)
σοφος, η, ον wise (ὁ σοφος, the wise person)
τρεις, τρια three
φοβος, ου m fear

CHAPTER ELEVEN

Preview

Conjunctions

The relative pronoun: ὅς, ἥ, ὁ

Participles: present and aorist

ἀκουων, ουσα, ον   ἀκουσας, ασα, αν

δεχομενος, η, ον   δεξαμενος, η, ον

The second aorist: imperatives and participles

The genitive absolute

Compound verbs

CHAPTER ELEVEN

Making connections

11.1 A feature of Greek which sometimes makes life difficult for the translator is its preference for long sentences. Where we would have shorter units of information Greek writers liked to join the units up. A classic example of this is in the first chapter of Paul's letter to the Ephesians, where verses 3 to 14 form one long, unbroken sentence in the original Greek.

Number two in the charts

11.2 In this chapter we are going to look at some of the ways Greek writers made these connections. One of the simplest ways was to use **conjunctions**. In a chart of the words which occur most frequently in the New Testament it is probably no surprise to find "the" (ὁ ἡ τo) at number one with 19,904 occurrences. The word which comes straight in at number two is a conjunction, "and" (καὶ), with a more modest 9,164 occurrences. Number three is the pronoun "he/she/it" (αὐτος, η, o), appearing 5,601 times, and at number four is another conjunction, δε, which can be translated "and" or "but", making 2,801 appearances.

11.3 Analyze carefully this extract from 1 John 1:2–3 and notice how many times John uses καὶ and δε.

²**καὶ** ἡ ζωὴ ἐφανερώθη, **καὶ** ἑωράκαμεν
καὶ μαρτυροῦμεν

καὶ ἀπαγγέλλομεν ὑμῖν τὴν ζωὴν τὴν αἰώνιον
ἥτις ἦν πρὸς τὸν πατέρα καὶ ἐφανερώθη ἡμῖν –
³ ὃ ἑωράκαμεν καὶ ἀκηκόαμεν, ἀπαγγέλλομεν
καὶ ὑμῖν,
ἵνα καὶ ὑμεῖς κοινωνίαν ἔχητε μεθ᾽ ἡμῶν.
καὶ ἡ κοινωνία δὲ ἡ ἡμετέρα μετὰ τοῦ πατρὸς
καὶ μετὰ τοῦ υἱοῦ αὐτοῦ Ἰησοῦ Χριστοῦ.

²And the life was revealed, and we have seen
and we testify
and we declare to you the eternal life
which was with the Father and was revealed to us –
³What we have seen and heard, we declare
also to you,
that you also may have fellowship with us.
And our fellowship [is] also with the Father
and with his Son Jesus Christ.

Even allowing for the fact that και can be translated
"also" as well as "and" there do seem to be too many
connectors to force into good English style. As a
general rule you should expect to ignore some of the
conjunctions you come across in Greek and you
should try to break down long units into shorter ones
where possible.

Leaders and followers

11.4   The conjunctions και and δε illustrate a difference we
find among such words. The word και likes to stand
at the front of a sentence or clause, whereas δε does
not; it is usually second, though it may come even
later than that, as it does in 1 John 1:3. Here are
some other words which do not like to take the lead
in a sentence.

γαρ for   οὐν so, therefore, then   τε and

11.5 Most connecting words are quite happy to be "leaders" in their sentences. Here are some of the main ones you will come across.

ἀλλα (sometimes abbreviated to ἀλλ'), but
ὁτι, because or that (You judge by the context.)
ἱνα, that, or so that
ἱνα μη, lest (so that . . . not)
ὡστε, so that
εἰ or ἐαν, if
ἠ, or, or than
καθως or ὡς, as
ἑως, while or until
μηποτε, otherwise
ὁτε or ποτε, when
που or ὁπου, where
δια τί (sometimes abbreviated to τί), why
τί, what (You judge by the context whether it is "what" or "why")
πως, how
ἀχρι or ἀχρι οὑ, until
διο, therefore
και . . . και, both . . . and
οὐδε . . . οὐδε or μηδε . . . μηδε, neither . . . nor
εἰτε . . . εἰτε, whether . . . or

A powerful connector

11.6 A device which is very useful for making connections is the relative pronoun. In this English example the relative pronouns are printed in bold type.

The man **whom** I met yesterday gave me the hat **which** I am wearing.

This could be expressed without relative pronouns like this:

I met **a man** yesterday. **The man** gave me **a hat**. I am wearing **the hat**.

The pronouns **whom** and **which** show that the men
and the hats actually "relate" to the same man, the
same hat.

Building up a photofit

11.7   The relative pronoun refers back to someone or
something else. Even in English the connection has
to be reflected in the word you use. So we do not say,
"the man **which** I met" or "the hat **whom** I am
wearing". In Greek there is even more scope for
making the two "related" words agree. First let's
look at the data which is available for creating a
photofit from the relative pronoun.

ὅς	ἥ	ὅ
ὅν	ἥν	ὅ
οὗ	ἧς	οὗ
ᾧ	ᾗ	ᾧ
οἵ	αἵ	ἅ
οὕς	ἅς	ἅ
ὧν	ὧν	ὧν
οἷς	αἷς	οἷς

11.8   Now let's look at an example, from 1 John 1:5.

Καὶ ἔστιν αὕτη **ἡ ἀγγελία** <u>ἥν</u> ἀκηκόαμεν ἀπ᾽ αὐτοῦ
καὶ ἀναγγέλλομεν ὑμῖν.
And this is **the message** <u>which</u> we heard from him and
declare to you.

Does that surprise you? The photofit is not an exact
one, is it? ἡ ἀγγελια is feminine singular, and it is in
the *nominative* case. ἥν is also feminine singular, but
it is in the *accusative* case.

So the rules are these. The relative pronoun must agree in number (singular or plural) and gender (masculine, feminine or neuter), but it does not necessarily agree in case (nominative, accusative, etc). You can see why if you break the sentence up into smaller units again.

(1) This is *the message* (complement, and so nominative).

(2) You received *it* (object, and so accusative).

Because you will be translating from Greek into English you need not worry about these rules. The hard work has all been done for you!

11.9　You may have noticed that the forms ὁ, ἡ, οἱ and αἱ are ambiguous. They may mean "who/which" or "the". This is not a great problem as the context usually makes it clear which it is, but there is another way of telling. Can you spot it? Look again: **ἡ ἀγγελία ἦν**.

When the forms ὁ, ἡ, οἱ and αἱ represent the definite article ("the") they have no accent. Compare this text from 1 John 1:1.

Ὅ ἦν ἀπ᾽ ἀρχῆς, ὃ ἀκηκόαμεν, ὃ ἑωράκαμεν τοῖς ὀφθαλμοῖς ἡμῶν, ὃ ἐθεασάμεθα καὶ αἱ χεῖρες ἡμῶν ἐψηλάφησαν περὶ τοῦ λόγου τῆς ζωῆς.

What was from the beginning, **what** we heard, **what** we saw with our eyes, **what** we looked at and our hands touched – concerning the word of life.

In practice, the parts of the relative pronoun which are illustrated in section 11.7 with an acute accent (e.g. ὅς, ἥ, ὅ) may have a grave accent, like ὃ in the text above. You will come across both ὃ (grave accent) and ὅ (acute accent), representing the neuter of the relative pronoun; but when you come across ὁ (no accent) it is the definite article, "the".

Some more examples

11.10   Because the relative pronoun is such a powerful part
of speech, with its ability to match case, number and
gender, it helps to create Greek sentences which are
not always easy to translate into English. Look at
these texts with their literal translation. Analyze
them to see how they are constructed and then see if
you can produce a better English translation.

Exercise 11.10

1. ἐν ᾧ γὰρ κρίματι κρίνετε κριθήσεσθε,
   καὶ ἐν ᾧ μέτρῳ μετρεῖτε μετρηθήσεται ὑμῖν.

   For with **what** judgment you judge you will be
   judged,
   and with **what** measure you measure it will be
   measured to you. (Matthew 7:2)

2. οὗτός ἐστιν ὑπὲρ **οὗ** ἐγὼ εἶπον·
   Ὀπίσω μου ἔρχεται ἀνὴρ **ὃς** ἔμπροσθέν μου γέγονεν,
   ὅτι πρῶτός μου ἦν.

   This is about **whom** I said,
   "After me comes a man **who** has been before me,
   because he was before me." (John 1:30)

3. τὸν δὲ ἀρχηγὸν τῆς ζωῆς ἀπεκτείνατε
   ὃν ὁ θεὸς ἤγειρεν ἐκ νεκρῶν, **οὗ** ἡμεῖς μάρτυρές
   ἐσμεν.

   And the author of life you killed
   whom God raised from the dead, of **which** we are
   witnesses. (Acts 3:15)

4. Ἀπόστειλον εἰς Ἰόππην
   καὶ μετάπεμψαι Σίμωνα τὸν ἐπικαλούμενον Πέτρον,
   ὃς λαλήσει ῥήματα πρὸς σὲ
   ἐν οἷς σωθήσῃ σὺ καὶ πᾶς ὁ οἶκός σου.

   "Send to Joppa
   and send for Simon the [one] called Peter,
   who will speak words to you
   by **which** you will be saved and all your house."

   (Acts 11:13–14)

Supercharged adjectives

11.12   There is a class of words in both English and Greek called **participles.** In English they often have the ending **-ing** in them, for example knowing, doing (present), having known, having done (past).

Greek participles are quite aptly named, being part-verb and part-adjective. In English a participle is rather a dull word, but in Greek it is extremely versatile and is used in many more ways than its English counterpart. Like all adjectives it can match the features of a noun it is describing – case, number and gender. Because it is also a verb it has added dimensions and can describe both the time and the type of action being done.

11.13   Like the imperative, which we looked at in chapter 9, the Greek participle comes in two main varieties, **present** and **aorist** participle, roughly equivalent to the present and past participle in English. They can be illustrated using the verb ἀκουω, hear. Both sets of endings follow the 3–1–3 pattern.

Present participle (hearing)

The present participle was formed by isolating the present stem (ἀκου in the illustration below) and adding the relevant endings.

MASCULINE	FEMININE	NEUTER
ἀκου ων	ἀκου ουσα	ἀκου ον
ἀκου οντα	ἀκου ουσαν	ἀκου ον
ἀκου οντος	ἀκου ουσης	ἀκου οντος
ἀκου οντι	ἀκου ουση	ἀκου οντι
ἀκου οντες	ἀκου ουσαι	ἀκου οντα
ἀκου οντας	ἀκου ουσας	ἀκου οντα
ἀκου οντων	ἀκου ουσων	ἀκου οντων
ἀκου ουσιν	ἀκου ουσαις	ἀκου ουσιν

Aorist Participle (having heard)

The aorist participle was formed by removing the augment or its equivalent and adding relevant endings (ἐ πιστευσ **α** becoming πιστευσ **ας**).

The endings of the aorist participle are exactly the same as those of πας, πασα, παν (chapter 7 section 7.10).

MASCULINE	FEMININE	NEUTER
ἀκουσ ας	ἀκουσ ασα	ἀκουσ αν
ἀκουσ αντα	ἀκουσ ασαν	ἀκουσ αν
ἀκουσ αντος	ἀκουσ ασης	ἀκουσ αντος
ἀκουσ αντι	ἀκουσ ασῃ	ἀκουσ αντι
ἀκουσ αντες	ἀκουσ ασαι	ἀκουσ αντα
ἀκουσ αντας	ἀκουσ ασας	ἀκουσ αντα
ἀκουσ αντων	ἀκουσ ασων	ἀκουσ αντων
ἀκουσ ασιν	ἀκουσ ασαις	ἀκουσ ασιν

Alternative endings

11.14   Verbs which follow the pattern of δεχομαι, receive, have endings like ἀγαθος, η, ον.

Receiving: δεχομενος, η, ον (δεχ **ομενος, η, ον**)

Having received: δεξαμενος, η, ον (δεξ **αμενος, η, ον**)

Supercharged adjectives in action

11.15   In these examples I have highlighted the participles
so that you can identify them and I have given an
over-literal translation so that you can analyze how
they work in the sentences. In addition to the verbs
listed above (ἀκουω and δεχομαι) participles from
the following verbs also appear in the examples.

πεμπω send	καταβαινω come down
μενω remain	βαπτιζω baptize
τιμαω honour	πιστευω believe (+ dat.)
ἀκολουθεω follow (+ dat.)	ἀποστελλω (aor. ἀπεστειλα) send
εὐχαριστεω give thanks	ἐρχομαι come

It is worth taking time to familiarize yourself with the
behaviour of participles. They feature prominently in
Greek.

From this point I will not include accents unless they
are helpful in determining the meaning.

---

1. Matthew 11:2–3

[2] Ὁ δε Ἰωαννης **ἀκουσας** ἐν τῳ δεσμωτηριῳ τα ἐργα
του Χριστου **πεμψας** δια των μαθητων αὐτου [3] εἰπεν
αὐτῳ·
Συ εἶ ὁ **ἐρχομενος** ἠ ἑτερον προσδοκωμεν;
[εἰ can mean 'if' or 'you (s) are'. The former is usually written
without any accent, the latter with a circumflex, as here.]

But John **having heard** in the prison the deeds of the
Christ **having sent** through his disciples, he said to
him,
"Are you the **coming** [one] or should we expect
another?"

2. John 1:33

κἀγω οὐκ ἤδειν αὐτον,
ἀλλ᾽ ὁ **πεμψας** με βαπτιζειν ἐν ὑδατι ἐκεινος μοι
εἶπεν·
᾽Εφ᾽ ὃν ἀν ἰδῃς το πνευμα **καταβαινον** και **μενον**
ἐπ᾽ αὐτον,
οὑτος ἐστιν ὁ **βαπτιζων** ἐν πνευματι ἁγιῳ.

And I did not know him,
but the **having sent** me to baptize with water he said
to me,
"Upon whom you see the Spirit **descending** and
remaining on him,
this is the **baptizing** with the Holy Spirit."

3. John 5:23–24

23 . . . ὁ μη **τιμων** τον υἱον οὐ τιμα τον πατερα
τον **πεμψαντα** αὐτον.
24 ᾽Αμην ἀμην λεγω ὑμιν ὁτι ὁ τον λογον μου **ἀκουων**
και **πιστευων** τῳ **πεμψαντι** με ἐχει ζωην αἰωνιον
και εἰς κρισιν οὐκ ἐρχεται,
ἀλλα μεταβεβηκεν ἐκ του θανατου εἰς την ζωην.

The not **honouring** the Son does not honour the
father the **having sent** him.
Truly truly I say to you that the **hearing** my word
and **believing** the **having sent** me has eternal life
and does not come into judgment,
but has passed from death into life.

4. John 5:30

Οὐ δυναμαι ἐγω ποιειν ἀπ᾽ ἐμαυτου οὐδεν·
καθως ἀκουω κρινω, και ἡ κρισις ἡ ἐμη δικαια ἐστιν,
ὁτι οὐ ζητω το θελημα το ἐμον ἀλλα το θελημα του
πεμψαντος με.

I am not able to do anything of myself;
As I hear I judge, and my judgment is just,
because I do not seek my will but the will of the
having sent me.

5. John 5:37

και ὁ **πεμψας** με πατηρ ἐκεινος μεμαρτυρηκεν περι ἐμου.

οὐτε φωνην αὐτου πωποτε ἀκηκοατε οὐτε εἰδος αὐτου ἐωρακατε.

And the **having sent** me Father he has testified about me.

You have neither at any time heard his voice nor seen his form.

6. Matthew 8:10

ἀκουσας δε ὁ Ἰησους ἐθαυμασεν και εἰπεν τοις **ἀκολουθουσιν**,

Ἀμην λεγω ὑμιν, παρ᾽ οὐδενι τοσαυτην πιστιν ἐν τῳ Ἰσραηλ εὑρον.

And **having heard** Jesus was amazed and said to the **following**,

"Truly I say to you, I have not found in anyone such faith in Israel."

7. John 1:40

Ἡν Ἀνδρεας ὁ ἀδελφος Σιμωνος Πετρου εἰς ἐκ των δυο των **ἀκουσαντων** παρα Ἰωαννου και **ἀκολουθησαντων** αὐτῳ·

Andrew the brother of Simon Peter was one of the two the **having heard** with John and **having followed** him.

8. Matthew 10:40-41

⁴⁰ Ὁ δεχομενος ὑμας ἐμε δεχεται,
και ὁ ἐμε **δεχομενος** δεχεται τον **ἀποστειλαντα** με.
⁴¹ ὁ **δεχομενος** προφητην εἰς ὀνομα προφητου
μισθον προφητου λημψεται,
και ὁ **δεχομενος** δικαιον εἰς ὀνομα δικαιου
μισθον δικαιου λημψεται.

The **receiving** you receives me,
and the **receiving** me receives the **having sent** me.
The **receiving** a prophet in the name of a prophet
will receive a prophet's reward,
and the **receiving** a righteous man in the name of a
righteous man will receive a righteous man's reward.

9. Luke 22:17

και **δεξαμενος** ποτηριον **εὐχαριστησας** εἰπεν·
Λαβετε τουτο και διαμερισατε εἰς ἑαυτους·

And **having received** [the] cup **having given thanks** he
said, "Take this and divide [it] among yourselves."

Exercise 11.15

Translate the texts again to make them better English. When you have made your own translation compare it with one of the modern English versions of the New Testament, or if possible with more than one. Can you see any principles to help you when translating Greek participles?

Trouble with the second aorist

11.16   In chapter 8 we encountered the second aorist. Some verbs quite unexpectedly adopt a different stem and construct the aorist in a different way. This difference affects the imperative and the participle as well. Compare these charts.

PRESENT

INDICATIVE	IMPERATIVE	PARTICIPLE
I believe, etc.	believe! etc.	believing
πιστευω πιστευεις πιστευει	πιστευε πιστευετω	
		πιστευων, ουσα, ον
πιστευομεν πιστευετε πιστευουσιν	πιστευετε πιστευετωσαν	

FIRST AORIST

INDICATIVE	IMPERATIVE	PARTICIPLE
I believed, etc.	believe! etc.	having believed
ἐπιστευσα ἐπιστευσας ἐπιστευσεν	πιστευσον πιστευσατω	
		πιστευσας, ασα, αν
ἐπιστευσαμεν ἐπιστευσατε ἐπιστευσαν	πιστευσατε πιστευσατωσαν	

SECOND AORIST

INDICATIVE	IMPERATIVE	PARTICIPLE
I saw, etc.	see! etc.	having seen
εἶδον		
εἶδες	ἴδε	
εἶδεν	ἰδετω	
		ἰδών, ἰδουσα, ἰδον
εἶδομεν		
εἶδετε	ἴδετε	
εἶδον	ἰδετωσαν	

11.17 The trouble with the second aorist is that its imperative and participle endings "copy" the endings of the present tense. As a result you have to know the verb well to be able to say whether its imperative or participle is present or aorist. The endings themselves do not give you enough information. The secret is in the stem. Here is another chart giving more details about the verbs which we met in chapter 8 (sections 8.9 and 8.10). I have also included the second aorist from γινομαι (section 8.13).

FROM	INDICATIVE	IMPERATIVE	PARTICIPLE
λεγω, say	εἰπον	εἰπε	εἰπων, ουσα, ον
	I said	say	having said
βαλλω, throw	ἐβαλον	βαλε	βαλων, ουσα, ον
	I threw	throw	having thrown
ἐρχομαι, come	ἠλθον	ἐλθε	ἐλθων, ουσα, ον
	I came	come	having come
λαμβανω, accept	ἐλαβον	λαβε	λαβων, ουσα, ον
	I accepted	accept	having accepted
ὁραω, see	εἰδον	ἰδε	ἰδων, ουσα, ον
	I saw	see	having seen
ἁμαρτανω, sin	ἡμαρτον	ἁμαρτε	ἁμαρτων, ουσα, ον
	I sinned	sin	having sinned
μανθανω, learn	ἐμαθον	μαθε	μαθων, ουσα, ον
	I learned	learn	having learned
γινομαι, become	ἐγενομην	γενου	γενομενος, η, ον
	I became	become	having become

Exercise 11.17

Match these texts to the correct translations. Do not go on to the next section until you have completed the exercise.

1. ὁτι ὁ θεος ὁ εἰπων· Ἐκ σκοτους φως λαμψει, ὁς ἐλαμψεν ἐν ταις καρδιαις ἡμων προς φωτισμον της γνωσεως της δοξης του θεου ἐν προσωπῳ Ἰησου Χριστου.

2. ἀκουσας δε ὁ ἑκατονταρχης προσελθων τῳ χιλιαρχῳ ἀπηγγειλεν λεγων· Τί μελλεις ποιειν; ὁ γαρ ἀνθρωπος οὑτος Ῥωμαιος ἐστιν. προσελθων δε ὁ χιλιαρχος εἰπεν αὐτῳ· Λεγε μοι, συ Ῥωμαιος εἶ; ὁ δε ἐφη· Ναι.

3. εἰ τις ἀρετη και εἰ τις ἐπαινος, ταυτα λογιζεσθε·
ἃ και ἐμαθετε και παρελαβετε και ἠκουσατε και
εἰδετε ἐν ἐμοι, ταυτα πρασσετε· και ὁ θεος της
εἰρηνης ἐσται μεθ᾽ ὑμων.

4. Γυνη ἐν ἡσυχιᾳ μανθανετω ἐν πασῃ ὑποταγῃ·
διδασκειν δε γυναικι οὐκ ἐπιτρεπω οὐδε αὐθεντειν
ἀνδρος, ἀλλ᾽ εἰναι ἐν ἡσυχιᾳ. Ἀδαμ γαρ πρωτος
ἐπλασθη, εἰτα Εὑα.

5. και εἰπεν αὐτῳ Ναθαναηλ· Ἐκ Ναζαρετ δυναται τι
ἀγαθον εἰναι; λεγει αὐτῳ ὁ Φιλιππος· Ἐρχου και
ἰδε. εἰδεν ὁ Ἰησους τον Ναθαναηλ ἐρχομενον
προς αὐτον και λεγει περι αὐτου· Ἰδε ἀληθως
Ἰσραηλιτης ἐν ᾧ δολος οὐκ ἐστιν.

6. Και ἐσθιοντων αὐτων λαβων ἀρτον εὐλογησας
ἐκλασεν και ἐδωκεν αὐτοις και εἰπεν· Λαβετε,
τουτο ἐστιν το σωμα μου. και λαβων ποτηριον
εὐχαριστησας ἐδωκεν αὐτοις, και ἐπιον ἐξ
αὐτου παντες.

7. παντες γαρ ἡμαρτον και ὑστερουνται της δοξης
του θεου δικαιουμενοι δωρεαν τῃ αὐτου χαριτι δια
της ἀπολυτρωσεως της ἐν Χριστῳ Ἰησου· ὃν
προεθετο ὁ θεος ἱλαστηριον δια της πιστεως ἐν
τῳ αὐτου αἱματι.

8. και λαβοντες αὐτον ἐδειραν και ἀπεστειλαν
κενον. και παλιν ἀπεστειλεν προς αὐτους ἀλλον
δουλον· κἀκεινον ἐκεφαλιωσαν και ἠτιμασαν.
και ἀλλον ἀπεστειλεν· κἀκεινον ἀπεκτειναν.

A. And they took him, beat him and sent him away
empty-handed. And again he sent to them
another servant; and that one they beat about
the head and treated shamefully. And he sent
another, and they killed that one (Mark 12:3–5).

B. And while they were eating he took bread. When he had given thanks he broke it and gave it to them. He said, "Take it, this is my body." And he took the cup. When he had given thanks he gave it to them, and they all drank from it (Mark 14:22–23).

C. And Nathanael said to him, "Can there be anything good from Nazareth?" Philip said to him, "Come and see." Jesus saw Nathanael coming to him and he said of him, "Look, truly an Israelite in whom there is no guile" (John 1:46–47).

D. When the centurion heard he came to the commander and spoke up saying, "What are you about to do? For this man is a Roman citizen." The commander came and said to him, "Tell me, are you a Roman citizen?" He said, "Yes" (Acts 22:26–27).

E. For all have sinned and fall short of the glory of God, being justified as a gift by his grace through the redemption which is in Christ Jesus, whom God put forward as an atoning sacrifice though faith by his blood (Romans 3:23–25).

F. For [it is] the God who said, "Light will shine out of darkness," who has shone in our hearts to give the light of the knowledge of the glory of God in the face of Jesus Christ (2 Corinthians 4:6).

G. If there is any excellence, if there is anything praiseworthy, think about these things; the things which you learned and received and heard and saw in me, do these things, and the God of peace will be with you (Philippians 4:8–9).

> H. Let a woman learn quietly in all submission. And
> I do not permit a woman to teach nor to domi-
> neer over a man, but to be in quietness. For
> Adam was created first, then Eve
> (1 Timothy 2:11–13).

When it absolutely has to be genitive

11.18   A literal translation of Acts 22:26 (2/D) is "And the
centurion, having heard (ἀκουσας), having approached (προσελθων) the commander, spoke up
saying (λεγων) . . .". Each of the participles is **nominative** singular masculine. They agree with ὁ
ἑκατονταρχης, the centurion, which is the subject of
the sentence, and so nominative singular masculine.
These "supercharged" adjectives describe their noun
the having-heard having-approached centurion.

11.19   If you look closely at the beginning of Mark 14:22
(6/B) you will find another text heavily loaded
with participles. Literally it says, "And them eating (ἐσθιοντων), having taken (λαβων) bread, having
given thanks (εὐλογησας), he broke . . ." This time
we have two participles which are nominative singular masculine, λαβων and εὐλογησας, referring to the
subject "he", i.e. Jesus. But look at ἐσθιοντων
αὐτων, "them eating". Both words are **genitive** plural
masculine. The reason for this is that they stand in an
absolute position at the beginning of the sentence;
they are not connected to the subject or object which
follows. You cannot make "them" agree with "he"
or with "the bread". When that happens Greek puts
the whole phrase into the genitive case, and the
technical name for it is **the genitive absolute**. We often
use a clause with "while" or "when" to translate it
into English.

11.20   Classical Greek is the form of the language which was used for the great classical literature of Greece. Its relationship to the Koine (common) Greek used in the New Testament is roughly analogous to the relationship between Shakespearean English and the language as we speak it today. In classical Greek they would have been more strict in making participles "agree". I wonder if you can see how they would have done it in Mark 14:22. Look at it again.

When the text says, ἐδωκεν αὐτοις, he gave to them, it is the same "them", the disciples, as the "them" who were eating at the beginning of the verse. So in classical Greek the first phrase would have been put into the dative case: και ἐσθιουσιν αὐτοις . . . ἐδωκεν αὐτοις. However, by New Testament times, the genitive absolute was used more frequently and more "loosely".

Exercise 11.20

Translate these texts from Mark chapter 6 using the vocabulary helps. You will probably find it easier to make a fairly literal translation first and then "polish it up".

1. και γενομενου σαββατου
   ἠρξατο διδασκειν ἐν τη συναγωγη,
   και πολλοι ἀκουοντες ἐξεπλησσοντο.

Helps

γινομαι be, become, come   σαββατον, ου n sabbath
ἀρχομαι begin   διδασκειν to teach   συναγωγη, ης f synagogue
ἐξεπλησσοντο they were amazed

2. Και γενομενης ημερας εὐκαιρου
ὀτε 'Ηρῳδης τοις γενεσιοις αὐτου δειπνον
ἐποιησεν
τοις μεγιστασιν αὐτου και τοις χιλιαρχοις
και τοις πρωτοις της Γαλιλαιας,
και εἰσελθουσης της θυγατρος αὐτου 'Ηρῳδιαδος
και ὀρχησαμενης
ἠρεσεν τῳ 'Ηρῳδῃ και τοις συνανακειμενοις.
εἰπεν ὁ βασιλευς τῳ κορασιῳ·
Αἰτησον με ὁ ἐαν θελῃς, και δωσω σοι.

Helps

ἡμερα, ας f day   εὐκαιρος, ον opportune, suitable
ὀτε when   'Ηρῳδης, ου m Herod   τοις γενεσιοις
αὐτου at his birthday   δειπνον, ου n feast, supper
(δ. ποιεω give a feast)   μεγισταν, ανος m courtier
χιλιαρχος, ου m commander, senior officer
πρωτος, η, ον first (οἱ πρ. the leading men)
Γαλιλαια, ας f Galilee   εἰσερχομαι, aor. εἰσηλθον
come in   θυγατηρ, θυγατρος f daughter   'Ηρῳδιας,
αδος f Herodias   ὀρχεομαι dance
ἀρεσκω, aor. ἠρεσα (+ dat.) please
συνανακεινενος, ου m guest
βασιλευς, εως m king   κορασιον, ου n girl
αἰτεω ask   ὁ ἐαν θελῃς whatever you want
διδωμι, fut. δωσω give

Compound actions

11.21   In both Greek and English we find compound verbs,
verbs which have started as a simple verb and been
added to, often with a preposition. For example in
English from stand we have *with*stand and *under-*
stand.   In Greek we have ἐρχομαι (come),
εἰσερχομαι (come in, enter) and προσερχομαι (come
to, approach).

11.22 A feature of these Greek verbs which we need to be
aware of is that changes which usually take place at
the **beginning** of a verb take place at the beginning of
the **simple** verb. Look at this table.

Simple verb

| ἔρχομαι | I come | ἦλθον | I came |
| ἐρχομενος | coming | ἐλθων | having come |

Compound verb

| **εἰσερχομαι** | I come in | **εἰσηλθον** | I came in |
| εἰσερχομενος | coming in | εἰσελθων | having come in |

The compound, εἰσερχομαι, is made up of εἰς +
ἔρχομαι. When you add or remove an augment it is
not the εἰς part which is affected; it is the "simple"
verb ἔρχομαι.

11.23 Recognizing compound verbs comes with practice
rather than by learning lists of prefixes, but the
prepositions that are used with verbs as well as in
their own right are as follows. They are sometimes
abbreviated and I have included the abbreviations in
brackets.

ἀνα, ἀντι (ἀντ', ἀνθ'), ἀπο (ἀπ', ἀφ'), δια (δι'),
εἰς, ἐκ (ἐξ), ἐν, ἐπι (ἐπ', ἐφ'), κατα (κατ', καθ'),
μετα (μετ', μεθ'), παρα (παρ'), περι, προ, προς,
συν, ὑπερ, ὑπο (ὑπ', ὑφ').

Answers to exercises

Exercise 11.10

There are usually a number of ways in which texts can be translated, and so in addition to my suggestions I have given the references so that you can look them up in a modern English version.

1. For you will be judged by the judgment you give, and the measure which you use will be used for you
   (Matthew 7:2).

2. This is the one I was talking about when I said, "A man is coming after me but he is greater than I am, because he existed before me"
   (John 1:30).

3. You killed the author of life,
   but God raised him from the dead.
   We are witnesses to this
   (Acts 3:15).

4. Send to Joppa
   and ask Simon called Peter to come.
   He will bring you a message
   by which you will be saved – you and your entire household
   (Acts 11:13–14).

Exercise 11.15

If you have not done so already look up the texts in a modern translation and compare it with your own translation.

If you analyze the way participles are used in these verses you will see that on most occasions they are linked with the definite article. When that happens they are usually translated by a clause with "who" in it (a relative clause). When they occur without the article they are either translated as participles or by a clause with "when" in it (a temporal clause). Sometimes it is best to translate as a statement in its own right, e.g. "he said" rather than "saying".

Here is my analysis.

With the article

1. ὁ ἐρχομενος	the one **who** is coming
2. ὁ πεμψας	he **who** sent
ὁ βαπτιζων	the one **who** baptizes
3. ὁ μη τιμων	he **who** does not honour
τον πεμψαντα	**who** sent
ὁ ἀκουων και	he **who** hears and
πιστευων	believes
τῳ πεμψαντι	him **who** sent
4. του πεμψαντος	of him **who** sent
5. ὁ πεμψας	**who** sent
6. τοις ἀκολουθουσιν	to those **who** followed
7. των ἀκουσαντων	**who** heard and followed
και ἀκολουθησαντων	
8. ὁ δεχομενος	the one **who** receives
(4 times)	
τον ἀποστειλαντα	him **who** sent

Without the article

1. ἀκουσας	**When** John heard
πεμψας	he sent [and]
2. καταβαινον	descending
μενον	remaining
6. ἀκουσας	**When** Jesus heard
9. δεξαμενος	He received the cup/Having received
εὐχαριστησας	he gave thanks [and]

Exercise 11.17

1/F, 2/D, 3/G, 4/H, 5/C, 6/B, 7/E, 8/A

Exercise 11.20

1. When the sabbath had come
   he began to teach in the synagogue,
   and many were astonished when they heard him
   (Mark 6:2).

2. A convenient day arrived
   when Herod held a feast on his birthday
   for his courtiers and the senior officers
   and the leading men of Galilee.
   When his daughter Herodias came in and danced
   she pleased Herod and the guests.
   The king said to the girl,
   "Ask me for anything you want, and I will give it
   to you" (Mark 6:21–22).

   This is not the only way these texts may be
   translated. Again, look them up in as many modern versions as you can, and see if you can make
   further improvements.

REVIEW QUESTIONS

1. What feature of Greek can pose problems for translators?

2. What kind of words are καὶ and δε?

3. What feature of γαρ, δε, οὐν and τε is worth noting?

4. How do relative pronouns work in English?

5. Why is there more scope in Greek for making relative pronouns agree with the words they relate to?

6. Which parts of the relative pronoun might be ambiguous and how can they be distinguished?

7. Does the power of the Greek relative pronoun make it easier or harder to translate into English?

8. How would you describe a Greek participle and why is it more versatile than its English counterpart?

9. How are the present and aorist participles formed from ἀκουω?

10. How are the present and aorist participles formed from δεχομαι?

11. Why could the imperatives and participles of the second aorist cause confusion?

12. Where does the term "genitive absolute" come from and when is the genitive absolute used?

13. What are compound verbs?

14. What happens to a compound verb in Greek when an augment or its equivalent is added?

15. Which Greek prepositions are used to form compound verbs?

REVIEW EXERCISES

SELECT CONNECT

The text of 1 John 4:18–21 is given below. Where there is a choice of connecting word you have to select the correct one.

1 φοβος οὐκ ἐστιν ἐν τη ἀγαπη
2 [ἀλλ᾽/ὡστε] ἡ τελεια ἀγαπη ἐξω βαλλει τον φοβον,
3 [ὀτε/ὀτι] ὁ φοβος κολασιν ἐχει,
4 [ὁ/ὁς] δε φοβουμενος οὐ τετελειωται ἐν τη ἀγαπη.
5 ἡμεις ἀγαπωμεν, [ἐαν/ὀτι] αὐτος πρωτος ἠγαπησεν ἡμας.
6 [ἐαν/ὀτι] τις εἰπη ὀτι Ἀγαπω τον θεον
7 [γαρ/και] τον ἀδελφον αὐτου μιση,
8 ψευστης ἐστιν·
9 ὁ [γαρ/και] μη ἀγαπων τον ἀδελφον αὐτου
10   [ὁν/τον] ἑωρακεν,
11   τον θεον [ὁν/τον] οὐχ ἑωρακεν
12 οὐ δυναται ἀγαπαν.
13 [γαρ/και] ταυτην την ἐντολην ἐχομεν ἀπ᾽ αὐτου,
14 [ἐαν/ἱνα] ὁ ἀγαπων τον θεον ἀγαπᾳ και τον ἀδελφον αὐτου.

1 There is no fear in love
2 but perfect love casts out fear
3 for fear has [to do with] punishment,
4 and the one who fears has not been perfected in love.
5 We love, because he first loved us.
6 If anyone says, "I love God,"
7 and hates his brother
8 he is a liar;
9 for he who does not love his brother
10   whom he has seen
11   God whom he has not seen
12 cannot love.
13 And we have this command from him,
14 that he who loves God should love his brother also.

COMPREHENSION QUESTIONS

Matthew 14:23–34 describes the occasion when Jesus came to the disciples walking on the water. Without referring to an English translation see if you can answer the questions on this passage. There is one question for each line of the text.

1 ²³καὶ ἀπολυσας τους ὀχλους
2 ἀνεβη εἰς το ὀρος κατ᾽ ἰδιαν προσευξασθαι.
3 ὀψιας δε γενομενης μονος ἦν ἐκει.
4 ²⁴το δε πλοιον ἠδη σταδιους πολλους ἀπο της γης ἀπειχεν
5 βασανιζομενον ὑπο των κυματων,
6 ἦν γαρ ἐναντιος ὁ ἀνεμος.
7 ²⁵τεταρτη δε φυλακη της νυκτος ἠλθεν προς αὐτους
8 περιπατων ἐπι την θαλασσαν.
9 ²⁶οἱ δε μαθηται ἰδοντες αὐτον ἐπι της θαλασσης περιπατουντα
10 ἐταραχθησαν λεγοντες ὁτι Φαντασμα ἐστιν,
11 και ἀπο του φοβου ἐκραξαν.
12 ²⁷εὐθυς δε ἐλαλησεν ὁ Ἰησους αὐτοις λεγων·
13 Θαρσειτε, ἐγω εἰμι· μη φοβεισθε.
14 ²⁸ἀποκριθεις δε αὐτῳ ὁ Πετρος εἰπεν·
15 Κυριε, εἰ συ εἶ,
16 κελευσον με ἐλθειν προς σε ἐπι τα ὑδατα.
17 ²⁹ὁ δε εἰπεν· Ἐλθε.
18 και καταβας ἀπο του πλοιου
19 ὁ Πετρος περιεπατησεν ἐπι τα ὑδατα
20 και ἠλθεν προς τον Ἰησουν.
21 ³⁰βλεπων δε τον ἀνεμον ἰσχυρον ἐφοβηθη,
22 και ἀρξαμενος καταποντιζεσθαι ἐκραξεν λεγων·
23 Κυριε, σωσον με.
24 ³¹εὐθεως δε ὁ Ἰησους ἐκτεινας την χειρα ἐπελαβετο αὐτου
25 και λεγει αὐτῳ· Ὀλιγοπιστε, εἰς τί ἐδιστασας;
26 ³²και ἀναβαντων αὐτων εἰς το πλοιον ἐκοπασεν ὁ ἀνεμος.
27 ³³οἱ δε ἐν τῳ πλοιῳ προσεκυνησαν αὐτῳ λεγοντες·

28 Ἀληθῶς θεου υἱός εἶ.

29 ³⁴Και διαπερασαντες ἦλθον ἐπι την γην εἰς Γεννησαρετ.

1. Jesus dismissed the crowds. What part of the verb ἀπολυω is used?

2. Where did Jesus go by himself in order to pray?

3. Which genitive absolute means "when evening came"?

4. What distance in stadioi (furlongs) was the boat from the land?

5. The boat was beaten by the waves. What preposition means "by" and what case follows it?

6. The wind was against them. Which word has to be understood in the Greek text?

7. What happened in the fourth watch of the night?

8. How is Jesus described?

9. What happened next?

10. The disciples were troubled, thinking it was a ghost. What did they do?

11. Why did the disciples cry out?

12. What did Jesus immediately do?

13. Jesus told them to take heart and not be afraid. What reason did he give?

14. Who replied to Jesus?

15. How did he address him?

16. What command did he want to hear: to step out of the boat, to walk on the lake, or to come to Jesus on the waters?

17. What did Jesus say?

18. Where did Peter come down (cf. line 4)?

19. What happened next?

20. What did Peter do?

21. Why was Peter afraid (cf. line 6)?

22. What happened when Peter began to sink (cf. line 11)?

23. What did he say?

24. Jesus immediately reached out his hand and caught him. What are the two compound verbs in this line, and what case follows them?

25. Jesus asked, "Why did you doubt?" What other rebuke did Peter receive?

26. Where were they when the wind ceased?

27. Who worshipped Jesus?

28. What did they say?

29. Where did they come to land when they had crossed over?

WORDS TO LEARN

ἀκολουθεω + dative   follow

ἀνηρ, ἀνδρος m   man, husband

γνωσις, εως f   knowledge

δε   and, but (often not translated)

δικαιος, α, ον   righteous, just

δοξα, ης f   glory

ἐαν   if

εἰ   if

ἱνα   that

κριμα, τος n   judgment

κρισις, εως f   judgment

μαρτυρεω   witness, testify

μαρτυρια, ας f testimony, witness

μαρτυς, μαρτυρος m witness (i.e. the person who witnesses)

νεκρος, α, ον dead

ὅς, ἥ, ὅ who, which, that

ὁτι that, because, (introducing direct speech)

περιπατεω, aorist περιεπατησα walk (often figuratively of lifestyle)

πρωτος, η, ον first

ῥημα, τος n word

SUPPLEMENT TO WORDS
ALREADY GIVEN
(Chapter numbers in brackets)

ἀποκαλυπτω (6), reveal, is a compound of ἀπο + καλυπτω. Its aorist is ἀπεκαλυψα.

ἀποστελλω (2), send, is a compound of ἀπο + στελλω. Its aorist is ἀπεστειλα.

CHAPTER TWELVE

Preview

Verbs and voice

Active middle and passive

Present passive: πιστευομαι πιστευου πιστευομενος

Aorist passive: ἐπιστευθην πιστευθητι πιστευθεις

Future passive: πιστευθησομαι

Deponent verbs

Redundant language

CHAPTER TWELVE

On the receiving end

Active and passive

12.1 Up to this point we have concentrated on the way verbs express the action which somebody does. Here are some simple examples using the verb θεραπευω, *heal*. Our English word "therapy" will help you to remember it.

θεραπευει ὁ 'Ιησους τον παραλυτικον.	Jesus is healing the paralytic.
θεραπευσει ὁ 'Ιησους τον παραλυτικον.	Jesus will heal the paralytic.
ἐθεραπευσεν ὁ 'Ιησους τον παραλυτικον.	Jesus healed the paralytic.

12.2 In each of the examples the subject of the verb (Jesus) is doing something – healing. However if we want to we can say the same thing in a different way.

The paralytic is being healed by Jesus.
The paralytic will be healed by Jesus.
The paralytic was healed by Jesus.

It is the same action which is being described, but from a different perspective. We might want to emphasize the experience of the paralytic rather than the action of Jesus. Then we would want to say that he came to Jesus and *was healed*.

12.3 This difference of emphasis and perspective is achieved by using either the **active** or the **passive** voice. The first set of statements were active, the second passive. In the active the subject is doing something; in the passive something is being done to the subject. "He healed" is active; "he was healed" is passive.

12.4   When we speak about a verb being active or passive we are talking about the **voice** of the verb, to use the technical term. The "voice" of the Greek verb is made more complicated by the fact that it has not two but three voices: not just active and passive but a voice called **middle** as well. Before you get too worried you will be pleased to know that in most instances the "middle" voice is just another kind of active voice. In fact we are now able to put technical terms to something that you know already.

● The endings of πιστευω and the forms that develop from it are the endings of the **active** voice, expressing the action of the subject.
πιστευει   he believes

●The endings of δεχομαι and the forms that develop from it are the endings of the **middle** voice, also expressing the action of the subject.
δεχεται   he receives

A lost distinction

12.5   In classical Greek there was a distinction between the active and the middle. It can be illustrated from the verb νιπτω, *wash*.

νιπτει (active) τον υιον αυτου. He washes his son.
νιπτεται (middle). He washes (i.e. he washes himself).

The active was used to describe something the subject did to someone else; the middle was used to describe something he did for or to himself.

By the time of the New Testament that distinction had largely disappeared. There are a few places where it still occurs. John 13 is one of them, where Jesus washed (active) the disciples' feet, but said to Peter, "The one who has had a bath has no need to wash (middle), except his feet." However it is best to think of the middle voice simply as another active.

Introducing the passive

12.6 In English we form a passive by using the auxiliary verb, "to be". So "he heals" (active) becomes "he **is** healed" (passive). In Greek it is done with the endings.

he heals θεραπευει   he is healed θεραπευεται

No, your eyes are not deceiving you. That *is* the passive. In the **present** tense Greek uses exactly the same endings for both middle and passive.

This means that when you see the endings, ομαι, η, εται, ομεθα, εσθε, ονται and ου, εσθω, εσθε, εσθωσαν and ομενος, η, ον at the end of a verb they may indicate middle or passive, and so the *sense* may be active or passive. Look at these verses from Matthew 7.

¹⁹παν δενδρον μη ποιουν καρπον καλον
   ἐκκοπτεται και εἰς πυρ **βαλλεται.**
²⁰ ἀρα γε ἀπο των καρπων αὐτων **ἐπιγνωσεσθε**
   αὐτους.

Every tree not producing good fruit
is cut down and **is thrown** into the fire.
For by their fruits **you will know** them.

The verbs ἐκκοπτεται and βαλλεται are passive, but the verb ἐπιγνωσεσθε is middle. It means "you will know", not "you will be known".

The good news is: you don't have a new set of endings to learn. The bad news? How do you know if the endings indicate middle (active meaning) or passive?

Sorting them out

12.7   You get strong clues from the context, of course, but
       also you have to know which verb you are dealing
       with. If a verb has a "proper" active, like θεραπευω,
       the alternative endings are used to indicate the
       passive.

θεραπευει   he heals
θεραπευεται   he is healed

If a verb has an active meaning but is actually middle,
like δεχομαι, there are no alternative endings available and it cannot be used as a passive.

δεχεται   he receives
[   ]   he is received

A quick review

12.8   Here is a reminder of the pattern for active and
       middle. The full version is in chapters 8 and 9.

	STATEMENTS/ QUESTIONS	COMMANDS	PARTICIPLE
ACTIVE			
PRESENT	πιστευω	πιστευε	πιστευων, ουσα, ον
AORIST	ἐπιστευσα	πιστευσον	πιστευσας, ασα, αν
MIDDLE			
PRESENT	δεχομαι	δεχου	δεχομενος, η, ον
AORIST	ἐδεξαμην	δεξω	δεξαμενος, η, ον

12.9 We can now add the passives in summary form, the present (which is identical to the middle) and the aorist.

PASSIVE			
PRESENT	πιστευομαι	πιστευου	πιστευομενος, η, ον
	I am believed	be believed!	being believed
AORIST	ἐπιστευθην	πιστευθητι	πιστευθεις, εισα, εν
	I was be-lieved	be believed!	having been be-lieved

12.10 If you compare the formation of the active ἐπιστευσα with the passive ἐπιστευθην you will see a similar pattern. Each has four ingredients: an augment or its equivalent, a stem, an identifier, and a set of endings.

ἐ πιστευ σ α   ἐ πιστευ θ ην

The passive "identifier" is **θ**, and it is often a good clue that you are dealing with an aorist passive. However it is not always used. For example the aorist passive of γραφω, *write* is ἐγραφην (no **θ**!) What is more, the stem often changes slightly (or in some instances drastically). Look at these examples.

ἀκουω → ἠκουσθην   λεγω → ἐρρηθην

Rely on the endings

12.11 The dictionary entry for a verb will list any unusual forms which you could not predict from the basic present tense, and not many verbs are as wildly unpredictable as λεγω. What is reliable is the set of aorist passive endings.

Exercise 12.11

Analyze these texts and complete the chart which follows.

Matthew 3:16

βαπτισθεις δε ὁ Ἰησους εὐθυς ἀνεβη ἀπο του
ὑδατος·
και ἰδου ἠνεῳχθησαν αὐτῳ οἱ οὐρανοι,
και εἰδεν το πνευμα του θεου καταβαινον ὡσει
περιστεραν
και ἐρχομενον ἐπ᾽ αὐτον·

And after Jesus was baptized he immediately
came up from the water;
and behold the heavens were opened to him,
and he saw the Spirit of God descending like a
dove
and coming upon him.

Mark 1:9

Και ἐγενετο ἐν ἐκειναις ταις ἡμεραις
ἠλθεν Ἰησους ἀπο Ναζαρετ της Γαλιλαιας
και ἐβαπτισθη εἰς τον Ἰορδανην ὑπο Ἰωαννου.

And it came to pass in those days
Jesus came from Nazareth of Galilee
and was baptized in the Jordan by John.

Acts 2:38

Μετανοησατε, φησιν, και βαπτισθητω ἑκαστος
ὑμων
ἐπι τῳ ὀνοματι Ἰησου Χριστου εἰς ἀφεσιν των
ἁμαρτιων ὑμων
και λημψεσθε την δωρεαν του ἁγιου πνευματος.

"Repent," he said, "and let each of you be
baptized
in the name of Jesus Christ for the forgiveness of
your sins
and you will receive the gift of the Holy Spirit."

Acts 19:3–5

³εἶπεν τε· Εἰς τί οὖν ἐβαπτισθητε;
οἱ δε εἶπαν· Εἰς το Ἰωαννου βαπτισμα.
⁴εἶπεν δε Παυλος· Ἰωαννης ἐβαπτισεν βαπτισμα
μετανοιας
τῳ λαῳ λεγων
εἰς τον ἐρχομενον μετ' αὐτον
ἵνα πιστευσωσιν,
τουτ' ἐστιν εἰς τον Ἰησουν.
⁵ἀκουσαντες δε ἐβαπτισθησαν εἰς το ὀνομα του
κυριου Ἰησου.

³And he said, "Into what then were you
baptized?"
They said, "Into John's baptism."
⁴Paul said, "John baptized [with a] baptism of
repentance,
saying to the people
in the one coming after him
that they should believe,
that is, in Jesus."
⁵When they heard they were baptized in the
name of the Lord Jesus.

Romans 6:3

ἡ ἀγνοειτε ὁτι, ὁσοι ἐβαπτισθημεν εἰς Χριστον
Ἰησουν,
εἰς τον θανατον αὐτου ἐβαπτισθημεν;

Or do you not know that, we who were baptized into
Christ Jesus, were baptized into his death?

I was baptized	ἐβαπτισθ_ην____
you (s) were baptized	ἐβαπτισθ_ης____
he/she was baptized	ἐβαπτισθ_____
we were baptized	ἐβαπτισθ_____
you (p) were baptized	ἐβαπτισθ_____
they were baptized	ἐβαπτισθ_____
be baptized (s)	βαπτισθ_ητι____
let him be baptized	βαπτισθ_ητω____
be baptized (p)	βαπτισθ_ητε____
let them be baptized	βαπτισθ_ητωσαν__

12.12   The participle follows the 3–1–3 pattern.

βαπτισθ εις	βαπτισθ εισα	βαπτισθ εν
βαπτισθ εντα	βαπτισθ εισαν	βαπτισθ εν
βαπτισθ εντος	βαπτισθ εισης	βαπτισθ εντος
βαπτισθ εντι	βαπτισθ ειση	βαπτισθ εντι
βαπτισθ εντες	βαπτισθ εισαι	βαπτισθ εντα
βαπτισθ εντας	βαπτισθ εισας	βαπτισθ εντα
βαπτισθ εντων	βαπτισθ εισων	βαπτισθ εντων
βαπτισθ εισιν	βαπτισθ εισαις	βαπτισθ εισιν

Looking to a passive future

12.13 Once you know the aorist passive you can safely predict the **future** passive. Look at these examples and see if you can formulate some rules to describe how the future passive is formed.

AORIST		FUTURE	
ἐπιστευθην	I was believed	πιστευθησομαι	I will be believed
ἐβαπτισθην	I was baptized	βαπτισθησομαι	I will be baptized
ἠκουσθην	I was heard	ἀκουσθησομαι	I will be heard

1. From the four constituent parts of the aorist passive ἐ-πιστευ-θ-ην you remove the first part, taking away the augment or adjusting the vowel.
2. You remove the ending.
3. To the remaining parts (πιστευ-θ) you add **ησ** + the regular **ομαι** endings.

Exercise 12.13

See if you can complete this chart. You have been given the aorist passive and the verb from which it comes. You have to supply the appropriate future passive.

You were justified	ἐδικαιωθης (δικαιοω)
You will be justified	_____
He was raised	ἠγερθη (ἐγειρω)
He will be raised	_____
They were shaken	ἐσαλευθησαν (σαλευω)
They will be shaken	_____

You were baptized	ἐβαπτισθητε (βαπτιζω)
You will be baptized	_____
We were saved	ἐσωθημεν (σῳζω)
We will be saved	_____
I rejoiced	ἐχαρην (χαιρω)
I will rejoice	_____

12.14   Work through these examples to practise your reading skill. You can also check the accuracy of your work in Exercise 12.13.

Matthew 12:37

ἐκ γαρ των λογων σου δικαιωθησῃ, και ἐκ των λογων σου καταδικασθησῃ.

For by your words you will be justified and by your words you will be condemned.

καταδικαζω condemn

Matthew 17:23

και ἀποκτενουσιν αὐτον, και τῃ τριτῃ ἡμερᾳ ἐγερθησεται. και ἐλυπηθησαν σφοδρα.

And they will kill him, and on the third day he will be raised. And they were very sorrowful.

ἀποκτεινω, fut. ἀποκτενῶ, kill   λυπεομαι be sad, sorrowful

Matthew 24:29

Εὐθεως δε μετα την θλιψιν των ἡμερων ἐκεινων
ὁ ἡλιος σκοτισθησεται, και ἡ σεληνη οὐ δωσει το
φεγγος αὐτης,
και οἱ ἀστερες πεσοῦνται ἀπο του οὐρανου,
και αἱ δυναμεις των οὐρανων σαλευθησονται.

Immediately after the tribulation of those days
the sun will be darkened, and the moon will not give
its light,
and the stars will fall from heaven,
and the powers of the heavens will be shaken.

σκοτιζομαι be darkened   διδωμι, fut. δωσω give
πιπτω, fut. πεσοῦμαι fall

Mark 10:39

οἱ δε εἰπαν αὐτῷ· Δυναμεθα. ὁ δε Ἰησους εἰπεν
αὐτοις·
Το ποτηριον ὃ ἐγω πινω πιεσθε
και το βαπτισμα ὃ ἐγω βαπτιζομαι βαπτισθησεσθε.

And they said to him, "We are able." Jesus said to
them,
"The cup which I drink you will drink
and the baptism with which I am baptized you will be
baptized with."

δυναμαι, be able   πινω, fut. πιομαι drink

Romans 5:9

πολλῳ οὐν μαλλον δικαιωθεντες νυν ἐν τῳ αἱματι
αὐτου
σωθησομεθα δι᾽ αὐτου ἀπο της ὀργης.

How much more then having now been justified
by his blood we will be saved through him from
wrath.

πολλῳ μαλλον how much more   νυν now

Philippians 1:18

Τί γαρ; πλην ὁτι παντι τροπῳ, εἰτε προφασει εἰτε ἀληθειᾳ, Χριστος καταγγελλεται, και ἐν τουτῳ χαιρω. Ἀλλα και χαρησομαι,

What then? Only that in every way, whether in pretence or truth,
Christ is proclaimed, and in this I rejoice. Yes and I shall rejoice.

More words with an identity crisis

12.15   In chapter 10 we met two adjectives which did not seem to know what category they should belong to. There are some verbs which have a similar problem. The technical way of describing them is **deponent** verbs. They take middle or passive endings, but their meaning is active.

As we have seen, most middle verbs fall into this category, having lost any "reflexive" meaning (something I do to or for myself). There are also some notable passive verbs which turn out to have an active meaning. Here are some of them.

βουλομαι, wish, aor. ἐβουληθην
πορευομαι, go, aor. ἐπορευθην
φοβεομαι (φοβοῦμαι) fear, aor. ἐφοβηθην

Some verbs which are active in meaning "pretend" to be middle or passive but can't make their minds up which they want to be!

ἀποκρινομαι, answer, aor. ἀπεκριναμην *or* ἀπεκριθην
[Note that it is a compound, ἀπο + κρινομαι]
γινομαι, be, become, fut. γενησομαι, aor. ἐγενομην *or* ἐγενηθην

Conversations and quotations

12.16 Much of the material in the gospels is a record of conversations. One feature of the reporting of these conversations is a certain amount of redundant language. An example will make this clearer.

Matthew 22:1–2

¹Καὶ **ἀποκριθεὶς** ὁ Ἰησοῦς παλιν **εἶπεν** ἐν παραβολαις αὐτοις λεγων·
²Ὡμοιωθη ἡ βασιλεια των οὐρανων ἀνθρωπῳ βασιλει, ὁστις ἐποιησεν γαμους τῳ υἱῳ αὐτου.

An over-literal translation of verse 1 gives us:

¹And **in answer** Jesus again **said** in parables to them **saying**,
²"The kingdom of heaven is like a [man] king, who gave a wedding banquet for his son."

The participles **ἀποκριθεὶς** (aorist passive, ἀποκρινομαι) and **λεγων** (present active, λεγω) are redundant; they are not strictly necessary for the sense. We do not need to reproduce this feature in English. The Revised English Bible says simply, "Jesus spoke to them again in parables."

12.17 A similar thing sometimes happens with quotations.

Exercise 12.17

Use the information given to translate this text literally, and then put it into more acceptable English.

τοτε ἐπληρωθη το ρηθεν δια Ἰερεμιου του προφητου λεγοντος· Φωνη ἐν Ῥαμα ἠκουσθη.

τοτε then πληροω fulfil ρηθεν, aor. ptc. pass. of λεγω
δια + gen. through Ἰερεμιας, ου m Jeremiah
προφητης, ου m prophet φωνη, ης f voice, sound
ἐν + dat. in Ῥαμα Ramah

Answers to Exercises

Exercise 12.11

I was baptized	ἐβαπτισθ_ην_
you (s) were baptized	ἐβαπτισθ_ης_
he/she was baptized	ἐβαπτισθ_η_
we were baptized	ἐβαπτισθ_ημεν_
you (p) were baptized	ἐβαπτισθ_ητε_
they were baptized	ἐβαπτισθ_ησαν_
be baptized (s)	βαπτισθ_ητι_
let him be baptized	βαπτισθ_ητω_
be baptized (p)	βαπτισθ_ητε_
let them be baptized	βαπτισθ_ητωσαν_

Exercise 12.13

You will be justified	**δικαιωθησῃ**
He will be raised	**ἐγερθησεται**
They will be shaken	**σαλευθησονται**
You will be baptized	**βαπτισθησεσθε**
We will be saved	**σωθησομεν**
I will rejoice	**χαρησομαι**

Exercise 12.17
The text is Matthew 2:17–18a.

Literal translation
Then was fulfilled what was spoken through Jeremiah the prophet saying, "A voice was heard in Ramah."

το ῥηθεν is nominative singular neuter of the article ὁ ἡ το with the nominative singular neuter of the aorist passive participle of λεγω – ἐρρηθην (I was said) – leading to ῥηθεις, εισα, εν (having been said).

Improved translation
Compare these two modern translations.

So the words spoken through Jeremiah the prophet were fulfilled, "A voice was heard in Rama" [Revised English Bible].

In this way what the prophet Jeremiah had said came true: "A sound is heard in Ramah" [Good News Bible].

REVIEW QUESTIONS

1. What is meant by the active and passive voice?

2. Is the meaning of the Greek middle voice nearer to the active or the passive?

3. What was the distinction between active and middle in classical Greek?

4. How far is this distinction relevant for New Testament Greek?

5. How does Greek differ from English in the way the passive is formed?

6. Why is it possible to confuse the middle and passive voices and how may this confusion be avoided?

7. What are the constituent parts of the aorist passive of πιστευω, meaning "I was believed"?

8. What is the aorist passive "identifier" and is it always used?

9. What is the full pattern of endings following
(a) ἐβαπτισθην (b) βαπτισθητι (c) βαπτισθεις?

10. How is the future passive formed?

11. What is meant by "deponent" verbs?

12. What is unusual about the deponent verbs ἀποκρινομαι and γινομαι?

13. What is meant by redundant language?

14. When does Greek use redundant language and how should it be translated?

REVIEW EXERCISES

JUDGE RIGHTLY

In this exercise you have been given eight texts all containing the verb κρινω, *judge*. Attach the correct meanings to the relevant texts and then check your answers in an English translation.

---

(1) I judge (2) I will judge (3) you (s) judged
(4) judge [●] (5) do not judge [―――]
(6) judging (nom. pl.) (7) he is judged
(8) you (p) will be judged (9) they were judged

Matthew 7:2

ἐν ᾧ γαρ κριματι <u>κρινετε</u> <u>κριθησεσθε</u>.

Luke 7:43

ὁ δε εἶπεν αὐτῷ, Ὀρθως <u>ἐκρινας</u>.

Luke 19:22

λεγει αὐτῷ, Ἐκ του στοματος σου <u>κρινῶ</u> σε, πονηρε δουλε.

Luke 22:30

και καθησεσθε ἐπι των θρονων, τας δωδεκα φυλας <u>κρινοντες</u> του Ἰσραηλ.

John 3:18

ὁ πιστευων εἰς αὐτον οὐ <u>κρινεται</u>.

John 5:30

καθως ἀκουω <u>κρίνω</u>, και ἡ κρισις ἡ ἐμη δικαια ἐστιν.

Acts 4:19

Εἰ δικαιον ἐστιν ἐνωπιον του θεου ὑμων ἀκουειν μαλλον
ἢ του θεου, κρινατε.

Revelation 20:13

και ἐκριθησαν ἑκαστος κατα τα ἐργα αὐτων.

HEAR HEAR

This is a similar exercise to the last one, based on the verb
ἀκουω. This time you have been given the Greek words to be
inserted in the correct spaces.

Ἀκουε Ἀκουεις ἀκουεται ἀκουσαντες ἀκουσατε
ἀκουσατω ἀκουσατωσαν ἀκουσει ἀκουσετε
ἀκουσθεισιν ἀκουσθησεται ἀκουων ἠκουσατε ἠκουσθη

Matthew 21:16

και εἰπαν αὐτῳ, ___(1)___ τί οὑτοι λεγουσιν;
And they said to him, "*Do you hear* what these are saying?"

Matthew 21:33

Ἀλλην παραβολην ___(2)___ .
Hear [●] another parable.

Matthew 21:45

Και ___(3)___ οἱ ἀρχιερεις και οἱ Φαρισαιοι τας παραβολας
αὐτου ἐγνωσαν ὁτι περι αὐτων λεγει.
And *when* the chief priests and Pharisees *heard* his parables
they knew that he was speaking about them.

Matthew 26:65

τί ἔτι χρειαν ἔχομεν μαρτυρων; ἰδε νυν ___(4)___ την βλασφημιαν.

What further need have we of witnesses? See now, *you have heard* the blasphemy.

Mark 12:29

___(5)___ ᾿Ισραηλ, κυριος ὁ θεος ἡμων κυριος εἰς ἐστιν.

Hear [---], O Israel, the Lord our God, the Lord is one.

Luke 12:3

ἀνθ᾿ ὧν ὅσα ἐν τη σκοτιᾳ εἰπατε ἐν τῳ φωτι ___(6)___.

Therefore whatever you have said in the dark *will be heard* in the light.

Luke 16:29

᾿Εχουσιν Μωϋσεα και τους προφητας· ___(7)___ αὐτων.

They have Moses and the prophets; *let them hear* [●] them.

John 5:24

᾿Αμην ἀμην λεγω ὑμιν ὅτι ὁ τον λογον μου ___(8)___ και πιστευων τῳ πεμψαντι με ἐχει ζωην αἰωνιον και εἰς κρισιν οὐκ ἐρχεται.

Truly truly I say to you that *He who hears* my word and believes him who sent me has eternal life and does not come into judgment.

John 9:32

ἐκ του αἰωνος οὐκ ___(9)___ ὅτι ἠνεῳξεν τις ὀφθαλμους τυφλου γεγεννημενου.

It has not *been heard* ever that someone opened the eyes of a man born blind.

John 16:13

ὅσα __(10)__ λαλησει και τα ἐρχομενα ἀναγγελεῖ ὑμιν.

Whatever *he will hear* he will speak and he will declare to you the things to come.

Acts 28:26

Πορευθητι προς τον λαον τουτον και εἰπον, Ἀκοῃ __(11)__ και οὐ μη συνητε και βλεποντες βλεψετε και οὐ μη ἰδητε.

Go to this people and say, "*You will* surely *hear* but never understand and you will surely see but never perceive."

1 Corinthians 5:1

ὅλως __(12)__ ἐν ὑμιν πορνεια.

It is actually *heard* [that there is] immorality among you.

Hebrews 2:1

δια τουτο δει περισσοτερως προσεχειν ἡμας τοις __(13)__ .

Therefore we must pay all the more attention *to the things which have been heard*.

Revelation 2:7

ὁ ἐχων οὐς __(14)__ τί το πνευμα λεγει ταις ἐκκλησιαις.

He who has an ear *let him hear* [●] what the Spirit is saying to the churches.

WORDS TO LEARN

αἷμα, τος n blood

ἀληθεια, ας f truth

ἀποκρινομαι, aor. ἀπεκριναμην or ἀπεκριθην answer

ἀποκτεινω, fut. ἀποκτενῶ (εω), aor. ἀπεκτεινα kill

ἀρχιερευς, εως m high priest, pl. chief priests

ἀστηρ, ἀστερος m star

ἀφεσις, εως f forgiveness

γενναω give birth, be father to (used of both male and female)

ἐγειρω, fut. ἐγερῶ (εω), aor. act. ἠγειρα, aor. pass. ἠγερθην raise.

The passive can mean "rise" as well as "be raised".

ἐπι (ἐπ᾽, ἐφ᾽) + accusative, genitive or dative, upon.

This is a very common preposition with a variety of meanings.

εὐθυς, εὐθεως immediately

ἡλιος, ου m sun

μετα (μετ᾽, μεθ᾽) + accusative, after (cf μετα + gen. in chapter 9)

ὀργη, ης f anger, wrath

παραλυτικος, ου m paralytic, cripple

πιπτω, fut. πεσοῦμαι (εομαι), aor. ἐπεσον fall

στομα, τος n mouth

τριτος, η, ον third

ὑπο (ὑπ᾽, ὑφ᾽) + genitive by

χαιρω, aor. pass. (with active meaning), ἐχαρην rejoice

CHAPTER THIRTEEN

Preview

Verbs: mood
  Indicative – actual
  Subjunctive – potential

Verbs: tense
  Present – continuous
  Aorist – neutral

Verb analysis

The use of the subjunctive

The infinitive

δυναμαι

Accusative and infinitive

Matthew 1:18–25

CHAPTER THIRTEEN

Purpose and potential

13.1 Read through these pairs of texts paying particular attention to the words in bold type.

1 (a) ὁ πιστευων εἰς τον υἱον **ἐχει** ζωην αἰωνιον.

He who believes in the Son **has** eternal life (John 3:36).

(b) οὑτως ὑψωθηναι δει τον υἱον του ἀνθρωπου,
ἱνα πας ὁ πιστευων ἐν αὐτῳ **ἐχῃ** ζωην αἰωνιον.

So the Son of Man must be lifted up,
that everyone who believes in him **may have**
eternal life (John 3:14–15).

2 (a) Δικαιωθεντες οὐν ἐκ πιστεως
εἰρηνην **ἐχομεν** προς τον θεον
δια του κυριου ἡμων Ἰησου Χριστου.

Therefore being justified by faith
we have peace with God
through our Lord Jesus Christ (Romans 5:1).

(b) Ἐν τουτῳ τετελειωται ἡ ἀγαπη μεθ' ἡμων,
ἱνα παρρησιαν **ἐχωμεν**
ἐν τῃ ἡμερᾳ της κρισεως.

In this love has been perfected with us,
that **we may have** confidence
on the day of judgment (1 John 4:17).

3 (a) και τον λογον αὐτου οὐκ **ἐχετε** ἐν
ὑμιν μενοντα,
ὁτι ὁν ἀπεστειλεν ἐκεινος, τουτῳ ὑμεις
οὐ πιστευετε.

And **you** do not **have** his word remaining in
you,
because the one whom he has sent, you do not
believe him (John 5:38).

(b) και οὐ θελετε ἐλθειν προς με ἱνα ζωην **ἐχητε**.

And you do not want to come to me that **you
may have** life (John 5:40).

4 (a) οὑτοι **ἐχουσιν** την ἐξουσιαν κλεισαι τον
οὐρανον.

These **have** power to shut the sky (Revelation
11:6).

(b) ὁ κλεπτης οὐκ ἐρχεται εἰ μη
ἱνα κλεψῃ και θυσῃ και ἀπολεσῃ·
ἐγω ἠλθον ἱνα ζωην **ἐχωσιν**
και περισσον **ἐχωσιν**.

The thief does not come except
that he may steal and kill and destroy;
I have come that **they may have** life
and **have** [it] more abundantly (John 10:10).

13.2 The texts marked (a) use the present tense of ἐχω
with endings you should recognize. The texts marked
(b) use a different set of endings. The translations
bring out the difference in English: you have, you
may have, etc.

Another mode

13.3 What we have here is another "mode" or "mood" of
the verb, a subject we looked at first in chapter 9. To
use the technical terms, "you have" is **indicative**

mood; "you may have" is **subjunctive**. In English "you may" carries the idea of uncertainty, but that is not a feature of the Greek subjunctive. It is better to think of it as the mood of **potential** action.

The two ways of looking at things

13.4   In these charts you will find the subjunctive forms of πιστευω and δεχομαι. Note that just like commands there are always two alternatives, which we can represent as [---] and [●].

	PRESENT [---]	AORIST [●]
I may believe	πιστευ ω	πιστευσ ω
you (p) may believe	πιστευ ης	πιστευσ ης
he may believe	πιστευ η	πιστευσ η
we may believe	πιστευ ωμεν	πιστευσ ωμεν
you (p) may believe	πιστευ ητε	πιστευσ ητε
they may believe	πιστευ ωσιν	πιστευσ ωσιν

	PRESENT [---]	AORIST [●]
I may receive	δεχ ωμαι	δεξ ωμαι
you (s) may receive	δεχ η	δεξ η
he may receive	δεχ ηται	δεξ ηται
we may receive	δεχ ωμεθα	δεξ ωμεθα
you (p) may receive	δεχ ησθε	δεξ ησθε
they may receive	δεχ ωνται	δεξ ωνται

Exercise 13.4

Can you work out a set of rules to describe the formation of the subjunctive endings?

13.5   The passive endings have a little surprise in store for us. Look at this chart.

	PRESENT [---]	AORIST [●]
I may be believed	πιστευ ωμαι	πιστευθ ω
you (p) may be believed	πιστευ ῃ	πιστευθ ῃς
he may be believed	πιστευ ηται	πιστευθ ῃ
we may be believed	πιστευ ωμεθα	πιστευθ ωμεν
you (p) may be believed	πιστευ ησθε	πιστευθ ητε
they may be believed	πιστευ ωνται	πιστευθ ωσιν

The surprise is in the aorist passive, which uses the same endings as the present and aorist active. Only the stem (usually with its characteristic **θ**) gives the clue you need.

Neutral or continuous

13.6   The choice of aorist or present tense can make a difference. All the moods – indicative (actual), subjunctive (potential), imperative (commands), etc., can be expressed by means of the aorist [●] or present [---] tense. Look closely at these verses from John 12:35–36, which record the climax of Jesus' public ministry in John's Gospel. I have put symbols above the verbs to show the type of action and added a more formal analysis.

³⁵ εἶπεν οὖν αὐτοις ὁ Ἰησους·	So Jesus **said** to them,
Ἐτι μικρον χρονον	"Yet a little time
το φως ἐν ὑμιν ἐστιν.	the light **is** among you.
περιπατειτε ὡς το φως ἐχετε,	**Walk** while you **have** the light,
ἱνα μη σκοτια ὑμας	that darkness may not
καταλαβῃ·	**overtake** you;
και ὁ περιπατων ἐν τῃ σκοτιᾳ	and he who **walks** in the darkness
οὐκ οἰδεν που ὑπαγει.	does not **know** where he **is going**.
³⁶ ὡς το φως ἐχετε,	While you **have** the light
πιστευετε εἰς το φως,	**believe** in the light,
ἱνα υἱοι φωτος γενησθε.	that you may **become** sons of light."
ταυτα ἐλαλησεν Ἰησους,	Jesus **spoke** these things,
και ἀπελθων ἐκρυβη ἀπ᾽ αὐτων.	and **having left** was **hidden** from them.

Verb analysis

When verbs are analyzed grammatically the main categories are

- **tense**, e.g. present, future, aorist
- **mood**, e.g. indicative, subjunctive, imperative
- **voice**, e.g. active, middle, passive

If a verb form is present indicative active that is usually regarded as a "default". In other words, if no information is given about the tense you can assume it is present; if no information is given about the mood you can assume it is indicative; if no information is given about the voice you can assume it is active (unless the verb has an -ομαι ending, when you assume it is middle).

In the first example below, εἰπεν, you are told only the tense (2nd aorist). That means you are to assume that the mood is indicative (making a statement or question), and the voice is active.

εἰπεν, 2nd aor. λεγω.

ἐστιν, pres. εἰμι, an irregular verb.

περιπατειτε, imperative, περιπατεω.

ἐχετε, ἐχω.

καταλαβῃ, 2nd aor. subjunctive, from the compound verb κατα-λαμβανω, aor. κατ-ελαβεν.

περιπατων, participle, περιπατεω.

οἰδεν, from οἰδα, which will be dealt with in chapter 15.

ὑπαγει, from the compound verb ὑπ-αγω.

ἐχετε, as above.

πιστευετε, imperative, πιστευω.

γενησθε, 2nd aor. subjunctive, γινομαι.

ἐλαλησεν, aor., λαλεω.

ἀπελθων, 2nd aor. participle, from the compound verb ἀπ-ερχομαι.

ἐκρυβη, aor. passive, κρυπτω.

Exercise 13.6

In your opinion is there anything significant to say about the choice of **tenses** in John 12:35–36?

Recognizing potential when you see it

13.7 There are several situations in which Greek uses the subjunctive, the mood of potential action. The first should be easily recognizable from the examples given in section 13.1. Note that the connecting words ἵνα (that, so that) and ἐαν (if) are *always* followed by a verb in the subjunctive.

1. After ἵνα (sometimes ὅπως) expressing purpose or result (= so that)
2. After ἵνα describing something (= namely that)
3. After ἐαν meaning "if"
4. Expressions with ἀν or ἐαν: whoever, whatever, whenever, wherever, until.
5. Exhortations (i.e. "Let us . . .")
6. Deliberative questions (e.g. What are we to do?)
7. οὐ μη + aorist subjunctive, strong negative future statements
8. μη + aorist subjunctive, prohibitions (negative commands)

Exercise 13.7

In the texts below you will find illustrations of all these situations where a subjunctive mood is used. Link each verb to the number of the correct description above.

Matthew 1:20

ταυτα δε αὐτου ἐνθυμηθεντος
ἰδου ἀγγελος κυριου κατ᾽ ὀναρ ἐφανη αὐτῷ λεγων·
᾽Ιωσηφ υἱος Δαυιδ, μη **φοβηθῃς** παραλαβειν Μαριαν
την γυναικα σου·
το γαρ ἐν αὐτῃ γεννηθεν ἐκ πνευματος ἐστιν ἁγιου.

And when he had considered these things
behold an angel of the Lord appeared to him in a
dream saying,
"Joseph, son of David, don't be afraid to take Mary
as your wife;
for the [child] conceived in her is of the Holy Spirit."

A. φοβηθῃς

Matthew 2:8

και πεμψας αὐτους εἰς Βηθλεεμ εἰπεν·
Πορευθεντες ἐξετασατε ἀκριβως περι του παιδιου·
ἐπαν δε **εὑρητε**, ἀπαγγειλατε μοι,
ὁπως κἀγω ἐλθων **προσκυνησω** αὐτῷ.

He sent them to Bethlehem and said,
"Go and search carefully for the child;
And whenever you find [him], bring me word,
that I also may come and worship him."

B. εὑρητε   C. προσκυνησω

Matthew 10:11

εἰς ἡν δ᾽ ἀν πολιν ἡ κωμην **εἰσελθητε**,
ἐξετασατε τίς ἐν αὐτῃ ἀξιος ἐστιν·
κἀκει μεινατε ἑως ἀν **ἐξελθητε**.

And into whichever town or village you enter,
find out who is worthy in it;
and remain there until you go out.

D. εἰσελθητε   E. ἐξελθητε

John 6:37

παν ὃ διδωσιν μοι ὁ πατηρ προς ἐμε ἡξει,
και τον ἐρχομενον προς ἐμε οὐ μη **ἐκβαλω** ἐξω.

Everyone [lit. thing] whom the Father gives to me
will come to me, and the one who comes to me I will
never cast out.

F. ἐκβαλω

John 19:15

ἐκραυγασαν οὖν ἐκεινοι· Ἀρον ἀρον, σταυρωσον
αὐτον.
λεγει αὐτοις ὁ Πιλατος· Τον βασιλεα ὑμων
σταυρωσω;
ἀπεκριθησαν οἱ ἀρχιερεις· Οὐκ ἐχομεν βασιλεα
εἰ μη Καισαρα.

So they shouted, "Away away! Crucify him."
Pilate said to them, "Am I to crucify your king?"
The chief priests answered, "We have no king but
Caesar."

G. σταυρωσω

1 Thessalonians 5:6

ἀρα οὖν μη **καθευδωμεν** ὡς οἱ λοιποι ἀλλα **γρηγορωμεν** και **νηφωμεν**.

So then let us not sleep like the rest but let us watch
and be sober.

H. καθευδωμεν   *I.* γρηγορωμεν   *J.* νηφωμεν

1 John 1:8

ἐαν **εἰπωμεν** ὁτι ἁμαρτιαν οὐκ ἐχομεν, ἑαυτους
πλανωμεν και ἡ ἀληθεια οὐκ ἐστιν ἐν ἡμιν.

If we say that we have no sin, we deceive ourselves
and the truth is not in us.

K. εἰπωμεν

1 John 3:23

Και αὐτη ἐστιν ἡ ἐντολη αὐτου,
ἱνα **πιστευσωμεν** τῳ ὀνοματι του υἱου αὐτου ᾽Ιησου
Χριστου και **ἀγαπωμεν** ἀλληλους, καθως ἐδωκεν
ἐντολην ἡμιν.

And this is his command,
that we should believe in the name of his Son Jesus
Christ and love one another, as he has given command to us.

L. πιστευσωμεν   *M.* ἀγαπωμεν

Another way of expressing purpose

13.8   In English the most common way of expressing
purpose is with the **infinitive**.
e.g. Christ Jesus came into the world **to save** sinners.

In Greek the most common way is to use ἱνα or ὁπως
+ the subjunctive. But Greek does have infinitives
and sometimes they are used to express purpose. For
example, the Greek of 1 Timothy 1:15 (quoted
above) is

Χριστος ᾽Ιησους ἠλθεν εἰς τον κοσμον ἁμαρτωλους
σωσαι.

The two varieties

13.9   Once again we find when we look at the infinitive that
it comes in two basic varieties, present [---] and
aorist [●]. We need a double set for active, middle
and passive. Here is a chart.

	to believe	to receive	to be believed
PRESENT	πιστευ **ειν**	δεχ **εσθαι**	πιστευ **εσθαι**
1st AORIST	πιστευσ **αι**	δεξ **ασθαι**	πιστευθ **ηναι**

Infinitives are fairly easy to spot. They usually end with ειν or some combination ending with αι. Verbs with a second aorist use the endings of the **present** infinitive attached to their own second aorist stem. So we have εἰπειν, "to say", ἰδειν, "to see", and γενεσθαι, "to become". See chapter 11 section 11.17.

Infinitives in action

13.10 Some uses of the infinitive are straightforward and similar to English usage, such as expressing purpose. Here are some more examples where Greek and English are similar.

John 6:6

αὐτος γαρ ἠδει τί ἐμελλεν **ποιειν**.
For he knew what he was going **to do**.

The verb μελλω means "I am about to" or "I intend to" and is followed by an infinitive.

John 8:44

και τας ἐπιθυμιας του πατρος ὑμων θελετε **ποιειν**.
And you want **to do** the desires of your father.

The verb θελω means "I wish" or "I want" and is followed by an infinitive.

1 John 3:9

και οὐ δυναται **ἁμαρτανειν**, ὁτι ἐκ του θεου γεγεννηται.
And he is not able **to sin**, because he is born of God.

This is an interesting example because the choice of ἁμαρτανειν [– – –] rather than ἁμαρτειν [●] allows us to translate, "he cannot **go on sinning**," which throws a helpful light on a difficult verse.

The verb which John uses is δυναμαι, which means "I am able" or "I can". The meaning "I am able" helps us to see how the infinitive fits the construction – "able to . . .". Technically it is a passive, but it is a little irregular.

Exercise 13.10

Here is the present tense, but not in the correct order. See if your "instincts" enable you to sort them correctly. Check your results with the examples below.

δυνασαι	δυναμαι	δυναμεθα	δυνασθε
δυναται	δυνανται		

Matthew 8:2

και ἰδου λεπρος προσελθων προσεκυνει αὐτῳ λεγων·
Κυριε, ἐαν θελῃς δυνασαι με καθαρισαι.
[καθαρισαι is aorist infinitive of καθαριζω, cleanse.]

And behold a leper came to him and worshipped him saying,"Lord, if you are willing you are able to make me clean."

Matthew 9:28

ἐλθοντι δε εἰς την οἰκιαν προσηλθον αὐτῳ οἱ τυφλοι,
και λεγει αὐτοις ὁ Ἰησους, Πιστευετε ὀτι δυναμαι
τουτο ποιησαι; λεγουσιν αὐτῳ· Ναι κυριε.

When he came into the house the blind men approached him,
and Jesus said to them, "Do you believe that I can do this?"
They said to him, "Yes, Lord."

Matthew 20:22

ἀποκριθεὶς δε ὁ ᾽Ιησους εἶπεν· Οὐκ οἴδατε τί αἰτεισθε.
δυνασθε πιειν το ποτηριον ὃ ἐγω μελλω πινειν;
λεγουσιν αὐτῳ· Δυναμεθα.

Jesus answered, "You do not know what you are asking.
Can you drink the cup which I am to drink?"
They said to him, "We can."

Matthew 27:42

ἀλλους ἐσωσεν, ἑαυτον οὐ δυναται σωσαι.

He saved others, himself he cannot save.

Mark 2:19

και εἶπεν αὐτοις ὁ ᾽Ιησους· Μη δυνανται οἱ υἱοι του νυμφωνος
ἐν ᾧ ὁ νυμφιος μετ᾽ αὐτων ἐστιν νηστευειν;
ὁσον χρονον ἐχουσιν τον νυμφιον μετ᾽ αὐτων οὐ δυνανται νηστευειν.

And Jesus said to them, "Can the wedding guests fast while the bridegroom is with them?
As long as they have the bridegroom with them they cannot fast."

Some different uses

13.11   The Greek infinitive is also used in ways which have
no exact parallel in modern English. This can be
illustrated from constructions with δει (it is necessary) and ὡστε (so that).

In 1 Corinthians 15:25 we read "For he must reign."
In Greek it is δει γαρ αὐτον **βασιλευειν**.
In Greek the English "he must" is something like "it
is necessary him to," or, using archaic language, "it
behoves him to".

Here is another familiar text, Acts 16:30.
The English is "Sirs, what must I do to be saved?"
The Greek says literally, "Sirs what is it necessary me
to do that I may be saved?"

Κυριοι, τί με **δει ποιειν** ἱνα σωθω;

Accusative and infinitive

13.12   When the Greek infinitive is used in this way the
Greek noun or pronoun associated with it is put in
the **accusative** case, giving us the rule

ACCUSATIVE AND INFINITIVE

He must reign   but   δει **αὐτον** βασιλευειν
What must **I** do?   but   τί **με** δει ποιειν;

Here is another example, from Matthew 12:22, this
time using ὡστε followed by the infinitive to express
the result of something.

"And he healed him, so that the dumb man spoke
and saw."
και ἐθεραπευσεν αὐτον, **ὡστε** τον κωφον **λαλειν** και
βλεπειν.
Literally, "so that the dumb man to speak and to
see".

13.13 A fairly common verb which is followed by an infinitive is ἔξεστιν, meaning "it is lawful". In Matthew 12:2 the Pharisees said to Jesus, "Look, your disciples are doing what it is not lawful to do on the sabbath." The Greek text reads,

Ἰδου οἱ μαθηται σου ποιουσιν ὃ οὐκ **ἔξεστιν ποιειν** ἐν σαββατῳ.

Another identity crisis

13.14 By now you should not be too surprised when words have a grammatical identity crisis. The infinitive, every inch a verb, also likes to act as a noun. In fact this is not too shocking. If you think of the English phrase "to obey is better than sacrifice" the infinitive "to obey" is acting rather like a noun. You could replace it with the noun "obedience" and not alter the meaning: "obedience is better than sacrifice".

When the Greek infinitive does this it takes on the identity of a neuter noun with the definite article **το**. The infinitive itself does not have any changing endings but the article does (το, το, του, τῳ). Look at these examples where I have given an over-literal translation to show you what is going on and a more "polished" one.

Philippians 2:6

οὐχ ἁρπαγμον ἡγησατο το εἰναι ἰσα θεῳ.
not something-to-be-grasped he-considered the to-be equally with-God.

He did not consider equality with God something to be grasped.

Matthew 6:8

οἶδεν γαρ ὁ πατηρ ὑμων ὧν χρειαν
ἐχετε
he-knows [for] the father of-you of-what need
you have

προ του ὑμας αἰτησαι αὐτον.
before the you to-ask him.

For your Father knows what you need before you
ask him.

Romans 15:13

ὁ   δε   θεος   της   ἐλπιδος   πληρωσαι   ὑμας
The [but] God of hope may-he-fill you

πασης   χαρας   και εἰρηνης   ἐν   τῳ
πιστευειν.
[with] all joy and peace in the to-believe.

May the God of hope fill you with all joy and
peace in believing.

Because this construction is so different from English
it is difficult to sort out. Fortunately it is not very
frequent, but that is all the more reason to be ready
for it when it does appear.

Familiarity helps

13.15   Few people find languages easy to learn and Greek is
certainly no exception, but we have the incentive of
discovering the treasures of the New Testament in its
original language. Being familiar with it in English
does give us an advantage.

Exercise 13.15

In this translation exercise we shall look at one of the most familiar stories about Jesus, the Nativity, from Matthew 1:18–25. The dictionary form of the Greek words is given and you have to supply the English meanings. This is an "open book" exercise, and you may use any resources you need, including English translations.

¹⁸Του δε Ἰησου Χριστου ἡ γενεσις οὑτως ἠν.
μνηστευθεισης της μητρος αὑτου Μαριας τω Ἰωσηφ,
πριν ἠ συνελθειν αὑτους
εὑρεθη ἐν γαστρι ἐχουσα ἐκ πνευματος ἁγιου.

γενεσις, εως f _____ οὑτως _____ ἠν, past

tense of εἰμι _____ μνηστευομαι (pass.)

_____ μητηρ, μητρος f _____ Μαρια, ας f

_____ Ἰωσηφ m _____ πριν ἠ (+ infinitive)

_____ συνερχομαι _____ εὑρισκω, aor. pass.

εὑρεθην _____ γαστηρ, γαστρος f _____ ἐν

γαστρι ἐχειν = _____ ἐκ (+ gen.) _____

πνευμα, τος n _____ ἁγιος, α, ον _____

¹⁹Ἰωσηφ δε ὁ ἀνηρ αὑτης,
δικαιος ὢν και μη θελων αὑτην δειγματισαι,
ἐβουληθη λαθρα ἀπολυσαι αὑτην.

ἀνηρ, ἀνδρος m _____ δικαιος, α, ον _____

ὢν οὑσα ὀν, participle of εἰμι _____

δειγματιζω, aor. ἐδειγματισα _____ βουλομαι,

aor. ἐβουληθην _____ λαθρα _____ ἀπολυω

_____

²⁰ταυτα δε αυτου ἐνθυμηθεντος
ἰδου ἀγγελος κυριου κατ' ὀναρ ἐφανη αὐτῳ λεγων·
'Ιωσηφ υἱος Δαυιδ, μη φοβηθῃς παραλαβειν Μαριαν
την γυναικα σου·
το γαρ ἐν αὐτῃ γεννηθεν ἐκ πνευματος ἐστιν ἁγιου.

ταυτα, from οὑτος αὑτη τουτο _____
ἐνθυμεομαι _____
ἀγγελος, ου m _____   κυριος, ου m _____
ὀναρ n _____
(κατ' ὀναρ = _____) φαινομαι, aor. ἐφανην
_____   υἱος, ου m _____   Δαυιδ m _____
φοβεομαι _____   παραλαμβανω _____
γυνη, γυναικος f _____   το γεννηθεν (article +
aor. pass. participle of γενναω _____) _____

²¹τεξεται δε υἱον, και καλεσεις το ὀνομα αὐτου
'Ιησουν·
αὐτος γαρ σωσει τον λαον αὐτου ἀπο των ἁμαρτιων
αὐτων.

τικτω, fut. τεξομαι _____   καλεω _____
ὀνομα, τος n _____   'Ιησους, ου m _____
σῳζω, fut. σωσω _____   λαος, ου m _____
ἀπο (+ gen.) _____   ἁμαρτια, ας f _____

²²τουτο δε ὁλον γεγονεν ἱνα πληρωθῃ το ῥηθεν ὑπο
κυριου δια του προφητου λεγοντος·

ὁλος, η, ον _____   γεγονεν, from γινομαι
_____   ἱνα _____   πληροω, aor. pass.
ἐπληρωθην _____   το ῥηθεν (article + aor.
pass. participle of λεγω _____) _____   ὑπο (+
gen.) _____
δια (+ gen.) _____   προφητης, ου m _____

²³ Ἰδου ἡ παρθενος ἐν γαστρι ἑξει και τεξεται υἱον,
και καλεσουσιν το ὀνομα αὐτου Ἐμμανουηλ,
ὃ ἐστιν μεθερμηνευομενον μεθ' ἡμων ὁ θεος.

ἰδου _____ παρθενος, ου f _____ (γαστηρ,
γαστρος f _____) ἐχω, fut. ἑξω (note the
change of breathing) _____
ἐν γαστρι ἐχειν = _____ Ἐμμανουηλ _____
μεθερμηνευω _____ μετα, μεθ' (+ gen.)
_____ θεος, ου m _____

²⁴ ἐγερθεις δε ὁ Ἰωσηφ ἀπο του ὑπνου
ἐποιησεν ὡς προσεταξεν αὐτῳ ὁ ἀγγελος κυριου
και παρελαβεν την γυναικα αὐτου,

ἐγειρω, aor. pass. ἠγερθην, passive meaning =
_____ ὑπνος, ου m _____ ποιεω _____ ὡς
_____ προστασσω, aor. προσεταξα (+ dat.)
_____

²⁵ και οὐκ ἐγινωσκεν αὐτην ἑως οὑ ἐτεκεν υἱον·
και ἐκαλεσεν το ὀνομα αὐτου Ἰησουν.

γινωσκω _____ (here = _____) ἑως οὑ
_____ τικτω, aor. ἐτεκον _____

Answers to Exercises

Exercise 13.4

1. The endings are all based on **present** tense indicative endings (ω, εις, ει, ομεν, ετε, ουσιν & ομαι, η, εται, ομεθα, εσθε, ονται).
2. Where possible, the initial vowel is lengthened, e.g. ομεν → ωμεν.
3. The iota in ει is written under the line, e.g. εις → ῃς.
4. The υ in ου is dropped, e.g. ουσιν → ωσιν.

Exercise 13.6

Most of the tenses are continuous present, representing the continuing opportunities to believe in Jesus, the Light of the World, and to live for him. The aorist καταλαβῃ in verse 35 is in stark contrast to the surrounding present tenses, highlighting the sudden fall of darkness when the light is taken away. Becoming "sons of light" is also represented by an aorist, γενησθε, in verse 36. The emphasis is on "becoming" rather than simply "being" the people of the light.

Exercise 13.7

A. μη φοβηθης	8. Prohibition.
B. ἐπαν εὑρητε	4. Whenever (ἐπαν = ἐπει ἀν)
C. ὁπως προσκυνησω	1. Purpose
D. εἰς ἡν ἀν εἰσελθητε	4. Into whichever
E. ἑως ἀν ἐξελθητε	4. Until
F. οὐ μη ἐκβαλω	7. Strong future negative
G. σταυρωσω	6. Deliberative question
H. μη καθευδωμεν	5. Exhortation
I. γρηγορωμεν	5. Exhortation
J. νηφωμεν	5. Exhortation
K. ἐαν εἰπωμεν	3. Condition with ἐαν
L. ἱνα πιστευσωμεν	2. Description with ἱνα
M. ἱνα ἀγαπωμεν	2. Description with ἱνα

Exercise 13.10

δυναμαι, δυνασαι, δυναται, δυναμεθα, δυνασθε, δυνανται

Exercise 13.15

Check your translation with a fairly literal English version such as the Revised Standard Version and with a more dynamic translation such as the Good News Bible.

γενεσις, εως f birth   οὑτως in this way
ἦν, past tense of εἰμι I am
μνηστευομαι (pass.) be betrothed
μητηρ, μητρος f mother
Μαρια, ας f Mary   Ἰωσηφ m Joseph
πριν ἤ (+ infinitive) before
συνερχομαι come together
εὑρισκω, aor. pass. εὑρεθην find
γαστηρ, γαστρος f womb
ἐν γαστρι ἐχειν = to be pregnant
ἐκ (+ gen.) from   πνευμα, τος n spirit
ἁγιος, α, ον holy   ἀνηρ, ἀνδρος m man
δικαιος, α, ον righteous
ὠν οὑσα ὀν, participle of εἰμι I am
δειγματιζω, aor. ἐδειγματισα disgrace βουλομαι,
aor. ἐβουληθην wish   λαθρᾳ secretly
ἀπολυω divorce

ταυτα, from οὑτος αὑτη τουτο this
ἐνθυμεομαι consider   ἀγγελος, ου m angel
κυριος, ου m Lord   ὀναρ n dream
(κατ' ὀναρ = in a dream)
φαινομαι, aor. ἐφανην appear
υἱος, ου m son   Δαυιδ m David
φοβεομαι fear   παραλαμβανω take
γυνη, γυναικος f wife
το· γεννηθεν (article + aor. pass. participle of
γενναω conceive) what is conceived

τικτω, fut. τεξομαι bear, give birth to
καλεω call   ὀνομα, τος n name
'Ιησους, ου m Jesus   σῳζω, fut. σωσω save
λαος, ου m people   ἀπο (+ gen.) from
ἁμαρτια, ας f sin

ὁλος, η, ον whole, all   γεγονεν, from γινομαι
happen   ἱνα that πληροω, aor. pass. ἐπληρωθην
fulfil   το ῥηθεν (article + aor. pass. participle of
λεγω say) what was said   ὑπο (+ gen.) by
δια (+ gen.) through   προφητης, ου m prophet

ἰδου behold
παρθενος, ου f virgin   (γαστηρ, γαστρος f
womb)
ἐχω, fut. ἑξω (note the change of breathing) have
ἐν γαστρι ἐχειν = conceive
'Εμμανουηλ God with us   μεθερμηνευω translate
μετα, μεθ' (+ gen.) with   θεος, ου m God

ἐγειρω, aor. pass. ἠγερθην, passive meaning =
rise
ὑπνος, ου m sleep
ποιεω do   ὡς as   προστασσω, aor. προσεταξα
(+ dat.) command

γινωσκω know (here = have sexual relations)
ἑως οὑ until   τικτω, aor. ἐτεκον bear, give birth
to

REVIEW QUESTIONS

1. What is the difference between the meaning of the subjunctive mood in English and Greek?

2. Subjunctive endings are similar to present indicative endings, but with some changes. What are the changes?

3. What is unusual about the subjunctive endings of the aorist passive?

4. What are the main categories into which verbs can be analyzed?

5. What is a "default" and what information is regarded as a default when verbs are analyzed?

6. In what situations is the subjunctive used in Greek?

7. Which connecting words are always followed by a verb in the subjunctive?

8. What is the most common way of expressing purpose (a) in Greek (b) in English?

9. What are the infinitives derived from πιστευω and δεχομαι?

10. What kind of endings are attached to second aorist infinitives?

11. What do μελλω and θελω mean and what construction follows them?

12. What is the full pattern of δυναμαι and what does it mean?

13. What case is associated with the infinitive in constructions where English would give the verb a subject, e.g. "*he* must reign"?

14. What is the meaning of δει, ὡστε and ἐξεστιν, and what do they have in common?

15. When the infinitive is used as a noun what gender is it and how does it represent the different cases?

REVIEW EXERCISES

COMPREHENSION QUIZ

Read through the Greek text of Matthew 24:20–28 with the English translation and then answer the following questions.

²⁰προσευχεσθε δε
ἱνα μη γενηται ἡ φυγη ὑμων
χειμωνος μηδε σαββατῳ.

And pray
that your flight may not be
during winter or on the
sabbath.

²¹ἐσται γαρ τοτε θλιψις
μεγαλη
οἱα οὐ γεγονεν
ἀπ' ἀρχης κοσμου

For then there will be great
tribulation
such as has not been
from the beginning of the
world

ἑως του νυν
οὐδ' οὐ μη γενηται.

until now
nor ever shall be.

²²και εἰ μη ἐκολοβωθησαν
αἱ ἡμεραι ἐκειναι,
οὐκ ἀν ἐσωθη πασα σαρξ·

And if those days had not
been shortened
no person would have been
saved;

δια δε τους ἐκλεκτους
κολοβωθησονται αἱ ἡμεραι
ἐκειναι.

but because of the elect
those days will be shortened.

²³Τοτε ἐαν τις ὑμιν εἰπη,
Ἰδου ὡδε ὁ Χριστος,
ἠ Ὡδε,
μη πιστευσητε·

Then if anyone says to you,
"Look, the Christ is here,"
or "Here,"
do not believe [them];

²⁴ἐγερθησονται γαρ ψευδοχριστοι	for false Christs will rise
και ψευδοπροφηται	and false prophets
και δωσουσιν σημεια μεγαλα	and they will give great signs
και τερατα	and wonders
ὡστε πλανησαι, εἰ δυνατον,	so as to deceive, if possible,
και τους ἐκλεκτους.	even the elect.
²⁵ἰδου προειρηκα ὑμιν.	See, I have told you beforehand.
²⁶ἐαν οὐν εἰπωσιν ὑμιν,	So if they say to you,
Ἰδου ἐν τη ἐρημῳ ἐστιν,	"Look, he is in the desert,"
μη ἐξελθητε·	do not go out;
Ἰδου ἐν τοις ταμειοις,	"Look, in the inner rooms,"
μη πιστευσητε·	do not believe;
²⁷ὡσπερ γαρ ἡ ἀστραπη ἐξερχεται	For as the lightning goes out
ἀπο ἀνατολων	from the east
και φαινεται	and shines
ἑως δυσμων,	as far as the west,
οὑτως ἐσται ἡ παρουσια	so will be the coming
του υἱου του ἀνθρωπου·	of the Son of Man.
²⁸ὁπου ἐαν το πτωμα,	For wherever the corpse [is],
ἐκει συναχθησονται οἱ ἀετοι.	there the vultures will be gathered.

---

1. προσευχεσθε, verse 20, is a present imperative. What is its aspect and does it add anything to the meaning?

2. The word γενηται occurs in verses 20 and 21. Which verb is it from and is the construction the same in both verses?

3. Greek uses the cases to represent some concepts of time. Which cases are used for "time within which" and "time at which" (verse 20)?

4. θλιψις, εως means "tribulation". What gender is it (verse 21)?

5. In verse 22 the verb κολοβοω is used twice. What tense and voice are used?

6. Which is nearest the literal equivalent of "no person would have been saved" (verse 22)? (a) no one would have been saved (b) all flesh would not have been saved (c) no flesh would have been saved.

7. Which words in verse 23 are subjunctive mood and why is it used each time?

8. Is ἐγερθησονται, verse 24, active, middle or passive?

9. The verb πλαναω means "deceive". What construction is ὡστε πλανησαι (verse 24)?

10. ἐρημος, ου means "desert". What gender is it (verse 26)?

11. Why is the subjunctive used in the expressions μη ἐξελθητε and μη πιστευσητε (verse 26), and are they present or aorist tense?

12. Which mood follows ὡσπερ (verse 27), indicative, subjunctive or infinitive?

13. ἀνατολη, ης f means "rising". What other meaning does it have (verse 27)?

14. What is the meaning of δυσμη, ης f, and is it used in the singular or plural (verse 27)?

15. ἐαν is used in verses 23, 26 and 28. Does it have the same meaning in all these verses?

TOO MANY MOODS

In these texts you have been given an indicative, subjunctive, infinitive and participle, but only one is correct. Select the correct mood. I have not provided an English translation, but if you need it I have given the references.

Matthew 12:34

πως δυνασθε ἀγαθα [*] πονηροι ὀντες;
[λαλειτε / λαλητε / λαλειν / λαλουντες]

Mark 9:37

ὁς ἀν ἐν των τοιουτων παιδιων [*] ἐπι τῳ ὀνοματι μου, ἐμε δεχεται.
[ἐδεξατο / δεξηται / δεξασθαι / δεξαμενος]

Luke 14:3

Ἐξεστιν τῳ σαββατῳ [*] ἠ οὐ;
[ἐθεραπευσεν / θεραπευσῃ / θεραπευσαι / θεραπευσαντι]

John 12:47

οὐ γαρ [*] ἱνα κρινω τον κοσμον, ἀλλ' ἱνα σωσω τον κοσμον.
[ἠλθον / ἐλθω / ἐλθειν / ἐλθων]

John 18:8

[*] Ἰησους, Εἰπον ὑμιν ὁτι ἐγω εἰμι.
[ἀπεκριθη / ἀποκριθῃ / ἀποκριθηναι / ἀποκριθεις]

John 21:24

οὗτος ἐστιν ὁ μαθητης ὁ μαρτυρων περι τουτων και ὁ [*] ταυτα.
[ἐγραψεν / γραψῃ / γραψαι / γραψας]

Romans 14:3

ὁ δε μη ἐσθιων τον [*] μη κρινετω.
[ἐσθιει / ἐσθιῃ / ἐσθιειν / ἐσθιοντα]

1 John 2:1

Τεκνια μου, ταυτα γραφω ὑμιν ἱνα μη [*].
[ἡμαρτετε / ἁμαρτητε / ἁμαρτειν / ἁμαρτων]

WORDS TO LEARN

ἀλληλους (ων, οις)   one another.
   ἀγαπατε ἀλληλους = Love one another.
ἁμαρτωλος, ου m sinner
δει it is necessary.
   δει με ποιειν τουτο = I must do this.
δυναμαι be able
εἰρηνη, ης f peace
ἐξεστιν it is lawful.   ἐξεστιν μοι = It is lawful for me.
εὑρισκω, fut. εὑρησω, aor. act. εὑρον, aor. pass.
   εὑρεθην find
μελλω be about to, intend.
   μελλει ἐλθειν = He is about to go.
ναι yes
οὐ no
παιδιον, ου n child
πλαναω deceive
πορευομαι, aor. ἐπορευθην go

προσκυνεω + dative   worship
σταυροω   crucify
τεκνον, ου n   child
φοβεομαι (φοβοῦμαι), aor. ἐφοβηθην   fear
χρεια, ας f   need
χρονος, ου m   time
ὣστε   so that (expressing result)

CHAPTER FOURTEEN

Preview

Questions

How? what? when? where? why?

Who?

Someone anyone

Questions expecting the answer "yes"

Questions expecting the answer "no" and hesitant
  questions

CHAPTER FOURTEEN

Questions questions

14.1   In Chapter 2 we learned that Greek makes no
distinction in word order between statements and
questions. Only the presence of a Greek question
mark (;) tells us that we are dealing with a question.
In the earliest manuscripts of the New Testament
they did not use any punctuation and so there are
some texts which could have been either statements
or questions.

Did he or didn't he?

14.2   In John 12:27–28 there is an account of Jesus praying
to his Father.

> Νυν ἡ ψυχη μου τεταρακται,
> και τί εἰπω;
> Πατερ, σωσον με ἐκ της ὡρας ταυτης;
> ἀλλα δια τουτο ἠλθον εἰς την ὡραν ταυτην.
> πατερ, δοξασον σου το ὀνομα.

Most English versions translate it along these lines:

> Now is my soul troubled,
> and what shall I say?
> "Father, save me from this hour"?
> But for this reason I came to this hour.
> Father, glorify your name.

Notice the use of the deliberative subjunctive in τί
εἰπω; (what am I to say?) Notice also the aorist
imperatives σωσον (save) and δοξασον (glorify, from
δοξαζω).

A different translation

14.3   The New English Bible has a different approach at this point. It reads,

> 'Now my soul is in turmoil,
> and what am I to say?
> Father save me from this hour.
> No, it was for this that I came to this hour.
> Father, glorify thy name.'

The middle line of the five has become a statement. The NEB is following a punctuation of the Greek text that has

Πατερ, σωσον με ἐκ της ὡρας ταυτης.

14.4   Did Jesus pray this prayer or not? If a full stop is correct then the prayer is a real request. His prayer in Matthew 26:39 would support such an interpretation. If a question mark is the correct punctuation then the request was only considered, and rejected. Jesus was probably using the words of Psalm 6:3–4 at this point, a psalm which he applied to himself in Matthew 7:23.

Unambiguous questions

14.5   Most questions give a clear signal that they are questions because they are introduced by words like who, what, when, why, where and how.

Exercise 14.5

Analyze these texts and identify the various Greek words which are used to introduce questions. Then fill in the chart.

Matthew 2:1–2

¹Του δε Ἰησου γεννηθεντος ἐν Βηθλεεμ της Ἰουδαιας
ἐν ἡμεραις Ἡρῳδου του βασιλεως,
ἰδου μαγοι ἀπο ἀνατολων παρεγενοντο εἰς Ἰεροσολυμα
²λεγοντες, **Που** ἐστιν ὁ τεχθεις βασιλευς των Ἰουδαιων;
εἰδομεν γαρ αὐτου τον ἀστερα ἐν τη ἀνατολη
και ἡλθομεν προσκυνησαι αὐτῳ.

¹When Jesus was born in Bethlehem of Judea
in the days of Herod the king,
behold magi from the east came to Jerusalem
²saying, "Where is the one who was born king of the Jews?
For we have seen his star in the east
and we have come to worship him."

Matthew 24:3

Καθημενου δε αὐτου ἐπι του Ὀρους των Ἐλαιων
προσηλθον αὐτῳ οἱ μαθηται κατ᾽ ἰδιαν λεγοντες,
Εἰπε ἡμιν, **ποτε** ταυτα ἐσται
και **τι** το σημειον της σης παρουσιας και συντελειας του
αἰωνος;

As he sat on the Mount of Olives
the disciples came to him privately saying,
"Tell us, when will these things be
and what [will be] the sign of your coming and the end of the
age?"

John 9:19

και ἡρωτησαν αὐτους λεγοντες,
Οὑτος ἐστιν ὁ υἱος ὑμων, ὁν ὑμεις λεγετε ὁτι τυφλος
ἐγεννηθη;
πως οὐν βλεπει ἀρτι;

And they asked them saying,
"Is this your son, whom you say that he was born blind?
How then does he see now?"

John 13:37

λεγει αὐτῷ ὁ Πετρος,
Κυριε, **δια τί** οὐ δυναμαι σοι ἀκολουθησαι ἀρτι;
την ψυχην μου ὑπερ σου θησω.

Peter said to him,
"Lord, why can I not follow you now?
I will lay down my life for you."

John 18:23

ἀπεκριθη αὐτῷ ᾽Ιησους,
Εἰ κακως ἐλαλησα, μαρτυρησον περι του κακου·
εἰ δε καλως, **τί** με δερεις;

Jesus answered him,
"If I have spoken wrongly, testify about the wrong;
but if [I have spoken] well, why do you strike me?"

HOW   _____

WHAT   _____

WHEN   _____

WHERE   _____

WHY   _____ or _____ _____

14.6   When the words πότε, ποῦ, πῶς and τί are used to ask
       questions they are printed with an accent. They are
       also used without an accent but with different mean-
       ings. ποτε means *once, ever*. που means *somewhere*.
       πως means *somehow*, and τι will be dealt with in
       section 14.10.

Who what and why

14.7 You will see from the chart that the same word can be used for "what" and "why", that there are two ways of saying "why", and that I have not said anything yet about "who". There is a connection between all these words. Look at these examples.

Matthew 12:48

ὁ δε ἀποκριθεις εἶπεν τῳ λεγοντι αὐτῳ,
Τίς ἐστιν ἡ μητηρ μου
και τίνες εἰσιν οἱ ἀδελφοι μου;

But he answered the man who was speaking to him,
"**Who** is my mother
and **who** are my brothers?"

Mark 12:16

και λεγει αὐτοις, Τίνος ἡ εἰκων αὑτη και ἡ ἐπιγραφη;
οἱ δε εἶπαν αὐτῳ, Καισαρος.

And he said to them, "**Whose** [is] this image and inscription?"
And they said to him, "Caesar's."

Another photofit word

14.8 What we have here is another photofit word. It follows the 3–3 pattern (Chapter 10 section 10.9). In Matthew 12:48 the need for singular and plural forms is illustrated. In Mark 12:16 we see the need for different cases, e.g. genitive. Here is the full pattern.

		MASCULINE/ FEMININE	NEUTER
SINGULAR	Nom	τίς	τί
	Acc	τίνα	τί
	Gen	τίνος	τίνος
	Dat	τίνι	τίνι
PLURAL	Nom	τίνες	τίνα
	Acc	τίνας	τίνα
	Gen	τίνων	τίνων
	Dat	τίσιν	τίσιν

Exercise 14.8

Identify the correct form of τίς, τί in the following texts.

John 18:4

Ἰησους οὖν εἰδὼς παντα τα ἐρχομενα ἐπ' αὐτον ἐξηλθεν και λεγει αὐτοις, __(1)__ ζητειτε;

So Jesus, knowing everything which was coming upon him, went out and said to them, "**Whom** do you seek?"

Hebrews 1:5

__(2)__ γαρ εἰπεν ποτε των ἀγγελων,
  Υἱος μου εἶ συ,
    ἐγω σημερον γεγεννηκα σε;

For **to which** of the angels did he ever say,
  "You are my Son,
    today I have become your Father"?

[Notice ποτε without an accent here.]

Hebrews 3:18

___(3)___ δε ὤμοσεν μη εἰσελευσεσθαι εἰς την καταπαυσιν αὐτου
εἰ μη τοις ἀπειθησασιν;

And **to whom** did he swear that they would not enter into his rest if not to those who disobeyed?

14.9 The question "what" is usually τί. The question "why" is δια τί. The preposition δια, followed by the accusative, means "because of / on account of"; hence δια τί is "because of what?" or "why?" This was often abbreviated simply to τί.

Who is anyone with an accent

14.10 I have written τίς, meaning "who", with an accent. The same word is used **without an accent** to mean someone/something, or anyone/anything. τις can be used on its own, meaning "someone". It can also be used with a noun, as in the expression ἀνθρωπος τις, "a certain man", and often it is not translated, i.e. "a man".

Look at these examples.

Matthew 16:28

ἀμην λεγω ὑμιν ὁτι εἰσιν **τινες** των ὡδε ἑστωτων
οἵτινες οὐ μη γευσωνται θανατου
ἑως ἀν ἰδωσιν τον υἱον του ἀνθρωπου
ἐρχομενον ἐν τῃ βασιλειᾳ αὐτου.

Truly I tell you that there are **some** of those standing here
who will certainly not taste death
until they see the Son of Man
coming in his kingdom.

[In line two you will see an alternative form of the relative pronoun ὁστις. The interesting thing about it is that both constituent parts change; ὁς becomes οἵ and τις becomes τινες.]

Mark 9:38

Ἐφη αὐτῷ ὁ Ἰωαννης·
Διδασκαλε, εἰδομεν **τινα** ἐν τῳ ὀνοματι σου ἐκβαλλοντα
δαιμονια και ἐκωλυομεν αὐτον, ὁτι οὐκ ἠκολουθει ἡμιν.

John said to him,
"Teacher, we saw **someone** casting out demons in your name and
we tried to stop him, because he was not following us."

Mark 12:13

Και ἀποστελλουσιν προς αὐτον
τινας των Φαρισαιων και των Ἡρῳδιανων
ἱνα αὐτον ἀγρευσωσιν λογῳ.

And they sent to him
some of the Pharisees and the Herodians
that they might trap him by a word.

[There are two ways of understanding the third line, depending on whether λογῳ
refers to Jesus' words or those of his opponents. So the Good News Bible says they
were sent "to trap him with questions," and the New Revised Standard Version.
says they were sent "to trap him in what he said".]

Acts 16:1

Κατηντησεν δε και εἰς Δερβην και εἰς Λυστραν.
και ἰδου μαθητης **τις** ἠν ἐκει ὀνοματι Τιμοθεος,
υἱος γυναικος Ἰουδαιας πιστης, πατρος δε Ἑλληνος.

And he came also to Derbe and Lystra.
And behold a **certain** disciple was there, Timothy by name,
the son of a believing Jewish woman, but of a Greek father.

Loaded questions

14.11　Two words are used for "not" in Greek, οὐ and μη.
Roughly speaking, **οὐ** is used when verbs are making
statements or asking questions (the indicative mood),
and **μη** is used for everything else (subjunctive,
imperative, infinitive, etc).

The two forms of the negative have another use. They have a special function when they appear in questions.

Questions expecting the answer "yes"

14.12 When οὐ is used in a question it means the question expects the answer "yes". It is not always easy to make this clear in an English translation and so a knowledge of the Greek text is a distinct advantage. "Yes" is the answer expected by the person asking the question – not necessarily the answer given.

Matthew 7:22

πολλοι ἐροῦσιν μοι ἐν ἐκεινῃ τῃ ἡμερᾳ,
Κυριε, κυριε, οὐ τῳ σῳ ὀνοματι ἐπροφητευσαμεν,
και τῳ σῳ ὀνοματι δαιμονια ἐξεβαλομεν,
και τῳ σῳ ὀνοματι δυναμεις πολλας ἐποιησαμεν;

Many will say to me on that day,
"Lord, lord, did we not prophesy in your name,
and cast out demons in your name,
and do many miracles in your name?"

They expected the answer "yes", but the reply of Jesus was to be, "I never knew you."

Questions expecting the answer "no"

14.13 When μη is used in a question it means the question expects the answer "no". Again, this is the answer expected by the person putting the question.

John 3:4

λεγει προς αὐτον ὁ Νικοδημος·
Πῶς δυναται ἀνθρωπος γεννηθηναι γερων ὤν;
μη δυναται εἰς την κοιλιαν της μητρος αὐτου
δευτερον εἰσελθειν και γεννηθηαι;

Nicodemus said to him,
"How can a man be born when he is old?
Can he enter his mother's womb a second time
and be born?"

Clearly, Nicodemus expected the answer "no" to this
question.

Hesitant questions

14.14   **Μη** is also used in hesitant questions. Only the
context makes it clear whether a negative answer is
expected or whether the questioner is unsure what
the answer should be.

John 18:17

λεγει οὐν τῳ Πετρῳ ἡ παιδισκη ἡ θυρωρος,
Μη και συ ἐκ των μαθητων εἶ του ἀνθρωπου τουτου;
λεγει ἐκεινος· Οὐκ εἰμι.

The maid who kept the door said to Peter,
"Aren't you one of this man's disciples as well?"
He said, "I am not."

Exercise 14.14

Match the following texts to the appropriate translations, and then identify the type of question as
expecting the answer "yes" (Y), "no" (N), or a
hesitant question (H). Use an English Bible to help
you put the texts in context. The first one has been
done as an example.

1. Are you not worth more than they?
   (Matthew 6:26)

2. Will he give him a stone?
   (Matthew 7:10)

3. Have you not read what David did when he was hungry, and those with him?
   (Matthew 12:3)

4. Is this not the carpenter's son?
   (Matthew 13:55)

5. Are you greater than our father Jacob?
   (John 4:12)

6. Can this be the Christ?
   (John 4:29)

7. When the Christ comes, will he do more signs than this man has done? (John 7:31)

8. Are you also from Galilee? (John 7:52)

9. Can a demon open the eyes of the blind?
   (John 10:21)

10. Are all apostles?
    (1 Corinthians 12:29)

A. Οὐκ ἀνεγνωτε τί ἐποιησεν Δαυιδ ὁτε ἐπεινασεν και οἱ μετ' αὐτου;

B. μη δαιμονιον δυναται τυφλων ὀφθαλμους ἀνοιξαι;

C. Μη και συ ἐκ της Γαλιλαιας εἶ;

D. μη λιθον ἐπιδωσει αὐτῳ;

E. Οὐχ οὑτος ἐστιν ὁ του τεκτονος υἱος;

F. μητι οὑτος ἐστιν ὁ Χριστος;

G. μη παντες ἀποστολοι;

H. μη παντες γλωσσαις λαλουσιν;

I. μη συ μειζων εἶ του πατρος ἡμων Ἰακωβ;

J. οὐχ ὑμεις μαλλον διαφερετε αὐτων;

11. Do all speak in
    tongues?
    (1 Corinthians 12:30)

K. Ὁ Χριστος ὁταν ἐλθῃ
   μη πλεονα σημεια
   ποιησει ὡν οὑτος
   ἐποιησεν;

1	2	3	4	5	6	7	8	9	10	11
J										
Y										

Answers to Exercises

Exercise 14.5

HOW	πῶς
WHAT	τί
WHEN	πότε
WHERE	ποῦ
WHY	τί or δια τί

Exercise 14.8

(1) τίνα   (2) τίνι   (3) τίσιν

Exercise 14.14

1	2	3	4	5	6	7	8	9	10	11
J	D	A	E	I	F	K	C	B	G	H
Y	N	Y	Y	N	H	N	N	N	N	N

REVIEW QUESTIONS

1. What punctuation was used in the earliest Greek manuscripts?

2. What difference, apart from punctuation, does Greek make between statements and questions?

3. In what way do most questions signal clearly that they are questions?

4. What is the meaning of διὰ τί, πότε, ποῦ, πῶς, τί?

5. What is the meaning of ποτε, που and πως?

6. What is the connection between the Greek for "who", "what", and "why" in questions?

7. What is the full pattern of τίς?

8. What does τις mean when written without an accent?

9. When is οὐ used as a negative and when is μη used?

10. What are the special functions of οὐ and μη when used in questions?

11. How can you tell whether a question is hesitant or expecting the answer "no"?

REVIEW EXERCISES

A PUNCTUATION PROBLEM

The text of Matthew 11:7–9 is printed below with an English translation. What is the difference in punctuation in the second version and how should it be translated?

A. Τουτων δε πορευομενων
   ἠρξατο ὁ Ἰησους λεγειν τοις ὀχλοις περι Ἰωαννου,
   Τί ἐξηλθατε εἰς την ἐρημον θεασθαι;
   καλαμον ὑπο ἀνεμου σαλευομενον;
   ἀλλα τί ἐξηλθατε ἰδειν;
   ἀνθρωπον ἐν μαλακοις ἠμφιεσμενον;
   ἰδου οἱ τα μαλακα φορουντες ἐν τοις οἰκοις των
   βασιλεων εἰσιν.
   ἀλλα τί ἐξηλθατε ἰδειν; προφητην;
   ναι λεγω ὑμιν, και περισσοτερον προφητου.

As these people were going
Jesus began to speak to the crowds about John:
"What did you go out into the desert to see?
A reed shaken by the wind?
But what did you go out to see?
A man dressed in soft clothes?
Listen, those who wear soft clothes are in kings' houses.
But what did you go out to see? A prophet?
Yes, I tell you, and much more than a prophet."

B. Τουτων δε πορευομενων
ηρξατο ὁ Ἰησους λεγειν τοις ὀχλοις περι Ἰωαννου,
Τί ἐξηλθατε εἰς την ἐρημον;
θεασθαι καλαμον ὑπο ἀνεμου σαλευομενον;
ἀλλα τί ἐξηλθατε;
ἰδειν ἀνθρωπον ἐν μαλακοις ἠμφιεσμενον;
ἰδου οἱ τα μαλακα φορουντες ἐν τοις οἰκοις των
βασιλεων εἰσιν.
ἀλλα τί ἐξηλθατε; ἰδειν προφητην;
ναι λεγω ὑμιν, και περισσοτερον προφητου.

WHEN WHERE HOW

In this exercise you have to supply the correct word, πότε,
ποῦ or πῶς. English translations are provided but not in the
same order as the Greek texts.

1. ἀλλα ἐρεῖ τις, [*] ἐγειρονται οἱ νεκροι; ποιῳ δε σωματι
ἐρχονται;

2. εἰ ὁλον το σωμα ὀφθαλμος, [*] ἡ ἀκοη; εἰ ὁλον ἀκοη,
[*] ἡ ὀσφρησις;

3. εἰ οὖν Δαυιδ καλει αὐτον κυριον, [*] υἱος αὐτου ἐστιν;

4. εἶπεν δε αὐτοις, [*] ἡ πιστις ὑμων; φοβηθεντες δε
ἐθαυμασαν.

5. ἐλεγον οὖν αὐτῳ, [*] ἐστιν ὁ πατηρ σου;

6. οἱτινες ἀπεθανομεν τη ἁμαρτιᾳ, [*] ἐτι ζησομεν ἐν αὐτη;

7. [*] δε σε εἰδομεν ἀσθενουντα ἡ ἐν φυλακη και ἠλθομεν
προς σε;

8. [*] θελεις ἀπελθοντες ἐτοιμασωμεν ἱνα φαγης το πασχα;

So if David calls him lord, how is he his son? (Matthew 22:45).

When did we see you ill or in prison and come to you? (Matthew 25:39).

Where do you want us to go and prepare for you to eat the passover? (Mark 14:12).

And he said to them, "Where is your faith?" And they were afraid and amazed. (Luke 8:25).

So they said to him, "Where is your father?" (John 8:19).

We who have died to sin, how shall we still live in it? (Romans 6:2).

If the whole body were an eye, where would the hearing be? If the whole were hearing, where would the sense of smell be? (1 Corinthians 12:17).

But someone will say, "How are the dead raised? With what kind of body do they come?" (1 Corinthians 15:35).

TO SEE OR NOT TO SEE
THAT IS THE QUESTION

The lines of John 9:13–17 have been jumbled up. Can you put them back into the correct order? Use an English translation if it is too difficult without one. The first line is in the right place.

1. Ἀγουσιν αὐτον προς τους Φαρισαιους

2. αὐτοις. λεγουσιν οὐν τω τυφλω παλιν,

3. αὐτοις, Πηλον ἐπεθηκεν μου ἐπι τους

4. ἐλεγον, Πῶς δυναται ἀνθρωπος ἁμαρτωλος τοιαυτα

5. ἐν ἧ ἡμερᾳ τον πηλον ἐποιησεν ὁ

6. Ἰησους και ἀνεῳξεν αὐτου τους

7. ὅτι το σαββατον οὐ τηρει. ἀλλοι δε

8. Οὐκ ἐστιν οὑτος παρα θεου ὁ ἀνθρωπος,

9. οὐν ἐκ των Φαρισαιων τινες,

10. ὀφθαλμους και ἐνιψαμην και βλεπω. ἐλεγον

11. ὀφθαλμους; ὁ δε εἰπεν ὁτι Προφητης ἐστιν.

12. ὀφθαλμους. παλιν οὐν ἠρωτων αὐτον και οἱ

13. σημεια ποιειν; και σχισμα ἠν ἐν

14. Τί συ λεγεις περι αὐτου, ὁτι ἠνεῳξεν σου τους

15. τον ποτε τυφλον. ἠν δε σαββατον

16. Φαρισαιοι πῶς ἀνεβλεψεν. ὁ δε εἰπεν

WORDS TO LEARN

αἰων, αἰωνος m age. εἰς τον αἰωνα for ever

ἀλλος, η, ο other

γαρ for (never first in its sentence)

γυνη, γυναικος f woman, wife. Vocative γυναι

ἑως until. ἑως πότε (until when?) how long?

μη not

οὐν therefore (never first in its sentence)

ὀφθαλμος, ου m eye

παρουσια, ας f coming, presence

πότε when?

ποῦ where?

πῶς how?

σαββατον, ου n sabbath (often in plural). Dative plural, σαββασιν

σημειον, ου n sign

τις, τι someone, any one, etc.

τίς, τί who? what? τί and δια τί why?

τυφλος, η, ον blind
ψυχη, ης f soul, life
ὡρα, ας f hour
ὡς as (also καθως)

CHAPTER FIFTEEN

Preview

The optative mood

The moods of the present and aorist tenses compared

The imperfect tense

The perfect tense

The pluperfect tense

The meanings of the four past tenses

γινωσκω, οἰδα and ἐγνωκα

The perfect tense: infinitive and participle

CHAPTER FIFTEEN

Getting the right nuance

Completing the picture

15.1 We have now been formally introduced to all the moods of the verb with one exception, and that is the **optative** mood. It is very rare in the New Testament and where it does occur it is mainly in the writings of Paul and Luke. It is used for wishes or indirect questions and in its endings there is usually a diphthong – **αι, ει** or **οι**. Here are some samples.

Luke 1:38

εἶπεν δε Μαριαμ· Ἰδου ἡ δουλη κυριου· **γενοιτο** μοι κατα το ρημα σου.

Mary said, "See, [I am] the servant of the Lord. **May it be** to me according to your word."

Luke 8:9

Ἐπηρωτων δε αὐτον οἱ μαθηται αὐτου τίς αὐτη **εἴη** ἡ παραβολη.

His disciples asked him what this parable **might be** [i.e. mean].

1 Thessalonians 3:12

ὑμας δε ὁ κυριος **πλεονασαι** και **περισσευσαι** τη ἀγαπη εἰς ἀλληλους και εἰς παντας καθαπερ και ἡμεις εἰς ὑμας.

May the Lord **make** you **increase** and **abound** in love to one another and to all just as we [do] to you.

In Paul's letter to the Romans, 10 of the 12 occurrences are in the phrase, μη γενοιτο, literally "may it not happen". It can be translated, "Certainly not!" or "By no means!" (e.g. Romans 3:4,6).

15.2   It is helpful to see the moods of the present and aorist set out side by side. It draws attention to the importance of the **aspect** of the two tenses, continuous [---] and neutral [●].

Active

	INDICATIVE	SUBJUNCTIVE	IMPERATIVE	*	INFINITIVE	PARTICIPLE
PRESENT ---	πιστευω πιστευεις πιστευει πιστευομεν πιστευετε πιστευουσιν	πιστευω πιστευης πιστευη πιστευωμεν πιστευητε πιστευωσιν	 πιστευε πιστευετω πιστευετε πιστευετωσαν		πιστευειν	πιστευων ουσα ον
AORIST ●	επιστευσα επιστευσας επιστευσεν επιστευσαμεν επιστευσατε επιστευσαν	πιστευσω πιστευσης πιστευση πιστευσωμεν πιστευσητε πιστευσωσιν	 πιστευσον πιστευσατω πιστευσατε πιστευσατωσαν		πιστευσαι	πιστευσας ασα αν

* Optative not included

This chart of approximate English equivalents shows that the type of action is a much more relevant concept than time of action, except with the indicative and participle.

	INDICATIVE	SUBJUNCTIVE	IMPERATIVE	[ ]	INFINITIVE	PARTICIPLE
PRESENT ---	I believe you believe he believes we believe you believe they believe	I may b. you may b. he may b. we may b. you may b. they may b.	 believe let him b. believe let them b.		to believe	believing
AORIST ●	I believed you believed he believed we believed you believed they believed	I may b. you may b. he may b. we may b. you my b. they may b.	 believe let him b. believe let them b.		to believe	having believed

Not forgetting the middle and passive

15.3   Πιστευω, of course, is active. The same basic layout
of moods is duplicated for middle and passive forms.
Here is a brief outline. A fuller chart is given in the
Reference Section at the end of the book.

Middle

	INDICATIVE	SUBJUNCTIVE	IMPERATIVE	[ ]	INFINITIVE	PARTICIPLE
PRES ---	δεχομαι	δεχωμαι	δεχου		δεχεσθαι	δεχομενος η ον
AOR ●	ἐδεξαμην	δεξωμαι	δεξω		δεξασθαι	δεξαμενος η ον

	INDICATIVE	SUBJUNCTIVE	IMPERATIVE	[ ]	INFINITIVE	PARTICIPLE
PRES	I receive	I may receive	receive		to receive	receiving
AOR ●	I received	I may receive	receive		to receive	having received

Passive

	INDICATIVE	SUBJUNCTIVE	IMPERATIVE	[ ]	INFINITIVE	PARTICIPLE
PRES –––	πιστευομαι	πιστευωμαι	πιστευου		πιστευεσθαι	πιστευομενος η ον
AOR ●	ἐπιστευθην	πιστευθω	πιστευθητι		πιστευθηναι	πιστευθεις εισα εν

	INDICATIVE	SUBJUNCTIVE	IMPERATIVE	[ ]	INFINITIVE	PARTICIPLE
PRES –––	I am believed	I may be believed	be believed		to be believed	being believed
AOR ●	I was believed	I may be believed	be believed		to be believed	having been believed

More options for reporting the past

15.4   The indicative mood is the one which is most closely linked to the **time** of the action. In Chapter 2 we looked at action in the present; in Chapter 6 we examined action in the future and in Chapter 8 we saw how past action is handled, noting that the name of the tense for past action was "aorist" rather than "past".

The reason for this is that Greek has not just one but four past tenses, and each has its own "aspect" or special nuance in addition to the time reference. They are called **aorist**, **imperfect**, **perfect** and **pluperfect**.

15.5   Here is a reminder of the way the aorist is constructed.

> ἐ* + stem + σ* + endings
> (* or equivalent)

There are four elements, giving us, for example, ἐπιστευσα.

Exercise 15.5

Fill in the gaps in these descriptions of the imperfect, perfect and pluperfect. (For now we shall just consider the active voice.)

The Imperfect Indicative

> ἐ* + stem + endings
> (* or equivalent)

- There are _____ elements, giving us, for example, ἐπίστευον.
- The personal endings are ον, ες, εν, ομεν, ετε, ον. They are the same as the endings of the

  _____ _____.

  So, for example, from βαλλω (throw) we get
  Imperfect   ἐβαλλον   I was throwing
  2nd aorist   ἐβαλον   I threw

The Perfect Indicative

> (First letter + ε*) + stem + κ + endings
> (* or equivalent)

- There are four elements, giving us, for example, πεπιστευκα.
- The first letter of the stem is doubled and the letters are joined by ε. So πιστευ becomes πε πιστευ.
- Verbs beginning with a vowel cannot double the first letter. They simply lengthen the vowel.

  For example, from αἰτεω (ask) we get ᾐτηκα, I have asked.

- When a stem begins with χ, φ or θ, these changes happen:

  χ becomes κεχ-, φ becomes πεφ-, θ becomes τεθ-. From φιλεω (love) we get πεφιληκα, I have loved.

- The personal endings are α, ας, εν, αμεν, ατε, ασιν. They are the same as the _____ endings except for the "they" ending (ασιν).

The Pluperfect Indicative

> [ἐ] + (first letter + ε*) + stem + κ + endings
> (* or equivalent)

- There are _____ elements, giving us, for example, ἐπεπιστευκειν. The initial augment is not always used.

- Where the beginning of the perfect tense differs from the standard format the pluperfect behaves in the same way.

  For example ᾔτηκα, I have asked (perfect)
  ᾔτηκειν, I had asked (pluperfect)

- The personal endings are ειν, εις, ει, ειμεν, ειτε, εισαν.

- The pluperfect is not very common in the New Testament.

Layers of meaning

15.6 The aorist tense can be seen as the basic tense – straightforward, neutral, no frills. The imperfect, perfect and pluperfect each add a layer of meaning to the basic description. Before we look at some New Testament examples read through these sentences in English.

1. Last year **I went** on holiday to Frinton.
2. As **I was going** to the beach I lost my money somewhere.
3. When I came home my neighbour said, "You've got a great tan." "Yes, I said, **I have been** on holiday."
4. I'm rather pale now but last September I was really brown after **I had been** on holiday.

15.7   These English verbs illustrate the meanings of the four past tenses in Greek.

1. *I went*. That is equivalent to an aorist, a plain statement. We can use the symbol [●] for it.
2. *I was going*. That is equivalent to an imperfect, describing an event that was continuing. It was as I was going [---] that I lost [●] the money.
3. *I have been*. That is equivalent to a perfect. The action is in the past but it has consequences in the present [●→]. The emphasis is not so much on the holiday but its results – the tan.
4. *I had been*. That is equivalent to a pluperfect. Again the emphasis is on the consequences of the action, but this time the results as well as the action are in the past. We can represent this by the symbol [●→ ●].

The extra layer of meaning provided by the imperfect tense is the idea of the action **continuing**. The extra layer provided by the perfect and pluperfect tenses is the idea of the **consequences** of the action.

Watch and learn

15.8   The rules outlined in section 15.5 are a necessary starting point but they apply to verbs which behave in a regular way, and unfortunately many verbs are irregular in some way. However a dictionary will give information about any irregularities.

Exercise 15.8

Aorist and imperfect

In this part of the exercise you are given pairs of texts containing a verb used in both the aorist and the imperfect tenses (indicated by the appropriate symbols). Explain briefly why those tenses have been selected. You may use an English Bible to check the contexts.

1. θεραπευω, *heal*

και ἐξεβαλεν τα πνευματα λογῳ, και παντας τους κακως ἐχοντας ἐθεραπευσεν [●].	And he cast out the demons with a word, and all who were sick he healed (Matthew 8:16).
ὁ δε ἑνι ἑκαστῳ αὐτων τας χειρας ἐπιτιθεις ἐθεραπευεν [---] αὐτους.	And on each one of them he laid his hands and healed them (Luke 4:40).

2. ἀποθνησκω, *die*, 2nd aor. ἀπεθανον (compound of ἀπο + θνησκω)

θυγατηρ μονογενης ἠν αὐτῳ ὡς ἐτων δωδεκα και αὐτη ἀπεθνησκεν [---].	He had an only daughter about twelve years old and she was dying (Luke 8:42).
Ἐτι αὐτου λαλουντος ἐρχονται ἀπο του ἀρχισυναγωγου λεγοντες ὁτι, Ἡ θυγατηρ σου ἀπεθανεν [●].	While he was still speaking they came from the synagogue ruler saying, "Your daughter has died" (Mark 5:35).

3. γινωσκω, *know*, aor. ἐγνων.

This verb has a completely irregular aorist indicative: ἐγνων, ἐγνως, ἐγνω, ἐγνωμεν, ἐγνωτε, ἐγνωσαν.

και οὐκ ἐγινωσκεν [---] αὐτην ἑως οὑ ἑτεκεν υἱον και ἐκαλεσεν το ὀνομα αὐτου Ἰησουν.	And he did not know her until she had borne a son and he called his name Jesus (Matthew 1:25).

Και ακουσαντες οι αρχιερεις και οι Φαρισαιοι τας παραβολας αυτου εγνωσαν [●] οτι περι αυτων λεγει.	And when the chief priests and the Pharisees heard his parables they knew that he was speaking about them (Matthew 21:45).

4. αναγινωσκω, _read_ (compound of ανα + γινωσκω)

ο δε ειπεν αυτοις, Ουκ ανεγνωτε [●] τι εποιησεν Δαυιδ;	And he said to them, "Have you not read what David did?" (Matthew 12:3).
ην τε υποστρεφων και καθημενος επι του αρματος αυτου και ανεγινωσκεν [– – –] τον προφητην Ησαϊαν.	He was returning and sitting in his chariot and he was reading the prophet Isaiah (Acts 8:28).

5. εχω, _have_, impf. ειχον; 2nd aor. εσχον.

και λεγει αυτοις, Ουδεποτε ανεγνωτε τι εποιησεν Δαυιδ οτε χρειαν εσχεν [●] και επεινασεν αυτος και οι μετ' αυτου;	And he said to them, "Have you never read what David did when he had need and he was hungry and his companions? . . ." (Mark 2:25).
ος την κατοικησιν ειχεν [– – –] εν τοις μνημασιν.	. . . who had his dwelling among the tombs (Mark 5:3).

Aorist and perfect

In this part of the exercise pairs of texts have been selected containing the same verb used with the aorist and perfect tenses. Give a brief explanation for the choice of tenses.

6. σωζω, _save_, aor. εσωσα; perf. σεσωκα

ο δε Ιησους στραφεις και ιδων αυτην ειπεν, Θαρσει, θυγατερ· η πιστις σου σεσωκεν [●→] σε.	When Jesus turned and saw her he said, "Take heart, daughter; your faith has saved you" (Matthew 9:22).
Αλλους εσωσεν [●], εαυτον ου δυναται σωσαι.	"He saved others, himself he cannot save" (Matthew 27:42).

7. πιστευω, *believe*

και ἐφανερωσεν την δοξαν αὐτου και ἐπιστευσαν [●] εἰς αὐτον οἱ μαθηται αὐτου.	And he revealed his glory and his disciples believed in him (John 2:11).
λεγει αὐτῳ, Ναι κυριε, ἐγω πεπιστευκα [●→] ὁτι συ εἶ ὁ Χριστος ὁ υἱος του θεου ὁ εἰς τον κοσμον ἐρχομενος.	She said to him, "Yes Lord, I believe that you are the Christ, the Son of God who is coming into the world" (John 11:27).

8. γραφω, *write*; aor. ἐγραψα; perf. γεγραφα.

The perfect does not have the characteristic κ, but it does double the first letter, and the endings are regular.

και αἰτησας πινακιδιον ἐγραψεν [●] λεγων, Ἰωαννης ἐστιν ὀνομα αὐτου. και ἐθαυμασαν παντες.	And he asked for a writing tabl(and wrote, saying, "John is his name." And they were all amazed (Luke 1:63).
ἀπεκριθη ὁ Πιλατος, Ὁ γεγραφα, γεγραφα [●→].	Pilate answered, "What I have written, I have written" (John 19:22).

9. πιπτω, *fall*, 2nd aor. ἐπεσον; perf. πεπτωκα.

και ἀκουσαντες οἱ μαθηται ἐπεσαν [●] ἐπι προσωπον αὐτων και ἐφοβηθησαν σφοδρα.	And when the disciples heard it they fell down on their faces and were greatly afraid (Matthew 17:6).
μνημονευε οὐν ποθεν πεπτωκας [●→] και τα πρωτα ἐργα ποιησον.	Remember then from where you have fallen and do the former works (Revelation 2:5).

10. ἀποστελλω, *send*, aor. ἀπεστειλα; perf. ἀπεσταλκα
(compound of ἀπο + στελλω)

και ἀπεστειλεν [●] αὐτον εἰς οἰκον αὐτου λεγων, Μηδε εἰς την κωμην εἰσελθῃς.	And he sent him to his home saying, "Do not enter the village" (Mark 8:26).
τον υἱον αὐτου τον μονογενη ἀπεσταλκεν [●→] ὁ θεος εἰς τον κοσμον ἱνα ζησωμεν δι' αὐτου.	His only Son God sent into the world that we might live through him (1 John 4:9).

All the action

15.9   We can now add the middle and passive forms and set out all six tenses in a chart. For generations writers of Greek Grammars have used λυω, I loose, as a model of the regular verb. It is a very convenient "coat hanger" for displaying the different "outfits" worn by the stem of the verb.

ACTIVE	MIDDLE	PASSIVE
PRESENT		
λυω	λυομαι	λυομαι
λυεις	λυῃ	λυῃ
λυει	λυεται	λυεται
λυομεν	λυομεθα	λυομεθα
λυετε	λυεσθε	λυεσθε
λυουσιν	λυονται	λυονται

ACTIVE	MIDDLE	PASSIVE
FUTURE		
λυσω	λυσομαι	λυθησομαι
λυσεις	λυσῃ	λυθησῃ
λυσει	λυσεται	λυθησεται
λυσομεν	λυσομεθα	λυθησομεθα
λυσετε	λυσεσθε	λυθησεσθε
λυσουσιν	λυσονται	λυθησονται

IMPERFECT

ἔλυον	ἐλυομην	ἐλυομην
ἔλυες	ἐλυου	ἐλυου
ἔλυεν	ἐλυετο	ἐλυετο
ἐλυομεν	ἐλυομεθα	ἐλυομεθα
ἐλυετε	ἐλυεσθε	ἐλυεσθε
ἔλυον	ἐλυοντο	ἐλυοντο

AORIST

ἔλυσα	ἐλυσαμην	ἐλυθην
ἔλυσας	ἐλυσω	ἐλυθης
ἔλυσεν	ἐλυσατο	ἐλυθη
ἐλυσαμεν	ἐλυσαμεθα	ἐλυθημεν
ἐλυσατε	ἐλυσασθε	ἐλυθητε
ἔλυσαν	ἐλυσαντο	ἐλυθησαν

PERFECT

λελυκα	λελυμαι	λελυμαι
λελυκας	λελυσαι	λελυσαι
λελυκεν	λελυται	λελυται
λελυκαμεν	λελυμεθα	λελυμεθα
λελυκατε	λελυσθε	λελυσθε
λελυκασιν	λελυνται	λελυνται

PLUPERFECT

ἐλελυκειν	ἐλελυμην	ἐλελυμην
ἐλελυκεις	ἐλελυσο	ἐλελυσο
ἐλελυκει	ἐλελυτο	ἐλελυτο
ἐλελυκειμεν	ἐλελυμεθα	ἐλελυμεθα
ἐλελυκειτε	ἐλελυσθε	ἐλελυσθε
ἐλελυκεισαν	ἐλελυντο	ἐλελυντο

A philosophical question

15.10　One of the issues that has engaged the minds of the great philosophers is the nature of knowledge and its relationship to thought and reality. Ancient Greece produced some of the earliest of the world's leading philosophical thinkers and so perhaps we should not be surprised to find a philosophical twist to their concept of knowledge.

We have already come across two verbs which mean "I know". One is our old friend γινωσκω. The other is οἰδα. Its meaning is exactly the same, "I know", but it is actually a perfect tense. If you think about it, anything you know is in your mind because you have come to know it, even if you came to know it only a split second before. So the perfect tense [●→] is particularly apt. I have come to know and as a result I know – οἰδα.

This concept of knowledge also influences γινωσκω at times. The Good News Bible translates 1 John 2:3–4 like this:

"If we obey God's commands, then we are sure that we know him. If someone says that he knows him, but does not obey his commands, such a person is a liar and there is no truth in him."

Here is the Greek text with a more literal translation alongside.

Και ἐν τουτῳ γινωσκομεν [–––]　And by this **we know**
ὁτι ἐγνωκαμεν [●→] αὐτον,　that **we know** him,
ἐαν τας ἐντολας αὐτου τηρωμεν.　if we keep his commands.
ὁ λεγων ὁτι, Ἐγνωκα [●→] αὐτον　He who says, "**I know** him,"
και τας ἐντολας αὐτου μη τηρων,　and does not keep his commands,
ψευστης ἐστιν και ἐν τουτῳ　is a liar and in him
ἡ ἀληθεια οὐκ ἐστιν.　the truth is not.

The perfect tense of γινωσκω is ἐγνωκα, but its meaning is sometimes the same as the present tense.

More about the perfect tense

15.11 The Greek perfect tense also has an **infinitive** and a **participle**. This is how they behave, using λυω as a model.

PERFECT INFINITIVE	ACTIVE	MIDDLE & PASSIVE
	λελυκεναι	λελυσθαι

PERFECT PARTICIPLE	ACTIVE [3–1–3]	MIDDLE & PASSIVE [2–1–2]
MASCULINE	λελυκως, οτος	λελυμενος
FEMININE	λελυκυια, ας	λελυμενη
NEUTER	λελυκος, οτος	λελυμενον

EXAMPLES

1 Corinthians 2:2

ου γαρ εκρινα τι **ειδεναι** εν υμιν ει μη Ἰησουν Χριστον και τουτον **εσταυρωμενον**.

For I decided **to know** nothing among you except Jesus Christ and him **crucified**.

εἰδεναι is the (perfect) infinitive of οἰδα, and εσταυρωμενον is the perfect participle passive of σταυροω, crucify.

Acts 16:34

και ηγαλλιασατο πανοικει **πεπιστευκως** τω θεω.

And he rejoiced with all his household **having believed** in God.

The perfect participle emphasizes that his faith is permanent.

Another attempt to complete the picture

15.12 The most difficult thing to master in New Testament Greek is the complexity of the verb system. In this section I have tried to give a visual representation of the material in the earlier sections of this chapter.

The bold lines indicate the combinations of tense and mood which are common in the New Testament. The dotted lines show some which are extremely rare. I have used double lines to highlight the present and aorist tenses, which are most important in my view.

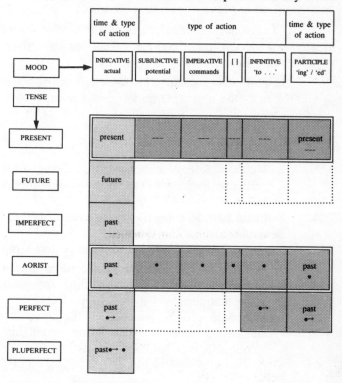

This pattern has to be repeated for active, middle and passive.

Answers to Exercises

Exercise 15.5

The imperfect indicative has *three* elements.
Its personal endings are the same as the endings of the *second aorist*.

The personal endings of the perfect indicative are the same as the *aorist* endings except for the "they" ending (ασιν).

The pluperfect indicative has *five* elements, although the first (the augment) is not always used.

Exercise 15.8

1. Matthew 8:16 describes what happened on a particular evening and so the aorist is appropriate.
   Luke 4:40 describes the same event, but Luke wants to stress that Jesus gave individual attention to each sufferer, hence the imperfect tense.

2. In Luke 8:42 Jairus, the synagogue ruler, was unaware that his daughter had died, though he knew that she "was dying" (imperfect).
   Mark 5:35 records a later stage in the story, when messengers came from his house to tell him, "Your daughter has died" (aorist).

3. In Matthew 1:25 the verb γινωσκω is used to describe intimate marital relationships (or rather the absence of them) between Joseph and Mary during the time before Jesus was born. This use of the imperfect is sometimes called "durative".
   Matthew 21:45 is describing the reaction of the Pharisees to a particular parable of Jesus. They recognized that he was speaking about them, and the aorist is used.

4. In Matthew 12:3 the emphasis does not lie on the reading but on what David did. A simple aorist is sufficient.

   Acts 8:28 describes a long journey when the time was taken up with reading the prophet Isaiah. This time an imperfect brings out the meaning better.

5. In Mark 2:25 Jesus describes an event in David's life when he had a specific need: he was hungry. The aorist draws attention to the specific occasion.

   In Mark 5:3 the reference is not to a specific occasion but the lifestyle of the man who was demon-possessed. The imperfect highlights this.

6. In Matthew 9:22 the result of Christ's saving action is in view as well as the action itself, hence the perfect.

   Matthew 27:42 records the words of the Jewish religious leaders when Jesus was on the cross. They were not intending anything other than to taunt Jesus, hence the simple aorist.

7. The context of John 2:11 links this statement to the occasion of Christ's first miracle at Cana in Galilee. Their believing was a reaction to what Christ had done.

   John 11:27 is an interesting verse, in which the perfect tense is used. Martha's "Yes" is amplified by what sounds like a formal confession of faith, which may have been used in the church of John's time as a baptismal confession. It sounds more like a liturgical statement than a spontaneous reaction.

8. The aorist in Luke 1:63 gets us straight to the point of Zechariah's decisive action.

   Pilate's use of the perfect tense in John 19:22 implies that he understands the implications of what he has written and stands by them.

9. Matthew 17:6 records the transfiguration of Jesus and the aorist is used to tell us what happened next.

   The perfect tense in Revelation 2:5 carries an extra layer of meaning. You have fallen and you are still down!

10. Mark 8:26 is a narrative passage, again telling us what happened next in the story.

    1 John 4:9 has more theological overtones, reminding the readers that the sending of Christ was not a random event but had a clear end in view.

REVIEW QUESTIONS

1. How common is the optative mood in the New Testament?

2. In what kind of constructions is the optative mood used?

3. What does μη γενοιτο mean?

4. In which moods of the verb is the time of action most important?

5. In which moods of the verb is the type of action most important?

6. Why is it necessary to speak about "the aorist tense" rather than simply "the past tense"?

7. How is the regular aorist indicative constructed?

8. How is the regular imperfect indicative constructed?

9. How is the regular perfect indicative constructed?

10. How is the regular pluperfect indicative constructed?

11. What is the difference in meaning between aorist, imperfect, perfect and pluperfect?

12. In which tenses of the verb are the middle and passive forms identical?

13. Why is a perfect tense often used to convey the meaning "I know"?

14. What is the most difficult thing to master in New Testament Greek?

REVIEW EXERCISES

SELECT A SYMBOL

Each of the verbs underlined is either aorist, imperfect, perfect or pluperfect. You are given the present tense form of the verb and you have to choose the appropriate symbol for the tense used.

- •　　　Aorist
- ---　　Imperfect
- •→　　Perfect
- •→ •　Pluperfect

Matthew 3:6 [βαπτιζω]

και ἐβαπτιζοντο ἐν τῳ ᾽Ιορδανῃ ποταμῳ ὑπ᾽ αὐτου ἐξομολογουμενοι τας ἁμαρτιας αὐτων.

And they were baptized [   ] by him in the Jordan river confessing their sins.

Matthew 19:2 [ἀκολουθεω θεραπευω]

και ἠκολουθησαν αὐτῳ ὀχλοι πολλοι, και ἐθεραπευσεν αὐτους ἐκει.

And large crowds followed [   ] him, and he healed [   ] them there.

Mark 1:9 [γινομαι ἐρχομαι βαπτιζω]

και ἐγενετο ἐν ἐκειναις ταις ἡμεραις ἠλθεν ᾽Ιησους ἀπο Ναζαρετ της Γαλιλαιας και ἐβαπτισθη εἰς τον ᾽Ιορδανην ὑπο ᾽Ιωαννου.

And it came to pass [   ] in those days Jesus came [   ] from Nazareth in Galilee and was baptized [   ] in the Jordan by John.

Mark 1:21 [εἰσερχομαι διδασκω]

και εὐθυς τοις σαββασιν <u>εἰσελθων</u> εἰς την συναγωγην
<u>ἐδιδασκεν</u>.

And immediately on the sabbath he entered [   ] the
synagogue and taught [   ].

Luke 7:50 [λεγω σῳζω]

<u>εἰπεν</u> δε προς την γυναικα, Ἡ πιστις σου <u>σεσωκεν</u>
σε· πορευου εἰς εἰρηνην.

And he said [   ] to the woman, "Your faith has made you
well [   ]; go in peace."

John 3:18 [κρινω πιστευω]

ὁ πιστευων εἰς αὐτον οὐ κρινεται· ὁ δε μη πιστευων ἠδη
<u>κεκριται</u>, ὁτι μη <u>πεπιστευκεν</u> εἰς το ὀνομα του μονογενους
υἱου του θεου.

He who believes in him is not condemned; he who does not
believe is condemned [   ] already, because he has not
believed [   ] in the name of the only Son of God.

John 7:5 [πιστευω]

οὐδε γαρ οἱ ἀδελφοι αὐτου <u>ἐπιστευον</u> εἰς αὐτον.

For not even his brothers believed [   ] in him.

John 7:48 [πιστευω]

μη τις ἐκ των ἀρχοντων <u>ἐπιστευσεν</u> εἰς αὐτον ἠ ἐκ των
Φαρισαιων;

Has any of the authorities or of the Pharisees believed [   ]
in him?

John 8:28–29 [διδασκω πεμπω]

καθως ἐδιδαξεν με ὁ πατηρ ταυτα λαλω και ὁ πεμψας με μετ' ἐμου ἐστιν.

As the Father taught [   ] me I speak these things and he who sent [   ] me is with me.

John 16:27 [φιλεω πιστευω ἐξερχομαι]

αὐτος γαρ ὁ πατηρ φιλει ὑμας, ὁτι ὑμεις ἐμε πεφιληκατε και πεπιστευκατε ὁτι ἐγω παρα του θεου ἐξηλθον.

For the Father himself loves you, because you have loved [   ] me and believed [   ] that I came [   ] from God.

Acts 14:23 [πιστευω]

προσευξαμενοι μετα νηστειων παρεθεντο αὐτους τῳ κυριῳ εἰς ὁν πεπιστευκεισαν.

When they had prayed with fasting they committed them to the Lord in whom they had believed [   ].

1 John 5:10 [ποιεω πιστευω μαρτυρεω]

ὁ πιστευων εἰς τον υἱον του θεου ἐχει την μαρτυριαν ἐν ἑαυτῳ, ὁ μη πιστευων τῳ θεῳ ψευστην πεποιηκεν αὐτον, ὁτι οὐ πεπιστευκεν εἰς την μαρτυριαν ἡν μεμαρτυρηκεν ὁ θεος περι του υἱου αὐτου.

He who believes in the Son of God has the testimony in himself; he who does not believe God has made [   ] him a liar, because he has not believed [   ] in the testimony which God has testified [   ] concerning his Son.

MIX AND MATCH

The text of John 6:59–69 is printed below. Some of the words have been highlighted and their English meanings listed, but not in the same order. By analyzing the text match the Greek words to their correct meanings.

⁵⁹ Ταυτα εἶπεν ἐν συναγωγῃ διδασκων ἐν ⸂Καφαρναουμ.⸃

⁶⁰ Πολλοι οὖν ἀκουσαντες ἐκ των μαθητων αὐτου εἶπαν, ⸂Σκληρος⸃ ἐστιν ὁ λογος οὗτος· τίς δυναται αὐτου ἀκουειν;

⁶¹ ⸂εἰδως⸃ δε ὁ 'Ιησους ἐν ἑαυτῳ ὁτι ⸂γογγυζουσιν⸃ περι τουτου οἱ μαθηται αὐτου εἶπεν αὐτοις, Τουτο ὑμας ⸂σκανδαλιζει⸃;

⁶² ἐαν οὖν ⸂θεωρητε⸃ τον υἱον του ἀνθρωπου ⸂ἀναβαινοντα⸃ ὁπου ἠν ⸂το προτερον⸃;

⁶³ το πνευμα ἐστιν το ⸂ζῳοποιουν⸃, ἡ σαρξ οὐκ ⸂ὠφελει⸃ οὐδεν· τα ⸂ρηματα⸃ ἁ ἐγω λελαληκα ὑμιν πνευμα ἐστιν και ζωη ἐστιν.

⁶⁴ ἀλλ' εἰσιν ἐξ ὑμων τινες οἳ οὐ πιστευουσιν. ⸂ἠδει⸃ γαρ ἐξ ἀρχης ὁ 'Ιησους τίνες εἰσιν οἱ μη πιστευοντες και τίς ἐστιν ⸂ὁ παραδωσων⸃ αὐτον.

⁶⁵ και ἐλεγεν, Δια τουτο ⸂εἰρηκα⸃ ὑμιν ὁτι οὐδεις δυναται ἐλθειν προς με ἐαν μη ἠ ⸂δεδομενον⸃ αὐτῳ ἐκ του πατρος.

⁶⁶ ἐκ τουτου πολλοι ἐκ των μαθητων αὐτου ἀπηλθον εἰς τα ὀπισω και ⸂οὐκετι⸃ μετ' αὐτου περιεπατουν.

⁶⁷εἶπεν οὖν ὁ Ἰησους τοις δωδεκα,
Μη και ὑμεις θελετε ὑπαγειν ;

⁶⁸ἀπεκριθη αὐτῳ Σιμων Πετρος,
Κυριε, προς τίνα ἀπελευσομεθα ;
ῥηματα ζωης αἰωνιου ἐχεις,

⁶⁹και ἡμεις πεπιστευκαμεν και ἐγνωκαμεν
ὁτι συ εἶ ὁ ἁγιος του θεου.

---

the one who would betray ● is of benefit ●
Capernaum ● formerly ● given ● giving life ● hard
● holy ● we will go ● to go ● ascending ● he
knew ● we know ● knowing ● no longer ● they
murmur ● it offends ● I said ● you see ● words

WORDS TO LEARN

ἀναγινωσκω (compound of ἀνα + γινωσκω) read
ἀποθνησκω, aor. ἀπεθανον (compound of ἀπο +
  θνησκω) die
ἐθνος, ους n nation. Plural τα ἐθνη often means "the
  gentiles".
ἑκαστος, η, ον each
θαυμαζω wonder, be amazed
θεωρεω see
Ἰουδαιος, ου m Jew
καλεω, fut. καλεσω, aor. ἐκαλεσα, aor. pass. ἐκληθην
  call
κατα (κατ', καθ') + accusative according to. (+ genitive
  = against)
    κατα τον νομον according to the law
    ἐχει τι κατα σου He has something against you.
κωμη, ης f village
λαος, ου m people

μονογενης, ες   only (i.e. an only child)
οἰδα, participle εἰδως, plupf. ἠδειν   know
οὑτως   in this way
ὀχλος, ου m   crowd
παρα (παρ') + accusative   beside (+ gen. = from; +
  dat. = with)
    παρα την θαλασσαν beside the sea
    παρα του πατρος   from the Father
    παρα τῳ πατρι   with the Father
περισσευω   abound, increase
σαρξ, σαρκος f   flesh (i.e. body, human nature, etc)
χειρ, χειρος f   hand. Dative plural χερσιν.
ψευστης, ου m   liar

CHAPTER SIXTEEN

Preview

The MI-verbs

εἰμί

εἰ and ἐαν

διδωμι

τιθημι

ἱστημι

ἱημι ἀφιημι συνιημι

ἀπολλυμι φημι δεικνυμι

CHAPTER SIXTEEN

Counterintelligence

The Secret Services

16.1 Spying and intelligence work have given novel writers almost as much scope for the imagination as the limitless possibilities of science fiction. The world of military intelligence, MI5 and MI6, has been a rich source of fictional fantasy.

If you are wondering what this has to do with New Testament Greek, the connection lies in a subject kept secret by most writers of Greek Grammar for as long as possible. I refer to the dreaded MI-verbs! Most of the verbs we have been looking at are "O" verbs. like λυω, πιστευω, etc. But there are some verbs which end in MI (μι) and it is these which we must now identify.

MI–1 εἰμι

16.2 The verb "to be" is so common that it almost teaches itself to you, and by this stage it should have a familiar ring to it. Here is a "scrambled" list of present tense endings. See if you can put them in the correct order.

Exercise 16.2

| εἶ | εἰμι | εἰσιν | ἐσμεν | ἐστε | ἐστιν |

Subjunctive imperative infinitive and participle

16.3   The subjunctive and participle of εἰμι are easy. They are simply the endings that are used by other verbs to form the present active, but on their own, i.e. without any stem.

SUBJUNCTIVE: ὦ ᾖς ᾖ ὦμεν ἦτε ὦσιν

PARTICIPLE: ὤν οὖσα ὄν (genitive ὄντος οὔσης ὄντος)

Only three parts of the **imperative** occur in the New Testament, ἴσθι be (singular), ἔστω let him be, and ἔστωσαν let them be.

The INFINITIVE is εἶναι.

Future and imperfect

16.4   The **future** of εἰμι has almost the same endings as -ομαι verbs:

ἔσομαι ἔσῃ ἔσται ἐσόμεθα ἔσεσθε ἔσονται

Exercise 16.4

Which of the future endings of εἰμι is the odd one out in comparison with regular middle endings?

16.5   The only past tense of εἰμι is the **imperfect**. Sometimes the aorist and perfect tenses of γινομαι are used where those tenses are called for, since it can be used with the meaning "to be".

Exercise 16.5

The Imperfect of εἰμι. Here is another "scrambled" list to decode, but be warned. It is not as simple as it looks.

> ἤμεν he was   ἤμεθα I was   ἤμην you (s)
> were   ἤν you (p) were   ἦς they were
> ἦσαν we were   ἦσθα ἦτε

16.6 Here are some examples containing εἰμι in different guises. Match the Greek texts to the correct English translations.

Exercise 16.6

1. και λεγετε, Εἰ **ἤμεθα** ἐν ταις ἡμεραις των πατερων ἡμων, οὐκ ἀν **ἤμεθα** αὐτων κοινωνοι ἐν τῳ αἱματι των προφητων.

2. ἐαν δε ὁ ὀφθαλμος σου πονηρος **ᾖ**, ὁλον το σωμα σου σκοτεινον **ἐσται**. εἰ ουν το φως το ἐν σοι σκοτος **ἐστιν**, το σκοτος ποσον.

3. ὑμεις ἐκ του πατρος του διαβολου **ἐστε** και τας ἐπιθυμιας του πατρος ὑμων θελετε ποιειν. ἐκεινος ἀνθρωποκτονος **ἦν** ἀπ' ἀρχης.

4. ὁ δε ὁπισω μου ἐρχομενος ἰσχυροτερος μου **ἐστιν**, οὑ οὐκ **εἰμι** ἱκανος τα ὑποδηματα βαστασαι.

5. λεγει οὐν αὐτῳ ἡ γυνη ἡ Σαμαριτις, Πως συ Ἰουδαιος **ὢν** παρ' ἐμου πειν αἰτεις γυναικος Σαμαριτιδος **οὐσης**;

6. **ἐστω** δε ὁ λογος ὑμων ναι ναι, οὑ οὑ· το δε περισσον τουτων ἐκ του πονηρου **ἐστιν**.

7. ὁ μὴ **ὢν** μετ' ἐμου κατ' ἐμου **ἐστιν**, και ὁ μὴ συναγωγων μετ' ἐμου σκορπιζει.

8. ἐγω **εἰμι** ὁ ἀρτος ὁ ζων ὁ ἐκ του οὐρανου καταβας. και ὁ ἀρτος δε ὁν ἐγω δωσω ἡ σαρξ μου **ἐστιν** ὑπερ της του κοσμου ζωης.

9. οὐ γαρ **εἰσιν** δυο ἠ τρεις συνηγμενοι εἰς το ἐμον ὀνομα, ἐκει **εἰμι** ἐν μεσῳ αὐτων.

10. ἀποκριθεις δε ὁ Πετρος εἰπεν τῳ Ἰησου, Κυριε, καλον **ἐστιν** ἡμας ὡδε **εἰναι**· εἰ θελεις, ποιησω ὡδε τρεις σκηνας.

A. But the one who is coming after me is more powerful than I, whose sandals I am not worthy to carry (Matthew 3:11).

B. When you speak let your "yes" be "yes" and your "no" be "no". Anything beyond this comes from the evil one (Matthew 5:37).

C. But if your eye is bad your whole body will be full of darkness (Matthew 6:23).

D. He who is not with me is against me, and he who does not gather with me scatters (Matthew 12:30).

E. And Peter said to Jesus, "Lord, it is good for us to be here; if you wish, I will make three shelters here" (Matthew 17:4).

F. For where two or three are gathered together in my name, I am there with them (Matthew 18:20).

G. And you say, "If we had been in the days of our fathers, we would not have taken part with them in [shedding] the blood of the prophets" (Matthew 23:30).

H. So the Samaritan woman said to him, "How is it that you being a Jew ask for [something] to drink from me being a Samaritan woman?" (John 4:9).

I. I am the living bread which came down from heaven. And the bread which I will give for the life of the world is my flesh (John 6:51).

J. You are of your father the devil and you want to do the desires of your father. He was a murderer from the beginning (John 8:44).

An "iffy" situation

16.7 The Greek text of numbers 1, 2 and 10 above contains the equivalent of our word "if". You will see that it is εἰ in numbers 1 and 10, but ἐαν in number 2.

These words have a different effect on the verb which follows them. When εἰ is used the following verb is indicative, e.g. εἰ θελεις. When ἐαν is used the following verb is subjunctive, e.g. ἐαν ἦ.

Number 1 illustrates a construction which you can only do with εἰ. To represent a condition that is contrary to fact you use εἰ in the "if-clause" and the little word ἀν in the "then-clause". The concept behind the sentence is this:

We *didn't* live in the days of the prophets, but if we *had*, we would not have joined in the killing.

This is the only construction in which ἀν is linked to a verb in the indicative. Normally it goes with a subjunctive (chapter 13, section 13.7).

MI–2 διδωμι

16.8 The verb διδωμι means "I give". It occurs frequently in the New Testament, coming in at number 9 in the chart of the most common verbs after εἰμι (to be), λεγω (say), ἐχω (have), γινομαι (become), ἐρχομαι (come), ποιεω (make, do), ὁραω (see) and ἀκουω (hear). It also occurs in compound verbs, including ἀποδιδωμι (give, give back, pay, repay) and παραδιδωμι (hand over, betray, entrust).

16.8   Its **future** is δωσω. The **aorist** active is ἐδωκα and the
perfect active is δεδωκα. (It is not difficult to mistake
ἐδωκα for a perfect; so watch out for it.) The **passive**
of the aorist is ἐδοθην. The perfect passive is δεδομαι.
The endings of all these parts are predictable, following the expected pattern.

16.9   So far so good, but the fun begins when we compare
the different moods of the present and aorist tenses.
A bit of counterintelligence is definitely called for
here to penetrate MI–2's heavy disguise.

PRESENT TENSE

Indicative	Subjunctive	Imperative	Infinitive	Participle
διδωμι	διδω			
διδως	διδῳς	διδου		
διδωσιν	διδῳ	διδοτω		
			διδοναι	διδους -ουσα -ον
διδομεν	διδωμεν			διδοντος
διδοτε	διδωτε	διδοτε		-ουσης -οντος
διδοασιν	διδωσιν	διδοτωσαν		

AORIST TENSE

Indicative	Subjunctive	Imperative	Infinitive	Participle
ἐδωκα	δῳ			
ἐδωκας	δῳς	δος		
ἐδωκεν	δῳ	δοτω		
			δουναι	δους δουσα δον
ἐδωκαμεν	δωμεν			δοντος δουσης
ἐδωκατε	δωτε	δοτε		δοντος
ἐδωκαν	δωσιν	δοτωσαν		

It is mainly the active which is used, but where
middle forms occur they are fairly easy to recognize,
διδομαι (present) and ἐδομην (aorist).

MI–3 τιθημι

16.10 It is difficult to assign an English equivalent for τιθημι. The ones that are usually given are "to place, set, appoint", but these do not cover the full range of meanings. For example τιθημι την ψυχην means "I lay down my life" and τιθημι τα γονατα means "I kneel down", literally, placing or putting the knees. Like διδωμι it occurs in several compound verbs, such as ἐπιτιθημι (place upon).

16.11 The **future** is θησω, the **aorist** active ἐθηκα, and the aorist passive ἐτεθην. The **perfect** active is τεθεικα, and the perfect middle/passive is τεθειμαι. Again it is the various moods of the present and aorist that need to be noted carefully.

PRESENT TENSE

Indicative	Subjunctive	Imperative	Infinitive	Participle
τιθημι	τιθω			
τιθης	τιθης	τιθει		
τιθησιν	τιθη	τιθετω		
			τιθεναι	τιθεις -εισα -εν
τιθεμεν	τιθωμεν			-εντος -εισης
τιθετε	τιθητε	τιθετε		-εντος
τιθεασιν	τιθωσιν	τιθετωσαν		

AORIST TENSE

Indicative	Subjunctive	Imperative	Infinitive	Participle
ἐθηκα	θω			
ἐθηκας	θης	θες		
ἐθηκεν	θη	θετω		
			θειναι	θεις θεισα θεν
ἐθηκαμεν	θωμεν			θεντος θεισης
ἐθηκατε	θητε	θετε		θεντος
ἐθηκαν	θωσιν	θετωσαν		

16.12   Here are some examples of διδωμι and τιθημι in real
New Testament contexts. Study them carefully.

1. οὐδε καιουσιν λυχνον και **τιθεασιν** αὐτον ὑπο τον μοδιον
ἀλλ' ἐπι την λυχνιαν, και λαμπει πασιν τοις ἐν τη οἰκιᾳ.

Nor do [people] light a lamp and put it under a basin
but on a lampstand, and it gives light to all in the house
(Matthew 5:15).

2. εἰ οὖν ὑμεις πονηροι ὀντες
οἰδατε δοματα ἀγαθα **διδοναι** τοις τεκνοις ὑμων,
ποσῳ μαλλον ὁ πατηρ ὑμων ὁ ἐν τοις οὐρανοις
δωσει ἀγαθα τοις αἰτουσιν αὐτον.

If you then being evil
know [how] to give good gifts to your children,
how much more your Father in heaven
will give good things to those who ask him
(Matthew 7:11).

3. ὁ δε ἀποκριθεις εἰπεν αὐτοις, **Δοτε** αὐτοις ὑμεις φαγειν.
και λεγουσιν αὐτῳ,
Ἀπελθοντες ἀγορασωμεν δηναριων διακοσιων ἀρτους
και **δωσομεν** αὐτοις φαγειν;

But he answered them, "You give them [something] to eat."
And they said to him,
"Are we to go and buy bread worth two hundred denarii
and will we give [it] to them to eat?"
(Mark 6:37).

4. και ἐναγκαλισαμενος αὐτα κατευλογει
τιθεις τας χειρας ἐπ' αὐτα.

And he took them in his arms and blessed them
laying his hands upon them
(Mark 10:16).

5. καὶ ἐλθόντες λεγουσιν αὐτῷ,
   Διδασκαλε, οἴδαμεν ὅτι ἀληθης εἶ καὶ οὐ μελει σοι περι
   οὐδενος·
   οὐ γαρ βλεπεις εἰς προσωπον ἀνθρωπων,
   ἀλλ᾽ ἐπ᾽ ἀληθειας την ὁδον του θεου διδασκεις·
   ἐξεστιν **δουναι** κηνσον Καισαρι ἢ οὐ;
   δωμεν ἢ μη **δωμεν**;

   They came and said to him,
   "Teacher, we know that you are true and don't care about
   anyone;
   for you do not show partiality [lit. look into the face of men],
   but you teach the way of God in truth;
   is it lawful to give tribute to Caesar or not?
   Are we to give or are we not to give?"
   (Mark 12:14–15).

6. **διδοτε**, καὶ **δοθησεται** ὑμιν·
   μετρον καλον πεπιεσμενον σεσαλευμενον ὑπερεκχυννομενον
   δωσουσιν εἰς τον κολπον ὑμων·
   ᾧ γαρ μετρῳ μετρειτε ἀντιμετρηθησεται ὑμιν.

   Give, and it will be given to you;
   good measure, pressed down, shaken together, running over
   they will give into your lap.
   For with what measure you measure it will be measured back
   to you
   (Luke 6:38).

7. ἀπεκριθη ᾽Ιησους καὶ εἶπεν αὐτη,
   Εἰ ᾔδεις την δωρεαν του θεου
   καὶ τίς ἐστιν ὁ λεγων σοι· **Δος** μοι πειν,
   συ ἀν ἠτησας αὐτον
   καὶ **ἐδωκεν** ἀν σοι ὑδωρ ζων.

   Jesus answered her,
   "If you had known the gift of God
   and who it is who is telling you, 'Give me to drink,'
   you would have asked him
   and he would have given you living water"
   (John 4:10).

8. εἶπεν οὖν αὐτοῖς ὁ Ἰησους, Ἀμην ἀμην λεγω ὑμιν,
οὐ Μωϋσης **δεδωκεν** ὑμιν τον ἀρτον ἐκ του οὐρανου,
ἀλλ' ὁ πατηρ μου **διδωσιν** ὑμιν
τον ἀρτον ἐκ του οὐρανου τον ἀληθινον.

So Jesus said to them, "Truly truly I say to you,
Moses has not given you the bread from heaven,
but my Father gives you
the true bread from heaven"
(John 6:32).

9. Δια τουτο με ὁ πατηρ ἀγαπᾳ ὁτι ἐγω **τιθημι** την ψυχην μου,
ἱνα παλιν λαβω αὐτην. οὐδεις αἱρει αὐτην ἀπ' ἐμου,
ἀλλ' ἐγω **τιθημι** αὐτην ἀπ' ἐμαυτου.
ἐξουσιαν ἐχω **θειναι** αὐτην, και ἐξουσιαν ἐχω παλιν λαβειν
αὐτην.

This is why the Father loves me, because I lay down my life,
that I may take it again. No one takes it from me,
but I lay it down of my own accord.
I have power to lay it down, and I have power to take it
again
(John 10:17–18).

10. ὡς δε ἐτελεσαν παντα τα περι αὐτου γεγραμμενα,
καθελοντες ἀπο του ξυλου **ἐθηκαν** εἰς μνημειον.

And when they had fulfilled all that was written about him,
they took [him] down from the tree and laid [him] in a tomb
(Acts 13:29).

Exercise 16.12

Answer these questions on the material above. Numbers given in brackets refer to the number at the beginning of the texts.

1. Give the tense (present, future, aorist or perfect) of:

τιθεασιν (1), διδοναι (2), δωσομεν (3),
τιθεις (4), δουναι (5), διδοτε (6), Δος (7),
δεδωκεν (8), τιθημι (9), ἐθηκαν (10).

2. Give the meaning of:

ὑπο τον μοδιον (1), ποσῳ μαλλον (2), οὐ μελει σοι (5), ἐπ' ἀληθειας (5), Ἀμην ἀμην λεγω ὑμιν (8), ἀπ' ἐμαυτου (9).

3. What case is used to express the price of something, as in the phrase "worth 200 denarii" (3)?

4. Why is the subjunctive mood used for the following?

ἀγορασωμεν (3), δωμεν (5), λαβω (9)

5. ᾐδεις is the past tense of οἰδα. Is it an imperfect, an aorist or a pluperfect?

6. What kind of if-clause does εἰ introduce in number 7?

MI-4 ἱστημι

16.13 When it comes to disguises and multiple identities there is no verb to equal ἱστημι. In this section we can only hope to scratch the surface of its bizarre behaviour. The best place to start is with a basic meaning, "to stand". However, even this is not as simple as it appears. We can use "stand" in two ways, with or without an object.

WITH AN OBJECT:	I stood a vase of flowers on the table.
WITHOUT AN OBJECT:	When the queen entered the room everybody stood.

ἵστημι *with an object*

16.14   The first of these meanings is handled by the present, future and aorist active of ἵστημι.

The **present** is seen only in the compound συνιστημι (commend).

● Συνιστημι δε ὑμιν Φοιβην την ἀδελφην ἡμων.
   I commend to you Phoebe, our sister (Romans 16:1).

At other times ἵστημι disguised itself as an "O" verb, ἱστανω.

● νομον ἱστανομεν.
   We uphold the law (Romans 3:31).

The **future** is στησω.

● στησει τα προβατα ἐκ δεξιων αὐτου.
   He will place the sheep on his right (Matthew 25:33).

The past tense is handled by the **aorist**, ἐστησα.

● και προσκαλεσαμενος παιδιον ἐστησεν αὐτο ἐν μεσῳ αὐτων.
   He called a child to him and stood him in the middle of them (Matthew 18:2).

ἵστημι *without an object*

16.15   This is by far the commonest use of ἵστημι, and we have to be ready to distinguish between the *sense* in English and the *tense* in Greek. We have already done this with οἰδα (know), where the tense is perfect but the **sense** is present. Not only that but we have to cope with forms that are *passive* in Greek and translated as *active* in English.

Here I stand, I can do no other

16.16 We start with the present **sense** of the verb. This is translated by the **perfect** tense.

Indicative: ἑστηκα   I stand
Participle: ἑστηκως, υια, ος *or* ἑστως, ωσα, ος
(γεν. -οτος)   (gen. -ωτος)
standing

- περι δε την ἑνδεκατην ἑξελθων εὑρεν ἀλλους **ἑστωτας** και λεγει αὑτοις, Τί ὡδε **ἑστηκατε** ὁλην την ἡμεραν ἀργοι;

  About the 11th hour he went out and found others standing and said to them, "Why are you standing here all the day idle?" (Matthew 20:6).

- τινες δε των ἑκει **ἑστηκοτων** ἀκουσαντες ἑλεγον ὁτι 'Ηλιαν φωνει οὑτος.

  Some of those standing there when they heard said, "He is calling for Elijah" (Matthew 27:47).

They were standing

16.17 The **pluperfect** tense, εἱστηκειν, is used as a past continuous [–––].

- 'Ετι αὑτου λαλουντος τοις ὁχλοις ἱδου ἡ μητηρ και οἱ ἀδελφοι αὑτου **εἱστηκεισαν** ἑξω ζητουντες αὑτῳ λαλησαι.

  While he was still speaking to the crowds behold his mother and brothers were standing outside seeking to speak to him (Matthew 12:46).

How will it stand?

16.18   The future sense is conveyed by the future **passive**,
σταθησομαι.

  ● και εἰ ὁ Σατανας τον Σαταναν ἐκβαλλει, ἐφ'
  ἑαυτον ἐμερισθη· πως οὑν **σταθησεται** ἡ βασιλεια
  αὑτου;

  And if Satan casts out Satan, he is divided against
  himself; how then will his kingdom stand? (Matthew
  12:26).

Standing in the past

16.19   To describe yourself or someone else standing in the
past you used the **aorist** tense of ἱστημι, but *not* the
aorist ἐστησα. There was an alternative form of the
active, ἐστην, and the **passive**, ἐσταθην. The endings
of both are the same, and both were used without any
distinction in meaning.

Indicative	Subjunctive	Imperative	Infinitive	Participle
ἐστην ἐσταθην	στω σταθω	———— στηθι	στηναι σταθηναι	στας στασα σταν σταθεις -εισα -εν

  ● ἠλθεν ὁ 'Ιησους και **ἐστη** εἰς το μεσον
  και λεγει αὑτοις, Εἰρηνη ὑμιν.

  Jesus came and stood in the middle
  and said to them, "Peace to you" (John 20:19).

  ● ὁ δε 'Ιησους **ἐσταθη** ἐμπροσθεν του ἡγεμονος.

  Jesus stood before the governor (Matthew 27:11).

- καὶ **στας** ὁ Ἰησους ἐφωνησεν αὐτους καὶ εἶπεν,
  Τί θελετε ποιησω ὑμιν;

  And Jesus stood and called them and said,
  "What do you want me to do for you?"
  (Matthew 20:32).

- **σταθεις** δε ὁ Ἰησους ἐκελευσεν αὐτον ἀχθηναι
  προς αὐτον.

  Jesus stood and commanded him to be brought to
  him (Luke 18:40).

We can see an example of both infinitives used with
the same meaning in the same context in these verses.

- καὶ ἐαν οἰκια ἐφ' ἑαυτην μερισθῃ,
  οὐ δυνησεται ἡ οἰκια ἐκεινη **σταθηναι**.
  καὶ εἰ ὁ Σατανας ἀνεστη ἐφ' ἑαυτον καὶ ἐμερισθη,
  οὐ δυναται **στηναι** ἀλλα τελος ἐχει.

  And if a house is divided against itself,
  that house will not be able to stand.
  And if Satan has risen against himself and is
  divided,
  he is not able to stand but he is finished
  (Mark 3:25–26).

16.20   Another endearing feature of ἰστημι is that of all the
        MI-verbs it is used most in forming compound verbs.
        There is an example of one in Mark 3:26, ἀνεστη
        from ἀνιστημι, meaning "raise" (with an object) and
        "rise" (without an object). From the same word
        group we get the noun ἀναστασις, εως f resurrection.

MI–5 ἰημι

16.21   In the New Testament ἰημι only occurs in com-
        pounds. The most important are ἀφιημι and συνιημι.

ἀφιημι

16.22   Present ἀφιημι, future ἀφησω, aorist ἀφηκα, aor.
imperative ἀφες, aor. passive ἀφεθην, perfect passive
("they have been forgiven") ἀφεωνται.

ἀφιημι has a variety of meanings, "allow, forgive,
leave". The first meaning is illustrated in the incident
at Jesus' baptism when Jesus persuaded John that it
was right to baptize him.

● ἀποκριθεις δε ὁ Ἰησους εἰπεν προς αὐτον, **Ἀφες**
ἀρτι, οὑτως γαρ πρεπον ἐστιν ἡμιν πληρωσαι
πασαν δικαιοσυνην. τοτε **ἀφιησιν** αὐτον.

But Jesus answered him, "**Let it be** [aorist impera-
tive] now, for in this way it is fitting for us to fulfil
all righteousness." Then **he permitted** [present]
him (Matthew 3:15).

The second meaning is seen in the Lord's Prayer.

● και **ἀφες** ἡμιν τα ὀφειληματα ἡμων,
ὡς και ἡμεις **ἀφηκαμεν** τοις ὀφειλεταις ἡμων· . . .
Ἐαν γαρ **ἀφητε** τοις ἀνθρωποις τα παραπτωματα
αὐτων, **ἀφησει** και ὑμιν ὁ πατηρ ὑμων ὁ οὐρανιος.

And **forgive** (aor. imperative) us our debts,
as **we** also **have forgiven** (aorist) our debtors. . . .
For if **you forgive** (aor. subjunctive) men their
trespasses, your heavenly Father **will forgive**
(future) you also (Matthew 6:12,14).

This meaning is linked to the noun ἀφεσις, εως f
forgiveness. The third meaning is illustrated in a
piece of narrative which comes at the end of the great
chapter of parables in Matthew 13.

● Τοτε **ἀφεις** τους ὀχλους ἡλθεν εἰς την οἰκιαν.

Then **having left** (aor. participle) the crowds he
went into the house (Matthew 13:36).

συνιημι

16.23 Present συνιημι or συνιω, future συνησω, aorist συνηκα.

- Ἀκουετε και **συνιετε**.
  Hear and **understand** (pres. imperative)
  (Matthew 15:10).

- Ἀκουσατε μου παντες και **συνετε**.
  Hear me all of you and **understand**
  (aor. imperative) (Mark 7:14).

  Associated with this verb is the noun συνεσις, εως
  f understanding.

MI–6 ἀπολλυμι, φημι, δεικνυμι

16.24 ἀπολλυμι is a compound verb (ἀπο + ὀλλυμι),
meaning "destroy, lose". Its future is ἀπολεσω or
ἀπολῶ (εω), the aorist ἀπωλεσα, and the perfect
participle ἀπολωλως, υια, ος means "lost".

- μελλει γαρ Ἡρῳδης ζητειν το παιδιον του
  ἀπολεσαι αὐτο.
  For Herod will seek the child to destroy him
  (Matthew 2:13).

- Συγχαρητε μοι, ὁτι εὑρον το προβατον μου το
  ἀπολωλος.
  Rejoice with me, for I have found my sheep which
  was lost (Luke 15:6).

It also has a set of middle tenses, which mean
"perish". The present is ἀπολλυμαι, the future
ἀπολουμαι (εομαι), and the aorist ἀπωλομην.

- και προσελθοντες ἠγειραν αὐτον λεγοντες, Κυριε,
  σωσον, **ἀπολλυμεθα**.
  And they went and roused him saying, "Lord,
  save [us], we are perishing" (Matthew 8:25).

16.25   Several of the MI-verbs use middle forms, sometimes in compound verbs, but they are generally easier to recognise and can be learned as you come to them.

16.26   The verb φημι is an alternative for λεγω, but much less common. It has only 4 parts in the New Testament, φημι I say, φησιν he says, φασιν they say, and ἐφη he said. In practice there is no difference between φησιν (present) and ἐφη (imperfect). They are both used in narrative and translated "he said".

16.27   The verb δεικνυμι means "show". Its future is δειξω, its aorist active ἐδειξα, and aorist passive ἐδειχθην. It illustrates a tendency seen in several MI-verbs, the tendency to fall in line with the "O" verbs. Compare these two texts. You will see that in the second δεικνυμι is behaving as if it were δεικνυω.

● Και ἐτι καθ' ὑπερβολην ὁδον ὑμιν **δεικνυμι**.
And I show you a yet more excellent way
(1 Corinthians 12:31).

● Τί σημειον **δεικνυεις** ἡμιν ὁτι ταυτα ποιεις;
What sign do you show us that you [will] do these things? (John 2:18).

16.28   In the following exercise you have been given the complete Greek text of Matthew 13:24–30 in numbered lines, but the order has been scrambled. The equivalent lines of the English translation are provided in the correct order. See how quickly you can sort the lines of the Greek text.

Exercise 16:28

A.   24 He put another parable before them saying,
B.   "The kingdom of God is like a man
C.   who sowed good seed in his field.
D.   25 While men were sleeping
E.   his enemy came and sowed weeds

F. among the wheat and went away.
G. 26When the shoot sprouted and bore fruit,
H. then the weeds also appeared.
I. 27The servants of the householder came and
J. said to him, 'Master, did you not sow good seed
K. in your field? How then does it have weeds?'
L. 28He said to them, 'An enemy [man] has done this.'
M. The servants said to him,
N. 'Do you want us to go and gather them?'
O. 29He said, 'No, lest in gathering the weeds
P. you uproot the wheat at the same time with them.
Q. 30Let them grow together until the harvest,
R. and at the time of the harvest I will say to the reapers,
S. "Gather the weeds first
T. and bind them into bundles to burn them,
U. but gather the wheat into my barn." ' "

1. ἀνα μεσον του σιτου και ἀπηλθεν.
2. Ἀλλην παραβολην παρεθηκεν αὐτοις λεγων·
3. ἀφετε συναυξανεσθαι ἀμφοτερα ἑως του θερισμου,
4. εἰπον αὐτῳ· Κυριε, οὐχι καλον σπερμα ἐσπειρας
5. ἐκριζωσητε ἁμα αὐτοις τον σιτον.
6. ἐν δε τῳ καθευδειν τους ἀνθρωπους
7. ἐν τῳ σῳ ἀγρῳ; ποθεν οὐν ἐχει ζιζανια;
8. ἠλθεν αὐτου ὁ ἐχθρος και ἐπεσπειρεν ζιζανια
9. τον δε σιτον συναγαγετε εἰς την ἀποθηκην μου.
10. και δησατε αὐτα εἰς δεσμας προς το κατακαυσαι αὐτα,
11. και ἐν καιρῳ του θερισμου ἐρῶ τοις θερισταις·
12. προσελθοντες δε οἱ δουλοι του οἰκοδεσποτου
13. ὁ δε ἐφη αὐτοις· Ἐχθρος ἀνθρωπος τουτο ἐποιησεν.
14. Θελεις οὐν ἀπελθοντες συλλεξωμεν αὐτα;
15. ὁ δε φησιν· Οὔ, μηποτε συλλεγοντες τα ζιζανια

16. ὅτε δε ἐβλαστησεν ὁ χορτος και καρπον
    ἐποιησεν,
17. Συλλεξατε πρωτον τα ζιζανια
18. σπειραντι καλον σπερμα ἐν τῳ ἀγρῳ αὐτου.
19. οἱ δε δουλοι λεγουσιν αὐτῳ·
20. τοτε ἐφανη και τα ζιζανια.
21. Ὡμοιωθη ἡ βασιλεια των οὐρανων ἀνθρωπῳ

Answers to exercises

Exercise 16.2

I am	εἰμι	we are	ἐσμεν
you (s) are	εἶ	you (p) are	ἐστε
he/she/it is	ἐστιν	they are	εἰσιν

Exercise 16.4

The odd one out is ἐσται. Compare δεξ<u>ε</u>ται.

Exercise 16.5

The solution to the problem of too many Greek equivalents is that two of the parts have an alternative. The pattern is:

I was	ἠμην	we were	ἠμεν or ἠμεθα
you were	ἠς or ἠσθα	you were	ἠτε
he was	ἠν	they were	ἠσαν

Exercise 16.6

1/G 2/C 3/J 4/A 5/H 6/B 7/D 8/I
9/F 10/E

Exercise 16.12

1. τιθεασιν (1) present   διδοναι (2) present
   δωσομεν (3) future   τιθεις (4) aorist
   δουναι (5) aorist   διδοτε (6) present
   Δος (7) aorist   δεδωκεν (8) perfect
   τιθημι (9) present   ἐθηκαν (10) aorist

2. ὑπο τον μοδιον, under a basin
   The Greek says literally "under *the* basin".

   ποσῳ μαλλον, how much more

   οὐ μελει σοι, you don't care
   The Greek says literally "it does not matter to you".

   ἐπ' ἀληθειας, in truth

   Ἀμην ἀμην λεγω ὑμιν, Truly truly I say to you
   ἀπ' ἐμαυτου, of my own accord, literally "from myself"

3. The genitive case is used with prices, δηναριων διακοσιων, "worth 200 denarii".

4. ἀγορασωμεν (3) and δωμεν (5) are both deliberative questions. λαβω (9) after ἱνα expresses purpose.

5. ἠδεις is pluperfect in form. It represents the past tense of the perfect verb, οἰδα.

6. It is an "if-clause" contrary to fact.

Exercise 16.28

A/2	B/21	C/18	D/6	E/8	F/1	G/16
H/20	I/12	J/4	K/7	L/13	M/19	N/14
O/15	P/5	Q/3	R/11	S/17	T/10	U/9

REVIEW QUESTIONS

1. What is the full pattern of the present tense of εἰμι?

2. What is the pattern of the subjunctive of εἰμι and why is it already familiar?

3. How are the infinitive and participle of εἰμι formed?

4. What are the future forms of εἰμι and which ending behaves in a slightly unexpected way?

5. What is the imperfect of εἰμι and why are there eight words instead of six?

6. Is εἰ followed by the indicative or subjunctive mood?

7. Is ἐαν followed by the indicative or subjunctive mood?

8. When is the construction εἰ . . . ἀν used?

9. What is the meaning of δίδωμι and how common is it in the New Testament?

10. Why is it important to distinguish carefully between the aorist and perfect active of δίδωμι?

11. What is the full pattern of the present indicative δίδωμι?

12. What distinguishes the present from the aorist tense in the subjunctive, imperative and participle of δίδωμι?

13. Why is it difficult to assign an English equivalent for τίθημι?

14. How does τίθημι behave (a) in the present tense (b) in the aorist?

15. In what two ways can we use the verb "stand"?

16. Which sense is conveyed by the present, future and aorist active of ἱστημι?

17. What sense is conveyed by the perfect and pluperfect forms, ἑστηκα and εἱστηκειν?

18. What sense is conveyed by the future passive, σταθησομαι?

19. What, if any, is the distinction between ἐστησα and ἐστην?

20. What, if any, is the distinction between ἐστην and ἐσταθην?

21. What is the noun, meaning "resurrection", from the same word group as ἀνιστημι?

22. What are the possible meanings of ἀφιημι?

23. What is the meaning of συνιημι and which noun belongs to the same word group?

24. What is the difference in meaning between the active ἀπολλυμι and the middle ἀπολλυμαι?

25. What do φημι and δεικνυμι mean?

REVIEW EXERCISES

STRAIGHT TRANSLATION

You should know enough to be able to translate the texts below. The references are given so that you can check your answers.

1. θησω το πνευμα μου ἐπ' αὐτον (Matthew 12:18).

2. και εἱστηκει ὁ λαος θεωρων (Luke 23:35).

3. ὁ νομος δια Μωϋσεως ἐδοθη, ἡ χαρις και ἡ ἀληθεια δια Ἰησου Χριστου ἐγενετο (John 1:17).

4. Δος δοξαν τῳ θεῳ· ἡμεις οἱδαμεν ὁτι οὑτος ὁ ἀνθρωπος ἁμαρτωλος ἐστιν (John 9:24).

5. Ἐγω εἰμι ὁ ποιμην ὁ καλος. ὁ ποιμην ὁ καλος την ψυχην αὐτου τιθησιν ὑπερ των προβατων (John 10:11).

6. εἰπε μοι ποῦ ἐθηκας αὐτον (John 20:15).

7. δωσει γαρ σοι ὁ κυριος συνεσιν ἐν πασιν (2 Timothy 2:7).

8. ἱδου ἐγω και τα παιδια ἁ μοι ἐδωκεν ὁ θεος (Hebrews 2:13).

ANOTHER CLOZE ENCOUNTER

In John 13:4–11 Jesus teaches his disciples about humility by washing their feet. Peter objects vehemently and Jesus explains why he too must have his feet washed. In the Greek text below key words have been removed. See if you can insert them in the correct places and see how much of the text you can understand without looking up any of the words.

4 ἐγειρεται ἐκ του δειπνου
και [1] τα ἱματια
και λαβων λεντιον
[2] ἑαυτον·
5 εἰτα βαλλει ὑδωρ εἰς [3] νιπτηρα
και ἠρξατο νιπτειν τους [4] των μαθητων
και ἐκμασσειν τῳ [5] ᾡ ἠν διεζωσμενος.
6 ἐρχεται οὐν [6] Σιμωνα Πετρον·
λεγει αὐτῳ, Κυριε, [7] μου νιπτεις τους ποδας;
7 ἀπεκριθη [8] και εἰπεν αὐτῳ,
Ὅ ἐγω [9] συ οὐκ οἰδας ἀρτι,
γνωσῃ [10] μετα ταυτα.
8 λεγει αὐτῳ ὁ [11],
Οὐ μη νιψῃς μου τους ποδας [12] τον αἰωνα.
ἀπεκριθη Ἰησους αὐτῳ,
[13] μη νιψω σε, οὐκ ἐχεις μερος [14] ἐμου.
9 λεγει αὐτῳ Σιμων Πετρος,
[15], μη τους ποδας μου μονον
ἀλλα και [16] χειρας και την κεφαλην.
10 λεγει [17] ὁ Ἰησους,
Ὁ λελουμενος οὐκ [18] χρειαν
εἰ μη τους ποδας [19],
ἀλλ' ἐστιν καθαρος ὁλος·
και [20] καθαροι ἐστε, ἀλλ' οὐχι παντες.
11 [21] γαρ τον παραδιδοντα αὐτον·
δια [22] εἰπεν ὁτι
Οὐχι παντες καθαροι ἐστε.

αὐτῳ	δε	διεζωσεν	Ἐαν	εἰς	ἐχει	ἠδει
Ἰησους	Κυριε	λεντιῳ	μετ'	νιψασθαι		
Πετρος	ποδας	ποιω	προς	συ	τας	
τιθησιν	τον	τουτο	ὑμεις			

WORDS TO LEARN

αἴρω, fut. ἀρῶ (εω), aor. ἦρα take, take up, remove
ἀνιστημι raise. ἀνισταμαι rise.
ἀπολλυμι destroy. ἀπολλυμαι perish
ἀφιημι forgive, allow, leave
διδωμι give
εἰμι I am
ἑτερος, α, ον other, another, different
ζαω, imperfect ἐζην live
ἰδιος, α, ον one's own

    ἐχω τον ἰδιον οἰκον. I have my own house.

    ἐχει τον ἰδιον οἰκον. He has his own house.

ἰστημι stand
νυν now
παλιν again
παραδιδωμι hand down, hand over, betray
παρακαλεω exhort, encourage
πους, ποδος m foot. Dative plural ποσιν
προσευχομαι pray
σπειρω, fut. σπερῶ (εω), aor. ἐσπειρα, aor. pass.

    ἐσπαρην sow

συνιημι understand
τιθημι put, place, lay down, appoint
τοτε then

CHAPTER SEVENTEEN

Preview

The need for new translations

Translation criteria

The process of translation: three steps

Different structures with the same meaning

The same structure with different meanings

Explicit and implicit information

The influence of feminism on translation

The versatile genitive

John 1:19–28

CHAPTER SEVENTEEN

Surface structure and deep meaning

So many translations

17.1 Have you ever wondered why we have so many translations of the Bible, and of the New Testament in particular? Part of the answer is that language is constantly evolving. Just think about the different meanings of the word "chips" that have emerged during the 20th century.

17.2 In the 17th century the translators of the King James Version used words which have changed their meaning. It's not just the archaic words like "thee" and "thou" but words which we still use, only with a different meaning. Mark 2:4 says, "they could not come nigh unto him FOR THE PRESS." The most obvious way of understanding that today would be in terms of reporters and photographers, but Mark is simply referring to a crowd of people. In Galatians 1:11 Paul writes, "I CERTIFY you, brethren." No, he was not committing them to a mental hospital; he was simply saying, "I want you to know . . ." In Matthew 17:25 we read that when Peter came into the house, "Jesus PREVENTED him." That sounds to us like an embarrassing tussle in the doorway, but in the 17th century "prevented" simply meant that Jesus spoke first.

17.3 So translations have to keep up with the changes in language. Another reason why there are so many translations is that there are different ideas about what makes a good translation. Here are some criteria to think about.

- keeping as close as possible to the original text
- using the same word in the English translation every time the same word is used in the original
- retaining the historical and cultural authenticity of the original
- preserving the dignity and sanctity of the text in language appropriate to traditional liturgical usage
- expressing the ideas of the original in today's idiom
- stimulating the same reaction in today's readers as the original text stimulated in its first readers
- presenting the text in language which can be easily understood by people of all ages and from all walks of life

All of these criteria have to a greater or lesser extent contributed to the wide variety of translations available today.

Unacceptable extremes

17.4   There are some approaches which fall outside the limits of an acceptable translation. One extreme is the translation which follows the structure of the original so closely that it is simply not English. Here is an example from Robert Young's *Literal Translation of the Bible*.

"and what I do, I also will do, that I may cut off the occasion of those wishing an occasion, that in that which they boast they may be found according as we also;" (2 Corinthians 11:12).

The other extreme is the translation which modernizes the text to the extent of placing the New Testament events in a 20th century culture – and a western one at that! In *The Cotton Patch Version*, by Clarence Jordan, Jesus is born in Gainesville, Georgia, grows up in Valdosta and is baptized in the Chattahoochee River. The angel's message to Joseph in Matthew 2:13 is

"Get moving, and take your wife and baby and highball it to Mexico."

Both of these approaches are unacceptable for different reasons, but between the two extremes there lies a broad range of legitimate possibilities.

The three steps

17.5   The process of translating from one language to another involves three steps.

Step 1 A full understanding of the structure of the original

Step 2 A thorough grasp of the underlying meaning conveyed by the surface structure

Step 3 A representation of that deep meaning in the appropriate structures and idioms of contemporary English

So far in this book I have concentrated on analyzing the surface structure of the Greek text of the New Testament and in my translations I have erred on the side of being too literal, to enable you to see what is happening in the Greek text. It is time now to encourage you beyond step 1 to steps 2 and 3.

Yea verily, tradition ruleth

17.6   For people familiar with the English Bible it is hard to recognize how far traditional phrasing and cadences still dictate the way the Bible is translated. The heading for this paragraph should be "Tradition rules OK" but I couldn't resist making the point more forcibly. In a similar way, when we try to put the Greek text of the New Testament into contemporary language the echo of the King James tradition never seems far away.

17.7   In Luke 2:10 the message of the angel to the shepherds begins, μη φοβηθης. The King James Version's "Fear not" has been reinforced in generations of Carol Services and Nativity Plays. More modern versions recognize that "Fear not" is unnatural in current English. The Revised Standard Version has "Be not afraid," which is not much better. The Good News Bible's "Don't be afraid" is better.

The real test of a translation is to imagine a contemporary scene in which you might say something similar. Suppose there is a severe thunder storm and you are trying to comfort a terrified child. What would you say? It is extremely unlikely that you would say, "Fear not" or "Be not afraid." You might well say, "Don't be frightened," which I think is better than "Don't be afraid," but it is even more likely that you would say, "Don't worry; it's all right. There's nothing to be afraid of."

Of course this raises the question of when a translation is expanded so much that it becomes a paraphrase. Also, it could be pointed out that a message from an angel is not in the same category as comforting a child, but I hope you see the issues which the translator has to consider. It is always worth trying to get away from the accepted, traditional phrasing and at least think about an alternative way of putting it.

Different structure same meaning

17.8   Sometimes different language structures can be used to express the same underlying meaning. Consider these New Testament phrases.

ὁ ἐχων   He who has (Matthew 13:9)
ὁστις ἐχει   Anyone who has (Matthew 13:12)

εἰ τις ἐχει   If anyone has (Mark 7:16)
ὁς ἀν ἐχῃ   Whoever has (Luke 8:18)
πας ὁ ἐχων Everyone who has (1 John 3:3)

Although they are all different on the surface the deep meaning is virtually the same in all of them. Look at this text from 1 John 3:17 with a fairly literal translation alongside.

ὁς δ' ἀν ἐχῃ	But whoever has
τον βιον του κοσμου	the life of the world
και θεωρῃ τον ἀδελφον αὐτου	and sees his brother
χρειαν ἐχοντα	having need
και κλεισῃ τα σπλαγχνα αὐτου	and shuts his internal organs
ἀπ' αὐτου,	from him,
πως ἡ ἀγαπη του θεου	how does the love of God
μενει ἐν αὐτῳ;	remain in him?

Exercise 17.8

What is wrong with the translation given above, and how could it be improved? You may refer to modern English versions for comparison.

Same structure different meaning

17.9   One of the most persistent misunderstandings about languages and translation is the view that there ought to be a one-for-one equivalence between words in both languages. This leads to the view, for example, that σαρξ, σαρκος f should always be translated "flesh" in the New Testament, and that somehow, because the same word is used, there should be a connection between its various meanings.

17.10   The fallacy of this can be seen if we take an example
         from our own language, the phrase "to put on".
         Think what we mean when we say these things.

> Put the electric blanket on.
> Put your coat on.
> Put the fire on.
> Put a brave face on.
> Put on a show.

Various alternatives make the differences clear:
switch on; wear; light; pretend to be happy even
though you're not; produce. If you were translating
these English phrases into another language you
would be foolish to insist on looking for a single
expression to equal the English "put on".

Exercise 17.10

Look at these texts, which contain the word σαρξ,
and select the most suitable English equivalents from
the list given.

John 1:14

και ὁ λογος **σαρξ** ἐγενετο και ἐσκηνωσεν ἐν ἡμιν.

And the Word became (1) and lived among us.

Romans 11:13–14

ἐφ' ὁσον μεν οὐν εἰμι ἐγω ἐθνων ἀποστολος,
την διακονιαν μου δοξαζω,
ἱνα παραζηλωσω μου **την σαρκα**
και σωσω τινας ἐξ αὐτων.

So, as long as I am an apostle of the Gentiles
I magnify my ministry,
that I may make my own (2) jealous
and may save some of them.

Galatians 5:19

φανερα δε ἐστιν τα ἐργα **της σαρκος**, ἀτινα ἐστιν
πορνεια, ἀκαθαρσια, ἀσελγεια . . .

But the works of (3) are plain, which are immorality,
filthiness, indecency . . .

Hebrews 5:7

ὁς ἐν ταις ἡμεραις **της σαρκος** αὐτου δεησεις τε και
ἱκετηριας προς τον δυναμενον σῳζειν αὐτον ἐκ
θανατου
μετα κραυγης ἰσχυρας και δακρυων προσενεγκας

Who in the days of his (4) | having offered | ←
prayers and requests to him who was able to
save him from death with
loud crying and tears [   ] . . .

+---+
| fallen human nature | a human being | life on |
| earth | fellow Jews |
+---+

Explicit and implicit information

17.11 Sometimes a language contains implicit information
because of its structures or the culture in which it is
used. When it is translated into another language that
information may need to be made explicit. Analyze
carefully this text from Galatians 4:23 with its English
counterpart and see how much implicit information
you think needs to be made more explicit.

ἀλλ'	ὁ	μεν	ἐκ της	παιδισκης
but	the	on-the-one-hand	of the	slave-girl

κατα	σαρκα	γεγεννηται,
according-to	flesh	was-born

ὁ	δε	ἐκ της ἐλευθερας	δι' ἐπαγγελιας.
the	on-the-other-hand	of the free	through promise

17.12   If you are not familiar with this verse then the amount of implicit information probably makes it very difficult to translate. "The of the slave-girl" is "the **son** of the slave-girl". "The (masculine) of the free (feminine)" is "the **son** of the free **woman**". The gender is clear in Greek but not in English. Κατα σαρκα, "according to the flesh," is an idiom that needs to be expressed in a different way in English. "The son who was born **in the usual way**" is one way of doing it, or "**in the ordinary course of nature**". "Through promise" can also be expanded. What does δια (through) mean here, and whose promise was it? The Good News Bible translates "as a result of God's promise".

17.13   The tiny words μεν and δε are inserted into the Greek to indicate a contrast. The translation "on the one hand . . . on the other hand" is clumsy and in English the contrast is clear without it. This is an example of information that is explicit in Greek but can be left implicit in English.

Useful trade-ins

17.14   Another fallacy we need to dispel is that a noun must always be translated by a noun, a verb by a verb, etc. Again, the structures of different languages operate differently and it may be best to translate a noun by a verb, or indeed by a much longer phrase. Here are some examples to consider.

Romans 9:33

καθως γεγραπται, 'Ιδου τιθημι ἐν Σιων
λιθον προσκομματος και πετραν σκανδαλου.

In this verse Paul takes up the language of Isaiah 8:14.

As it is written, Behold I lay in Zion
a stone of stumbling and a rock of offense.

The second line contains four nouns:

λιθος, ου m stone

προσκομμα, τος n something which makes someone stumble

πετρα, ας f rock

σκανδαλον, ου n something which makes someone stumble

It is no use trying to reproduce the surface structure of the Greek. The important thing is to find the deep meaning and express it in the best way possible in English. This is a better translation.

As it is written, See I am laying in Zion
a stone that will make people stumble,
a rock they will fall over.

Matthew 5:41

και ὁστις σε ἀγγαρευσει μιλιον ἑν, ὑπαγε μετ' αὐτου δυο.

This text contains the verb ἀγγαρευω, which could be defined in a concise dictionary as "force, compel, press into service". It refers to the forced transport of military baggage by the inhabitants of a country through which troops were passing. In this translation, taken from the Good News Bible, I have used bold type to show how the single Greek verb ἀγγαρευω is translated.

"And if **one of the occupation troops forces you to carry his pack** one kilometre, carry it two kilometres."

Note also, in passing, how this version has adopted the metric system of weights and measures in its British edition.

17.15 We have already seen that Greek may use a present tense in narrative where we need a past tense in English, e.g. λεγει, "he **said**". Another possible "trade-in" is active voice for passive. Take as an example one of the beatitudes, Matthew 5:4.

μακαριοι οἱ πενθουντες, ὅτι αὐτοι
παρακληθησονται.
Blessed [are] those who mourn, for **they will be comforted**.

Most commentators interpret this as a "theological passive"; that is, if the statement were made active God would be the subject. The Good News Bible treats this as another instance of implicit information that needs to be made explicit and translates accordingly:

> "Happy are those who mourn; God will comfort them!"

The feminist perspective

17.16 In recent years there has been a significant move towards equal opportunities and greater respect for women. Its influence has been felt in theology as well as other areas, and modern translators have been forced to rethink certain assumptions about the way women appear (or, more often, don't appear) in traditional translations. Women have rarely participated in major translation projects.

17.17 In English as in Greek when the reference is to any person, male or female, there is a grammatical preference for the masculine gender. So we have ὁ λεγων, "he who says". In most New Testament contexts where this kind of construction is used it is meant to include women, whereas ἡ λεγουσα, "she who says," would definitely exclude men. When Christians are referred to as members of God's family it is nearly always as υἱοι, "sons" or ἀδελφοι, "brothers". This use of masculine-oriented language is now seen as linguistic sexism and where possible it should be altered in favour of inclusive language.

17.18   To date, the version which has been most thorough-going in this direction is the New Revised Standard Version. It is fairly easy to change "he who" to "anyone who", "men" to "people" and "brothers" to "brothers and sisters", but the difficulty arises when a singular personal pronoun has to be used, for example 1 John 4:15.

ὃς ἐὰν ὁμολογήσῃ ὅτι Ἰησοῦς ἐστιν ὁ υἱὸς τοῦ θεοῦ, ὁ θεὸς ἐν αὐτῷ μενει καὶ αὐτὸς ἐν τῷ θεῷ.

Whoever confesses that Jesus is the Son of God, God remains in him and he in God.

Up till recently the problem for the translator would have been seen in the initial construction ὃς ἂν ὁμολογήσῃ. The sentence would sound better if it began, "If anyone confesses. . .". The translation of μενω in this context might also be a point of discussion, "abide" in older versions, "remain" in most modern ones. Neither of these really has a modern ring to it, and it may be better to say, "God lives in him and he in God."

17.19   In today's climate of opinion the dominant issue is how to eliminate the exclusive male-oriented language. The Good News Bible, published in 1976, was completed before the full force of the feminist debate hit translators. It has

"If **anyone** declares that Jesus is the Son of God, **he** lives in union with God and God lives in union with **him**" (emphasis mine).

The Revised English Bible is much more recent, coming out in 1989, but although it acknowledges the issue of inclusive gender reference in its preface, it does not solve the problem of the masculine pronoun. It has

"If **anyone** acknowledges that Jesus is God's Son, God dwells in **him** and **he** in God" (emphasis mine).

The New Revised Standard Version does find a way round the problem. It has

"God abides in **those** who confess that Jesus is the Son of God, and **they** abide in God" (emphasis again mine).

The way it is done is to turn the singular of the original text into a plural all the way through. The structure has also been altered, bringing the subject "God" to the beginning of the sentence.

Beware of the genitive

17.20   At the beginning of this book we saw how the Greek system of using cases makes it very different from English, which relies much more heavily on the order of words. One of the cases in particular, the genitive, has an enormous range of meanings and the English word "of" often fails to do justice to the meaning. Consider this text, 2 Corinthians 4:6.

ὅτι ὁ θεος ὁ εἰπων, ᾿Εκ σκοτους φως λαμψει,
ὃς ἐλαμψεν ἐν ταις καρδιαις ἡμων προς φωτισμον
της γνωσεως της δοξης του θεου
ἐν προσωπῳ ᾿Ιησου Χριστου.

For [it is] the God who said, "Let light shine out of darkness," who has shone in our hearts to give the light of the knowledge of the glory of God
in the face of Jesus Christ.

It is the third line with its three genitives which I want you to think about. What exactly do they mean? What could we replace each of them with? Here are some suggestions for you to try.

which consists of | which comes from | which leads to | which characterizes | which belongs to | which gives

Some translation practice

17.21 In this section you are given the Greek text of John
1:19–28, the testimony of John the Baptist. Use it to
practise the three steps outlined above in section
17.5, analyzing the structure, penetrating to the
meaning and expressing the meaning accurately in
modern idiom.Helps with vocabulary are given at the
end of the Greek text.

¹⁹Και αυτη εστιν ή μαρτυρια του Ἰωαννου,
  ὁτε ἀπεστειλαν προς αὐτον οἱ Ἰουδαιοι ἐξ
  Ἱεροσολυμων
  ἱερεις και Λευιτας
  ἱνα ἐρωτησωσιν αὐτον, Συ τίς εἰ;
²⁰και ὡμολογησεν και οὐκ ἠρνησατο, και
  ὡμολογησεν ὁτι
  Ἐγω οὐκ εἰμι ὁ Χριστος.
²¹και ἠρωτησαν αὐτον, Τί οὐν; συ Ἠλιας εἰ;
  και λεγει, Οὐκ εἰμι.
  Ὁ προφητης εἰ συ;
  και ἀπεκριθη, Οὔ.
²²εἰπαν οὐν αὐτῳ, Τίς εἰ;
  ἱνα ἀποκρισιν δωμεν τοις πεμψασιν ἡμας·
  τί λεγεις περι σεαυτου;
²³ἐφη,
      Ἐγω φωνη βοωντος ἐν τη ἐρημῳ·
      εὐθυνατε την ὁδον κυριου.
  καθως εἰπεν Ἠσαϊας ὁ προφητης.
²⁴Και ἀπεσταλμενοι ἠσαν ἐκ των Φαρισαιων.
²⁵και ἠρωτησαν αὐτον και εἰπαν αὐτῳ,
  Τί οὐν βαπτιζεις
  εἰ συ οὐκ εἰ ὁ Χριστος οὐδε Ἠλιας οὐδε
  ὁ προφητης;
²⁶ἀπεκριθη αὐτοις ὁ Ἰωαννης λεγων,
  Ἐγω βαπτιζω ἐν ὑδατι·
  μεσος ὑμων ἑστηκεν
  ὁν ὑμεις οὐκ οἰδατε,

²⁷ ὁ ὀπισω μου ἐρχομενος,
οὐ οὐκ εἰμι ἐγω ἀξιος
ἱνα λυσω αὐτου τον ἱμαντα του ὑποδηματος.
²⁸ ταυτα ἐν Βηθανιᾳ ἐγενετο περαν του Ἰορδανου,
ὁπου ἠν ὁ Ἰωαννης βαπτιζων.

Verse 19

μαρτυρια, ας f testimony   Ἰωαννης, ου m John
ὀτε when   ἀποστελλω, aor. ἀπεστειλα send
Ἰουδαιος, ου m Jew   ἐκ + gen. from
Ἱεροσολυμα (neut. pl.) Jerusalem
ἱερευς, εως m priest   Λευιτης, ου m Levite
ἐρωταω ask

Verse 20

ὁμολογεω confess   ἀρνεομαι deny
Χριστος, ου m Christ, Messiah

Verse 21

Ἠλιας, ου m Elijah   προφητης, ου m prophet
οὐ no

Verse 22

ἀποκρισις, εως f answer   διδωμι give
πεμπω send   περι + gen about
σεαυτον, ου yourself

Verse 23

φημι say   φωνη, ης f voice   βοαω cry, shout
ἐρημος, ου f desert   εὐθυνω, aor. εὐθυνα make
straight   ὁδος, ου f way
κυριος, ου m (the) Lord   καθως as
Ἠσαϊας, ου m Isaiah

Verse 24

ἀπεσταλμένοι, sent, perf. participle passive of ἀποστελλω. With imperfect of εἰμι = pluperfect, "they had been sent".
Φαρισαιος, ου m Pharisee

Verse 25

βαπτιζω baptize

Verse 26

ὑδωρ, ὑδατος n water
μεσος, η, ον in the middle, among
ἱστημι, perf. ἑστηκα stand
οἰδα know

Verse 27

ὀπισω + gen. after   ἐρχομαι come
ἀξιος, α, ον worthy   λυω loose, untie
ἱμας, ἱμαντος m strap (of a sandal)
ὑποδημα, τος n sandal, shoe

Verse 28

Βηθανια, ας f Bethany   γινομαι happen
περαν + gen. beyond
'Ιορδανης, ου m Jordan river   ὁπου where

Insights from the Greek text

17.22   Check your translation with one or more modern English versions. A first hand knowledge of the Greek text opens up issues which cannot be discussed just from the English text.

• **Verse 19** Και links this section with the Prologue to John's Gospel, and particularly the theme of μαρτυρια, cf. verse 7. "The Jews" here refers to the Jewish authorities. On its own τίς εἶ; would mean "Who are you?" The inclusion of Συ makes it emphatic, "Who are *you*?"

● **Verse 20** Attention is drawn to John's confession by the threefold statement expressed twice positively and once negatively. ὅτι is used here to introduce direct speech. Ἐγω is emphatic. ὁ Χριστος is probably best translated "the Messiah" in this context.

● **Verse 21** The question asked by the Jewish delegation can be punctuated in more than one way. As printed above it is "What then? Are you Elijah?" Alternatively it could be Τί οὖν συ; Ἠλιας εἶ; which means "What are you, then? Are you Elijah?" In this context the alteration makes little difference. The repetition of συ is again emphatic. ὁ προφητης was "THE prophet" like Moses, Deuteronomy 18:15, 18; compare John 6:14; 7:40.

● **Verse 22** ἵνα ἀποκρισιν δωμεν may be translated as expressing purpose; understand "**Tell us** so that we may give an answer". A sentence with ἵνα like this can also mean "We must give an answer . . ." The technical term for this is a "semi-imperatival" ἵνα. τοις πεμψασιν is dative plural of the definite article + the aorist participle of πεμπω, "to those who sent".

● **Verse 23** John quotes from Isaiah 40:3. We have to add the verb "to be", i.e. ἐγω [], "I [am]". βοωντος is the present participle of βοαω, genitive singular, "of one shouting". ἐρημος and ὁδος are both examples of **feminine** nouns from Family 2 with endings like λογος. κυριος without the definite article is used in the Greek Old Testament to represent the Hebrew YHWH, which English Bibles print as "the LORD" with capitals. This is sometimes reflected in the New Testament, as here.

- **Verse 24** The relationship between this verse and verse 19 is disputed. There are several possible interpretations.

(1) The Revised Standard Version translates, "Now they had been sent from the Pharisees." It seems strange that a delegation of priests would take orders from the Pharisees.

(2) Even stranger is the interpretation of the King James Version, which follows a different manuscript reading at this point: Καὶ οἱ ἀπεσταλμένοι ἦσαν ἐκ τῶν Φαρισαιων. "And they which were sent were of the Pharisees." This seems to identify the Pharisees with the Priests and Levites, whereas they were very different groups of people.

(3) A third interpretation, based on the text without οἱ added, takes ἐκ τῶν Φαρισαιων as the **subject** of the sentence. The Greek for "some of the Pharisees" is τινες ἐκ τῶν Φαρισαιων, but sometimes the word τινες was dropped, so that ἐκ τῶν Φαρισαιων on its own meant "some of the Pharisees". The text now reads, "Now some of the Pharisees had been sent and they asked," meaning that Pharisees formed part of the delegation, or possibly that they were a separate delegation.

- **Verse 25** Τί is equivalent to διὰ τί, "why?" Compare verses 21 and 22 where it meant "what?" Note also the occurrences of εἰ and εἶ, "if" and "you (s) are". The inclusion of συ is emphatic.

- **Verse 26** Ἐγω βαπτιζω ἐν ὑδατι. "I baptize with water." This is repeated in verses 31 and 33. The corollary of this, "he will baptize with the Holy Spirit" is not introduced until verse 33. This delay seems to draw attention to the subsidiary nature of John's role. οὐκ οἰδατε, "you do not know," ties in with verse 10 of the Prologue. The inclusion of the pronouns ἐγω and ὑμεις again adds emphasis.

- **Verse 27** This is a good example of the need to escape the original structure where it does not transfer easily to English. A literal translation reads, "the one coming after me, of whom I am not worthy that I should untie the strap of the sandal". The Jerusalem Bible has a neat translation of the second part: "and I am not fit to undo his sandal strap". Again, ἐγω is emphatic.

- **Verse 28** The plural subject ταυτα, "these things", is followed by a singular verb ἐγενετο, "took place". This illustrates the rule that *neuter* plural subjects are sometimes followed by a singular verb. "Where" when it is asking a question is always ποῦ. When it is just making a connection ποῦ may be used, but usually it is ὁπου, as here.

Answers to exercises

Exercise 17.8

- βιος, ου m means "life" but usually in the sense of the material things that make up life. Here there are no negative connotations to κοσμος, "world", and a better translation for the phrase τον βιον του κοσμου would be "material possessions".
- The idiom "having need" is not good English. It would be better to say simply "in need".
- In Greek the word σπλαγχνα (pronounced splang-ch-na) was used figuratively to express the idea of inner emotions, in much the same way as we say, "I love you with all my heart," not meaning the blood pump situated in the chest! We can say "and closes his heart" or "and refuses to have pity".
- "From" is a literal translation of ἀπο but it doesn't necessarily match the English idiom, "closes his heart **against**" or "refuses to have pity **on**".
- The "whoever" at the beginning of the verse does not lead naturally on to the question "how" at the

end. Most translators change it to "if anyone has". It is also more natural in English to say, "how **can** God's love be in him?"

Exercise 17.10

John 1:14	a human being
Romans 11:13–14	fellow Jews
Galatians 5:19	fallen human nature
Hebrews 5:7	life on earth

These verses illustrate the different nuances of the word σαρξ depending on the context. The use of the word in connection with Jesus refers to his real humanity but without any connotation of fallenness or bias towards evil, such as we find in Galatians 5.

REVIEW QUESTIONS

1. Why is the language of the 17th century inappropriate for today?

2. What different criteria have shaped the work of translators?

3. When does a translation go beyond acceptable limits?

4. What three steps are involved in the process of translation?

5. What is wrong with the translation "Fear not" for μη φοβηθης?

6. Do different structures always imply a difference in meaning?

7. If structures are identical is the meaning always identical?

8. How should the Greek word σαρξ be translated?

9. What factors lead to languages carrying implicit information?

10. What implicit information is contained in Galatians 4:23?

11. Should a noun always be translated by a noun, a verb by a verb, etc?

12. What does ἀγγαρευω mean and what is the best way to translate it?

13. What is meant by "theological passives" and what alternative is available for translating them?

14. Why is the masculine gender so prevalent in the tradition of English Bible translations?

15. What is meant by "linguistic sexism" and "inclusive language"?

16. Why is it too simplistic to say that the genitive case is equivalent to a construction containing the word "of"?

17. In what way may a change of punctuation alter the meaning of John 1:21?

18. How do differences in manuscript evidence affect the interpretation of John 1 verses 19 and 24?

19. When is ποῦ used and when is ὅπου used?

20. Which personal pronouns are emphatic in John 1:19–28?

REVIEW EXERCISES

THREE TO COMPARE

Evaluate these three translations of Matthew 21:8–11 in the light of the Greek text and the issues we have been discussing in this chapter.

⁸ὁ δε πλειστος ὀχλος ἐστρωσαν ἑαυτων τα ἱματια ἐν τη ὁδῳ, ἀλλοι δε ἐκοπτον κλαδους ἀπο των δενδρων και ἐστρωννυον ἐν τη ὁδῳ.
⁹οἱ δε ὀχλοι οἱ προαγοντες αὐτον και οἱ ἀκολουθουντες ἐκραζον λεγοντες·

    Ὡσαννα τῳ υἱῳ Δαυιδ·

    εὐλογημενος ὁ ἐρχομενος ἐν ὀνοματι κυριου·

    ὡσαννα ἐν τοις ὑψιστοις.

¹⁰Και εἰσελθοντος αὐτου εἰς Ἱεροσολυμα ἐσεισθη πασα ἡ πολις λεγουσα·

    Τίς ἐστιν οὑτος;

¹¹οἱ δε ὀχλοι ἐλεγον·

    Οὑτος ἐστιν ὁ προφητης Ἰησους ὁ ἀπο Ναζαρεθ της Γαλιλαιας.

Revised Version

⁸And the most part of the multitude spread their garments in the way; and others cut branches from the trees, and spread them in the way.
⁹And the multitudes that went before him, and that followed, cried, saying, Hosanna to the son of David: Blessed is he that cometh in the name of the Lord; Hosanna in the highest.
¹⁰And when he was come into Jerusalem, all the city was stirred, saying, Who is this?
¹¹And the multitudes said, This is the prophet, Jesus, from Nazareth of Galilee.

Revised English Bible

[8] Crowds of people carpeted the road with their cloaks, and some cut branches from the trees to spread in his path. [9] Then the crowds in front and behind raised the shout: 'Hosanna to the Son of David! Blessed is he who comes in the name of the Lord! Hosanna in the heavens!' [10] When he entered Jerusalem the whole city went wild with excitement. 'Who is this?' people asked, [11] and the crowds replied, 'This is the prophet Jesus, from Nazareth in Galilee.'

Contemporary English Version

[8] Many people spread clothes in the road, while others put down branches which they had cut from trees. [9] Some people walked ahead of Jesus and others followed behind. They were all shouting,

"Hooray for the Son of David!
God bless the one who comes
   in the name of the Lord.
Hooray for God
   in heaven above!"

[10] When Jesus came to Jerusalem, everyone in the city was excited and asked, "Who can this be?"

[11] The crowd answered, "This is Jesus, the prophet from Nazareth in Galilee."

IS THIS DIFFICULT OR
IS IT DIFFICULT?

Look at the Greek text of Romans 3:22–26 below. What makes it so difficult, and how far have the sample translations been successful in clarifying the meaning?

²²οὐ γαρ ἐστιν διαστολη,
²³παντες γαρ ἡμαρτον και ὑστερουνται της δοξης του θεου
²⁴δικαιουμενοι δωρεαν τη αὐτου χαριτι
δια της ἀπολυτρωσεως της ἐν Χριστῳ Ἰησου·
²⁵ὁν προεθετο ὁ θεος ἱλαστηριον δια της πιστεως
ἐν τῳ αὐτου αἱματι
εἰς ἐνδειξιν της δικαιοσυνης αὐτου
δια την παρεσιν των προγεγονοτων ἁμαρτηματων
²⁶ἐν τη ἀνοχη του θεου,
προς την ἐνδειξιν της δικαιοσυνης αὐτου ἐν τῳ νυν καιρῳ,
εἰς το εἰναι αὐτον δικαιον και δικαιουντα τον ἐκ πιστεως
Ἰησου.

Young's Literal Translation

²²– for there is no difference,
²³for all did sin, and are come short of the glory of God –
²⁴being declared righteous freely by His grace
through the redemption that is in Christ Jesus,
²⁵whom God did set forth a mercy seat, through the faith in his blood, for the shewing forth of His righteousness, because of the passing over of the bygone sins
²⁶in the forbearance of God –
for the shewing forth of His righteousness in the present time, for His being righteous, and declaring him righteous who is of the faith of Jesus.

William Barclay's Translation

²²There is no distinction. ²³All have sinned; all have lost the divine glory which they were meant to have. ²⁴And all can enter into a right relationship with God as a free gift, by

SURFACE STRUCTURE AND DEEP MEANING 423

means of his grace, through the act of deliverance which happened in Jesus Christ. 25 It was God's purpose that Jesus Christ should be the one through whose sacrificial death sin can be forgiven through faith. Such a sacrifice was necessary to demonstrate God's justice, because in his forbearance he had not exacted from the men of past generations the penalty which their sins deserved. 26 And it was necessary in order to demonstrate his justice at this present time, by showing that, although he is just, he nevertheless puts the man who has faith in Jesus into a right relationship with him.

Contemporary English Version

22 God treats everyone alike.23 All of us have sinned and fallen short of God's glory. 24 But God is really kind, and because of Jesus Christ, he freely accepts us and sets us free from our sins. 25-26 God sent Christ to be our sacrifice. Christ offered his life's blood, so that by faith in him we could come to God. And God did this to show that in the past he was right to be patient and forgive sinners. This also shows that God is right when he accepts people who have faith in Jesus.

WORDS TO LEARN

αἰτεω   ask (sometimes in the middle voice, αἰτεομαι)
ἀνοιγω, aor. ἀνεῳξα, ἠνεῳξα, ἠνοιξα, perf. ἀνεῳγα open
ἀπολυω (compound of ἀπο + λυω)   release, send away, divorce
γραμματευς, εως m   scribe, teacher of the Law
διακονια, ας f   service, ministry
δοκεω   think, suppose; seem
    δοκεις;   Do you think?
    τί δοκει σοι;   What do you think? (What does it seem to you?)
ἐρωταω   ask
ἱερον, ου n   temple
καθαρος, α, ον   clean, pure

καιρος, ου m   time, opportunity
κεφαλη, ης f   head
κηρυσσω   preach
νυξ, νυκτος f   night
    ἡμερας και νυκτος   by day and night
πλοιον, ου n   boat
πρεσβυτερος, ου m   elder
πυρ, πυρος n   fire
τηρεω   keep (with commandments = obey)
ὑδωρ, ὑδατος n   water
φερω, fut. οἰσω, aor. ἠνεγκον   bear, carry
χαρα, ας f   joy

CHAPTER EIGHTEEN

Preview

Revision

Progress

Using what you know

Vocabulary

CHAPTER EIGHTEEN

Taking off the L-plates

What next?

18.1 It is said that you only start learning to drive when you have passed your driving test. The test is not the end; it is just the beginning. You have to get out onto the roads and gain experience as a driver on your own. In a similar way this chapter does not mark the end of your course but the beginning. We have been driving largely on the quieter roads of New Testament Greek and there is a world of discovery awaiting you – busier traffic and tricky situations, but also the freedom to explore fascinating areas of truth and go further in your understanding.

Back to the beginning

18.2 In any subject area there is a core of essential knowledge and the key to progress is to understand those central elements as thoroughly as possible. The material we have covered so far constitutes that core, and it will be well worth while going over it again. Some things which you found difficult will seem much easier and you will be reinforcing the foundations of your knowledge of Greek. It will not take as long to go through it a second time.

The road ahead

18.3 However you will also want to investigate new passages and become more confident in using the language. What is the best way to proceed? You may be using a specific syllabus which will determine your choice, but even if you are it is helpful to know which parts of the New Testament are suitable for beginners and which are not.

18.4   The first book I ever read in the Greek New Testament was the First Letter of John, and in many ways it is ideal. It is fairly short (only 105 verses) and many of the words and constructions are repeated throughout the book. There are some difficult parts, but they don't prevent you from reading through it at a sitting and understanding most of it.

18.5   The only disadvantage of starting with 1 John is that much of the vocabulary of the Gospels is missing. It does not talk about disciples, parables, going fishing, crowds coming and being healed, and so on. John's Gospel, like the first letter, contains fairly accessible Greek. You may not think so as a beginner, but coming back to it from 2 Corinthians or Hebrews is like stepping back from deep waters to the shallows near the shore.

18.6   Mark's Gospel is a favourite first text because it is the shortest of the Synoptic Gospels and contains a good variety of content and style. I have found Matthew's Gospel a little easier, but it is longer and so more difficult to complete. Luke's Gospel is probably the most difficult at this stage.

18.7   The Greek in Paul's letters takes you to a more advanced level than the Greek of the Gospels. This is partly because he loves to write in long sentences and also because his style is often terse and compressed. Romans and 1 Corinthians are easier than 2 Corinthians, but to complete a whole letter it is probably better to start with one of the shorter ones like Philippians or Colossians.

Go where your motives lead you

18.8   Although it is satisfying to tackle a whole book it may
be more realistic to select shorter passages to read
and translate, even single verses. Start with something familiar. It is not "cheating" to use what you
know to help with what you don't know. We do it all
the time with our own language. Take the word
"druxy". Here are three possible meanings.

druxy	intoxicated
	half-asleep
	decayed

Which is correct? Unless it happens to be within your
field you probably won't know, but if I use it in a
sentence it will be obvious straight away.

> Don't use that timber. It looks OK but it's
> druxy.

What you know is the clue to what you don't know. It
means having decayed spots concealed by healthy
wood.

18.9   If your favourite text is John 3:16, or if your favourite
chapter is 1 Corinthians 13, or if your favourite
section is the Sermon on the Mount, then start there.
Your progress will be quicker simply because you are
familiar with the material.

Maps and maintenance manuals

18.10   In Chapter 8 I mentioned some reference books. If
you intend to take your knowledge of the Greek New
Testament further you will need a Greek-English
dictionary and I would strongly recommend a Gram-

matical Analysis. If you have decided which "route" you intend to take then you can buy a detailed "map" for that specific journey. In terms of the Greek New Testament that map is a good commentary on the original text.

18.11   You can drive a car without a very deep knowledge of how it works. It is only if you want to be a mechanic that you need to learn how everything works. In the same way it is possible to read a language without knowing much about its grammar, but if, for example, you want to work as a translator, you will need a much more sophisticated understanding of how the language works. There are more advanced books on Greek grammar if you need them, but they are for specialists. For the majority of people who want to read the Greek New Testament it is best to devote your time and energies to the New Testament itself rather than more advanced grammars.

Filling up with petrol

18.12   Just as you need plenty of petrol for a long journey the "fuel" for your journey into the Greek New Testament is vocabulary. You need to know what the words mean. The words to learn at the end of the chapters have been selected because they occur most frequently in the New Testament. They should be learned thoroughly and reviewed regularly so that you are "driving on a full tank". Here are some more word lists to add to them.

WORDS TO LEARN

1.

Ἀβρααμ Abraham
ἀγρος, ου m field
ἀληθως truly
βαπτισμα, τος n baptism
βαπτιστης, ου m baptist
δεικνυμι show
ἐγγιζω draw near, approach
ἐγγυς near
ἐλευθερος, α, ον free
θλιψις, εως f trouble, distress
ἱματιον, ου n garment
καθαριζω cleanse
λιθος, ου m stone
μακαριος, α, ον happy, blessed
μαρτυριον, ου n witness
ὁδος, ου f way
παντοτε always
παραδοσις, εως f tradition
σημερον today
σοφια, ας f wisdom

2.

ἁγιαζω consecrate, purify
ἀκαθαρτος, ον unclean
ἀναστασις, εως f resurrection
γαμεω marry
δεκα ten
εἰκων, εἰκονος f image

ἑκατον   a hundred
ἑκατονταρχος, ου m   centurion
ζητεω   seek
θυρα, ας f   door, gate
'Ιακωβος, ου m   James
κἀγω (= και ἐγω)   and I
κλαιω   weep, cry
λεπρος, ου m   leper
μαχαιρα, ης f   sword
νεος, α, ον   new
παλαιος, α, ον   old
παρθενος, ου f   virgin
συναγω   gather
συναγωγη, ης f   synagogue

3.
ἀγοραζω   buy
ἀμπελων, ωνος m   vineyard
ἀπερχομαι   leave
ἀριστερος, α, ον   left (opposite to right)
δεξιος, α, ον   right (opposite to left)
ἐκβαλλω   cast out
ἐκει   there
ἐλπιζω   hope
'Ηλιας, ου m   Elijah
ἱερευς, εως m   priest
καθημαι   sit
κριτης, ου m   judge
λυω   loose, destroy
μερος, ους n   part
ναος, ου m   sanctuary, temple

παραγγελλω + dative   command
πληρης, ες full
πλουσιος, α, ον rich
πτωχος, η, ον poor
τελος, ους n end

4.
ἀμην amen, truly
ἀνεμος, ου m wind
ἁπτομαι + genitive touch, hold
βασταζω carry
δευτερος, α, ον second
διωκω persecute, pursue
εἰτε..εἰτε whether..or
ἐλεεω have mercy on
ἐλεος, ους n mercy
ἐπερωταω ask
ἠδη already, now
ἰαομαι heal
ἰατρος, ου m doctor
καθιζω sit
κακος, η, ον bad
μισθος, ου m pay, reward
νεφελη, ης f cloud
οἰκοδομεω build
παις, παιδος m child, servant
σκευος, ους n jar

5.

ἀγω go, lead, bring
ἀναβαινω, aor. ἀνεβην ascend, go up
Ἀνδρεας, ου m Andrew
βλασφημεω blaspheme
διακονεω + dative serve
διακονος, ου m servant, deacon
δυνατος, η, ον possible, powerful
ἐκπορευομαι go out
ἐμος, η, ον my
ἐπιστολη, ης f letter
εὐλογεω bless
θυσια, ας f sacrifice
Ἱεροσολυμα n. pl. and f.sg. Jerusalem
Ἱερουσαλημ f Jerusalem
Ἰσραηλ m Israel
καθιστημι appoint
λοιπος, η, ον remaining
οἰνος, ου m wine
παραγινομαι come, arrive
σταυρος, ου m cross

6.

ἀδικεω do wrong
ἀδικια, ας f wrongdoing, evil
ἀνακειμαι be seated at table
βουλομαι wish, want
διδαχη, ης f teaching
διερχομαι go through
Ἑλλην, ηνος m Greek
ἐμπροσθεν + genitive before

ἐνδυω   put on
ἰδου   behold, see
ἱκανος, η, ον   sufficient
καινος, η, ον   new
καταβαινω   go down, descend
κατοικεω   live, live in
μαλιστα   especially
ὀλιγος, η, ον   small, pl. few
ὁπου   where
οὑς, ὡτος n   ear
παραλαμβανω   take, receive, accept
πεντε   five

7.

ἀπαγγελλω, fut. ἀπαγγελῶ, aor. ἀπηγγειλα   proclaim
ἁπας, ἁπασα, ἁπαν   all
ἀρα   therefore
γενεα, ας f   generation
δικαιοω   justify
ἐνωπιον + genitive   before, in the presence of
ἑξ   six
ἐπαγγελια, ας f   promise
Ἰουδαια, ας f   Judea
κατακειμαι   lie, be sick, recline at table
κειμαι   lie, be, stand
λογιζομαι   reckon, consider
ὁμοιος, α, ον   of the same nature as, like
    ὁμοιος αὐτῳ   like him
ὁταν   when, whenever
ὁτε   when
παριστημι   present, show, provide

πειραζω test, tempt
πειρασμος, ου m trial, temptation
σκανδαλιζω cause to sin, offend
σκανδαλον, ου n that which causes sin, stumbling

8.
ἀποδιδωμι give back, pay, repay
ἀποκαλυψις, εως f revelation
ἀρνεομαι deny
γενος, ους n race, sort, kind
ἐξω out, outside
ἐπιγινωσκω know, perceive
ἑπτα seven
'Ιουδας, α m Judas
καταλειπω, aor. κατελιπον leave
μαλλον rather
μυστηριον, ου n mystery, secret
ὁμολογεω confess
ὅστις, ἥτις, ὅτι who, whoever
οὐαι woe
πασχα n Passover
πασχω, aor. ἐπαθον suffer
προφητευω prophesy
τελωνης, ου m tax-collector
τεσσερακοντα forty
τοπος, ου m place

9.

ἀπαγω   lead, lead away
ἀργυριον, ου n   silver, money
ἀσθενεω   be ill, weak
ἀσθενης, ες   sick, weak
δοξαζω   glorify
ἐξερχομαι   come out
ἐπιστρεφω   turn, return
ἐσχατος, η, ον   last
καυχαομαι   boast, rejoice
μεσος, η, ον   middle, in the middle
ὀφειλω   owe, ought, be obliged
Παυλος, ου m   Paul
πληθος, ους n   crowd, number
πρασσω   do
σκοτος, ους n   darkness
στρεφω, aor. pass ἐστραφην   turn
συνερχομαι   come together
τεσσαρες, α   four
φιλος, ου m   friend
χρυσιον, ου n   gold

10.

ἀρτι   now
ἀρχω   rule, govern. ἀρχομαι (mid.)   begin
ἀρχων, οντος m   ruler, official
διο   therefore
ἐπιτιθημι   lay or put on
ἐργαζομαι   work
ἐργατης, ου m   workman
ἠ   or, than

κραζω, aor. ἐκραξα, perf. κεκραγα cry out, shout
μεν (with δε forms a contrast)
μηδε nor, and not, not even. μηδε..μηδε neither nor
οὐδε nor, and not, not even. οὐδε..οὐδε neither nor
οὐχι not, no (emphatic form of οὐ)
πειθω persuade. Perf. πεποιθα, be confident
πετρα, ας f rock
σπερμα, ατος n seed, offspring
συνεδριον, ου n Sanhedrin
σωτηρ, σωτηρος m saviour
τερας, τερατος n wonder, omen
φαινω shine. Aor. pass. ἐφανην. φαινομαι appear, be
  revealed

11.
ἀσπαζομαι greet
δεω bind, tie
ἐπιτιμαω + dative command, rebuke
ἐρημος, ου f desert
ἐτι still, yet
κρατεω hold, seize
μελος, ους n limb, member
μηκετι no longer
μην, μηνος m month
μνημειον, ου n grave, tomb
οὐκετι no longer
πλειων, ον more, most
ποιος, α, ον what? which?
ποταμος, ου m river
προ + genitive before
προσερχομαι approach, come to

τιμαω honour
τιμη, ης f honour, price
τοιουτος, τοιαυτη, τοιουτον such as this
ὑπακουω + dative obey

12.
ἑτοιμαζω prepare
ἑτος, ους n year
εὐ well
κρειττων, ον better (also, κρεισσων, ον)
ὁπως that, in order that
ὁσος, η, ον as much as
προσφερω offer, present
συνανακειμαι sit at table with
συνειδησις, εως f conscience, awareness
τε and
ὑπαγω go, depart
ὑποκριτης, ου m hypocrite
φανεροω make known, reveal
Φαρισαιος, ου m Pharisee
φευγω, aor. ἐφυγον flee
φημι say
χειρων, ον worse
χηρα, ας f widow
χιλιοι, αι, α thousand
ὡδε here

13.

ἀκροβυστια, ας f uncircumcision
ἀχρι until, as far as
ἐλαχιστος, η, ον least
εὐαγγελιζομαι preach the good news
εὐχαριστεω give thanks
ἐφιστημι approach, stand near
κρυπτω hide
μακροθυμια, ας f patience
περιτομη, ης f circumcision
στρατιωτης, ου m soldier
ταπεινος, η, ον humble
ὑπαρχω be
ὑπομονη, ης f steadfastness
ὑποστρεφω return, turn back
φυλακη, ης f prison, guard
φυλασσω guard
φωνεω call, summon
χιλιαρχος, ου m tribune, commander
χωρις + genitive without
ὡσπερ just as

REFERENCE SECTION

NOUNS

FEM	1.1 (f)	1.2 (f)	1.3 (f)	1.4 (m)	1.5 (m)	1.6 (m)
ἡ	γραφη	καρδια	γλωσσα	μαθητης	νεανιας	Σατανας
				μαθητα	νεανια	Σατανα
την	γραφην	καρδιαν	γλωσσαν	μαθητην	νεανιαν	Σαταναν
της	γραφης	καρδιας	γλωσσης	μαθητου	νεανιου	Σατανα
τη	γραφη	καρδιᾳ	γλωσση	μαθητη	νεανιᾳ	Σατανᾳ
αἱ	γραφαι	καρδιαι	γλωσσαι	μαθηται	νεανιαι	
τας	γραφας	καρδιας	γλωσσας	μαθητας	νεανιας	
των	γραφων	καρδιων	γλωσσων	μαθητων	νεανιων	
ταις	γραφαις	καρδιαις	γλωσσαις	μαθηταις	νεανιαις	

MASC	2.1 (m/f)	2.2 (m)	2.3 (n)	NEUT
ὁ	λογος	Ἰησους	ἐργον	το
	λογε	Ἰησου		
τον	λογον	Ἰησουν	ἐργον	το
του	λογου	Ἰησου	ἐργου	του
τῳ	λογῳ	Ἰησου	ἐργῳ	τῳ
οἱ	λογοι		ἐργα	τα
τους	λογους		ἐργα	τα
των	λογων		ἐργων	των
τοις	λογοις		ἐργοις	τοις

3.1 (m/f)	3.2 (m/f)	3.3 (m/f)	3.4 (f)	3.5 (m)	3.6 (n)	3.7 (n)
ἐλπις	πατηρ	ἰχθυς	πολις	βασιλευς	σωμα	ὀρος
	πατερ	ἰχθυ	πολι	βασιλευ		
ἐλπιδα	πατερα	ἰχθυν	πολιν	βασιλεα	σωμα	ὀρος
ἐλπιδος	πατρος	ἰχθυος	πολεως	βασιλεως	σωματος	ὀρους
ἐλπιδι	πατρι	ἰχθυι	πολει	βασιλει	σωματι	ὀρει
ἐλπιδες	πατερες	ἰχθυες	πολεις	βασιλεις	σωματα	ὀρη
ἐλπιδας	πατερας	ἰχθυας	πολεις	βασιλεις	σωματα	ὀρη
ἐλπιδων	πατερων	ἰχθυων	πολεων	βασιλεων	σωματων	ὀρων
ἐλπισιν	πατρασιν	ἰχθυσιν	πολεσιν	βασιλευσιν	σωμασιν	ὀρεσιν

ADJECTIVES

M	F	N	M	F	N	M/F	N
ἀγαθος	ἀγαθη	ἀγαθον	ἁγιος	ἁγια	ἁγιον	ἀληθης	ἀληθες
ἀγαθε			ἁγιε				
ἀγαθον	ἀγαθην	ἀγαθον	ἁγιον	ἁγιαν	ἁγιον	ἀληθη	ἀληθες
ἀγαθου	ἀγαθης	ἀγαθου	ἁγιου	ἁγιας	ἁγιου	ἀληθους	ἀληθους
ἀγαθῳ	ἀγαθη	ἀγαθῳ	ἁγιῳ	ἁγιᾳ	ἁγιῳ	ἀληθει	ἀληθει
ἀγαθοι	ἀγαθαι	ἀγαθα	ἁγιοι	ἁγιαι	ἁγια	ἀληθεις	ἀληθη
ἀγαθους	ἀγαθας	ἀγαθα	ἁγιους	ἁγιας	ἁγια	ἀληθεις	ἀληθη
ἀγαθων	ἀγαθων	ἀγαθων	ἁγιων	ἁγιων	ἁγιων	ἀληθων	ἀληθων
ἀγαθοις	ἀγαθαις	ἀγαθοις	ἁγιοις	ἁγιαις	ἁγιοις	ἀληθεσιν	ἀληθεσιν

M	F	N	M	F	N	M/F	N
μεγας	μεγαλη	μεγα	πολυς	πολλη	πολυ	πλειων	πλειον
μεγαν	μεγαλην	μεγα	πολυν	πολλην	πολυ	πλειονα	πλειον
μεγαλου	μεγαλης	μεγαλου	πολλου	πολλης	πολλου	πλειονος	πλειονος
μεγαλῳ	μεγαλη	μεγαλῳ	πολλῳ	πολλη	πολλῳ	πλειονι	πλειονι
μεγαλοι	μεγαλαι	μεγαλα	πολλοι	πολλαι	πολλα	πλειονες	πλειονα
μεγαλους	μεγαλας	μεγαλα	πολλους	πολλας	πολλα	πλειονας	πλειονα
μεγαλων	μεγαλων	μεγαλων	πολλων	πολλων	πολλων	πλειονων	πλειονων
μεγαλοις	μεγαλαις	μεγαλοις	πολλοις	πολλαις	πολλοις	πλειοσιν	πλειοσιν

M	F	N	M	F	N
πας	πασα	παν	εἱς	μια	ἑν
παντα	πασαν	παν	ἑνα	μιαν	ἑν
παντος	πασης	παντος	ἑνος	μιας	ἑνος
παντι	παση	παντι	ἑνι	μιᾳ	ἑνι
παντες	πασαι	παντα			
παντας	πασας	παντα			
παντων	πασων	παντων			
πασιν	πασαις	πασιν			

PRONOUNS

I	you	he, she, it			myself		yourself		him/her/itself		
ἐγω	συ	αὐτος	η	ο							
με, ἐμε	σε	αὐτον	ην	ο	ἐμαυτον	ην	σεαυτον	ην	ἑαυτον	ην	ο
μου, ἐμου	σου	αὐτου	ης	ου	ἐμαυτου	ης	σεαυτου	ης	ἑαυτου	ης	ου
μοι, ἐμοι	σοι	αὐτῳ	ῃ	ῳ	ἐμαυτῳ	ῃ	σεαυτῳ	ῃ	ἑαυτῳ	ῃ	ῳ

we	you	they			ourselves, yourselves, themselves		one another
ἡμεις	ὑμεις	αὐτοι	αι	α			
ἡμας	ὑμας	αὐτους	ας	α	ἑαυτους	ας α	ἀλληλους
ἡμων	ὑμων	αὐτων	ων	ων	ἑαυτων	ων ων	ἀλληλων
ἡμιν	ὑμιν	αὐτοις	αις	οις	ἑαυτοις	αις οις	ἀλληλοις

who, which			anyone*		this			that		
ὁς	ἡ	ὁ	τις	τι	οὑτος	αὑτη	τουτο	ἐκεινος	η	ο
ὁν	ἡν	ὁ	τινα	τι	τουτον	ταυτην	τουτο	ἐκεινον	ην	ο
οὑ	ἡς	οὑ	τινος	τινος	τουτου	ταυτης	τουτου	ἐκεινου	ης	ου
ᾡ	ᾑ	ᾡ	τινι	τινι	τουτῳ	ταυτῃ	τουτῳ	ἐκεινῳ	η	ῳ

					these			those		
οἱ	αἱ	ἁ	τινες	τινα	οὑτοι	αὑται	ταυτα	ἐκεινοι	αι	α
οὑς	ἁς	ἁ	τινας	τινα	τουτους	ταυτας	ταυτα	ἐκεινους	ας	α
ὡν	ὡν	ὡν	τινων	τινων	τουτων	τουτων	τουτων	ἐκεινων	ων	ων
οἱς	αἱς	οἱς	τισιν	τισιν	τουτοις	ταυταις	τουτοις	ἐκεινοις	αις	οις

*Without an accent τις is the indefinite pronoun, "someone", "anyone", etc.
With an accent τίς is the interrogative pronoun, "who?", "what?", etc.

οὑτος and ἐκεινος can be used as adjectives as well as pronouns.

THE REGULAR VERB: ACTIVE

	INDICATIVE	SUBJUNCTIVE	IMPERATIVE	INFINITIVE	PARTICIPLE
PRESENT	λυω λυεις λυει λυομεν λυετε λυουσιν	λυω* λυης λυη λυωμεν λυητε λυωσιν	λυε* λυετω λυετε λυετωσαν	λυειν*	λυων -ουσα -ον*
FUTURE	λυσω λυσεις λυσει λυσομεν λυσετε λυσουσιν				
IMPERFECT	ἐλυον* ἐλυες ἐλυεν ἐλυομεν ἐλυετε ἐλυον				
AORIST	ἐλυσα ἐλυσας ἐλυσεν ἐλυσαμεν ἐλυσατε ἐλυσαν	λυσω λυσης λυση λυσωμεν λυσητε λυσωσιν	λυσον λυσατω λυσατε λυσατωσαν	λυσαι	λυσας -ασα -αν
PERFECT	λελυκα λελυκας λελυκεν λελυκαμεν λελυκατε λελυκασιν			λελυκεναι	λελυκως -υια -ος
PLUPERFECT	ἐλελυκειν ἐλελυκεις ἐλελυκει ἐλελυκειμεν ἐλελυκειτε ἐλελυκεισαν				

*These endings are also used for the 2nd aorist

THE REGULAR VERB: MIDDLE

	INDICATIVE	SUBJUNCTIVE	IMPERATIVE	INFINITIVE	PARTICIPLE
PRESENT	λυομαι λυη λυεται λυομεθα λυεσθε λυονται	λυωμαι* λυη λυηται λυωμεθα λυησθε λυωνται	λυου* λυεσθω λυεσθε λυεσθωσαν	λυεσθαι*	λυομενος -η -ον*
FUTURE	λυσομαι λυση λυσεται λυσομεθα λυσεσθε λυσονται				
IMPERFECT	ἐλυομην* ἐλυου ἐλυετο ἐλυομεθα ἐλυεσθε ἐλυοντο				
AORIST	ἐλυσαμην ἐλυσω ἐλυσατο ἐλυσαμεθα ἐλυσασθε ἐλυσαντο	λυσωμαι λυση λυσηται λυσωμεθα λυσησθε λυσωνται	λυσαι λυσασθω λυσασθε λυσασθωσαν	λυσασθαι	λυσαμενος -η -ον
PERFECT	λελυμαι λελυσαι λελυται λελυμεθα λελυσθε λελυνται			λελυσθαι	λελυμενος -η -ον
PLUPERFECT	ἐλελυμην ἐλελυσο ἐλελυτο ἐλελυμεθα ἐλελυσθε ἐλελυντο				

*These endings are also used for the 2nd aorist.

THE REGULAR VERB: PASSIVE

	INDICATIVE	SUBJUNCTIVE	IMPERATIVE	INFINITIVE	PARTICIPLE
PRESENT	λυομαι λυῃ λυεται λυομεθα λυεσθε λυονται	λυωμαι λυῃ λυηται λυωμεθα λυησθε λυωνται	λυου λυεσθω λυεσθε λυεσθωσαν	λυεσθαι	λυομενος -η -ον
FUTURE	λυθησομαι λυθησῃ λυθησεται λυθησομεθα λυθησεσθε λυθησονται				
IMPERFECT	ἐλυομην ἐλυου ἐλυετο ἐλυομεθα ἐλυεσθε ἐλυοντο				
AORIST	ἐλυθην ἐλυθης ἐλυθη ἐλυθημεν ἐλυθητε ἐλυθησαν	λυθω λυθῃς λυθῃ λυθωμεν λυθητε λυθωσιν	λυθητι λυθητω λυθητε λυθητωσαν	λυθηναι	λυθεις -εισα -εν
PERFECT	λελυμαι λελυσαι λελυται λελυμεθα λελυσθε λελυνται				λελυσθαι	λελυμενος -η -ον
PLUPERFECT	ἐλελυμην ἐλελυσο ἐλελυτο ἐλελυμεθα ἐλελυσθε ἐλελυντο				

THE REGULAR VERB: PARTICIPLES

PRESENT

ACTIVE*			MIDDLE* / PASSIVE		
λυων	λυουσα	λυον	λυομενος	λυομενη	λυομενον
λυοντα	λυουσαν	λυον	λυομενον	λυομενην	λυομενον
λυοντος	λυουσης	λυοντος	λυομενου	λυομενης	λυομενου
λυοντι	λυουσῃ	λυοντι	λυομενῳ	λυομενη	λυομενῳ
λυοντες	λυουσαι	λυοντα	λυομενοι	λυομεναι	λυομενα
λυοντας	λυουσας	λυοντα	λυομενους	λυομενας	λυομενα
λυοντων	λυουσων	λυοντων	λυομενων	λυομενων	λυομενων
λυουσιν	λυουσαις	λυουσιν	λυομενοις	λυομεναις	λυομενοις

AORIST

ACTIVE			MIDDLE			PASSIVE		
λυσας	λυσασα	λυσαν	λυσαμενος	λυσαμενη	λυσαμενον	λυθεις	λυθεισα	λυθεν
λυσαντα	λυσασαν	λυσαν	λυσαμενον	λυσαμενην	λυσαμενον	λυθεντα	λυθεισαν	λυθεν
λυσαντος	λυσασης	λυσαντος	λυσαμενου	λυσαμενης	λυσαμενου	λυθεντος	λυθεισης	λυθεντος
λυσαντι	λυσασῃ	λυσαντι	λυσαμενῳ	λυσαμενη	λυσαμενῳ	λυθεντι	λυθεισῃ	λυθεντι
λυσαντες	λυσασαι	λυσαντα	λυσαμενοι	λυσαμεναι	λυσαμενα	λυθεντες	λυθεισαι	λυθεντα
λυσαντας	λυσασας	λυσαντα	λυσαμενους	λυσαμενας	λυσαμενα	λυθεντας	λυθεισας	λυθεντα
λυσαντων	λυσασων	λυσαντων	λυσαμενων	λυσαμενων	λυσαμενων	λυθεντων	λυθεισων	λυθεντων
λυσασιν	λυσασαις	λυσασιν	λυσαμενοις	λυσαμεναις	λυσαμενοις	λυθεισιν	λυθεισαις	λυθεισιν

PERFECT

ACTIVE			MIDDLE / PASSIVE		
λελυκως	λελυκυια	λελυκος	λελυμενος	λελυμενη	λελυμενα
λελυκοτα	λελυκυιαν	λελυκος	λελυμενον	λελυμενην	λελυμενα
λελυκοτος	λελυκυιας	λελυκοτος	λελυμενου	λελυμενης	λελυμενου
λελυκοτι	λελυκυιᾳ	λελυκοτι	λελυμενῳ	λελυμενη	λελυμενῳ
λελυκοτες	λελυκυιαι	λελυκοτα	λελυμενοι	λελυμεναι	λελυμενα
λελυκοτας	λελυκυιας	λελυκοτα	λελυμενους	λελυμενας	λελυμενα
λελυκοτων	λελυκυιων	λελυκοτων	λελυμενων	λελυμενων	λελυμενων
λελυκοσιν	λελυκυιαις	λελυκοσιν	λελυμενοις	λελυμεναις	λελυμενοις

*These endings are also used for the 2nd aorist.

CONTRACTED 'E' VERBS

ACTIVE

	INDICATIVE	SUBJUNCTIVE	IMPERATIVE	INFINITIVE	PARTICIPLE		
PRES	φιλω	φιλω			φιλων	φιλουσα	φιλουν
	φιλεις	φιλης	φιλει		φιλουντα	φιλουσαν	φιλουν
	φιλει	φιλη	φιλειτω		φιλουντος	φιλουσης	φιλουντος
	φιλουμεν	φιλωμεν		φιλειν	φιλουντι	φιλουση	φιλουντι
	φιλειτε	φιλητε	φιλειτε				
	φιλουσιν	φιλωσιν	φιλειτωσαν		φιλουντες	φιλουσαι	φιλουντα
					φιλουντας	φιλουσας	φιλουντα
					φιλουντων	φιλουσων	φιλουντων
					φιλουσιν	φιλουσαις	φιλουσιν
IMPF	ἐφιλουν						
	ἐφιλεις						
	ἐφιλει						
	ἐφιλουμεν						
	ἐφιλειτε						
	ἐφιλουν						

Fut. φιλησω, aor. ἐφιλησα, perf. πεφιληκα

MIDDLE / PASSIVE

	INDICATIVE	SUBJUNCTIVE	IMPERATIVE	INFINITIVE	PARTICIPLE		
PRES	φιλουμαι	φιλωμαι			φιλουμενος	-η	-ον
	φιλη	φιλη	φιλου		φιλουμενον	-ην	-ον
	φιλειται	φιληται	φιλεισθω		φιλουμενου	-ης	-ου
	φιλουμεθα	φιλωμεθα		φιλεισθαι	φιλουμενω	-η	-ω
	φιλεισθε	φιλησθε	φιλεισθε				
	φιλουνται	φιλωνται	φιλεισθωσαν		φιλουμενοι	-αι	-α
					φιλουμενους	-ας	-α
					φιλουμενων	-ων	-ων
					φιλουμενοις	-αις	-οις
IMPF	ἐφιλουμην						
	ἐφιλου						
	ἐφιλειτο						
	ἐφιλουμεθα						
	ἐφιλεισθε						
	ἐφιλουντο						

Aor. pass. ἐφιληθην, perf. mid/pass. πεφιλημαι

CONTRACTED 'A' VERBS

ACTIVE

	INDICATIVE	SUBJUNCTIVE	IMPERATIVE	INFINITIVE	PARTICIPLE		
PRES	ἀγαπω ἀγαπας ἀγαπα ἀγαπωμεν ἀγαπατε ἀγαπωσιν	ἀγαπω ἀγαπας ἀγαπα ἀγαπωμεν ἀγαπατε ἀγαπωσιν	ἀγαπα ἀγαπατω ἀγαπατε ἀγαπατωσαν	ἀγαπαν	ἀγαπων ἀγαπωντα ἀγαπωντος ἀγαπωντι ἀγαπωντες ἀγαπωντας ἀγαπωντων ἀγαπωσιν	ἀγαπωσα ἀγαπωσαν ἀγαπωσης ἀγαπωσῃ ἀγαπωσαι ἀγαπωσας ἀγαπωσων ἀγαπωσαις	ἀγαπων ἀγαπων ἀγαπωντος ἀγαπωντι ἀγαπωντα ἀγαπωντα ἀγαπωντων ἀγαπωσιν
IMPF	ἠγαπων ἠγαπας ἠγαπα ἠγαπωμεν ἠγαπατε ἠγαπων						

Fut. ἀγαπησω, aor. ἠγαπησα, perf. ἠγαπηκα

MIDDLE / PASSIVE

	INDICATIVE	SUBJUNCTIVE	IMPERATIVE	INFINITIVE	PARTICIPLE		
PRES	ἀγαπωμαι	ἀγαπωμαι			ἀγαπωμενος	-η	-ον
	ἀγαπᾳ	ἀγαπᾳ	ἀγαπω		ἀγαπωμενον	-ην	-ον
	ἀγαπαται	ἀγαπαται	ἀγαπασθω		ἀγαπωμενου	-ης	-ου
	ἀγαπωμεθα	ἀγαπωμεθα		ἀγαπασθαι	ἀγαπωμενῳ	-η	-ῳ
	ἀγαπασθε	ἀγαπασθε	ἀγαπασθε				
	ἀγαπωνται	ἀγαπωνται	ἀγαπασθωσαν		ἀγαπωμενοι	-αι	-α
					ἀγαπωμενους	-ας	-α
					ἀγαπωμενων	-ων	-ων
					ἀγαπωμενοις	-αις	-οις
IMPF	ἠγαπωμην						
	ἠγαπω						
	ἠγαπατο						
	ἠγαπωμεθα						
	ἠγαπασθε						
	ἠγαπωντο						

Aor. pass. ἠγαπηθην, perf. mid/pass. ἠγαπημαι

CONTRACTED 'O' VERBS

ACTIVE

	INDICATIVE	SUBJUNCTIVE	IMPERATIVE	INFINITIVE	PARTICIPLE		
PRES	πληρω	πληρω			πληρων	πληρουσα	πληρουν
	πληροις	πληροις	πληρου		πληρουντα	πληρουσαν	πληρουν
	πληροι	πληροι	πληρουτω		πληρουντος	πληρουσης	πληρουντος
	πληρουμεν	πληρωμεν		πληρουν	πληρουντι	πληρουση	πληρουντι
	πληρουτε	πληρωτε	πληρουτε				
	πληρουσιν	πληρωσιν	πληρουτωσαν		πληρουντες	πληρουσαι	πληρουντα
					πληρουντας	πληρουσας	πληρουντα
					πληρουντων	πληρουσων	πληρουντων
					πληρουσιν	πληρουσαις	πληρουσιν
IMPF	ἐπληρουν						
	ἐπληρους						
	ἐπληρου						
	ἐπληρουμεν						
	ἐπληρουτε						
	ἐπληρουν						

Fut. πληρωσω, aor. ἐπληρωσα, perf. πεπληρωκα

MIDDLE / PASSIVE

	INDICATIVE	SUBJUNCTIVE	IMPERATIVE	INFINITIVE	PARTICIPLE		
PRES	πληρουμαι	πληρωμαι			πληρουμενος	-η	-ον
	πληροι	πληροι	πληρου		πληρουμενον	-ην	-ον
	πληρουται	πληρωται	πληρουσθω		πληρουμενου	-ης	-ου
	πληρουμεθα	πληρωμεθα		πληρουσθαι	πληρουμενῳ	-ῃ	-ῳ
	πληρουσθε	πληρωσθε	πληρουσθε				
	πληρουνται	πληρωνται	πληρουσθωσαν		πληρουμενοι	-αι	-α
					πληρουμενους	-ας	-α
					πληρουμενων	-ων	-ων
					πληρουμενοις	-αις	-οις
IMPF	ἐπληρουμην						
	ἐπληρου						
	ἐπληρειτο						
	ἐπληρουμεθα						
	ἐπληρεισθε						
	ἐπληρουντο						

Aor. pass. ἐπληρωθην, perf. mid/pass. πεπληρωμαι

$$\boxed{\text{εἰμι}}$$

	INDICATIVE	SUBJUNCTIVE	IMPERATIVE	INFINITIVE	PARTICIPLE
PRESENT	εἰμι	ὦ			
	εἶ	ᾖς	ἰσθι		
	ἐστιν	ᾖ	ἐστω		
	ἐσμεν	ὦμεν		εἰναι	ὢν οὐσα ον
	ἐστε	ἠτε	ἐστε		(ὀντος)
	εἰσιν	ὦσιν	ἐστωσαν		
FUTURE	ἐσομαι				
	ἐσῃ				
	ἐσται				
	ἐσομεθα				
	ἐσεσθε				
	ἐσονται				
IMPERFECT	ἠμην				
	ἠς or ἠσθα				
	ἠν				
	ἠμεν or ἠμεθα				
	ἠτε				
	ἠσαν				

IRREGULAR AORISTS

γινωσκω

INDICATIVE	SUBJUNCTIVE	IMPERATIVE	INFINITIVE	PARTICIPLE
ἐγνων	γνω			
ἐγνως	γνῳς	γνωθι		
ἐγνω	γνῳ	γνωτω		
ἐγνωμεν	γνωμεν		γνωναι	γνους γνουσα γνον
ἐγνωτε	γνωτε	γνωτε		(γνοντος)
ἐγνωσαν	γνωσιν	γνωτωσαν		

βαινω (always in compounds)

INDICATIVE	SUBJUNCTIVE	IMPERATIVE	INFINITIVE	PARTICIPLE
ἐβην	βω			
ἐβης	βης	βηθι or βα		
ἐβη	βη	βατω		
ἐβημεν	βωμεν		βηναι	βας βασα βαν
ἐβητε	βητε	βατε		(βαντος)
ἐβησαν	βωσιν	βατωσαν		

$$\boxed{\delta \iota \delta \omega \mu \iota}$$

ACTIVE

	INDICATIVE	SUBJUNCTIVE	IMPERATIVE	INFINITIVE	PARTICIPLE
PRESENT	διδωμι διδως διδωσιν διδομεν διδοτε διδοασιν	διδω διδῳς or διδοις διδῳ or διδοι διδωμεν διδωτε διδωσιν	διδου διδοτω διδοτε διδοτωσαν	διδοναι	διδους -ουσα -ον (διδοντος)
IMPERFECT	ἐδιδουν ἐδιδους ἐδιδου ἐδιδομεν ἐδιδοτε ἐδιδοσαν or ἐδιδουν				
AORIST	ἐδωκα ἐδωκας ἐδωκεν ἐδωκαμεν ἐδωκατε ἐδωκαν	δω δῳς or δοις δῳ or δοι δωμεν δωτε δωσιν	δος δοτω δοτε δοτωσαν	δουναι	δους δουσα δον (δοντος)

Fut. δωσω, perf. δεδωκα.

MIDDLE / PASSIVE

	INDICATIVE	SUBJUNCTIVE	IMPERATIVE	INFINITIVE	PARTICIPLE
PRESENT	διδομαι διδοσαι . . .	διδωμαι διδῳ . . .	διδοσο διδοσθω . . .	διδοσθαι	διδομενος -η -ον
IMPERFECT	ἐδιδομην ἐδιδοσο . . .				
AORIST MIDDLE	ἐδομην ἐδοσο . . .	δωμαι δῳ . . .	δου δοσθω	δοσθαι	δομενος -η -ον

Aor. pass. ἐδοθην, perf. mid/pass. δεδομαι.

In the middle and passive the short o, or long ω, in the ending of a mood is retained all the way through that mood.

τιθημι

ACTIVE

	INDICATIVE	SUBJUNCTIVE	IMPERATIVE	INFINITIVE	PARTICIPLE
PRESENT	τιθημι τιθης τιθησιν τιθεμεν τιθετε τιθεασιν	τιθω τιθης τιθη τιθωμεν τιθητε τιθωσιν	τιθει τιθετω τιθετε τιθετωσαν	τιθεναι	τιθεις -εισα -εν (τιθεντος)
IMPERFECT	ἐτιθην ἐτιθεις ἐτιθει ἐτιθεμεν ἐτιθετε ἐτιθεσαν or ἐτιθουν				
AORIST	ἐθηκα ἐθηκας ἐθηκεν ἐθηκαμεν ἐθηκατε ἐθηκαν	θω θης θη θωμεν θητε θωσιν	θες θετω θετε θετωσαν	θειναι	θεις θεισα θεν (θεντος)

Fut. θησω, perf. τεθεικα.

MIDDLE / PASSIVE

	INDICATIVE	SUBJUNCTIVE	IMPERATIVE	INFINITIVE	PARTICIPLE
PRESENT	τιθεμαι τιθεσαι . . .	τιθωμαι (then like λυωμαι)	τιθεσο τιθεσθω . . .	τιθεσθαι	τιθεμενος -η -ον
IMPERFECT	ἐτιθεμην ἐτιθεσο . . .				
AORIST MIDDLE	ἐθεμην ἐθου . . .	θωμαι (then like λυωμαι)	θου θεσθω	θεσθαι	θεμενος -η -ον

Aor. pass. ἐτεθην, perf. mid/pass. τεθειμαι.

In the middle the short ε is predominant, except in the subjunctive and the aorist middle forms, ἐθου and θου.

$$\boxed{ἵστημι}$$

ACTIVE

	INDICATIVE	SUBJUNCTIVE	IMPERATIVE	INFINITIVE	PARTICIPLE
PRESENT	ἵστημι ἵστης ἵστησιν ἵσταμεν ἵστατε ἵστασιν	ἱστῶ ἱστῆς ἱστῆ ἱστῶμεν ἱστῆτε ἱστῶσιν	not in the NT	ἱστάναι	ἱστάς -ασα -αν (ἱστάντος)
AORIST*	ἔστην ἔστης ἔστη ἔστημεν ἔστητε ἔστησαν	στῶ στῆς στῆ στῶμεν στῆτε στῶσιν	στῆθι (or στα) στήτω στῆτε στητωσαν	στῆναι	στας στασα σταν (σταντος)

*Also ἔστησα. Perf. ἕστηκα, plupf. εἱστήκειν.

MIDDLE / PASSIVE

	INDICATIVE	SUBJUNCTIVE	IMPERATIVE	INFINITIVE	PARTICIPLE
PRESENT	ἵσταμαι ἵστασαι . . .	ἱστῶμαι (then like λυωμαι)	ἵστασο ἱστασθω . . .	ἵστασθαι	ἱσταμενος -η -ον
IMPERFECT	ἱσταμην ἱστασο . . .				

Aor. mid. ἐστησαμην (like ἐλυσαμην throughout)
Aor. pass. ἐσταθην (like ἐλυθην throughout)

In the present and imperfect middle the α is predominant, except in the subjunctive.

DICTIONARY

A

ἀββα m Father (Aramaic)

Ἀβρααμ m Abraham

ἀγαθος, η, ον good

ἀγαλλιαω be extremely glad

ἀγαπαω love

ἀγαπη, ης f love

ἀγαπητος, η, ον beloved

ἀγγαρευω compel into service

ἀγγελια, ας f message

ἀγγελος, ου m angel, messenger

ἁγιαζω consecrate

ἁγιος, α, ον holy
οἱ ἁγιοι, the saints, God's people

ἀγκαλη, ης f arm

ἁγνεια, ας f purity

ἀγνοεω be ignorant

ἀγοραζω buy

ἀγρευω trap

Ἀγριππας, α m Agrippa

ἀγρος, ου m field

ἀγω lead, bring, go

ἀγωνια, ας f anguish

Ἀδαμ m Adam

ἀδελφη, ης f sister

ἀδελφος, ου m brother

ἀδημονεω be distressed

ἁδης, ου m Hades

ἀδικεω wrong, do wrong

ἀδικια, ας f wrongdoing

ἀει always

ἀετος, ου m vulture, eagle

Αἰγυπτος, ου f Egypt

αἱμα, τος n blood

αἱρω (fut. ἀρῶ, aor. ἠρα, pf ἠρκα, aor. pass. ἠρθην) take, take away

αἰτεω ask

αἰων, ωνος m age
εἰς τον αἰωνα for ever

αἰωνιος, ον eternal

ἀκαθαρσια, ας f impurity

ἀκαθαρτος, ον unclean

ἀκηκοα see ἀκουω

ἀκοη, ης f hearing, report

ἀκολουθεω + dat. follow

ἀκουω + acc. or gen.; (pf. ἀκηκοα, aor. pass. ἠκουσθην) hear

ἀκριβως accurately, carefully

ἀκροβυστια, ας f uncircumcision

ἀληθεια, ας f truth

ἀληθης, ες true

ἀληθινος, η, ον true, genuine

αληθως truly
αλιευς, εως m fisherman
αλιευω fish
αλλα but
αλληλους, ων (no nom.)
one another
αλλος, η, ο another, other
αμα together, at the same
time
αμαρτανω (aor. ημαρτον) sin
αμαρτημα, τος n sin
αμαρτια, ας f sin
αμαρτωλος, ου m sinner
αμην truly, amen
αμπελων, ωνος m vineyard
αμφιεννυμι (pf. pass.
ημφιεσμαι) clothe, dress
αμφοτεροι, αι, α both, all
αν small word indicating
contingency in certain
constructions
ανα + acc. each, apiece
ανα δυο two by two
αναβαινω (aor. ανεβην, pf.
αναβεβηκα) go up, ascend
αναγγελλω (fut. αναγγελω,
aor. ανηγγειλα) tell,
proclaim
αναγινωσκω (aor. ανεγνων)
read
αναθεμα, τος n cursed
ανακειμαι be seated at table
αναλαμβανω (aor. ανελαβον)
take up, carry
αναμνησις, εως f reminder,
remembrance
Ανανιας, ου m Ananias

αναστασις, εως f
resurrection
ανατελλω (aor. ανετειλα)
dawn, rise
ανατολη, ης f rising, dawn;
pl. ανατολαι east
Ανδρεας, ου m Andrew
ανεγιν-, ανεγν- see
αναγινωσκω
ανελαβον see αναλαμβανω
ανεμος, ου m wind
ανετειλα see ανατελλω
ανεῳγ-, ανεῳξ- see ανοιγω
ανηρ, ανδρος m man,
husband
ανθιστημι (aor. αντεστην)
resist, oppose
ανθρωποκτονος, ου m
murderer
ανθρωπος, ου m man,
human being
ανιστημι (ανα + ιστημι)
raise, appoint; rise
ανοιγω (aor. ανεῳξα [ηνεῳξα,
ηνοιξα], pf. ανεῳγα, pf.
pass. ανεῳγμαι, aor. pass.
ανεῳχθην [ηνεῳχθην,
ηνοιχθην, ηνοιγην]) open
ανομια, ας f lawlessness,
wickedness
ανοχη, ης f forbearance
αντι, ανθ', αντ' + gen. for
ανθ' ων therefore
αντιμετρεω measure out in
return
αντιστην- see ανθιστημι
Αντιοχεια, ας f Antioch

ἄξιος, α, ον worthy
ἀπαγγελλω (fut. ἀπαγγελῶ,
aor. ἀπηγγειλα) proclaim,
tell
ἀπαγω (aor. ἀπηγαγον) lead
away
ἁπας, ασα, αν all, whole
ἀπειθεω disobey, be an
unbeliever
ἀπεκδυσις, εως f putting
off
ἀπερχομαι (fut. ἀπελευσομαι,
aor. ἀπηλθον) go, go
away
ἀπεσταλκ-, ἀπεσταλμ- see
ἀποστελλω
ἀπεστειλα see ἀποστελλω
ἀπεχω be distant
ἀπιστια, ας f unbelief,
unfaithfulness
ἀπιστος, ον unbelieving,
unfaithful
ἀπο, ἀπ', ἀφ' + gen. from
ἀποδιδωμι give, give back
ἀποθηκη, ης f barn
ἀποθνησκω (fut. ἀποθανοῦμαι,
aor. ἀπεθανον) die
ἀποκαλυπτω (aor. pass.
ἀπεκαλυφθην) reveal
ἀποκαλυψις, εως f
revelation
ἀποκρινομαι (aor. pass.
ἀπεκριθην) answer
ἀποκρισις, εως f answer
ἀποκτεινω (fut. ἀποκτενῶ,
aor. ἀπεκτεινα) kill
ἀπολλυμι (fut. ἀπολεσω, aor.
ἀπωλεσα, pf. ptc.

ἀπολωλως) destroy; mid.
perish, be lost.
ἀπολογια, ας f defense
ἀπολυτρωσις, εως f
redemption
ἀπολυω release, send away,
divorce
ἀποστελλω (fut. ἀποστελῶ,
aor. ἀπεστειλα, pf.
ἀπεσταλκα, aor. pass.
ἀπεσταλην) send
ἀποστολος, ου m apostle,
messenger
ἁπτομαι + gen. (aor.
ἡψαμην) touch, take hold
of
ἄρα therefore
ἆρα small word expecting a
negative response
ἀργος, η, ον idle,
unemployed
ἀργυριον, ου n silver, money
ἀρεσκω (aor. ἠρεσα) please
ἀρετη, ης f moral excellence
ἀριθμος, ου m number
ἀρισταω eat breakfast
ἀριστερος, α, ον left (opp.
right)
ἀρνεομαι deny
ἀρνιον, ου n lamb
ἁρπαγμος, ου m something
to grasp after, or hold
ἁρπαζω take by force, take
away
ἀρτι now
ἀρτος, ου m bread, loaf
ἀρχη, ης f beginning
ἀρχηγος, ου m founder

ἀρχιερευς, εως m high priest, chief priest

ἀρχισυναγωγος, ου m ruler of the synagogue

ἀρχω rule; mid. ἀρχομαι begin

ἀρχων, οντος m ruler

ἀρωμα, τος n aromatic spice, or oil

ἀσελγεια, ας f indecency

ἀσθενεω be sick, weak

ἀσθενης, ες sick, weak

ἀσκος, ου m wine-skin

ἀσπαζομαι greet

ἀστηρ, ερος m star

ἀστραπη, ης f lightning

ἀτενιζω fix one's eyes on

ἀτιμαζω dishonour, treat shamefully

αὐθεντεω domineer, have authority over

αὐξανω grow, increase

αὐριον tomorrow, the next day

αὐτος, η, ο self; preceded by the article, the same; he, she, it

ἀφαιρεω (fut. ἀφελῶ, aor. ἀφειλον) take away

ἀφελῶ see ἀφαιρεω

ἀφεσις, εως f forgiveness

ἀφιημι (impf. ἠφιον, aor. ἀφηκα, pf. pass. 3rd pl. ἀφεωνται) forgive, allow, leave

ἀχειροποιητος, ον not made with hands

ἀχθηναι see ἀγω

ἀχρι, ἀχρις + gen. until, as far as

ἀχρι οὑ until, as long as

B

Βαβυλων, ωνος f Babylon

βαλλω (fut. βαλῶ, aor. ἐβαλον, pf. βεβληκα, aor. pass. ἐβληθην) throw, put, cast

βαπτιζω baptize

βαπτισμα, τος n baptism

βαπτιστης, ου m baptist

Βαρναβας, α m Barnabas

βασανιζω toss about (of waves), torment

βασιλεια, ας f kingdom

βασιλευς, εως m king

βασιλευω rule, reign

βασταζω carry, bear

Βηθανια, ας f Bethany

Βηθεεμ f Bethlehem

βιβλιον, ου n book

βιος, ου m life, livelihood, possessions

βλαστανω (aor. ἐβλαστησα) sprout, produce

βλασφημεω blaspheme

βλασφημια, ας f blasphemy, slander

βλεπω see, beware of

βοαω cry out

βοηθεω help

βοσκω tend, feed

βουλομαι (aor. ἐβουληθην) wish, want

βροντη, ης f thunder

Γ

Γαῖος, ου m Gaius
Γαλατια, ας f Galatia
γαληνη, ης f calm (of the sea)
Γαλιλαια, ας f Galilee
Γαλιλαιος, α, ον Galilean
γαμεω marry
γαμος, ου m wedding
γαρ for
γαστηρ, τρος f womb
  ἐν γαστρι ἐχω conceive, be pregnant
γεγενν- see γενναω
γενεα, ας f generation
γενεαλογια, ας f genealogy
γενεσια, ων n pl. birthday celebrations
γενεσις, εως f birth, lineage
γενναω be father of, give birth to
Γεννησαρετ f Gennesaret
γεννητος, η, ον born
γενος, ους n kind, family, race
γερων, οντος m old man
γευομαι taste
γη, ης f earth, land, region, soil
γινομαι (fut. γενησομαι, aor. ἐγενομην, pf. γεγονα, aor. pass. ἐγενηθην) be, become, happen, be born
γινωσκω (fut. γνωσομαι, aor. ἐγνων, pf. ἐγνωκα, aor. pass. ἐγνωσθην) know (of sexual relations Mt 1:25; Lk 1:34)

γλωσσα, ης f tongue, language, speech
γνωριζω make known
γνωσις, εως f knowledge
γογγυζω grumble, mutter
γονευς, εως m parent
γονυ, γονατος n knee
γραμμα, τος n letter (of the alphabet)
γραμματευς, εως m scribe, expert in the Law
γραφη, ης f writing, Scripture; γραφαι pl, the OT Scriptures
γραφω (pf. γεγραφα, pf pass. γεγραπται, "it is written", aor. pass. ἐγραφην) write
γρηγορεω watch, be alert
γυμνος, η, ον naked
γυνη, αικος f woman, wife
γωνια, ας f corner

Δ

δαιμονιον, ου n demon
δακρυον, ου n tear (as in weeping)
δακτυλος, ου m finger
Δαυιδ m David
δε and, but
δεδωκα see διδωμι
δεησις, εως f prayer
δει it is necessary, must, should
δειγματιζω disgrace, expose
δεικνυμι (fut. δειξω, aor. ἐδειξα) show

δειπνεω eat, dine
δειπνον, ου n feast, supper, meal
δεκα ten
δενδρον, ου n tree
δεξιος, α, ον right (opp. left)
Δερβη, ης f Derbe
δερω (aor. ἐδειρα) beat, strike
δεσμη, ης f bundle
δεσμωτηριον, ου n jail, prison
δευρο (adverb) come, come here
δευτερος, α, ον second
δεχομαι receive, accept, welcome
δεω bind, tie
δηναριον, ου n denarius (Roman coin)
δια, δι' + acc. because of, on account of; + gen. through
δια τί why? δια τουτο for this reason
διαβολος, ου m the Devil
διαδημα, τος n diadem, crown
διαζωννυμι (aor. διεζωσα, pf. pass. ptc. διεζωσμενος) put on (clothes)
διαθηκη, ης f covenant, will, testament
διαθησομαι see διατιθεμαι
διακονεω + dat. serve
διακονος, ου m servant, deacon, minister
διακοσιοι, αι, α two hundred

διακρινω (aor. pass. διεκριθην) judge, discern, make a distinction
διαλογισμος, ου m thought
διαμεριζω divide, distribute
διαπεραω cross over
διαστολη, ης f distinction, difference
διατασσω + dat. command, instruct
διατιθεμαι (fut. διαθησομαι, aor. διεθεμην) make (of covenants, wills)
διαφερω be worth more than
διδασκαλος, ου m teacher
διδασκω (fut. διδαξω, aor. ἐδιδαξα, aor. pass. ἐδιδαχθην) teach
διδαχη, ης f teaching, what is taught
διδωμι (fut. δωσω, aor. ἐδωκα, pf. δεδωκα, aor. pass. ἐδοθην) give
διεζωσα see διαζωννυμι
διεκριθ- see διακρινω
διερχομαι (fut. διελευσομαι, aor. διηλθον, pf. διεληλυθα) come, go, pass through
δικαιος, α, ον just, rightous
δικαιοσυνη, ης f righteousness
δικαιοω justify, acquit
διο therefore
δισταζω doubt
διψαω thirst
διωκω persecute, pursue

δοκεω (aor. ἐδοξα) think, seem

δοκιμαζω test, examine, approve

δολος, ου m deceit

δομα, τος n gift

δοξα, ης f glory

δοξαζω glorify, praise

δουλη, ης f female slave, servant

δουλος, ου m slave, servant

δουλοω + dat. enslave; pass. be bound (of marriage vows)

δραμων see τρεχω

δυναμαι can, be able

δυναμις, εως f power, miracle

δυνατος, η, ον possible, powerful

δυο dat. δυσι (ν) two

δυσμη, ης f west (always plural)

δωδεκα twelve

δωρεα, ας f gift

δωρεαν without cost, as a free gift

E

ἐαν if, when

ἐαυτον, ην, ο himself, herself, itself (reflexive); in plural serves for ourselves, yourselves and themselves according to context

ἐβδομηκοντα seventy

ἐγγιζω approach, draw near

ἐγγυς near

ἐγγυτερον nearer

ἐγειρω (fut. ἐγερῶ, aor. ἠγειρα, pf. pass. ἐγηγερμαι, aor. pass. ἠγερθην, fut. pass. ἐγερθησομαι) raise; pass. rise, or be raised

ἐγω (με, ἐμε, μου, ἐμου, μοι, ἐμοι) I (me, etc.)

ἐδειρα see δερω

ἐδωκα see διδωμι

ἐθνος, ους n nation; τα ἐθνη the Gentiles

ἐθρεψα see τρεφω

εἰ if, whether

εἰδον see ὁραω

εἰδεναι see οἰδα

εἰδος, ους n form

εἰδως, υια, ος knowing (pf ptc οἰδα)

εἰκοσι twenty

εἰκων, ονος f likeness, image

εἰμι (fut. ἐσομαι, impf. ἠμην) be, exist

εἰπ- see λεγω

εἰρηκα see λεγω

εἰρηνη, ης f peace

εἰς + acc. to, into, in, with a view to

εἰς, μια, ἐν one

εἰσερχομαι (fut. εἰσελευσομαι, aor. εἰσηλθον, pf. εἰσεληλυθα) come or go into, enter

εἰστηκ- see ἰστημι

εἰτα then

εἰτε .. εἰτε whether .. or

εἶχον impf. ἔχω

ἐκ, ἐξ + gen. from, out of, of

ἕκαστος, η, ον each, every

ἑκατον one hundred

ἑκατονταρχης, ου m (and ἑκατονταρχος, ου m) centurion

ἐκβαλλω (fut. ἐκβαλῶ, aor. ἐξεβαλον, aor. pass. ἐξεβληθην) cast out, bring out

ἐκει there

ἐκειθεν from there

ἐκεινος, η, ο that; he, she, it

ἐκερδησα see κερδαινω

ἐκκλησια, ας f church, assembly

ἐκκοπτω cut off

ἐκλασα see κλαω

ἐκλεγομαι choose

ἐκλεκτος, η, ον chosen, elect

ἐκμασσω wipe, dry

ἐκπλησσομαι be amazed

ἐκπορευομαι go or come out

ἐκραξα see κραζω

ἐκριζοω uproot

ἐκτεινω (fut. ἐκτενῶ, aor. ἐξετεινα) stretch out

ἐκτενως earnestly

ἑκτος, η, ον sixth

ἐκχωρεω go away

ἐκψυχω die

ἑκων, ουσα, ον of one's own free will

ἐλαβον see λαμβανω

ἐλαια, ας f olive tree, olive

ἐλαχιστος, η, ον least

ἐλεγχω show, convince, convict

ἐλεεω have mercy

ἐλεος, ους n mercy

ἐλευθερος, α, ον free

ἐλευσομαι see ἐρχομαι

ἐλθ-, ἐληλυθ- see ἐρχομαι

Ἐλισαβετ f Elizabeth

Ἑλλας, αδος f Greece

Ἑλλην, ηνος m a Greek

Ἑλληνιστι in the Greek language

ἐλπιζω hope

ἐλπις, ιδος f hope

ἐμαυτον, ην myself (reflexive)

ἐμε see ἐγω

ἐμεινα see μενω

ἐμοι see ἐγω

Ἐμμανουηλ m Emmanuel

ἐμος, η, ον my, mine

ἐμου see ἐγω

ἐμποριον, ου n trade, market

ἐμπροσθεν + gen. before, in front of

ἐμωρανα see μωραινω

ἐν + dat. in, by

ἐν see εἰς

ἐναγκαλιζομαι take into one's arms

ἐναντιος, α, ον contrary, hostile

ἐνατος, η, ον ninth

ἐνδειξις, εως f evidence

ἐνδεκα eleven

ἐνδεκατος, η, ον eleventh

ἐνδυμα, τος n clothing, garment

ἐνδυω dress

ἐνενηκοντα ninety

ἐνθυμεομαι think about, think

ἐννεα nine

ἐντολη, ης f command

ἐνωπιον + gen. before, in the presence of

ἑξ six

ἑξακοσιοι, αι, α six hundred

ἐξεβαλον see ἐκβαλλω

ἐξερχομαι (fut. ἐξελευσομαι, aor. ἐξηλθον, pf. ἐξεληλυθα) come or go out

ἐξεστιν it is lawful

ἐξεταζω look for, make a careful search

ἑξηκοντα sixty

ἐξηλθον see ἐξερχομαι

ἐξομολογεω agree; mid. ἐξομολογεομαι confess

ἐξουσια, ας f authority, right, power

ἐξω outside

ἑορτη, ης f feast

ἐπαγγελια, ας f promise

ἐπαινος, ου m praise

ἐπαν when

ἐπανισταμαι rebel against

ἐπεθηκα see ἐπιτιθημι

ἐπει since, otherwise

ἐπειδη since, because

ἐπερωταω ask, ask for

ἐπι, ἐπ', ἐφ' + acc. or gen. or dat. upon, etc.

ἐπιβαινω (aor. ἐπεβην, pf. ἐπιβεβηκα) go on board

ἐπιγειος, ον earthly

ἐπιγινωσκω (fut. ἐπιγνωσομαι, aor. ἐπεγνων, pf. ἐπεγνωκα, aor. pass. ἐπεγνωσθην) know, perceive, understand

ἐπιγνωσις, εως f knowledge

ἐπιγραφη, ης f inscription

ἐπιζητεω seek

ἐπιθυμεω long for, desire

ἐπιθυμια, ας f desire

ἐπικαλεω (aor. pass. ἐπηκληθην, pf. pass. ἐπικεκλημαι) call, name

ἐπιλαμβανομαι (aor. ἐπελαβομην) take hold of, arrest

ἐπιπλησσω rebuke

ἐπισκοπος, ου m overseer, bishop

ἐπισπειρω sow in addition

ἐπιστολη, ης f letter

ἐπιστρεφω (aor. pass. ἐπεστραφην) turn back, return

ἐπιτιθημι (fut. ἐπιθησω, aor. ἐπεθηκα) put on, place, add

ἐπιτιμαω + dat. rebuke, command

ἐπιτρεπω let, allow

ἐπλασθην see πλασσω

ἐπουρανιος, ον heavenly

ἑπτα seven

ἐργαζομαι (aor. εἰργασαμην) work, bring about

ἐργατης, ου m workman

ἔργον, ου n work, deed
ἐρευγομαι declare, tell
ἐρημος, ου f desert
ἐρρεθ- see λεγω
ἐρχομαι (fut. ἐλευσομαι, aor.
ἦλθον, pf. ἐληλυθα)
come, go
ἐρῶ see λεγω
ἐρωταω ask
ἐσθιω (fut. φαγοῦμαι, aor.
ἐφαγον) eat
ἐσπαρμενος see σπειρω
ἐσπερα, ας f evening
ἐστηκ- see ἱστημι
ἐστρωσα see στρωννυμι
ἐσχατος, η, ον last
ἐταραχθην see ταρασσω
ἑτερος, α, ον other, another,
different
ἐτι still, yet
ἐτοιμαζω prepare
ἐτος, ους n year
εὐ well
Εὑα, ας f Eve
εὐαγγελιζομαι preach the
good news
εὐαγγελιον, ου n good news,
gospel
εὐδοκεω be pleased
εὐθεως immediately
εὐθυνω make straight
εὐθυς immediately
εὐκαιρος, ον suitable
εὐλογεω bless
εὐλογια, ας f blessing
εὑρισκω (fut. εὑρησω, aor.
εὑρον) find
εὐχαριστεω give thanks

ἐφανην see φαινω
Ἐφεσος, ου f Ephesus
ἐφιστημι (aor. ἐπεστην)
approach, stand near
ἐχθρος, α, ον enemy
ἐχω (fut. ἐξω -note the
breathing, impf. εἰχον, aor.
ἐσχον) have
ἑωρακα see ὁραω
ἑως until
ἑως + gen. until
ἑως ἀρτι still, until now

Z

ζαω live
Ζεβεδαιος, ου m Zebedee
ζηλος, ου m zeal (also
ζηλος, ους n)
ζητεω seek
ζιζανιον ου n weed
ζωη, ης f life
ζωοποιεω give life to

H

ἠ or, than
ἠγαπ- see ἀγαπαω
ἠγεμων, ονος m governor
ἠγεομαι consider
ἠδειν see οἰδα
ἠδη already, now
ἠκολουθ- see ἀκολουθεω
ἠκω have come, be present
now
ἠλθον see ἐρχομαι
Ἠλιας, ου m Elijah
ἠλικια, ας f stature, age,
span of life

ἥλιος, ου m sun
ἡμεις (ἡμας, ἡμων, ἡμιν)
  we (us, of us, etc)
ἡμερα, ας f day
ἡμετερος, α, ον our
ἡμφιεσμαι see ἀμφιεννυμι
ἠνεῳξ-, ἠνεῳχ- see ἀνοιγω
ἠρεσα see ἀρεσκω
ἠρξ- see ἀρχομαι
Ἡρῳδης, ου m Herod
Ἡρῳδιανοι, ων m Herodians
Ἡρῳδιας, αδος f Herodias
ἠρωτ- see ἐρωταω
Ἡσαΐας, ου m Isaiah
ἡσυχια, ας f silence,
  quietness
ᾐτ- see αἰτεω
ηὑρισκ- see εὑρισκω

Θ

θαλασσα, ης f sea, lake
θανατος, ου m death
θανατοω put to death
θαρσεω take courage
θαυμαζω be surprised
θαυμαστος, η, ον wonderful
θεαομαι see, look at
θεατρον, ου n spectacle
θελημα, τος n will, desire
θελω (impf. ἠθελον) wish,
  want
θεος, ου m God
θεραπευω heal
θερισμος, ου m harvest
θεριστης, ου m reaper
θεωρεω see, watch
θησαυρος, ου m treasure

θλιψις, εως f trouble,
  distress
θριξ, τριχος f hair
θρονος, ου m throne
Θυατειρα, ων n Thyatira
θυγατηρ, τρος f daughter
θυρα, ας f door, gate
θυρωρος, ου m and f
  doorkeeper
θυσια, ας f sacrifice
θυω sacrifice, kill

I

Ἰακωβ m Jacob
Ἰακωβος, ου m James
ἰαομαι heal
ἰατρος, ου m doctor
ἰδ- see ὁραω
ἰδε look!
ἰδιος, α, ον one's own
  κατ᾽ ἰδιαν privately, alone
ἰδου look!
Ἰεραπολις, εως f Hierapolis
Ἰερεμιας, ου m Jeremiah
ἱερευς, εως m priest
ἱερον, ου n temple
Ἰεροσολυμα n. pl. and f. sing.
  Jerusalem
Ἰερουσαλημ f Jerusalem
Ἰησους, ου m Jesus
ἱκανος, η, ον sufficient
ἱκετηρια, ας f request
ἱλαστηριον, ου n means or
  place of forgiveness
ἱμας, αντος m strap (of a
  sandal)

ἱματιον, ου n garment, clothing

ἱνα in order that, so that, that

Ἰοππη, ης f Joppa

Ἰορδανης, ου m Jordan River

Ἰουδαια, ας f Judea

Ἰουδας, α m Judas

Ἰσαακ m Isaac

ἰσος, η, ον equal

Ἰσραηλ m Israel

Ἰσραηλιτης, ου m an Israelite

ἱστημι (fut. στησω, 1 aor. ἐστησα, 2 aor. ἐστην, pf. ἐστηκα, plpf. εἱστηκειν, aor. pass ἐσταθην) stand, set, place

ἰσχυρος, α, ον strong

ἰχθυς, υος m fish

Ἰωαννης, ου m John

Ἰωσηφ m Joseph

K

κἀγω (και ἐγω) and I

καθαιρεω (fut. καθελῶ, aor. καθειλον, aor. ptc καθελων) take down

καθαπερ just as

καθαριζω cleanse

καθαρος, α, ον pure, clean

καθεζομαι sit, sit down

καθελων see καθαιρεω

καθευδω sleep

καθημαι sit, sit down

καθιζω sit, cause to sit

καθιστημι (fut. καταστησω, aor. κατεστησα, aor. pass. κατεσταθην) appoint

καθως as, just as

και and, also, even; και .. και both .. and

καινος, η, ον new

καιρος, ου m opportunity

Καισαρ, ος m Caesar

καιω burn

κἀκει (και ἐκει) and there, there also

κἀκεινος (και ἐκεινος) and he, and that

κακος, η, ον bad

κακως badly

κακως ἐχω be sick

καλαμος, ου m reed

καλεω (fut. καλεσω, aor. ἐκαλεσα, pf. κεκληκα, aor. pass. ἐκληθην, fut. pass. κληθησομαι) call

καλος, η, ον good, fine

καλυπτω cover; pass. be swamped

καλως well

καμηλος, ου m and f camel

Κανα f Cana

καρδια, ας f heart

καρπος, ου m fruit

καρποφορεω bear fruit

κατα, καθ', κατ' + acc. according to; + gen. against

καταβαινω (fut. καταβησομαι, aor. κατεβην, pf. καταβεβηκα) come or go down

καταβολη, ης f beginning, creation

καταγγελλω (aor. κατηγγειλα) proclaim

καταδικαζω condemn

κατακαιω (fut. κατακαυσω, aor. κατεκαυσα) burn, burn up

κατακειμαι lie (in bed), be sick, recline at table

καταλαμβανω (aor. κατελαβον, pf. κατειληφα) overcome, understand

καταλειπω (aor. κατελιπον) leave

καταντaω come, arrive, reach

καταπαυσις, εως f rest

καταποντιζομαι sink

κατασκευαζω prepare

καταφαγομαι see κατεσθιω

καταφιλεω kiss

κατεσθιω (fut. καταφαγομαι, aor. κατεφαγον) eat up

κατευλογεω bless

κατηγορια, ας f charge, accusation

κατοικεω live, live in

κατοικησις, εως f home

καυχαομαι boast, be glad

Καφαρναουμ f Capernaum

κειμαι lie, be lying down

κεκλημενος see καλεω

κελευω order, command

κενος, η, ον empty

κεραμιον, ου n jar

κερδαινω (fut. κερδησω, aor. εκερδησα) gain, win

κεφαλη, ης f head

κεφαλιοω beat over the head

κηνσος, ου m tax

κηρυγμα, τος n what is preached, message

κηρυσσω proclaim, preach

κιβωτος, ου f ark (of a ship); box

κλαδος, ου m branch

κλαιω (aor. εκλαυσα) weep, cry

κλαω break (of bread)

κλειω shut, lock

κλεπτης, ου m thief

κλεπτω steal

κληθ- see καλεω

κληρονομεω inherit, gain possession of

κλητος, η, ον called

κοιλια, ας f stomach, womb

κοινωνια, ας f fellowship

κοινωνος, ου m partner

κολασις, εως f punishment

κολοβοω shorten

κολπος, ου m chest, bosom, lap

κοπαζω cease, stop

κοπτω cut

κορασιον, ου n girl

κοσμος, ου m world

κραζω (aor. εκραξα, pf. with pres. meaning κεκραγα) call, cry out

κρανιον, ου n skull

κρατεω hold, take hold of

κραυγαζω call out, shout

κραυγη, ης f shout, outcry

κρειττων, ον (also κρεισσων, ον) better

κρεμαννυμι hang; mid.

κρεμαμαι depend

κριμα, τος n judgment

κρινω (fut. κρινω, aor. εκρινα, pf. κεκρικα, aor. pass. εκριθην) judge, condemn

Κρισπος, ου m Crispus

κριτης, ου m judge

κρυπτω (pf. pass. κεκρυμμαι, aor. pass. εκρυβην) hide

κτημα, τος n possession, property

κυλλος, η, ον crippled

κυμα, τος n wave (of the sea)

κυριακος, η, ον belonging to the Lord

κυριος, ου m Lord, master, sir

κωλυω hinder, prevent

κωμη, ης f village

κωφος, η, ον dumb, mute, deaf

Λ

λαβ- see λαμβανω

Λαζαρος, ου m Lazarus

λαθρα secretly, quietly

λαλεω speak

λαλια, ας f what is said

λαμβανω (fut. λημψομαι, aor. ελαβον, pf. ειληφα) take, receive, accept

λαμπω shine

Λαοδικεια, ας f Laodicea

λαος, ου m people

λαρυγξ, γγος m throat

λεγω (fut. ερω, aor. ειπον, pf. ειρηκα, aor. pass. ερρεθην or ερρηθην) say

λειτουργια, ας f service, worship

λεντιον, ου n towel

λεπρος, ου m leper, person with skin disease

Λευιτης, ου m a Levite

λευκαινω make white

λιθος, ου m stone

λογεια, ας f collection

λογια, ων n oracle

λογιζομαι count, think

λογος, ου m word, message, account, matter

λοιπος, η, ον remaining

λουω wash, bathe

λυκος, ου m wolf

λυπεω grieve; pass. be sorrowful, sad

Λυστρα f and n. pl. Lystra

λυχνια, ας f lampstand

λυχνος, ου m lamp

λυω loose, destroy

M

Μαγδαληνη, ης f woman of Magdala

μαγος, ου m wise man

μαθητης, ου m disciple

μακαριος, α, ον blessed, happy

Μακεδονια, ας f Macedonia

μακρος, α, ον long, far off

μαλακος, η, ον soft, luxurious

μαλιστα especially

μαλλον more, rather

μαμμη, ης f grandmother

μανθανω (aor. ἐμαθον) learn

μανια, ας f madness

Μαρθα, ας f Martha

Μαρια, ας f and Μαριαμ f Mary

μαρτυρεω witness

μαρτυρια, ας f witness, testimony

μαρτυριον, ου n witness, testimony

μαρτυς, υρος m witness (one who witnesses)

μαχαιρα, ης f sword

με see ἐγω

μεγας, μεγαλη, μεγα great, large

μεγισταν, ανος m person of high status

μεθερμηνευω translate

μειζων, ον greater, greatest

μελει it matters

μελλω be going to, be about to, intend to

μελος, ους n bodily part, member

μεν (with δε) indicating a contrast

μενω (fut. μενῶ, aor. ἐμεινα) remain, stay, live

μεριζω divide

μερος, ους n part

μεσος, η, ον middle, in the middle

ἀνα μεσον among; ἐν μεσῳ among

μετα, μεθ’, μετ’ + acc. after; + gen. with

μεταβαινω (fut. μεταβησομαι, aor. μετεβην, pf. μεταβεβηκα) cross over

μεταιρω (aor. μετηρα) go away, leave

μετανοεω repent

μετανοια, ας f repentance

μεταπεμπομαι send for, summon

μετεχω share in

μετηρα see μεταιρω

μετοικεσια, ας f deportation

μετρεω measure

μετρον, ου n measure

μετωπον, ου n forehead

μη not

μηδε and not, not even, nor

μηδεις, μηδεμια, μηδεν no one, nothing

μηκετι no longer

μην, μηνος m month

μηποτε lest, otherwise

μητε .. μητε neither .. nor

μητηρ, τρος f mother

μητι used in questions expecting the answer no, or hesitant questions

μια see εἰς

μικρος, α, ον small

μιμητης, ου m imitator

μισεω hate

μισθιος, ου m hired worker

μισθος, ου m pay, reward
μνημα, τος n grave
μνημειον, ου n grave
μνημονευω remember
μνηστευομαι be promised in
  marriage
μοδιος, ου m bucket, basket
μοιχαομαι commit adultery
μοι see ἐγω
μοιχευω commit adultery
μονη, ης f room
μονογενης, ες only (child)
μονος, η, ον only, alone
μονον only
μου see ἐγω
μυριοι, αι, α ten thousand
μυριος, α, ον countless
μυστηριον, ου n mystery,
  secret
μωραινω (aor. ἐμωρανα)
  make foolish
μωρια, ας f foolishness
μωρος, α, ον foolish
  το μωρον foolishness
Μωϋσης, εως m Moses

N

Ναζαρεθ or Ναζαρετ f
  Nazareth
Ναθαναηλ m Nathanael
ναι yes
νεανιας, ου m young man
νεανισκος, ου m young man
νεκρος, α, ον dead
νεος, α, ον new
νεφελη, ης f cloud
νηστεια, ας f fasting

νηστευω fast, go without
  food
νηφω be sober
Νικολαϊτης, ου m Nicolaitan
νιπτηρ, ηρος m washbasin
νιπτω (aor. ἐνιψα) wash
νομος, ου m law
νυμφων, ωνος m wedding
  hall
  ὁ υἱος του νυμφωνος the
  wedding guest
νυν, νυνι now
νυξ, νυκτος f night
νωτος, ου m back

Ξ

ξυλον, ου n wood, tree

O

ὁ, ἡ, το the
ὁδος, ου f way
ὁδους, ὁδοντος m tooth
ὁθεν from where, for which
  reason
οἰδα (subj. εἰδω, inf. εἰδεναι,
  ptc. εἰδως, υια, ος; plupf.
  ἠδειν) know
οἰκεω live, live in
οἰκια, ας f house, household
οἰκοδεσποτης, ου m
  householder, master
οἰκοδομεω build
οἰκοδομη, ης f upbuilding,
  building
οἰκονομια, ας f task,
  responsibility, plan

οἶκος, ου m house, household

οἰκουμενη, ης f world

οἶνος, ου m wine

οἶος, α, ον such as

οἶσω see φερω

ὀκτω eight

ὀλιγοπιστος, ον of little faith

ὀλιγος, η, ον small; pl. few

ὅλος, η, ον whole, all

ὀμνυω and ὀμνυμι (aor. ὤμοσα) swear, vow

ὅμοιος, α, ον like

ὁμοιοω + dat. be like

ὁμοιως in the same way

ὁμολογεω confess

ὀναρ n dream

κατ᾽ ὀναρ in a dream

ὀνειδιζω reproach, insult

Ὀνησιμος, ου m Onesimus

ὀνομα, τος n name

ὀνος, ου m and f donkey

ὀπισω + gen. after

ὁπου where

ὁπως that, in order that

ὁραω (fut. ὀψομαι, aor. εἶδον, stem ἰδ-, pf. ἑωρακα or ἑορακα, aor. pass. ὤφθην) see

ὀργη, ης f wrath, anger

ὀρθως rightly

ὀρος, ους n mountain

ὀρφανος, ου m orphan

ὀρχεομαι dance

ὅς, ἥ, ὅ who, which, that (relative pronoun)

ὁσακις as often as

ὁσος, η, ον as much as

ἐφ᾽ ὁσον inasmuch as

ὀστεον, ου n bone

ὅστις, ἥτις, ὅτι who, which, whoever, etc.

ὀσφρησις, εως f nose, sense of smell

ὀσφυς, υος m waist

ὀταν (ὁτε ἀν) when, whenever

ὁτε when

ὁτι that, because, (marking direct speech)

οὔ no

οὐ, οὐκ, οὐχ not

οὐαι horror

οὐδε and not, not even; οὐδε .. οὐδε neither .. nor

οὐδεις, οὐδεμια, οὐδεν no one, nothing, no

οὐδεποτε never

οὐκετι no longer

οὐν therefore

οὐπω not yet

οὐρανιος, ον heavenly

οὐρανος, ου m heaven (often pl.)

οὖς, ὠτος n ear

οὖτε .. οὖτε neither .. nor

οὖτος, αὐτη, τουτο this

οὖτω, οὖτως in this way

οὐχι emphatic form of οὐ

ὀφειλετης, ου m debtor, one under obligation

ὀφειλημα, τος n debt, wrong

ὀφειλω owe, ought

ὀφθαλμος, ου m eye

ὀχλος, ου m crowd

όψια, ας f evening

όψις, εως f face
κατ' όψιν by outward
appearances

όψομαι see όραω

Π

παιδιον, ου n child

παιδισκη, ης f slave
(female)

παις, παιδος m and f
servant, child

παλαιος, α, ον old

παλιν again

πανοικει with one's entire
household

πανοπλια, ας f armour

πανταχου everywhere

παντοκρατωρ, ορος m the
Almighty

παντοτε always

παντως by all means,
doubtless

παρα, παρ' + acc. alongside;
+ gen. from ; + dat. with
τα παρα τινος what
someone has given

παραβολη, ης f parable

παραγγελλω (aor.
παρηγγειλα) command,
give orders

παραγινομαι (aor.
παρεγενομην) come, arrive

παραγομαι disappear, pass
away

παραδιδωμι (fut. παραδωσω,
aor. παρεδωκα, pf.

παραδεδωκα, aor. pass.
παρεδοθην) hand over,
betray, deliver, pass on

παραδοσις, εως f tradition

παραζηλοω make jealous

παρακαλεω (fut. pass.
παρακληθησομαι)
encourage, comfort

παρακλητος, ου m helper,
advocate

παραλαμβανω (fut.
παραλημψομαι, aor.
παρελαβον) receive,
accept

παραλλαγη, ης f variation,
change

παραλυτικος, η, ον
paralyzed

παραλυτικος, ου m paralytic

παραπτωμα, τος n
transgression, sin

παρατιθεμαι (aor.
παρεθεμην) commit

παρεδιδ- see παραδιδωμι

παρεδωκα see παραδιδωμι

παρεθ- see παρατιθημι

παρελαβον see παραλαμβανω

παρεσις, εως f passing by,
overlooking

παρθενος, ου f virgin

παριστημι (fut. παραστησω, 1
aor. παρεστησα, 2 aor.
παρεστην, pf. παρεστηκα,
plpf. παρειστηκειν)
present, be present

παρουσια, ας f coming,
arrival

παρρησια, ας f confidence

πας, πασα, παν all, every, whole

πασχα n Passover

πατηρ, τρος m father

πατρις, ιδος f home town

Παυλος, ου m Paul

παχυνομαι grow insensitive

πειθω (aor. ἐπεισα, pf. πεποιθα, pf. pass. πεπεισμαι) persuade; pf. act. and pass. be confident

πειν see πινω

πειναω be hungry

πειραζω test, tempt

πειρασμος, ου m trial, test, temptation

πεμπω send

πενθερα, ας f mother-in-law

πενθερος, ου m father-in-law

πενθεω mourn

πεντε five

πεντηκοντα fifty

πεπιεσμενος see πιεζω

περαν + gen. across, beyond

Περγαμος, ου f and Περγαμον, ου n Pergamum

περι + acc. and gen. about, around

περιβαλλω (aor. περιεβαλον, pf. pass. περιβεβλημαι) put on, clothe

περιλυπος, ον very sad

περιπατεω walk, live

περισσευω increase, abound

περισσος, η, ον more

περισσοτερος, α, ον greater

περισσοτερως even more so

περιστερα, ας f dove, pigeon

περιτεμνω (aor. περιετεμον, pf. pass. περιτετμημαι, aor. pass. περιετμηθην) circumcise

περιτομη, ης f circumcision

πετρα, ας f rock

Πετρος, ου m Peter

πηλος, ου m mud, clay

πιεζω (pf. pass. ptc. πεπιεσμενος) press down

Πιλατος, ου m Pilate

πινακιδιον, ου n writing tablet

πινω (fut. πιομαι, aor. ἐπιον, a. inf. πιειν or πειν, pf. πεπωκα) drink

πιπτω (fut. πεσοῦμαι, aor. ἐπεσον, 3rd p. ἐπεσαν, pf. πεπτωκα) fall

πιστευω + dat. believe

πιστις, εως f faith

πιστος, η, ον faithful, believing

πλαναω lead astray, deceive

πλασσω (aor. ἐπλασα, aor. pass. ἐπλασθην) mould, form

πλειστος, η, ον (superlative of πολυς) most, greatest

πλειων, ον or πλεον, gen. πλειονος (comparative of πολυς) more

πλεοναζω increase, cause to increase

πλευρα, ας f side (of the body)

πλην nevertheless

πληρης, ες full, complete
πληροω fill, fulfil
πληρωμα, τος n fullness
πλησιον + gen. near
  ὁ πλησιον neighbour,
  fellow human being
πλοιον, ου n boat
πλουσιος, α, ον rich
πνευμα, τος n Spirit (of
  God), spirit
ποθεν from where
ποιεω do, make, produce
ποιμαινω (aor. ἐποιμανα)
  tend, shepherd
ποιμην, ενος m shepherd
ποιμνη, ης f flock
ποιος, α, ον what kind of
πολις, εως f city, town
πολυς, πολλη, πολυ much,
  many
πονηρος, α, ον evil
πορευομαι (aor. ἐπορευθην)
  go
πορνεια, ας f sexual
  immorality
πορνη, ης f prostitute
ποσος, η, ον how great
  ποσῳ μαλλον how much
  more
ποταμος, ου m river
ποτε once
πότε when?
  ἑως πότε how long?
ποτηριον, ου n cup
ποτιζω give to drink
ποῦ where?
που somewhere
πους, ποδος m foot

πραξις, εως f deed, action
πρασσω (pf. πεπραχα) do
πραΰς, πραεια, πραΰ humble,
  meek, gentle
πραΰτης, ητος f humility,
  meekness, gentleness
πρεπει it is fitting
  πρεπον ἐστιν it is fitting
πρεσβυτερος, α, ον elder,
  eldest
πριν or πριν ἡ before
προ + gen. before
προαγω go before
προβατον, ου n sheep
προγινομαι happen
  previously
  προγεγονατα ἁμαρτηματα
  former sins
προδηλος, ον obvious,
  evident
προειρηκα see προλεγω
προΐστημι be a leader
προκοπτω advance, progress
προλεγω (aor. προειπον, pf.
  προειρηκα) say or warn in
  advance
προς + acc. to, near, for
προσδοκαω wait for, look
  for
προσενεγκον see προσφερω
προσερχομαι (fut.
  προσελευσομαι, aor.
  προσηλθον, pf.
  προσεληλυθα) come to
προσευχη, ης f prayer
προσευχομαι pray
προσεχω (aor. προσεσχον)
  pay close attention to

προσκαλεομαι summon, invite

προσκομμα, τος n cause of stumbling, offense

προσκυνεω + dat. worship

προστασσω + dat. command

προσφερω (aor. προσηνεγκα or προσηνεγκον, pf. προσενηνοχα, aor. pass. προσηνεχθην) offer, present (especially sacrifices)

προσωπον, ου n face

προτερος, α, ον former
το προτερον before, previously

προτιθεμαι (aor. προεθεμην) plan, intend

προφασις, εως f pretense

προφητευω prophesy

προφητης, ου m prophet

πρωτοκλισια, ας f place of honour (at a feast)

πρωτος, η, ον first

πτωμα, τος n corpse

πτωχος, η, ον poor

πυγμη, ης f fist

πυρ, πυρος n fire

πωλεω sell

πωποτε ever, at any time

πῶς how?

πως somehow

Ρ

ῥαββι m rabbi, teacher

Ῥαμα f Ramah

Ῥεβεκκα, ας f Rebecca

ῥημα, τος n word, matter

ῥιζα, ης f root

Ῥωμαιος, ου m Roman

Σ

σαββατον, ου n (often in plural; dat. pl. σαββασιν) Sabbath

σαλευω shake

σαλπιγξ, ιγγος f trumpet

Σαμαριτης, ου m Samaritan

Σαμαριτις, ιδος f Samaritan (woman)

Σαουλ m Saul

Σαρδεις, εων f Sardis

σαρξ, σαρκος f flesh, physical body, human nature, lower nature

Σατανας, α m Satan

σεαυτον, ην yourself (sing. reflexive pronoun)

σεισμος, ου m storm, earthquake

σειω shake

σεληνη, ης f moon

σημειον, ου n sign, miracle

σημερον today

σιαγων, ονος f cheek

Σιδων, ωνος f Sidon

Σιλας, α m Silas

Σιμων, ωνος m Simon

σιτος, ου m grain, wheat

Σιων f Zion

σκανδαλιζω cause to sin

σκανδαλον, ου n cause of sin

σκελος, ους n leg

σκευος, ους n jar, container (pl. one's goods)

σκηνη, ης f tent, shelter

σκηνοω live, dwell

σκια, ας f shadow

σκορπιζω scatter

σκοτεινος, η, ον dark, in darkness

σκοτια, ας f darkness

σκοτιζομαι be or become darkened

σκοτος, ους n darkness

Σμυρνα, ης f Smyrna

Σολομων, ωνος m Solomon

σος, η, ον your (sing.)

Σουσαννα, ης f Susanna

σοφια, ας f wisdom

σοφος, η, ον wise

σπειρω (aor. pass. ἐσπαρην, pf. pass. ἐσπαρμαι) sow

σπερμα, τος n seed, offspring

σπλαγχνιζομαι be moved with pity

σπλαγχνον, ου n one's inmost feelings, affections (often pl.)

σταδιοι, ων m stades, furlongs (about 607 feet)

σταθ- see ἱστημι

σταυρος, ου m cross

σταυροω crucify

Στεφανος, ου m Stephen

στεφανος, ου m crown, wreath

στηθος, ους n chest, breast

στιγμα, τος n mark, scar

στομα, τος n mouth

στρατιωτης, ου m soldier

στρεφω (aor. pass. ἐστραφην) turn

στρωννυμι (aor. ἐστρωσα) spread

συ (σε, σου, σοι) you (your, etc)

συγγενεια, ας f relatives

συγχαιρω rejoice with

συζητητης, ου m skilful debater

συκη, ης f fig tree

συλλεγω gather (of crops)

συμπορευομαι go with

συν + dat. with

συναγω (aor. συνηγαγον, fut. pass. συναχθησομαι) gather, assemble

συναγωγη, ης f synagogue

συνανακειμαι sit at table with

ὁ συνανακειμενος guest

συναυξανομαι grow together

συναχθησ- see συναγω

συνεδριον, ου n council, Sanhedrin

συνειδησις, εως f conscience

συνεργος, ου m fellow-worker

συνερχομαι (aor. συνηλθον, pf. συνεληλυθα) come together

συνεσις, εως f understanding

συνετος, η, ον intelligent

συνευδοκεω be willing

συνιημι (fut. συνησω, aor. συνηκα) understand

συνιστημι (aor. συνεστησα, pf. συνεστηκα) commend

συντελεια, ας f end, completion

συντελεω (fut. συντελεσω) establish, make (a covenant), end

συντριβω (pf. pass. ptc. συντετριμμενος) crush

σφοδρα greatly

σχισμα, τος n division

σωζω (fut. σωσω, aor. ἐσωσα, pf. σεσωκα, aor. pass. ἐσωθην) save, heal

σωμα, τος n body

σωτηρ, ηρος m Saviour

σωτηρια, ας f salvation

T

ταμειον, ου n inner room, storeroom

ταρασσω (pf. pass. τεταραγμαι, aor. pass. ἐταραχθην) trouble, disturb

τασσω (pf. pass. τεταγμαι) appoint

ταφος, ου m grave

ταχιον quickly

ταχος, ους n speed
  ἐν ταχει speedily

τε and

τεκνιον, ου n little child

τεκνον, ου n child

τεκτων, ονος m carpenter

τελειος, α, ον mature, perfect

τελειοω make perfect, complete

τελος, ους n end

τελωνης, ου m tax-collector

τεξομαι see τικτω

τερας, ατος n object of wonder

τεσσερακοντα forty

τεσσαρες, τεσσαρα four

τεταρτος, η, ον fourth

τετρακοσιοι, αι, α four hundred

τεχθεις see τικτω

τηλικουτος, αυτη, ουτο so great, so terrible

τηρεω keep, observe, obey

τιθημι (fut. θησω, aor. ἐθηκα, pf. τεθεικα) put, place, lay down

τικτω (fut. τεξομαι, aor. ἐτεκον, aor. pass. ἐτεχθην) bear, give birth to

τιμαω honour

τιμη, ης f honour, price

Τιμοθεος, ου m Timothy

τί why? (also δια τί)

τίς, τί who? which? what?

τις, τι someone, anyone, anything, etc.

τιτλος, ου m title, inscription

Τιτος, ου m Titus

τοιγαρουν therefore

τοιουτος, αυτη, ουτον of such a kind

τοπος, ου m place

τοσουτος, αυτη, ουτον so much, so great

τοτε then

τραυμα, τος n wound

τραχηλος, ου m neck

τρεις, τρια three

τρεφω (aor. ἐθρεψα, pf. pass. τεθραμμαι) feed

τρεχω (aor. ἐδραμον) run

τριακοντα thirty

τριακοσιοι, αι, α three hundred

τριτον or το τριτον the third time

τριτος, η, ον third

τριχ- see θριξ

Τρῳας, αδος f Troas

τυφλος, η, ον blind

τυφλοω make blind

Υ

ὑδωρ, ὑδατος n water

υἱος, ου m son

ὑμεις (ὑμας, ὑμων, ὑμιν) you (your, etc)

ὑπαγω go, depart

ὑπακουω + dat. obey

ὑπαντησις, εως f meeting

ὑπαρχω be at one's disposal τα ὑπαρχοντα possessions

ὑπερ + acc beyond, more than; + gen. on behalf of

ὑπερβολη, ης f surpassing quality καθ' ὑπερβολην beyond measure

ὑπερεκχυννομαι overflow

ὑπερνικαω be completely victorious

ὑπνος, ου m sleep

ὑπο, ὑπ', ὑφ' + acc. under; + gen. by

ὑποδημα, τος n sandal

ὑποκατω + gen. under

ὑποκριτης, ου m hypocrite

ὑπομονη, ης f endurance

ὑποστρεφω return

ὑποταγη, ης f obedience, submission

ὑστερεω lack

ὑψιστος, η, ον highest ἐν ὑψιστοις in the highest heaven

ὑψοω lift up

Φ

φαγ- see ἐσθιω

φαινω (aor. pass. ἐφανην) shine; midd. and pass. appear, be seen

φανερος, α, ον known, plain

φανεροω make known, reveal

φαντασμα, τος n ghost

Φαρισαιος, ου m Pharisee

φαυλος, η, ον evil

φεγγος, ους n light

φερω (fut. οἰσω, aor. ἠνεγκα, aor. pass. ἠνεχθην) carry, bring, bear (fruit)

φευγω (aor. ἐφυγον) flee

φημη, ης f report, news

φημι say

Φηστος, ου m Festus

Φιλαδελφεια, ας f
 Philadelphia

φιλαδελφια, ας f brotherly
 love

φιλανθρωπια, ας f kindness

φιλεω love

Φιλιππος, ου m Philip

φιλος, ου m friend

φιλοσοφια, ας f philosophy

φοβεομαι (aor. ἐφοβηθην)
 fear

φοβος, ου m fear

Φοιβη, ης f Phoebe

φονευω murder

φορεω wear

φρεαρ, ατος n well

φρισσω tremble with fear

φυγη, ης f flight

φυλακη, ης f prison, watch
 (of the night)

φυλασσω guard, keep

φυλη, ης f tribe

φωνεω call, call out,
 summon

φωνη, ης f voice, sound

φως, φωτος n light

φωτισμος, ου m bringing to
 light

X

χαιρω (fut. χαρησομαι, aor.
 pass. ἐχαρην) rejoice

χαρα, ας f joy

χαρακτηρ, ηρος m exact
 representation

χαρις, ιτος f grace

χασμα, τος n chasm, pit

χειλος, ους n lip

χειμων, ονος m winter

χειρ, χειρος f (dat. pl.
 χερσιν) hand

χειρων, ον (gen. ονος)
 worse

χηρα, ας f widow

χιλιαρχος, ου m
 commander, tribune

χιλιας, αδος f (group of) a
 thousand

χιλιοι, αι, α thousand

χορτος, ου m grass, shoot

χρεια, ας f need

χρηζω need

Χριστος, ου m Christ,
 Messiah

χρονος, ου m time

χρυσιον, ου n gold

χωρα, ας f country, region

χωριζω separate

χωρις + gen. without, apart
 from

Ψ

ψαλμος, ου m psalm

ψευδομαι lie, speak untruth

ψευδομαρτυρεω give false
 evidence

ψευδοπροφητης, ου m false
 prophet

ψευδος, ους n lie

ψευδοχριστος, ου m false-
 Christ

ψευστης, ου m liar

ψηλαφαω touch, feel

ψυχη, ης f   life, soul
ψωμιον, ου n   piece of bread

Ω
ὠ   oh!
ὡδε   here
ᾠκοδομησα see οἰκοδομεω
ὡμοιωθ- see ὁμοιοω
ὡμολογησα see ὁμολογεω
ὠμος, ου m   shoulder
ὠμοσα see ὀμνυω

ᾠον, ου n   egg
ὡρα, ας f   hour
ὡς   as, like
ὡσαννα   hosanna!
ὡσαυτως   in the same way
ὡσει   like, as, approximately
ὡσπερ   just as
ὡστε   so that
ὠτιον, ου n   ear
ὠφελεω   gain, achieve,
   benefit